A Portable Cosmos

A Portable Cosmos

Revealing the Antikythera Mechanism,
Scientific Wonder of the Ancient World

ALEXANDER JONES

OXFORD
UNIVERSITY PRESS

OXFORD
UNIVERSITY PRESS

Oxford University Press is a department of the University of Oxford. It furthers the University's objective of excellence in research, scholarship, and education by publishing worldwide. Oxford is a registered trade mark of Oxford University Press in the UK and certain other countries.

Published in the United States of America by Oxford University Press
198 Madison Avenue, New York, NY 10016, United States of America.

© Oxford University Press 2017

Library of Congress Cataloging-in-Publication Data
Names: Jones, Alexander, author.
Title: A portable cosmos: revealing the Antikythera Mechanism, scientific wonder of the ancient world / Alexander Jones.
Description: New York, NY: Oxford University Press, 2017.
Identifiers: LCCN 2016045108 | ISBN 9780199739349 (hardback)
Subjects: LCSH: Antikythera mechanism (Ancient calculator) | Astronomy, Ancient—Greece. | Calendar, Greek. | Science—Greece—History—To 1500. | Technology—Greece—History—To 1500. | Greece—Intellectual life—To 146 B.C. | Greece—Antiquities. | Antikythera Island (Greece)—Antiquities. | BISAC: HISTORY / Ancient / Greece.
Classification: LCC QB107 .J65 2017 | DDC 681.1/11—dc23
LC record available at https://lccn.loc.gov/2016045108https://lccn.loc.gov/2016045108

9 8 7 6 5 4 3 2 1

Printed by Sheridan Books, Inc., United States of America

For Elizabeth and Martin Jones

Contents

Preface

In the name of his master Theoderic, king of the Ostrogoths, Cassiodorus wrote a letter to the philosopher Boethius about AD 506, commissioning him to arrange to have two time-telling devices made, a sundial and a water clock; they were to be a present to dazzle Gundobad, the king of the Burgundians.[1] A rhetorical manner was expected in such official correspondence, and Cassiodorus expands floridly on the astonishing works of which the mechanical art is capable: it can raise water, move fire, cause the organ to make music, defend cities, drain flooded buildings, and fashion sounding effigies of singing birds and hissing snakes. Nay, it even creates a means of imitating the heavens with no risk of impiety, through something called the "sphere of Archimedes," in which the mechanical art

> has made a second Sun take its course; it has fashioned another zodiacal circle by human cogitation; it has shown the Moon restored from its eclipse by the light of the art— it has set in revolution a little machine, pregnant with the cosmos, a portable sky, a compendium of all that is, a mirror of nature, in the image of the ether in its unimaginable mobility. . . . What a thing it is for a human being to make this thing, which can be a marvel even to understand!

Perhaps a still greater marvel is that a specimen of such a portable cosmos, which Cassiodorus had probably read about only in books, was found a little over a century ago off the small Greek island of Antikythera, where it had been lost 2000 years ago in a shipwreck. It may now be seen on public display in the National Archaeological Museum in Athens, bearing the inventory number X 15087.

During the first half century following its discovery, hardly anyone even in the scholarly world had heard of the Antikythera Mechanism. News reports, magazine articles, and television documentaries have now rendered these tiny fragments of bronze plate, bristling with gears and inscribed texts, one of the most familiar artifacts from the ancient Greek world. Much of this recent attention has focused on the technologies applied to studying the Mechanism's fragmentary remains, and on the personalities of the researchers. By now the enigmas of what it did and how it worked are largely solved. Yet the impression is still widely held that the Mechanism is a thing mysteriously foreign to Greco-Roman civilization as we know it, echoing Derek de Solla Price's 1959 statement that "from all we know of science and technology in the Hellenistic age [late fourth to late first centuries BC] we should have felt that such a device could not exist."[2]

I hope that this book will convince the reader that this impression is false. The Mechanism does indeed represent a level of technology exceeding anything else of the kind for which we have either physical remains or detailed descriptions from antiquity, but the devices it employed were a plausible extension of simpler inventions that we do know about. This technology was applied to displaying a profusion of astronomical and time-related functions, all of which were grounded in ancient Greek science. They would, with a little guidance from the Mechanism's operator, have been meaningful to an educated layman of the day, because they connected in diverse ways with Hellenistic society and with the prevailing understanding of cosmology and the physical environment. Changing one word in the title of Price's classic monograph on the Mechanism, *Gears from the Greeks*, we could fairly describe the Mechanism as "Gears *for* the Greeks."

The story of how the Mechanism was found and how we have come to know as much as we do about it is told in the first two chapters of this book. We would not have had this singular object to study had it not been for repeated instances of foresight, persistence, and luck, starting with a team of sponge divers' chance discovery of an ancient shipwreck in a part of the sea where they would not normally have been working, and the vision of a financially straitened government to fund an unprecedented undersea salvage operation, and to continue it well after the pace of "big" finds had slowed down. The investigation of the shattered and corroded fragments was a gradual, interdisciplinary process, involving the efforts of archeologists, historians, scientists, and technicians, and culminating by late 2006 in a reconstruction of much of its appearance and workings. This reconstruction was supported by extensive evidence and internal consistency, and, with very slight modifications, it has earned the acceptance of the entire community of researchers on the Mechanism.

The rest of this book takes this reconstruction as its starting point and seeks to make sense of the Mechanism as a product of its world, going from outside in. Chapter 3 provides a general picture of what the Mechanism looked like and how it operated, from the point of view of a nonexpert observer, when it was intact. Chapters 4 through 7 explore contexts of ancient astronomy and its cultural role and applications that relate to the displays and functions that were on the Mechanism's outside, while the Mechanism's inner workings and their background in the Greco-Roman technology of practical instruments and wonder-working devices are the subject of chapter 8. The book closes with a tentative exploration of the broader tradition of astronomical mechanisms in antiquity and the impact they may have had on ancient thought.

A prominent theme of my book is the public face of Greek astronomy in the Hellenistic period: the numerous ways in which specialists and populariz-ers sought to make the science visible, intelligible, and relevant to the layman. Following their example, I have tried to explain the astronomy and technol-ogy behind the Mechanism by using a minimum of specialized jargon and assuming no more than grade-school science. The central chapters on the Mechanism's displays and gearwork are more thematic than cumulative, and it should not be necessary for the reader to absorb the more technical discussions in full detail in order to follow my main lines of argument. A glossary at the end provides brief explanations of key terms.

Fruitful work continues to be done on many aspects of the Mechanism, but with respect to the largest questions we probably now have learned what we *can* learn from the known fragments. There remains the prospect that more frag-ments may be found. The sponge divers who salvaged the Antikythera ship-wreck in 1900–1901 brought up only part of the Mechanism, comprising what may have been little more than half the internal gearwork and a much smaller fraction of the exterior with its dials and inscriptions. All they would have seen was a piece or pieces of corroded metal, which was all that they had to notice to make this an item worth picking up, and they had neither the training nor the time to record where they found it. Jacques Cousteau and Frédéric Dumas dove briefly at the shipwreck site in 1953, and Cousteau returned in 1976 in a col-laboration with the Greek Institute of Marine Archeology, but new fragments of the Mechanism were not among the objects that they recovered. In 2012, a team of divers of the Hellenic Ephorate of Underwater Antiquities and the Woods Hole Oceanographic Institution began surveying the wreck site, using up-to-date methods and technology, and in 2014 they began a new, multiyear scientific excavation of the wreck. Finding more pieces of the Mechanism is not their primary goal, and it may seem a long shot, but if there still are significant pieces of bronze gears, dial plates, or pointers on the sea bottom, their under-water metal detectors stand a good chance of locating them. The excavations will in any event tell us much more than we now know about the voyage on which the Mechanism was lost to its ancient owner and saved for us.

Acknowledgments

Like all students and admirers of the Antikythera Mechanism, I am indebted in the first instance to the National Archaeological Museum for its stewardship of the delicate fragments since their discovery, and for encouraging and facilitating the work of a succession of researchers. I am also deeply grateful to the Antikythera Mechanism Research Project (AMRP) for inviting me to join in their ongoing research following the publication of their first results in late 2006. Among the original members of the AMRP team, I have especially profited from exchanges with Mike Edmunds, John Seiradakis, Xenophon Moussas, Tony Freeth, Yanis Bitsakis, Agamemnon Tselikas, Tom Malzbender, Andrew Ramsey, and Mary Zafeiropoulou, and among those who (like me) joined later, John Steele and Magdalini Anastasiou. I have also gained enormously from conversations and correspondence with other scholars working on the Mechanism: first and foremost Michael Wright, and also James Evans, Christián Carman, Paul Iversen, and John D. Morgan. Brendan Foley has generously shared news of the ongoing archeological surveying and excavation at the Antikythera shipwreck site.

For access to archival materials, I thank the National Archaeological Museum; the Historical Archive of Antiquities and Monuments (Hellenic Ministry of Culture and Sports, National Archive of Monuments); the National Hellenic Research Foundation; the Bayerische Staatsbibliothek, Munich; the archives of the Athens Department and Berlin Office of the Deutsches Archäologisches Institut; the Antikensammlung, Staatliche Museen zu Berlin Preussischer

Kulturbesitz; the Archivzentrum of the Goethe Universität, Frankfurt am Main; the Adler Planetarium, Chicago; and the heirs of Derek de Solla Price.

Stefan Vranka, my editor with the Oxford University Press (OUP), suggested in 2009 that I should write a book presenting the Antikythera Mechanism as a gateway to exploring broader aspects of ancient science and society, and he showed astonishing patience with a project that I repeatedly put off until I felt that the groundwork of current research was firm enough to build on. Mike Edmunds and OUP's anonymous reader gave me long and very helpful lists of suggestions for improving the first draft.

My profoundest gratitude remains to my wife, Catherine Haines, my book's first and most supportive reader.

1

The Wreck and the Discovery

Disaster

Around 60 BC, a ship was wrecked off the northeast coast of a small island called Aigila in the straits between Crete and the Peloponnese (fig. 1.1). The exact character of the ship is not known, but it was probably a large merchant vessel, perhaps about 40 meters long, and in addition to the usual amphorae containing wine or other commodities, it bore a cargo of bronze and marble statuary and fine glassware. The life-size bronzes were antiques, a century or more old, but the other prestige objects were of recent manufacture. There were apparently also passengers—we know that a woman was aboard, the probable owner of two pairs of elegant golden earrings.[1]

When the ship's remains were discovered and partly salvaged in 1900–1901, most or all of the sculptures were initially supposed to be much older than the ship that carried them, and an idea gained currency that it was bearing treasures looted from a Greek city by the Romans in the early first century BC. Though this theory still finds adherents, more careful study of the recovered objects has rendered it much more probable that this was a commercial voyage whose cargo came from diverse sources and perhaps was also headed for diverse destinations.[2]

We can identify or guess at the places of origin of many of the items on board. There were amphorae of types made in Rhodes and Kos in the Dodecanese, near Ephesus in Asia Minor, and probably also on the Adriatic coast of Italy. The marble of the statues is Parian, so they probably came from a workshop in the Aegean region, perhaps Delos or Pergamon. The glass is Syro-Palestinian or Egyptian. One of the people on board had his savings in the form of 32 silver coins from Pergamon and Ephesus, and someone was carrying some less valuable bronze coins from Ephesos as well as rather old ones from Katane in Sicily and Cnidos in Asia Minor. (The latest of the silver

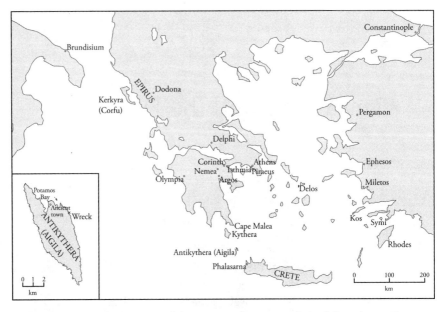

FIG. 1.1. Antikythera, Greece, and the Aegean. (large map derived from http://d-maps .com/m/mediterranean/meditmin/meditmino4.svg)

coins were minted between 76 and 67 BC, providing the firmest evidence that the shipwreck occurred after 76 and likely within a span of one or two decades after that year.)[3]

It need not be supposed that the ship had stopped at all these places on its last voyage. Parts of the cargo could have been brought by smaller vessels to a major port of transit such as Delos, there to be consolidated for long-distance transport on a larger ship that in any case would be limited by its size to the major harbors. The presence of passengers on such a vessel would not have been unusual, since in an age when specialized passenger transport did not exist, travelers too had to be opportunistic. And while the majority of amphorae in a cargo would probably have originated in the same places as their contents, some were surely reused. What is beyond doubt is that the ship was laden at one or more of the great ports of the Aegean: on the coast of Asia Minor, at one or more of the islands, or both. The location of its wreck shows that it was headed for the western Mediterranean, to deliver its cargo in ports of the Adriatic or farther west.

One item on the ship has not yet been mentioned: a mechanical object composed of wood and metal, about the shape and dimensions of a shoebox. Though it probably lacked the visual appeal of the statues and glassware, it was delicate and precious, and one hopes it was packed securely in a crate or container to protect it from casual damage and from the elements. That it would have been sent on a long voyage unaccompanied is highly improbable. Unless it was part of its owner's baggage—and this was not an object one would casu-ally subject to the risks of travel—we may conjecture that it was in the care of a technician trained to operate it and maintain it in working order. As I will argue later in this book, it is likely that he was escorting it on its journey from the workshop to its intended owner.[4]

A fellow passenger would not have had an easy time persuading this mechanic to unpack and show his treasure, but if he succeeded, he would have seen a box consisting of rectangular bronze plates forming its front and back faces, framed by a wooden casing, and a knob or crank protruding from the middle of one of the wooden sides (see fig. 3.9). The dominant feature of the front face would have been a circular dial surrounded by two concentric ring-shaped scales and having a complicated assemblage of pointers radiating from its center. Most of the back face would have been taken up by two spiral slots with scales inscribed along them and radial pointers of rather complicated con-struction, and three smaller circular dials, with simpler pointers. All around the dial scales, in the spaces around the dials, and also on separate bronze plates that were stored against the machine's faces and may have functioned as covers, one would have seen texts engraved in Greek letters, similar to the lettering of stone inscriptions but much tinier. The mechanic just might have twisted the knob on the side a little to show that all the pointers were somehow moved by it, though in different amounts and directions. If in an exceptionally compliant mood (or offered a sufficiently generous tip), he might also have removed the front plate to show, behind it, a mechanism of interconnected gears. Let us hope that he did offer someone such a demonstration; a bad accident was to happen quite soon, and it would have been a pity if no one outside the shop got a decent look at one of the wonders of the ancient world while it was intact.

Aigila, an island of approximately 20 square kilometers now known by the name Antikythera, was doubly dangerous in antiquity for vessels mak-ing the passage between Crete and the Greek mainland, by far the most direct route around Greece or generally between the Aegean and the western Mediterranean.[5] Though not capable of supporting large populations, it was a base for pirates within the sphere of the Cretan piratical stronghold Phalasarna. In the mid-third century BC, Rhodes had waged a campaign against Aigila, seeking to put a stop to depredations against her naval commerce, but in the long term this did not impede local piracy and the prosperity that it brought the island, as witnessed by the flourishing Hellenistic settlement on the heights overlooking the sheltered Potamos Bay, the island's harbor. However, in 69–67 BC the Roman general Quintus Caecilius Metellus harshly but effectively sup-pressed the pirates of Phalasarna—he was rewarded with a triumph and the cognomen Creticus—and as a result Aigila was substantially depopulated for the next four centuries.

Our merchant ship was thus probably safe from pirates, but not from the physical dangers and treacherous weather of the straits. The precise cause of its sinking cannot be determined, but the location, off a precipitous part of the island's coast east of Potamos Bay and well away from the passages around the island, suggest that the ship was driven by a storm and failed to reach shelter before it foundered. With its heavy load it must have sunk rapidly, and at least four of the people on board (two men, one woman, and one individual of uncertain sex, known from skeletal remains) went down with it. We do not know whether anyone got safely to shore, or whether news of the ship's fate reached anyone concerned, including the owner of the gearwork mechanism.

Around the wreck site, the cliffs of the island continue almost as steeply below the sea as above it. Although the ship was only about 25 meters from shore, it came to rest on a steeply sloping bottom at a depth ranging from about 45 to 61 meters, where it remained, probably undisturbed by humans, for close to 2000 years. Obviously the ship and its contents were in very different condition at the end of this interval from when the ship was still afloat. The sinking was a violent event, and much damage to objects must have been caused not only in the first impact but also through subsequent falling and rolling of heavy objects, especially the marble statues; such events would have occurred intermittently over the years as whatever was beneath them shifted or decayed away. More gradually, prolonged immersion in the sea resulted in physical, chemical, and biological processes attacking most of the materials represented in the wreck. Wood, when exposed and not in contact with metal, was eaten away by the mollusc *Teredo navalis* ("shipworm"); marble, unless protected by the muck of the seabed, was encrusted, pitted, and eroded by stone-boring organisms such as mussels and sea urchins; metal was also encrusted and chemically corroded and, if consisting of thin plate, turned into fragile chalk-like material.[6] Small objects and fragments would have been moved about, damaged, or broken by currents and especially by marine life.

In the meantime, the island underwent cycles of depopulation and repopulation. After the fourth crusade (1202–1204) and until 1800 it was ruled by the Venetian Republic and acquired the new name of Cerigotto—at least on charts, though transformations of its ancient name (Lioi or Singilio) continued to be used locally. Along with the other Ionian islands, it changed hands several times during the Napoleonic Wars before coming under British rule in 1809; in 1815 it became part of the United State of the Ionian Islands under British administration. During this period the island was used as a place of exile for Ionian radicals, and it appears that Ionian patriots were responsible for giving it the new, imitation-classical name Antikythera ("Opposite to Kythera") at the same time that they revived the ancient name Kythera for its larger neighbor to the north, known to the Venetians as Cerigo. The Ionian Islands were ceded to the young Greek state in 1865, and until 1913 Antikythera was the southernmost part of Greece, a seldom visited and little regarded spot though not much more than 200 kilometers from the Athenian port of Piraeus, a day's journey by steamship.

Salvage

The modern discovery of the wreck in 1900 came about through another, less severe bout of bad weather. Sponge diving had long been a principal industry in many of the Greek islands, especially in the Dodecanese, and about 1870 the divers of Symi had been among the first to adopt the new "hard hat gear," that is, brass helmets and dry suits with air pumped from the surface by way of a hose. Before this, and in fact since classical antiquity, nude diving was practiced: a diver would plunge to the bottom head-first, holding a heavy stone tied to the boat by a cord that served as both a signaling line and the means of rapidly hauling the diver back to the surface. Nude divers could reach depths of nearly 50 meters (it was said that some could even reach 70), but an entire dive would normally last only a minute and a half to two minutes, allowing scarcely a minute at the bottom, though experienced divers could reportedly stay below water for up to four minutes. A nude diver could make 10 or more dives in a day. With helmet and hose, divers could routinely reach greater depths, down to about 70 meters, and more crucially, they could stay at the bottom for longer periods, for example an average of about a quarter of an hour at 50 meters' depth in calm weather. Two dives a day was the usual limit—diving with deep sea gear was dangerous, especially from decompression sickness, which could result in paralysis or death, and the casualty rates in the Greek sponge fisheries were appalling. Despite this, the technology enabled the industry to expand both geographically and in intensity, and by the end of the 19th century about 50 teams of helmet divers, most of them Greek (under Greek or Ottoman rule) were annually operating off the coast of Libya for a season that extended from April to October. It was one of these teams that chanced on the wreck site in 1900, while pausing for shelter at Antikythera.[7]

The party consisted of two boats (a "mother ship," *Efterpi*, about 15 meters long, carrying the supplies and accumulated sponge harvest, and a diving boat, *Kalliopi*, about 10 meters long), owned by Fotios Lindiakos and captained by his brother-in-law Dimitrios Kontos, along with about six or seven divers and crews for the two vessels (fig. 1.2).[8] The precise circumstances of what happened are somewhat obscure, starting with the question of whether the wreck was discovered at the beginning or the end of the harvesting season. One published report, from 1902, says that it was late in the year, while another, from 1903, says that it was at Eastertide,[9] but confusingly adds that the party was making its return journey. In favor of the earlier, springtime date is a curious story published half a century after the event: a few days after Easter 1900, the operator of an optical telegraph station that had been set up on Antikythera to provide a communications link between Crete and Kythera during the Greco-Turkish War of 1897 urgently signaled that a treasure had been found offshore, but the government authorities in Athens dismissed the report, believing that the man must have been drunk.[10]

FIG. 1.2. Kontos's sponge divers and their boat *Efterpi* at Antikythera. Spyridon Stais and Emmanouil Lykoudis (legal adviser to the Greek government) stand in the small boat in the foreground. (Photographic Archive of the National Archaeological Museum, Athens)

The discovery was made by one of the divers, Ilias Stadiatis (formally Ilias Lykopantis), who saw fragments of bronze statuary at a depth reported as 35 fathoms (i.e., over 60 meters). (In some more recent retellings the figure is reduced to between 42 and 50 meters.) Kontos is supposed to have made a dive to confirm the find and establish its position securely, and either Kontos or Stadiatis brought up a life-size bronze arm, which has since been identified as belonging to the statue known as the "philosopher." That was all that they did at the site, according to what they told the authorities in Athens later that year; but in the 1960s the marine archeologist Peter Throckmorton was told by descendants of Kontos's men on Symi that some bronze statuettes were also recovered at this time and in due course were sold to dealers in Alexandria.[11]

Though Symi was part of the Ottoman Empire, the sponge divers emphatically regarded themselves as Greeks, and besides, it made sense for them to approach the Greek government with their discovery, not only because Antikythera was Greek territory but also because the government could be hoped to have both the inclination and the means to assist the divers in recovering the larger artifacts, which were obviously beyond their ability to bring to the surface by themselves. The divers also naturally wanted to be sure that they would themselves carry out the undersea operations and be paid for them. At this time, archeology came within the scope of the Greek Ministry of Education and Ecclesiastical Affairs. Accordingly, in early November Kontos brought a delegation of his men to Athens where they enlisted Antonios Oikonomos (1850–1902), a professor of archeology at the University of Athens and a fellow Symiote, to arrange a meeting with the minister of education, Spyridon Stais (1859–1932). They gave out that they had discovered ancient statuary in the sea between Cape Malea and the island of Kythera, probably mislocating the site intentionally to protect their interest in it, and that they were ready to dive for the artifacts if the government would pay them and provide the naval resources needed for the salvage.

The years between the Greco-Turkish War, which went badly for Greece both militarily and financially, and its great territorial expansion resulting from the Balkan Wars of 1912–1913 and the international recognition of its union with Crete in 1913 were an interval of comparatively low national morale and unstable governments. In compensation, it was a good time for archeology, in terms of both accomplishments and public interest. Stais, a former schoolteacher with scientific training and broad culture, must have consulted the archeologists of the government service (who immediately recognized that what the divers had found was a Greco-Roman shipwreck) and then worked quickly, promising the divers generous payment if they proved capable of recovering objects from the site, and arranging with the Greek navy for the loan of a transport ship. The newspapers of Athens followed every development, and stories on the "archeo-logical treasure in the deep" continued to be printed, often on the front page (most newspapers consisted of only four pages), through the duration of the project. They are in fact among our most useful informants for what was going on from week to week. Newspapers in other countries intermittently carried reports of the discoveries too, though they were generally less detailed.[12]

Thus on November 24, the newspaper *To Asty* reported that Kontos and his men had closed the deal with the government by handing over the bronze arm, and that the naval transport ship *Mykali* had just set out with the diving team (and their boats) and Professor Oikonomos to oversee their work (fig. 1.2). It was perhaps only after setting out that Kontos revealed the correct location of the wreck, since the name Antikythera first shows up in newspaper reports after Oikonomos returned to the Piraeus on the *Mykali* on November 27 with the first finds. The experience of these first days of official work gave a good indication of how things would proceed over the following months. Winds and choppy seas prevented the divers from working for more than three hours in total, and individual dives had to be kept to not longer than five minutes. The *Mykali* turned out to be too large to get close to the site, limiting its ability to help with raising objects—in the future, smaller navy vessels, the steamship

(a)   (b)

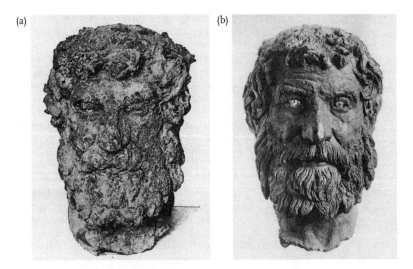

FIG. 1.3. The late-third-century BC bronze head of the "philosopher" (National Archaeological Museum X 13400), before and after cleaning. (Svoronos 1903a, 29 and plate III)

Syros (joined by a freighter with a crane) and the torpedo boat *Aigialeia*, would do this work, while the *Mykali* returned from time to time to bring artifacts to Athens and carry archeologists and other officials back and forth. Yet, despite the adverse conditions, the yield of these first dives was impressive: they included several fragments both of bronze and marble statuary, among which the most remarkable was a bronze head, initially thought to represent a boxer but recognized after cleaning to be a philosopher of unknown identity (fig. 1.3).

Over the following months, the work continued in a stop-and-start manner, with interruptions caused not only by weather but also by an investigation—there had been accusations in the Greek press that the divers were carelessly handling or even deliberately breaking their finds (the ministerial delegation exonerated them). The conditions under which the divers worked would have made it impossible for them to survey the wreck in an archeologically scientific way, even if they had had the training to do this; it was simply a salvage operation carried out under oversight by the ministry and its archeologists. Systematic records do not appear to have been preserved of the items as they were brought up. Intermittently, telegrams were sent from Kythera—no direct line of communication from Antikythera existed—reporting the finds, and these were usually summarized in the next day's newspapers.

At least from a layman's point of view, the most exciting discoveries were the bronze statues. Though shattered into pieces, they were otherwise in a comparatively good state of preservation, and at least some of them appeared to be late Classical or early Hellenistic work, from the fourth and third centuries BC. Not much bronze statuary has survived in general from antiquity, because the metal was recycled once statues were no longer wanted, and the fragments from the Antikythera wreck were a substantial addition to what was known at the time. Many of them were recovered during the first weeks of the salvage, both because there was so much interest in them and because they were easy for the divers to recognize and bring up. The biggest fragments of the most famous of the Antikythera bronzes, the so-called Ephebe (or Youth) of Antikythera, were retrieved already in late December 1900; it was the only one of which nearly all the pieces were eventually found. Some of the marble statues were brought up in the early weeks, including a life-size boy whose head and right side had been buried in sediment and so were protected from the stone-eating organisms; this piece required four dives to establish what it was, and a further three to bind it with cords so it could be hauled up to the *Syros*. The bulk of many of the marble fragments of larger-than-life-size men, gods, and horses made their lifting a still more laborious and slower affair. Some were simply too deep for the divers to reach with their hauling cables. Moreover, they were something of a disappointment because their surfaces were mostly eaten away, and it was not long before the archeologists realized that they were not original masterpieces of the Classical period but were late Hellenistic copies and imitations.

Gradually the balance of kinds of object recovered shifted more and more toward the smaller or mundane objects—less fine art, more amphorae and other ceramics, and also pieces of the ancient ship itself. Whereas in February 1901, Stais (paying a visit to the site following the investigation of the alleged mishandling of objects; fig. 1.4) found himself pleading with the demoralized divers to continue their work, by the summer it was the divers who were urging that the search should continue in the face of complaints of diminishing returns. The last noteworthy sculptural find had been announced in a telegram on June 23, a handsome bronze statuette of a young male. Toward the end of July, Stais wrote a memorandum instructing Kontos to stop work immediately because the recent finds ("vase fragments and pieces of wood from the shipwreck") were archeologically worthless.[13] Apparently, however, he relented and the operations went on for a further few weeks. In fact, the archeologist overseeing the salvage had recently sent a more positive report to the minister:

> The labors of the divers in bringing up the sunken treasure progress slowly but in a proper manner and more systematically than before. The seabed is being excavated by the divers to a depth of 1 meter from its surface and fine-scale searches are being made, so that the least archeological object cannot escape the divers' notice, unless it is undersea at a much greater depth than 35–40 fathoms [63–72 meters], which is how far down the Symiote divers reach.[14]

It does seem that the divers were trying not to miss anything. But one can understand why the minister was unimpressed by what they were finding. The

FIG. 1.4. The sponge divers, officers, and crew of the *Mykali*, and delegation from the Ministry of Education on board the *Mykali*, February 1901. Spyridon Stais stands on the upper deck, between the ropes, wearing a fedora and with his hand on the head of one of the divers; to the right of him, also in a fedora and with one hand on the rail, is Kavvadias. Directly below Stais, in a wide-brimmed hat, is Fotios Lindiakos, and to the left of Lindiakos and immediately left of the ropes is Kontos. (Lykoudis 1901, 390)

day after *To Asty* published this report, the same newspaper reported from a telegram that three days of diving, managed despite bad weather, had brought up "three little ceramic vessels, a ceramic vase, and various little fragments of bronze." Ten days later, on June 24, *To Asty* published a telegram that appeared on the face of it scarcely more exciting:

> There has been found . . . one slab with an inscription, whose letters however could not be copied. Besides this were found vases, fragments of sculptures, and other ancient objects.

A rival newspaper, *Skrip*, described the first item as "a *marble* slab bearing an inscription that is difficult to read," but this was almost certainly a mistake, since no inscription on stone is known to have been found in the shipwreck. (Unfortunately the original telegram has not survived in the archives of the Ministry of Education's archeological service.) In any case, no one in Athens seems to have thought this slab was very important: the evening newspaper *Estia* had summarized the same telegram the day before slightly differently, listing "various ancient objects, vases, fragments of sculptures, and *other things* [italics added]" as having been brought up on July 22.

One can scour the scientific and popular literature on the antiquities from the Antikythera wreck, from the contemporaneous newspaper accounts and the first scholarly surveys of 1902–1903 through to the excellent catalog of the National Archaeological Museum's 2012–2014 Antikythera exhibition, without finding many objects of any kind bearing inscriptions: a few stamps on ampho rae, various coins (all found in 1976), a sounding weight scratched with what appears to be a Roman numeral (also from 1976), a terra-cotta roof tile bearing a circular seal stamp with some partly legible Greek letters, *and the fragments of the ancient gearwork mechanism*. It deserves to be noted that when these frag- ments began to get serious attention nearly a year later, they were repeatedly described in the newspapers with practically the same words: an "inscribed slab" with difficult-to-read writing.

If this "slab" was a part of the Mechanism (we may as well give it the dignity of a capital letter from now on), and there really does not seem to be another plausible candidate, the absence of any mention of wheels or gears is striking. When the fragments came to notice in 1902, the gears were as obvi- ous, and as obviously interesting, as the inscription. (Incidentally, the authori- ties at the museum knew, presumably from records that no longer exist, that the fragments had been recovered toward the end of the salvage operations.) It would seem, therefore, that the object as brought out of the sea had a different appearance; it was likely an aggregate comprising several of the pieces as they were later known, and the mechanical components were still hidden inside.

Wishing to get a better sense of whether there was any point in prolong- ing the divers' search, Stais himself arrived at the site on July 30 on board the *Mykuli*. He was sufficiently encouraged by the finds that had been made earlier that summer—in a telegram to Athens he singled out the bronze statu- ette and a marble horse's head, but not a word about the inscribed slab—to authorize the work to continue for a few more weeks. It was finally shut down a few days before September 23, after the divers declared that there was little more that they could do: what remained consisted chiefly of immovable marble fragments.

Stais took on board the *Mykali* the antiquities that were waiting to be trans- ported to Athens, and it is at this time that an incident reported in print only many years later must have happened, if it happened at all. According to the admiral Ioannis Theofanidis (whom we will presently reencounter as a partici- pant in our story), a fellow naval officer named Periklis Rediadis (1875–1938), who had been aboard the *Mykali* on several of its visits to the wreck site and who will also soon reappear in our story in a different capacity, prevented the crew member who was loading the antiquities on the deck of the *Mykali* from tossing an apparently worthless encrusted lump—our Mechanism!—back into the sea, because he saw a bit of metal projecting from a fracture on its surface.[15] The anecdote may well be true, though it is odd that Rediadis did not mention it in his various publications on the Mechanism, and it is hard not to suspect in it a bit of modern mythologizing. However that may be, when Stais landed at the Piraeus on August 2, it was the statuette that he personally carried to the ministry offices like a prized article of booty, leaving one of the archeologists to oversee the unloading and transport of the other antiquities, among them the coy Mechanism.

Stais had been fortunate to hold office in one of the longer-lived governments of this period of Greek history. He had been appointed minister of education on May 27, 1900, and left office with the fall of Georgios Theotokis's government on November 25, 1901, following the violent "Gospel Riots" protesting a proposed publication of the Bible translated into modern Greek (Stais, whose ministry embraced ecclesiastical affairs, was deeply involved in these unfortunate events). Thus, he saw through the entire salvage campaign at Antikythera from the original negotation with Kontos in November 1900 to the promised payment, finally settled at 150,000 drachmas (equivalent to something less than 30,000 American dollars of the day), made to Kontos on behalf of his team of about 20 men in late October 1901.[16] The divers had earned this reward through diligence and brave risk-taking even as measured by the standards of their calling: by the end, two of them had been seriously injured and one, Georgios Kritikos, had died from the effects of decompression sickness.

Yet, despite recognition that the Symiote divers had gone to the limits of what they could do to find and recover the treasures of the shipwreck, there remained a sense that it would be worthwhile to return to the site with better resources. As early as the spring of 1901, the government had communicated with an Italian company, the Society for Promoting Submarine Recoveries, but negotiations in 1902–1903 foundered on the company's insistence on a promise of compensation exceeding what was allowed by Greek archeological law.[17] Other approaches also came to nothing. In 1905 the mayor of the island of Spetses, Dimitrios Leonidas, sponsored a campaign of diving that involved some kind of submersible machine, but after some discouraging first experiments at the site, the archeologists departed in frustration and the government withdrew its support; Leonidas afterwards claimed that his divers had reached the wreck after the archeologists had left, and even tied up seven marble statues for raising.[18] After this abortive effort, the site was left alone until Jacques Cousteau's visit in 1953 and his more extensive excavation for television in 1976.[19]

Meanwhile, even as Kontos's men were in the midst of their work in 1900–1901, the Greek archeological community had begun to think about the nature and date of the voyage that had ended in the shipwreck at Antikythera.

Gavriel Vyzantinos, an ephor (i.e., superintendent) in the Ministry of Education's archeological service, oversaw the operations at Antikythera from early December 1900, and early the following year he published a popular article on his experiences, soon afterwards republished in English translation in the New York magazine *The Independent*.[20] Relying on what at that point was a rather small body of recovered artifacts, he estimated that the shipwreck likely dated to the first century BC, and he raised the possibility that its cargo was Roman plunder from the Greek East. The second-century AD author Lucian of Samosata offered a suitable candidate for the voyage by referring to a shipload of Greek artistic treasures looted by the Roman general Sulla but lost in a shipwreck somewhere near Cape Malea in the mid-80s BC, though Vyzantinos admitted that it would be mere speculation to link the Antikythera wreck to this particular event. As evidence built up, in particular through the recovery of ceramics, a dating in or around the first century BC, the period of the late Roman Republic or the early Roman Empire, came to be more or less the consensus among his archeologist colleagues in the ministerial service. On the other hand, Ioannis Svoronos (1863–1922), the director of the Numismatic Museum—and a bitter and open enemy of Panayiotis Kavvadias (1850–1928), the head of the Ministry of Education archeological service— was quickly convinced that sculptures from the wreck could be matched with works that another second-century AD writer, Pausanias, described as existing at Argos in his day. He further proposed that the ship dated from the fourth century AD and was transporting the statues from Argos to adorn the newly founded imperial capital Constantinople. Svoronos made effective use of the press to publicize his progressively more elaborated theory, no doubt to the great exasperation of the archeologists.[21]

As the artifacts had arrived from the site, some had temporarily been stored and put on display at the Ministry of Education, but in due course everything was deposited at the National Archaeological Museum. An immense and difficult task of cleaning, conservation, and in some cases reconstruction lay ahead.[22] Most of the work was done out of the public eye; the Ephebe, however, was in the news for many months. It was regarded as the finest artwork recovered from the wreck; as a life-size bronze statue it was a rarity; and there were the enigmas of which mythological figure, if any, the youth represented and what lost object he had held aloft in his right hand. And most urgently, could the missing pieces be found, and who was best qualified to conserve the fragments and reconstruct the statue?

By the spring of 1902, the practical questions were becoming settled. In a pair of photographs that Kavvadias published in the previous year, we see the head, upper torso, and arms of the Ephebe as a single piece and about 20 separate fragments from the legs and lower body, some of them just a few square centimeters of plate (fig. 1.5). A space was allotted in the museum for unassigned bits of bronze so they could be sifted through for more missing pieces. Othon

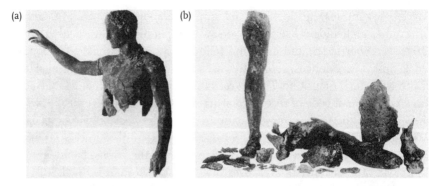

FIG. 1.5. Fragments of the mid-fourth-century BC bronze Ephebe (National Archaeological Museum X 13396) before assembly. (Kavvadias 1901, 206–7)

Rousopoulos (1856–1922), a noted chemist and pioneer of methods of cleaning bronzes, was entrusted with the conservation.[23] And after an international search and lengthy negotiations, the distinguished French conservator—and forger!—Alfred André (1839–1919) consented to come to Athens to reconstruct the Ephebe. He arrived to make an initial assessment of the job on May 6, and four days later he was heading back to Paris, with the intention of returning to begin the work that autumn.

In the context of these newsworthy developments, there was no reason it should have caused any fuss when Stais, now just a member of parliament for his native island, Kythera, made a Saturday morning visit to the museum on May 18 with his wife and sister-in-law. Though Stais's slightly older first cousin Valerios Stais (1857–1923) happened to be the museum's director, it appears that neither Valerios nor any of the other archeologists were there that day. The former minister had an obvious personal interest in seeing how the work on the materials from Antikythera was progressing, and so he was shown the room where the miscellaneous bronze fragments were kept. Of course, people had looked through them before, but they were searching specifically for bits of statuary and presumably did not pay too much attention to anything not shaped like flesh or clothing. Stais's eye was caught by a couple of fragments, probably lying side by side and evidently parts of a single slab-shaped object. One of them bore an inscription in Greek letters, difficult to make out in the afternoon light; the other had a system of interlocking gears visible on its surface.

This is the last time that Stais will figure in our story, but it is appropriate that he receives the title of "discoverer" of what we now call the Antikythera Mechanism, the most astonishing and historically significant object to have been recovered in the salvage operations that he had initiated and seen to successful completion—indeed, the most important artifact of ancient science that archeology has ever brought to light. He was not the first person to notice it;

that credit belongs to the sponge diver who brought it up from the seabed, followed probably by the archeologist who itemized the "inscribed slab" in the telegram, and perhaps also Periklis Rediadis if it is true that he prevented it from being chucked back into the water. But Stais seems to have been the first to observe the mechanical components, and, most important, he made sure that the fragments would at last receive attention from the archeologists.

2

The Investigations

Excitement in the museum

On the Monday following Spyridon Stais's visit to the National
Archaeological Museum, word of what had happened began to
spread, and Tuesday's newspapers carried reports with such headlines as *To Asty*'s "IMPORTANT DISCOVERY IN THE NATIONAL
ARCHAEOLOGICAL MUSEUM—Discovery of an inscribed bronze
slab—the things from Antikythera."[1] Whoever it was that told the
reporters about what had happened added a significant comment, that
examination of the inscribed lettering might cast light on the date of
the Antikythera shipwreck. This time the hard-to-read inscribed slab
was not going to fall back into obscurity, because it had the potential
to decide the outcome of the debate between Ioannis Svoronos and the
archeologists.

Greek inscriptions on stone survive in vast numbers from the
Archaic period through the late Roman Empire, and superficially they
look more or less the same regardless of when they were made: rows
of letters, mostly employing the "standard" 24-letter Greek alphabet, looking like the capital letters used in modern Greek printing
and scientific notations, with no spaces between words and rarely
anything like punctuation. On closer examination, however, there
are many variations in the way that letters were formed, and some
of these reflect changes of fashion. To take some easily recognized
examples, arc-shaped forms of epsilon and sigma (Ϲ as opposed to
E, Ϲ as opposed to Σ) are characteristic of inscriptions of the Roman
period—that is, "AD" centuries, while a "W-shaped" form of omega
(ω as opposed to Ω) becomes frequent not much earlier. Inscriptions
that contain dates, describe datable events, or were found in an archeological context from which we can determine when they were made
provide a basis of comparison against which one can attempt to estimate the date of a given inscription.

Epigraphers are often asked to provide bounds for the age of an inscription on the basis of the evidence of letter forms, and in older scholarship it is not uncommon to find dates assigned in this way with a precision of half a century or less. Nowadays the specialists tend to be more cautious. At any period, lettering styles could vary from one place to another within the Greek-speaking world, with the stonecutters of one place continuing to use "older" letter forms long after they had been abandoned elsewhere, and individual stonecutters could be active for decades using the forms that they learned in their youth—to say nothing of cases where old styles were consciously used to produce an antiquarian effect. For an inscription whose place of origin is unknown, it would now be considered prudent to qualify any date derived purely from letter forms with an uncertainty of as much as a century.[2] In the case of the texts preserved on the Antikythera Mechanism, the medium and technique are uncommon (ancient Greek inscriptions on bronze plate are rare, and the letters on them are usually punched, not engraved as on the Mechanism), the letters are exceptionally small, and the surfaces are corroded: additional reasons to be wary of making overly exact claims based on comparison with stone inscriptions.

Immediately upon Spyridon Stais's discovery of the Mechanism's fragments, an invitation was sent to Adolf Wilhelm (1864–1950), the secretary (i.e., director) of the Austrian Archaeological Institute in Athens and one of the leading Greek epigraphers of his day, to see what he could make of the inscribed letters.[3] In the meantime some of the archeologists, including Gavriel Vyzantinos, spent part of Tuesday looking at the fragments, which by this point we can definitely identify by the clues in the newspaper reports as the three fragments that would subsequently be named A, B, and C.[4] On Fragment A, the one with the conspicuous gears, they were able to discern a small area of exposed writing, of which they thought they could make out seven letters. In fact they got just four right. On Fragment B, there was a larger area of visible text, but curiously, it appeared to be a mirror image of normal Greek writing, as if they were seeing the back side of a thin and deeply inscribed plate (it was actually a layer of extraneous material that had kept the impress of a plate that had since disappeared). They did a bit better with this one, reading thirteen letters, of which nine were correctly identified, including a recognizable part of one ancient Greek word. The day's work cannot have felt encouraging, but after all they were experts on artifacts, not texts, and better could be expected on the morrow.

When Wilhelm arrived at the museum on Wednesday, Svoronos was also on the spot.[5] The reporter of the newspaper *Neon Asty* gives a lively picture of the epigrapher sitting elbow to elbow with the numismatist from 10 a.m. to noon and again for most of the afternoon, passing a big lens back and forth as they peered at the mirror text on Fragment B and intermittently calling for and leafing through big volumes of facsimiles of dated inscriptions from all periods. Toward the end of the day, Wilhelm, pressed by the reporters for his opinion, said cautiously that much more work would be needed before one could assign a definite date to the writing, but that it appeared to belong to the second or first century BC. He also revealed that a phrase meaning "ray of the Sun" could be read, suggesting that they were looking at the remains of a nautical instrument for astronomical observation. Svoronos, on the other hand, had a full prepared statement for the reporters, complete with a transcription of parts of seven lines of text—totaling 47 letters, all but one of them correct. While respectfully acknowledging Wilhelm's judgment that the letter forms were typical of the later Hellenistic period, he asserted that the presence of serifs terminating the strokes of the letters indicated a much later date, even as late as the third century AD. This rather audacious encroachment on Wilhelm's area of expertise was unfounded since there exist plenty of Hellenistic inscriptions with serifed letters, but Svoronos was confident of his theory about the voyage and he could not accept a dating of the Mechanism that would make it at least four centuries older than the ship that was carrying it.

Svoronos's statement is of considerable interest as the first attempt that anyone made to explain what the Mechanism was, drawing on both the physical features and the inscribed text. He begins by saying that he believes that it belonged to the general class of "astrolabes" or "shadow casters" used by ancient astronomers for their research and by mariners to determine their courses according to the observed positions of the Sun and stars. This sounds as if he was thinking of an observational instrument, an ancient counterpart of a Jacob's staff, mariner's astrolabe, or sextant, but what follows does not pursue this idea. Instead, he draws attention to the remains of a system of concentric metal rings on Fragment B and suggests that they could revolve and that the purpose of the gearwork was to drive the rings to represent the motions of the heavenly bodies—in a word, it was a planetarium, though Svoronos does not use that term. A key point was the reading in the inscription of part of "Aphrodite," the Greek name of the planet Venus. As for the layout of the device, Svoronos proposes that it was enclosed in a flat, hinged rectangular box like a diptych or a backgammon set, and when opened, one of the exposed faces showed the Mechanism while the other bore a metal plate inscribed with detailed instructions for the Mechanism's use. But, he goes on, the archeologists should call upon the knowledge of experts in astronomy, physics, and nautical science and meanwhile hold off on any chemical cleaning of the delicate fragments at least until they have been more closely studied. His concluding words hit the mark precisely: "what we have is a precious treasure, of interest to much wider circles than that of the archeologists."[6]

The next day, Konstantinos Rados (1862–1931), a teacher in the Royal Naval School and historian specializing in naval archeology and history, showed up in company with Wilhelm and the National Archaeological Museum's director, Valerios Stais.[7] Rados rapidly came to the conclusion that, while he had no clear idea of what the object could have been—were it not for the inscription, he would have suspected that it was something from a *modern* shipwreck that had accidentally got mixed up with the ancient one—it was definitely, *definitely* not an astrolabe, as he understood Svoronos to be claiming. By chance, the group ran into Svoronos and Periklis Rediadis in the courtyard of the museum, and Rados proceeded to explain to Svoronos everything that was wrong with his theory. The incident led to rival statements for the newspapers, and a few days later Rados gave a talk to the Archaeological Society of Athens in which he said that he had proved Svoronos wrong to his face, provoking an angry letter of rebuttal from Svoronos in *To Asty*.

The next steps tended to calm the furor.[8] The fragments were photographed and then put in a glass cabinet to wait until Othon Rousopoulos, a very busy man at this time, could undertake their cleaning and conservation. The minister of education (Antonios Momferratos) announced that a report would be commissioned from experts on how the Mechanism should be preserved and studied.[9] It is not clear that anything came of this initiative, and for almost three years the fragments appear to have been left in comparative peace in their cabinet.

An astrolabe?

In broad terms, the modern story of the Antikythera Mechanism divides into two periods. From 1902 to the 1960s, the only means of studying its remains were by examining it with one's own eyes or through photographs. The ensuing period, from the 1970s to the early 21st century, was distinguished by the availability of techniques for seeing *through* or *inside* the fragments. From this point on, each substantial leap in the detail and completeness of knowledge of the fragments went along with, and to a great extent resulted from, a new kind of imaging—though the technical advances operated in counterpoint with a succession of investigators who had varying talents, areas of competence, and ways of thinking. In the earlier period, by contrast, it was changes not in the ways of seeing but in the objects themselves that opened the way to significant progress. The work of skilled conservators in 1905 and 1953, as well as some accidental damage that occurred between these dates, made things visible that had previously been hidden behind other components of the fragments or underneath layers of accretion. Inevitably, some information was lost in the process, and old photographs and descriptions can take us only so far toward reconstructing the fragments' earlier states—though we would dearly like to find more of these witnesses from the past! With hindsight we might wish that Svoronos's plea had been followed, and that the fragments had been left in the condition they were found, or at most subjected to minimal conservation to protect them from further degradation. On the other hand, without some destruction of evidence at earlier times, scholars of more recent times would not have known enough about the Mechanism to motivate subjecting the fragments to sophisticated, nondestructive imaging methods that were not normally applied to antiquities.

The first accounts of the Mechanism, after the sparse details that one can extract from the newspaper reports of May 1902, described it "as it was removed from the sea," with the fragments still covered by a layer of accretion. The 1902 volume of the official journal of the Archaeological Society of Athens, *Efimeris Arheologiki*, contained a 25-page unsigned article on "The Finds of the Shipwreck of Antikythera," a collaboration of several of the ministry archeologists.[10] It is a rather dry catalog of the principal objects recovered, and while there is no explicit discussion of the date and nature of the wreck, date ranges are offered for several of the objects that would collectively imply that the ship was from the last two centuries BC or the first century AD. Almost the last object presented is the Mechanism; it gets just one paragraph, and a photograph of Fragment B bearing the mirror-writing inscription. We are told that it has gears, and an inscription that as yet eludes interpretation but that suggests that the Mechanism was something astronomical, and that is all except for the assertion that the inscription's letter forms can hardly be later than the middle of the first century AD.

If one gets the impression that this article was prepared in haste, an afterword confirms this: the journal's editorial committee (i.e., the archeologists under Panayiotis Kavvadias) considered that it was "most necessary" to publish as quickly as possible an issue containing images and brief descriptions of the objects recovered from the sea. Why this urgency? The explanation is surely that they had gotten wind that Svoronos was on the point of publishing a monograph of his own on the same subject, and felt that they had to get *something* into print first.

Svoronos's *The Hoard of Antikythera* came out in 1903 both in Greek and German editions, thus ensuring a worldwide readership.[11] With its item-by-item descriptions and its separate volume of plates, it has the look of an official catalog, but one can scarcely believe that this vehicle for Svoronos's most tendentious theories about the shipwreck was produced with the blessing of the museum and the Ministry of Education's archeological service. Yet, notwithstanding the book's biases, it is easily the best of the early publications on the wreck: detailed and informative, thoroughly documented, generally accurate on factual matters, and highly readable.

The chapter on the Mechanism—the first significant account of it published in a language other than Greek—is by Rediadis (fig. 2.1, on left).[12] Since those first heady days following the discovery of the fragments in the museum, Svoronos had established an informal alliance with Rediadis: Svoronos assumed the responsibility for reading and dating the inscriptions, while Rediadis took on the technical description and interpretation of the fragments. This explains why we hear no more of Svoronos's idea that the gearwork drove a planetarium.

(a)    (b)

FIG. 2.1. Two early investigators of the Mechanism: (*left*) the naval officer Periklis Rediadis, and (*right*) the philologist Albert Rehm, at the excavations at Miletus. (*left*, Modern Greek Visual Prosopography / National Hellenic Research Foundation; *right*, Antikensammlung, Staatliche Museen zu Berlin Preussischer Kulturbesitz, negative number Neg.PM 171)

By now four fragments had been identified, and in Svoronos's book they received the Roman letter designations A through D, which they have retained ever since (fig. 2.2). Rediadis's are the most detailed physical descriptions of the fragments that had yet appeared in print, and in fact they would not be superseded until Derek de Solla Price's *Gears from the Greeks* in 1974. Yet, they are strangely disappointing. Rediadis was capable of noticing small details, for example a tiny rectangular notch on one of the gears of Fragment A, which a century later was shown to be a key element of one of the Mechanism's most sophisticated functions (see p. 219). But he gives few measurements and makes no attempt to estimate the numbers of teeth on the gears that he saw, data without which one cannot begin a serious consideration of how the gearwork operated. The photographs, with one exception, are half-size, which is unhelpful given that the fragments were small to begin with, and the quality of their reproduction is poor.

Rediadis may have been the first person to realize that the proper approach to deducing what the Mechanism looked like when intact was by way of figuring out how the extant fragments fitted together. Unfortunately he based his answer on the false assumption that all the bits of text visible on Fragments A, B, and C belonged to a single inscribed plate; as we now know, these actually belonged to three distinct plates. As a result, he arrived at an arrangement that was entirely incorrect.

His interpretation of the Mechanism as an astrolabe was widely accepted in published scholarship until 1958. The Greek word *astrolabos*, meaning

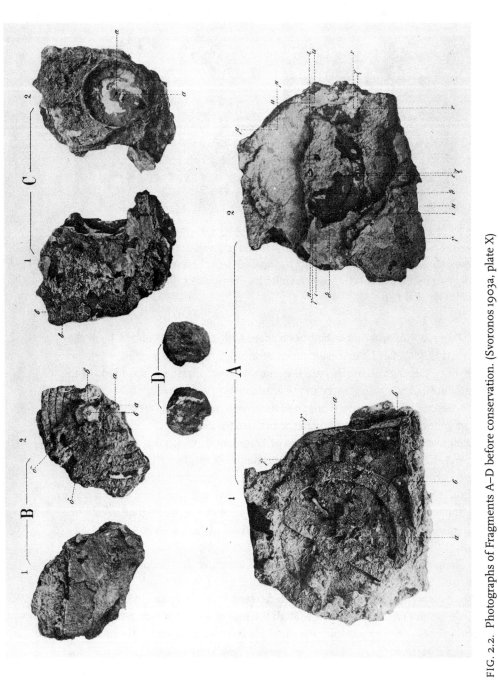

FIG. 2.2. Photographs of Fragments A–D before conservation. (Svoronos 1903a, plate X)

FIG. 2.3. Astrolabe made by Muhammad b. Abi Bakr in Isfahan, AD 1221/1222, Museum of the History of Science, Oxford, inv. 48213. This astrolabe, which was unknown to Rediadis, is exceptional in that it has a concealed gearwork mechanism displaying simple chronological cycles on the instrument's other face; see fig. 9.4. (Museum of the History of Science, University of Oxford)

"star taker," was used in antiquity as a general expression for an instrument designed to observe and measure the location of a heavenly body in the sky. When Rediadis asserted that the Mechanism was an astrolabe, he was thinking of an instrument that has been known by that name since about AD 400, the most important astronomical tool of the Middle Ages (fig. 2.3).[13] This medieval astrolabe, also called the "plane astrolabe," was shaped as a flat circular disk with attachments. One face of it was an observational instrument (hence the name), while the other was a calculator consisting of a kind of map of the observer's sky that can be adjusted to represent where the Sun and stars are in the sky at any date and time.

In pre-telescopic astronomy there was no way to see how far away a heavenly body is, but only its direction, and it was convenient to think of the sky as an enormous spherical shell with the Earth as its center. During the course of a day and night the Sun and stars are imagined as tracing out circular paths on this "celestial sphere," all of which are parallel and centered on a fixed point in the northern sky, the north celestial pole (this is assuming that the observer is somewhere in the Northern Hemisphere). On the slower time scale of months and years, the Sun is imagined to trace out a circular path relative to the stars, the "ecliptic," which runs through the middle of the zodiac belt and is on a tilt with respect to the axis of the circles of daily motion (see p. 107). The astrolabe uses a mathematical transformation called "stereographic projection," which maps the celestial sphere upon a planar surface in such a way that any circle on the sphere is represented by a circle on the map, and all circles that are centered on the north pole will be represented by concentric circles. Pivoted on the center of the disk is the "rete," a lattice of narrow bands of metal that represent the stars and the ecliptic circle. By rotating the rete, one can show how the Sun and stars are positioned in the observer's sky at an arbitrary date and time, and determine such quantities as the time interval from sunrise to sunset without having to make laborious calculations.

The origins of the plane astrolabe are obscure. Stereographic projection was already being used by the first century BC in the design of the display dials of water-driven mechanical clocks. We first encounter references to plane astrolabes toward the end of the fourth century AD, and the earliest surviving manual describing one is by the sixth-century Christian philosopher John Philoponus. No ancient astrolabe survives; the oldest ones known are Islamic and from the ninth century.

What considerations led Rediadis to identify the Mechanism as an astrolabe? He starts out by maintaining that the circumstance that it was found on board a ship implies that it was a marine instrument. He knew of one kind of mechanism described in an ancient text as being used for navigation, a sort of paddle-driven marine odometer described by Vitruvius, but this could be ruled out because the Mechanism was too small to serve such a purpose. On the other hand, the mentions of Venus and of the Sun's ray in the inscription linked it to astronomy, and hence (he reasons) it must have been used to determine a ship's location and bearing from the observed altitudes of the Sun and other heavenly bodies.

So far as Rediadis knew, the astrolabe was the only ancient astronomical instrument that had a complexity comparable to that which was apparent in the fragments of the Mechanism. To further establish a relation between them, he compiled a list of verbal parallels between the scraps of text that Svoronos and Wilhelm had been able to read on Fragment B and Philoponus' manual on the use of the astrolabe. Most of these are rather trivial, however; the most impressive was a sequence of letters that could have come from the middle of *moirognomonion*, a Greek word for the pointer of a graduated dial that occurs in Philoponus' manual. But even if one accepted this restoration, the coincidence of vocabulary would prove less than Rediadis thought, because the same word *moirognomonion* is used by other ancient authors, Heron and Pappus, for revolving pointers on diverse instruments.

And what about the gears? Rediadis realized that astrolabes such as the one described by Philoponus or the ones surviving from the Middle Ages had no gears. (There are in fact a very small number of medieval astrolabes fitted with gearwork, but he was unaware of them; for an example see p. 204 and figs. 2.3 and 9.4.) On the other hand, there seemed to be no visible remains on the Mechanism's fragments of stereographic projection. Rediadis therefore proposed that the Mechanism's gears served the same purpose as the stereographic mapping on conventional astrolabes; that is, they mechanically translated an observed altitude of the Sun or a star into angles displayed by pointers that represented the positional and temporal data that the ancient navigator required.

Rediadis did not try to show how a system of gears could convert an altitude angle into, say, the time of day. Generally speaking, one is struck by how little his interpretation of the Mechanism's purpose depended on his detailed observations of the fragments and his erroneous attempt to fit the fragments together. His lasting contribution was not to be the identification of the Mechanism as a mechanical counterpart of the astrolabe, which has turned out to be wrong, but the more general idea that the gears functioned as a device for calculating quantitative data by means of moving parts—that is, an analog computer.

A planetarium?

Three years after the appearance of Svoronos's book, Georg Karo (1872–1963), the secretary of the Athens branch of the German Archaeological Institute, gave a lecture on "The Finds of Antikythera," in which he announced a new interpretation of the Mechanism by a young classicist from Munich, Albert Rehm.[14] Up to this point, the Mechanism had been studied by specialists in the physical remains of antiquity (archeologists, a numismatist, an epigrapher) and authorities on naval history. Rehm (1871–1949; see fig. 2.1, on right) was a philologist—an expert on Greek and Latin texts—who had come to believe that a fully rounded student of antiquity should have experience with both the ancient texts handed down through the medieval manuscript tradition and the material remains recovered by modern archeology. For several years, therefore, he took part as an epigrapher in the German excavations at Miletus in Asia Minor and other sites. He also, as it happened, had a special interest in ancient astronomy, and he was intrigued by Rediadis's chapter on the Mechanism, sensing that there was more to be learned. Athens was on the way from Munich to Miletus, and so in September 1905 Rehm seized the opportunity, while passing through, to inspect the fragments.[15]

They were not quite the same fragments that Rediadis had described. By early 1905 Rousopoulos had apparently worked through much of the backlog of conservation work in the National Archaeological Museum and was ready to begin what he described as a "delicate task" entailing "difficulty and riskiness," the cleaning of the Mechanism.[16] He found that he could not treat the fragments with the same chemical or electrochemical processes as the bronze statuary from the shipwreck because they were composed of layers of plate so thin that two millennia of corrosion had left practically no free metal. Instead, Rousopoulos cautiously applied a wash of potassium cyanide to whichever surfaces he thought in need of cleaning, following this treatment with a layer of lacquer.

Meanwhile, a museum technician carefully pried off layers of plate or accretion that had become stuck to the fragments' surfaces, so that in addition to the four "original" Fragments A–D of Svoronos's 1903 book there were now a number of smaller bits, bearing either inscribed text or mirror-image offsets of text. A photograph of one particularly legible piece (now known as Fragment 19; fig. 2.4) was published by Valerios Stais, because it showed very clearly the typically late Hellenistic letter forms used in the Mechanism's inscriptions and so bolstered the argument that Svoronos was dating the shipwreck several centuries too late.[17] Stais thought that Rediadis had more or less solved the enigma of the Mechanism's nature, and had no inkling that the text on Fragment 19 contained clues that pointed in a quite different direction.

FIG. 2.4. Fragment 19, a portion of the "back cover" plate. At the time this photograph was made, soon after the fragment was separated from Fragment A, it was the most legible specimen of the Mechanism's inscriptions. (Stais 1905, 21)

Having only a few hours to look at the three main fragments, Rehm chose to concentrate on Fragment C, which hitherto had received little attention. It had an odd, flat cylindrical feature like an upside-down jar lid on one face (cf. fig. 2.2, top right), while the other face, according to Rediadis, had some illegible traces of inscription, though these were invisible in the published photograph. When Rehm saw Fragment C, this face was entirely transformed. An inscribed plate, itself mostly concealed behind a layer of accretion, had been fused to the rest of the fragment, and this had been carefully pried off in numerous pieces (the majority of them would later be reassembled into what we now call Fragment G). The surface now exposed was a *second* inscribed plate, and peeking out from behind its top edge was still another plate engraved with a graduated circular dial.

Because of its previously protected position, the new inscription was very well preserved, and entire lines of text could be read—quite a contrast to the miserable harvest obtained so far from Fragments A and B. But Rehm's luck did not stop there; the text turned out to be a special kind of astronomical document called a parapegma, and just the previous year Rehm had coauthored a paper devoted to several fragments of parapegmas inscribed on stone that had been excavated at Miletus.[18] Rehm knew, therefore, that these lists of the appearances and disappearances of constellations were tied to ancient methods of weather prediction, and that they were keyed to the Sun's annual cycle of motion through the zodiac.

Only a little of the dial was visible, but on it Rehm found a single Greek word, *Pachon*, which he recognized as the name of a month in the Egyptian calendar. The Egyptian calendar was unusual among ancient calendars in that its months had nothing to do with the phases of the Moon, but all were exactly 30 days long; the Egyptian year ended with five days that did not belong to any month, so the whole year was 365 days long, about a quarter-day shorter than the time it takes for the Sun to go around the zodiac (see p. 70). Shortly after Egypt became a province of the Roman Empire in 30 BC, the rules of the calendar were changed to add a leap day after every four years, in imitation of Julius Caesar's then-recent reform of the Roman calendar.

Rehm reasoned that a ring inscribed with the months and days of the Egyptian calendar *in this reformed version* would be a way of indirectly tracking the Sun's motion through the zodiac. By inference, the Mechanism must have had a revolving marker, driven by the gearwork, to represent the Sun's motion. But there were also clues that the Mechanism had something to do with the planets and the Moon. From the outset it had been recognized that the first letters of the Greek name of the planet Venus, Aphrodite, were legible on the Fragment B inscription. Now Rehm identified two numerals on the Fragment 19 inscription recently published by Valerios Stais that were intimately connected with the Moon and lunar calendars. Unaware that he had briefly been anticipated in this by Svoronos, Rehm guessed that the concentric rings in

Fragment B represented the orbits of the Sun, Moon, and planets around the Earth, and that a system of gears driven by a crank made each ring turn at a rate proportional to each heavenly body's period of revolution around the zodiac. No technical description of such a device exists in what survives of ancient Greek and Latin literature, but Rehm was able to point to passages in the Roman statesman and philosopher Cicero's writing that ascribe mechanized planetaria to Archimedes and to Cicero's older contemporary, the Stoic philosopher Posidonius (see pp. 129 and 182). Since he believed that the calendar ring represented the reformed version of the Egyptian calendar, Rehm supposed that the Mechanism must have been made not long after 30 BC, about half a century later than Posidonius' planetarium.

Rehm wrote up his observations and ideas about the Mechanism twice: first as part of a chapter of a book on ancient meteorology that he unsuccessfully submitted in a prize competition but never published; second, following another visit to Athens in 1906, as a separate manuscript paper that he referred to as his "Athens Lecture." It was the Athens Lecture that Georg Karo had presented on Rehm's behalf in December 1906.[19] The basics of Rehm's planetarium hypothesis were thus known to the Greek intellectuals who had taken an interest in the Mechanism, winning over Rados but provoking a rebuttal from Rediadis.[20] But Rehm never published his research, though Karo and other colleagues repeatedly urged him to do so. After 1906, when he was awarded a professorship at the University of Munich, he was increasingly occupied with pedagogy and university administration, and his primary scholarly mission was the publication of the inscriptions from the Miletus excavations. One suspects that he also sensed that more prolonged examination of the fragments, better measurements, and better photographs were necessary before a definitive interpretation of the Mechanism could be achieved.

The first person to attempt such an investigation was Ioannis Theofanidis (1877–1939), a naval officer whose career closely paralleled Rediadis's (by the mid-1920s, both had attained the rank of rear admiral) and who knew him well.[21] How much this connection had to do with Theofanidis's interest in the Mechanism is not clear; Rediadis wrote nothing on the topic after 1910, while Theofanidis's first published work on it dates from the late 1920s. It appeared in a curious context, an article on the voyages of Saint Paul that Theofanidis contributed to the *Great Military and Naval Encyclopedia*, a six-volume reference work in Greek that came out in 1929–1930.[22] Theofanidis took his subject as a springboard for a broad discussion of ancient navigational technology, and like most of the earlier investigators, he believed that the Mechanism was used on shipboard.

By 1934 Theofanidis had arrived—through study of the fragments combined with a good dose of imagination—at a very specific conception of what the Mechanism did, and he not only described his ideas in a short paper but also embodied them in a working model, which still exists though in a partly disassembled state.[23] According to his reconstruction, the Mechanism was a planetarium displaying the positions of the Sun, the Moon, and four of the five planets known to the Greeks. The detailed workings are very difficult to follow from his paper and its almost impenetrable diagrams. One notion he had, which we now know was mistaken, was that the displays of the Mechanism used stereographic projection to allow the user to read off the positions of the planets with respect both to the ecliptic and to the celestial equator, making an oblique link with the earlier speculations that the Mechanism was an astrolabe. On the other hand, his suggestion for systems of gears to produce the motions of Mars, Jupiter, and Saturn anticipate some elements of the reconstructions of planetary gearwork that have been proposed since 2001. Despite the fact that he published his paper in French, so that it was accessible to foreign scholars, its few pages had little impact, and more than 20 years would elapse before the Mechanism would again be the subject of original research. By then, practically everyone closely involved in studying the Mechanism had died, and the stage was clear for a new beginning.

A computer?

A young English physicist who had specialized in the physics of metals for his PhD as an external program student of the University of London, Derek de Solla Price (1922–1983) had become increasingly devoted to the history of science while holding a teaching post in applied mathematics in the late 1940s at Raffles College, Singapore (amalgamated in the University of Malaya in 1949).[24] Accordingly, he enrolled in 1951 as a doctoral student in the History of Science program at Cambridge, with his research topic initially defined as "The History of Scientific Instrument Making." Late that year he made the first discovery that would bring him fame, a 14th-century manuscript in the library of Peterhouse, Cambridge, containing a description in Middle English of an astronomical calculating instrument called an equatorium; Price argued on circumstantial grounds that this was a hitherto unknown work of Geoffrey Chaucer. Although he changed the research for his second doctorate, obtained in 1954, to an edition and study of this treatise, the broader topic of scientific instrumentation, and especially early "clockwork" mechanisms, retained its fascination. Price knew of the Mechanism from the 1903 description by Rediadis, Theofanidis's 1934 article, and a few less important secondhand references. Recognizing from these accounts that the fragments had to be evidence of a much more advanced Greco-Roman gearwork technology than anyone in the 1950s would have imagined on the basis of the surviving Greek and Latin literature, Price obtained from the National Archaeological Museum a new set of photographs of Fragments A, B, and C.

These photographs were not only clearer than any that Price had seen in print, but they showed the fragments in yet a third altered state. One cause was almost certainly accidental breakage, the most likely occasion of which was the Second World War.[25] When the Italian army invaded from the north in October

1940, bringing Greece into the war, the Greek government implemented plans for protecting the nation's archeological heritage. For the museum, this meant putting all the objects in the safest possible storage, a rather heroic operation. Statues and other large objects were buried in trenches under the galleries and in the courtyards of the museum; smaller objects, including the bronze artifacts—presumably the Mechanism among them—were boxed and deposited in the basement, in rooms that were subsequently filled with sand; and the most precious antiquities, such as the gold from Mycenae, and the inventory catalogs were transferred to the vaults of the Bank of Greece.

The redeployment of the museum's holdings after the German occupation of Athens and the Civil War took many years, and in the meantime certain treasures were given a new round of conservation and restoration. The Antikythera Ephebe, whose old reconstruction by Alfred André was thought to be unsatisfactory, was reassembled painstakingly by a team of sculptors and other experts, including the museum's master technician, Ioannis Bakoulis, between 1948 and 1953, after which Bakoulis turned to new conservation of the Mechanism.[26] Some damage was beyond repair: parts of the inscribed plates on the front face of Fragment C as well as a delicate patch of accretion layer with mirror writing on the back of Fragment A had shattered, with only isolated portions surviving as small separate bits. Bakoulis's work, so far as we can tell by comparing photographs from before and after, seems largely to have been a continuation of Rousopoulos's, clearing accreted matter from the faces of Fragments A, B, and C that Rousopoulos had left untouched. Between the breakage and the new cleaning, Price could see from his photographs that much new detail both of the mechanical elements and the inscriptions had become visible.

Price incorporated enthusiastic paragraphs on the Mechanism in articles that he wrote on the development of "clockwork before the clock" in the mid-1950s, but these were placeholders, drawing attention to the obvious complexity of the device and respectfully referencing Rediadis and Theofanidis but saying little more.[27] Wanting to inspect the fragments in person, but having little prospect of going to Athens, he made an application to have them brought to the British Museum's research laboratory, which had, he maintained, "the only complete facilities in the world for examining and restoring such corroded metal objects," but, to his disappointment, the Greek government would not allow the fragments to leave the country.[28] Then in 1957 he left England for the United States, holding temporary research positions first at the Smithsonian Institution and then, in 1958, in the School of Historical Studies at the Institute for Advanced Study, Princeton. Here he came in contact with two outstanding scholars in fields that complemented Price's expertise in early mechanical instrumentation: Otto Neugebauer, the 20th century's greatest historian of the mathematical sciences in antiquity, and Benjamin Dean Meritt, a specialist in the study of Greek inscriptions. Both were also members of the American Philosophical Society (APS), and it was likely at their suggestion, and certainly with Neugebauer's support, that he applied for and received a grant of $460 from the APS, with which he traveled to Athens and spent 10 summer days intensively studying the fragments in the National Archaeological Museum.[29]

Following their then recent conservation, they had not been put back on public display but were stored in several small flat boxes, some of them identifiable in Price's photographs as cigar boxes.[30] In addition to Fragments A, B, and C, they contained the inscribed plate that we now know as Fragment G— Price called it the "jigsaw" because it had been pieced together from numerous small bits separated from the front of Fragment C—many small fragments of plate (all of which had once probably been attached to A, B, or C), and a box half-filled with crumbs of corroded metal.[31] The museum's director, Hristos Karouzos, gave Price full access to the fragments and provided him with a workspace, where he was joined for part of the time by Georgios Stamiris (1914–1996), Meritt's research assistant, who, happening to be in Athens at the same time, assisted Price in reading the inscribed texts (since Price knew very little Greek).[32] Price's original notes from this visit are not known to have survived, but it is clear that he attempted to describe and measure every detail that he could. Among the many photographs that he brought back is one (fig. 2.5)

FIG. 2.5. Derek de Solla Price studying the fragments in the National Archaeological Museum in 1958. (© Derek de Solla Price heirs)

showing him seated smartly dressed at a table with a shelf of reference works behind him, measuring the inner radius of the large cross-spoked gear on the front of Fragment A with a pair of vernier calipers.

Once back in the United States, Price began to prepare a detailed scholarly book on the Mechanism, and in the interim he made a presentation on it on December 30 at the meeting of the American Association for the Advancement of Science (AAAS) in Washington, DC. Price had already shown a flair for publicity when a student at Cambridge—his "Chaucer" discovery had made both the *Times* and the *Times Literary Supplement*—and the AAAS meeting, though perhaps not the obvious venue if he had wanted to communicate to an audience of archeologists and historians of science and technology, was a good springboard for obtaining wider attention. Interviewed by the popular journal *Science News-Letter*, Price described his encounter with the fragments as "like opening a pyramid and finding an atomic bomb," adding that the Greeks who built the Mechanism "were not far behind where we are now."[33] A report by the Associated Press, widely printed in American newspapers, attributed to Price an only slightly less hyperbolic assessment that it "exhibits a stage of technological development perhaps more advanced than that of Europe in the 18th century."[34] Within days the story had also been picked up by the Greek press, while in the United States it got a brief and somewhat absurd lease on life when Karl Mohr, a retired professor of German at the University of Virginia, informed reporters that Dr. Price had been tragically deceived by mud and rust into an elementary blunder: the Mechanism was just a modern schoolroom model of the solar system, like the ones Mohr remembered from his elementary education in 1890s Austria, that had accidentally fallen off a boat and gotten mixed up with the ancient wreck.[35] (This story also reached Greece quickly, where it elicited an indignant rebuttal from the museum.)[36]

Despite the fanfare, Price had actually said little as yet about what the Mechanism was *for*, beyond describing it as a "computer" (a word that by the late 1950s already was associated in the popular mind with electronic, programmable computers, the acme of modern technological know-how), specifically a device for calculating planetary orbits—new words, but basically the planetarium hypothesis of Rehm and Theofanidis. Price was in fact deliberately shifting the focus of attention from the Mechanism's purpose, which remained a matter of informed guesswork, to the means by which it achieved that purpose; that is, the mechanical features that were there for anyone to see.

One person who was strongly impressed by the news of Price's researches was the science fiction and popular-science writer Arthur C. Clarke, who encouraged the editor of *Scientific American* to invite Price to write a popular article.[37] "An Ancient Greek Computer," the most important publication on the Mechanism since Rediadis's chapter, came out in the June 1959 issue, less than half a year after his AAAS presentation. It contained three crucial insights. First, Price had worked out exactly how Fragments A and B fitted together,

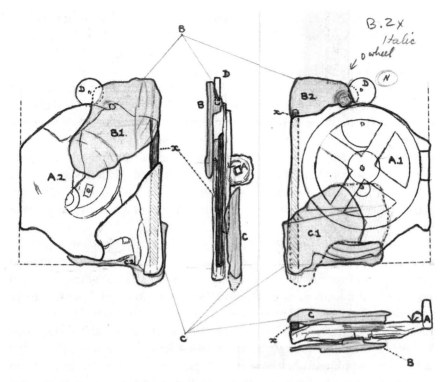

FIG. 2.6. Early 1970s drawing by Price showing how he believed that the principal fragments of the Mechanism fitted together. (© Derek de Solla Price heirs)

and also roughly how Fragment C was situated relative to them, and with this information he knew at last the exterior layout of the Mechanism with its front and back faces and dials (fig. 2.6). Second, contrary to the assumption of earlier investigators that the Mechanism's components had been badly crushed and distorted, Price realized that they largely preserved their original configuration, and that a larger fraction of the machine had survived than had previously been thought. Third, he grasped that the gearwork must have comprised a mechanical embodiment of various arithmetical relationships between periodically repeating time cycles involving the heavenly bodies. This last point seems to have come partly out of discussions with Neugebauer, who was able to identify for Price some of the key numbers connected with these astronomical periods in the inscription on Fragment 19.[38] So in Price's view, the Mechanism now seemed to be less about orbits in space than about cycles in time, less of a planetarium and more of a calculator.

Like Rehm before him, Price was convinced that the Mechanism was not a navigational instrument but rather a "wondrous device," designed to instruct and impress; the fact that it was found in a shipwreck site was an accidental consequence of its being transported, perhaps from its place of manufacture to its intended owner.[39] And there were clues suggesting to Price that it was fairly new when it sank to the sea bottom. Examining a sample of the inscriptions, Meritt judged that the lettering belonged to the first century BC, and vocabulary in the texts could be found in Greek scientific authors of that time.[40] A more precise date seemed to be offered by a small mark on Fragment C that Price thought was meant to show how the Egyptian calendar year lined up with the Sun's motion through the zodiac in the year the Mechanism was manufactured (see p. 76), and by a somewhat convoluted argument Price deduced that this "zero year" was approximately 82 BC and that the Mechanism was last reset about two years afterwards.[41] In later life, Price liked to suggest, only half-jokingly, that the Mechanism was a copy of the philosopher Posidonius' planetarium, lost en route to Rome with the baggage of the young Cicero after his eastern travels in 77 BC.[42]

At this stage Price seems to have got stuck.[43] He thought he had got what he could out of direct viewing of the fragments. He had measurements and estimated tooth counts for the 20 or so complete or partial gears that could easily be seen (mostly on the front and back of Fragment A), but other gears were hiding inside and still more were evidently lost. Stamiris had made a great advance in reading the inscribed texts, but the longer ones still had large gaps and many uncertain readings, and the noise-to-signal ratio was so high that only isolated words and phrases were intelligible. A second visit to the museum in 1961 only strengthened Price's conviction that he had come close to the limit of what could be accomplished by visual inspection.

The autumn following the *Scientific American* article's appearance, Price joined the faculty of Yale University, at first as a visiting professor and then from 1960 until his death in 1983 as a professor in Yale's new Department of the History of Science and Medicine. He published nothing specifically about the Mechanism between 1959 and 1974, and very little on the history of mechanism in general. This period of his career was most noteworthy for *Little Science, Big Science* (1963), his pioneering book on the growth of scientific activity, a strand of his interests that, as he told the story, went back to an occasion in his Singapore days when he stacked a two centuries' run of the Royal Society's *Philosophical Transactions* chronologically and noticed that the page count per decade increased more or less exponentially. But the Mechanism was still on his mind, and the year after *Little Science, Big Science* he wrote an essay on "Automata and the Origins of Mechanism and Mechanistic Philosophy," which argued for a sweeping thesis about the role in the history of thought and technology of devices such as the Mechanism that simulated the celestial motions as well as automata that mechanically imitated living beings. On this occasion Price declared that

> these two great varieties of automata go hand-in-hand and are indissolubly wedded in all their subsequent developments. In many ways they appear mechanically and historically dependent one upon the

other; they represent complementary facets of man's urge to exhibit the depth of his understanding and his sophisticated skills by playing the role of a do-it-yourself creator of the universe, embodying its two most noble aspects, the cosmic and the animate.[44]

The principles of these "despicable playthings and overly ingenious, impracticable scientific models and instruments" were eventually transferred to practical applications and thus came to be the "progenitors of the Industrial Revolution."

Seeing inside the fragments

Wilhelm Röntgen announced his discovery of X-rays in 1895, and already by the end of the 19th century, X-ray radiography was being applied to archeological and museum objects such as paintings and Egyptian mummies.[45] Radiography depends on the fact that the degree to which X-rays are attenuated by the matter through which they pass varies depending on the matter's density, composition, and thickness. X-rays can pass through a great deal of water or organic matter, but metals are much less permeable to them; it takes only a couple of millimeters of copper to attenuate X-rays by half. It was not at all clear whether subjecting the Mechanism's fragments by means of X-rays would yield useful results. Price's application for his 1958 travel grant from the American Philosophical Society shows that he hoped to make radiographs, but his inquiries at the National Archaeological Museum were turned down because the necessary equipment was not available and, even if it was, there would be problems with delivering the required electrical power in the museum.[46]

In the ensuing years, however, a few experiments were made with radiographing cast-bronze objects of cultural significance (such as the Great Buddha of Kamakura) by means of gamma rays emitted by radioactive materials.[47] Gamma-ray radiography had certain disadvantages compared to X-ray radiography: the radiation could not be controlled to the same extent as with X-rays, and it was difficult to obtain high contrast in the radiographs. On the other hand, gamma radiation penetrated metals much more effectively than X-rays and could be used in locations where not enough electricity was available to operate a sufficiently powerful X-ray source. When Price learned of this technology in 1971, he applied to the museum and to the Greek Atomic Energy Commission to see if something could be arranged, and this time his request was successful.[48]

Haralambos Karakalos, a physicist at the National Center of Scientific Research "Demokritos," undertook the radiography of the major fragments, initially using gamma radiation from a weak source of the isotope Thulium-170.[49] The resulting radiograms were of only fair quality but revealed some new

FIG. 2.7. Karakalos's 1971 X-ray setup with Fragment A. (Adler Planetarium, © Derek de Solla Price heirs)

gears. Deciding that X-ray radiography would be feasible after all, Karakalos brought two portable X-ray units to the museum (fig. 2.7) and produced a set of high-quality radiographs of Fragments A, B, C, and D.

For Price's purposes, the radiographs of A were the most important, since almost all the surviving gearwork is in that fragment. Twenty-seven gears were discernable in the images, of which six had been entirely invisible to direct inspection and another couple had been only barely visible. With the exception of the contrate (crown) gear that imparted the cranking input motion to the Mechanism, all the gears in Fragment A are parallel to the front and back faces and appeared in the radiographs as toothed circular arcs. The critical information that Price hoped to obtain was of two kinds: the tooth count of each gear, and the interconnections of the gears through common axles or meshing of teeth. It was anything but a straightforward task to extract either from the radiographs.

The tooth counts were carefully estimated by Karakalos and his wife, Emilia, though in the end Price sometimes chose to adopt different numbers. Price remarked on the way that the radiographs showed clear triangular outlines of teeth on gears that were barely noticeable to the eye. However, there was not one gear for which every single tooth could be made out, and in some instances less than half of the perimeter was extant. It was therefore necessary to determine the approximate center of each incomplete gear and then to extrapolate the tooth count from the number of surviving teeth and the arc that they subtended. Error could arise both from using the wrong center and from irregularities in the spacing of the teeth.

The radiographs of Fragment A were essentially the outlines of all the distinct components of the fragment projected along lines radiating from a focal point to the plane of the film. With more than 20 gears existing at varying depths in the fragment, each image was a complicated tangle of overlapping disks. In principle, two disks that showed up as concentric were likely to be joined by a common axle, and two disks that showed up as nearly touching—with the teeth of one projecting into the spaces between the other's teeth—were likely to be in the same plane and enmeshed, but the appearances could be deceptive. Karakalos tried unsuccessfully to obtain measurements of the depths of certain gears by making double exposures with the X-ray source moved from one position to another, though he was able to obtain some limited information about relative depths by comparing radiograms made at different focus-to-film distances.[50] Lost gears were a big further source of uncertainty.

Reconstructing the Mechanism was not a problem that could be solved purely from the radiographs, with their precious but incomplete and ambiguous evidence for the inner workings of the object. Knowledge of what the dials on the exterior were supposed to display might have given Price the constraints that he needed to resolve the uncertainties and to fill in the gaps in the gearwork, but he could determine the units and read the inscriptions on the scales of only the front dial, on the basis of which he could be sure that there was a revolving pointer indicating the Sun's annual motion through the zodiac. For the rest, all he could do was work out by trial and error what kinds of output would result from various hypothetical reconstructions, hoping that some of these would make sense in terms of astronomical reality and of what the ancient Greek astronomers were likely to assume about that reality.

Under the right conditions, this could work out astonishingly well. One series of gear-to-gear connections that Price reconstructed involved seven gears, beginning with the big cross-spoked gear, so conspicuous on the front of Fragment A, that was directly driven by the contrate gear transmitting the input motion.[51] Karakalos had provided estimates for the tooth counts, in two cases offering a range. Price's reconstruction assigns definite counts to all the gears, in all cases agreeing with Karakalos's specific figures or falling within his ranges except for one gear, where he gives the count as 127 teeth instead of Karakalos's 128. Price altered Karakalos's value not on the basis of the radiographs but because he realized that with 127 teeth, the train of gears would exactly translate 19 revolutions of the cross-spoked gear into 254 revolutions of the final gear in the train, and this would make astronomical sense if one turn of the big gear was meant to be one revolution of the Sun around the zodiac and one turn of the final gear was meant to be one zodiacal revolution of the Moon.[52] Price knew that this 19-year Sun-Moon cycle—which we will meet again in chapter 4 (see p. 78)—was referred to on the bit of inscribed plate we now (aptly if coincidentally) call Fragment 19, so everything appeared to fit; there must have been not only a pointer on the front dial representing the Sun, but also one for the Moon. This part of his reconstruction has been entirely vindicated by subsequent research, though we now know that there were further stages in the gearwork between what he thought was the last gear of the train and the Moon pointer.[53]

When it came to the gears leading to the dials of the back face, however, Price was less successful. One major difficulty was that several gears from the upper part of the Mechanism were lost. Some of these gears completed the train leading to the upper back dials, while others branched off from that train to drive the train leading to the lower back dials. The central component of the branch train is a large gear, visible on the back face of Fragment A, that has two tiers of teeth with differing tooth counts (it is like a pair of gears fused together) and that carries a little set of smaller gears on its face in an arrangement known as epicyclic gearing (see p. 216). We will refer to this for the time being as the "platform gear." This system is obviously something that had a special mechanical function. Price interpreted it as a "differential turntable," a device for subtracting one rate of revolution from another, in this case subtracting the Sun's motion around the zodiac from the Moon's to obtain a revolution with period equal to the lunar month.[54] He therefore guessed that the lower back dials displayed lunar months and lunar years, but to make this work, he had to alter Karakalos's tooth counts for two of the gears (which were in fact accurate to within one tooth) by a full 10 percent.

Karakalos's radiographs had given Price the impetus that he needed to finish his little book on the Mechanism, which he titled *Gears from the Greeks*, and in recognition of their sponsorship of his first trip to Athens, he gave it to the American Philosophical Society to publish in 1974 in one of their scholarly series. Compared to the attention the press had given to his AAAS talk and the wide readership his *Scientific American* article reached, this was, for Price, a low-key way to announce his findings; one wonders whether, notwithstanding the excitement that he expressed about the last puzzle-solving stages of the research, his interest in the Mechanism had not faded a little since 1959. His earlier work had already highlighted the astonishing technological sophistication of the object, and he may have felt less of a thrill in teasing out the fairly simple astronomical applications that his reconstruction implied for it. Be this as it may, *Gears from the Greeks* was noticed chiefly by historians of science and technology, who for the most part assumed that it was going to be the last word on its subject. Price's book had a greater impact in Greece, and by the mid-1970s the museum had again put the three main fragments on permanent display. (In chapter 9 we will see the impression it made on one famous visitor.) Most classical scholars and archeologists over the next three decades remained unaware of the Mechanism's existence and significance.

Toward a definitive reconstruction

In the years following the publication of *Gears from the Greeks*, a few people expressed doubts about whether Price's reconstruction was really viable. A particular focus of concern was that a comparatively slow rate of revolution representing the Sun's annual circuit of the zodiac was made to drive trains that "geared up" to much faster output rates representing the Moon's motion and the lunar month (see p. 207). In combination with Price's differential turntable, this would have put considerable strain on the gearwork, so that it was difficult to construct a working model that ran smoothly, especially if the gear teeth were made triangular as in the original.[55] A few speculative attempts were made to improve Price's reconstruction through comparatively minor modifications, but without direct reference to the physical evidence.

A fresh examination of the fragments was finally made by Michael T. Wright (born 1948) and Allan Bromley (1947–2002) during several visits to the museum in 1988–1993.[56] Wright, a curator at the Science Museum in London, had both trained as a physicist and acquired considerable practical experience and historical knowledge of clockwork mechanisms. Bromley, also originally a physicist, was a historian of computing at the University of Sydney who had previously studied Charles Babbage's designs for mechanical computers. In addition to painstaking visual study of the fragments (which brought to light many imprecisions and errors in Price's descriptions from 1958 to 1961), Wright and Bromley carried out new X-ray radiography. Realizing the importance of obtaining better information about the three-dimensional structure of the fragments and especially the relative depth of the tightly stacked gears and other components, they initially experimented with making stereo pairs of radiographs but achieved greater success with a technique known as linear tomography.

Linear tomography was developed between the two world wars as a method of X-ray radiography primarily for medical purposes.[57] In standard radiography, the X-ray source and the film must be kept stationary during the period of exposure to avoid blurring the image. If, however, the X-ray source is made to move along a straight path at a uniform rate, while the film moves in a parallel path at the same rate but in the opposite direction, all outlines of the object that lie in a plane halfway between the source and film paths will be sharp in the image, whereas outlines in other planes will be blurred. By adjusting the position of the object, one can produce radiographs in which any arbitrary plane is sharply imaged.

By the end of the 1980s, linear tomography had been almost wholly superseded by computed tomography and was a barely remembered technology. However, at that time, tomographic scanners powerful enough to scan a metallic object were rare and not portable, and their resolution was still too low to be able to capture the fine details of the Mechanism. Wright therefore built a table-top apparatus for linear tomography, with which he and Bromley produced numerous images of the fragments in the museum.

Bromley was prevented by illness from accomplishing much with the new data, and its significance became fully apparent only in a series of articles that Wright produced in 2002 and after, many of them published in journals dedicated to the history of watchmaking and scientific instruments. One example will suffice here to illustrate the remarkable progress that Wright made in recovering details of the Mechanism.[58]

We saw previously that among the first features to be seen on the fragments following their discovery in 1902 was what appeared to be the remains of a system of concentric circular bands, or annuli, of metal in Fragment B; later, another similar set was noticed in Fragment A. Some early investigators, such as Rehm, thought these might be mobile. Price's demonstration of how Fragments A and B fitted together led him to realize that these systems were two large dials occupying the top and bottom halves of the Mechanism's back face; he too thought that the annuli could be rotated.[59] Through precise measurements, Wright showed that, instead of sets of separate annuli, each dial was formed as a continuous spiral band of plate, making five complete turns in the upper dial and four in the lower, and of course the bands had to be fixed in position. The implication was that these dials displayed cycles that consisted of multiples, by five and four respectively, of a single revolution of their pointers.

Again, precise measurements together with considerations of simplicity led Wright to a conjecture about what gears were missing from the train leading to the upper back dials. For the link to the main spiral dial, only one lost gear had to be assumed, and its estimated tooth count, 53, would make the whole train translate exactly 3.8 revolutions of the big spoked gear into one revolution of the pointer of the upper back dial. From Price's work it was known that a revolution of the spoked gear represented a solar year, so one turn of the spiral dial's pointer should represent 3.8 solar years, and the spiral's five turns should represent exactly 19 years. This was the same cycle, equating 19 zodiacal revolutions of the Sun, 254 zodiacal revolutions of the Moon, and consequently 235 (254 – 19) lunar months, that Price had discovered as the foundation of the train leading to the Moon pointer of the front dial.[60] The bands of the upper dial, as Price had also noticed, were divided by engraved radial lines into cells containing illegible inscriptions, and the breadth of the cells was approximately what one would obtain if the entire spiral comprised 235 cells. Thus, even without deciphering any text in the cells, Wright had very strong confirmation that the upper spiral displayed a 19-year lunar calendar cycle and that his reconstruction of this train was correct.

Wright rejected Price's interpretation of the platform gear on the rear face of Fragment A as a differential turntable.[61] A differential by definition requires two input motions, but one of the inputs in Price's scheme had turned out not to be there. On the other hand, a closer examination suggested a different function for the epicyclic gearing. From his radiographs, Karakalos had suspected that at least one of the smaller gears lying on top of the platform gear was actually a stacked pair of distinct gears of similar size, and Wright confirmed that in fact there were two stacked pairs.[62] He believed that this epicyclic system was a device for obtaining a rate of rotation that would be hard to get through simple gear trains, in this instance most likely yielding a rate that enabled the lower back dials to display cycles of the Moon's motion in latitude (its alternating movement north and south of the ecliptic), one of the factors determining when eclipses occur. Wright's gearing scheme utilized only one of the two tiers of teeth on the platform gear; he accounted for the other tier as a relic of a previous use of the gear in a different mechanism.[63] This part of his reconstruction, as it stood in 2005, would turn out to be mistaken.

In the history of study of the Mechanism, the suggestion had repeatedly been made that it displayed the motions of the planets as well as the Sun and Moon. Svoronos had fleetingly toyed with the idea before committing himself to the "astrolabe" hypothesis. Rehm was committed to it, believing that it made sense of the apparent reference to the planet Venus in the mirror inscription on Fragment B and that it situated the Mechanism within a known category of ancient mechanical devices, the planetaria described by Cicero and other authors. Rehm also drew tentative sketches of what the gearwork of a simple planetarium might have looked like, though he did not build a physical model.[64] Theofanidis, as we saw, did construct a model of his more astronomically ambitious reconstruction, which attempted to take account of the visible features of the fragments.

It is not surprising, therefore, that when Price first went to Athens to examine the Mechanism, he was confident (as his grant application says) "that it was a planetarium, perhaps similar to that said to have been made by Archimedes." However, his findings concerning the original configuration of the fragments meant that the reconstructions of his predecessors could not be right, and in his *Scientific American* article he turned away from the planetarium idea, arguing instead that the Mechanism was, in his words, "an arithmetical counterpart of the much more familiar geometrical models of the solar system which . . . evolved into the orrery and the planetarium."[65] By this he appears to have meant that the displays exhibited not the actual varying motions of the planets but rather the current stage in their cycles of motion as a kind of time referent.

Gears from the Greeks, with its extensive reconstruction of the gear trains of the Mechanism on the basis of Karakalos's radiographs, represented a decisive step away from the conception of the Mechanism as a planetarium. It now appeared that all the roughly 30 surviving gears belonged to systems that were entirely related to the motions and phenomena of the Sun and Moon. In one place, where Price is summarizing the front-to-back arrangement of the Mechanism's plates and components, he indicates where there might have been "a block of planetary gearing if this is to be conjecturally restored," but this is just a passing remark; and it is not at all evident that he meant gearing that would mimic variable motions of the planets through the zodiac.[66] On the contrary, when toward the end of the book he attempts to set the Mechanism in the context of the astronomical mechanisms known from Cicero and other ancient authors, he writes that the advance of Greek astronomical theories since Archimedes' time "might well have made the planetary geared model virtually unobtainable in practice from that time until the highly elaborate constructions of Richard of Wallingford [1292–1336] and Giovanni de Dondi [ca. 1330–1388] restored the Archimedean intentions in the later Middle Ages."[67] Hence, he was no longer content to designate the Mechanism as a "computer"; it was now a "calendar computer," an expression that effectively excluded any serious representation of planetary motion.

To Wright it appeared that there were three persuasive arguments that the Mechanism ought to have had a planetarium display: first, the absence in ancient literature of any references to any mechanical device specifically dedicated to tracking chronological cycles; second, the mention of Venus in the inscription; and third, the presence of physical features on the front side of Fragment A whose purpose had not been accounted for.[68] It was still true in Wright's reconstruction that every surviving gear, except for an isolated one in Fragment D, had to do with the Sun, the Moon, and the calendar, but nearly the entirety of this complicated lunisolar system was *behind* the big spoked solar-year gear, and it did not supply an explanation of why the solar-year gear should have been made so big. But on the spokes and rim of the gear, there are the remains of several protuberances and mountings, which hinted to Wright at the former existence of a substantial further apparatus, likely involving epicyclic gearing.

The term "reconstruction" has appeared in our story frequently with reference to the Mechanism, and it will appear many more times. It carries a range of senses. A reconstruction can be (1) a diagrammatic representation of what someone thinks that the Mechanism looked like, which may be as generalized or as detailed as one wishes, or (2) a conceptual or mathematical model describing its operation in abstract terms, or (3) a physical model, whether built using modern resources and methods or, so far as is practicable, with the materials and tools supposedly available in antiquity, or (4) a digital model, in which the arrangement, motions, and possibly also the physical behavior of the components are simulated by computer. In his research on the Mechanism, Wright has always stressed the value of physical reconstructions made by means of reasonable approximations of ancient tools and materials, maintaining that working models provide the only convincing proof that a hypothetical reconstruction could be built and made to work.[69] He has accordingly built and, where necessary, modified working models of the Mechanism that include both the completed lunisolar gearwork and a conjectural gearwork representing the motions of the five ancient planets according to theories of their motion appropriate for the Greek astronomy of about 100 BC (at least so far as we know what those theories would be like). The planetarium displays of his models are not offered as definitive recreations of the lost gearwork but aim to be consistent with the physical evidence while conforming to the most sophisticated and accurate level of astronomy that it would be reasonable to suppose the ancient designer would have sought to emulate.

The most recent examination of the fragments was carried out in 2005 by a research team called the Antikythera Mechanism Research Project (AMRP) in collaboration with the National Archaeological Museum.[70] The AMRP was organized through the initiative of Mike Edmunds, an astrophysicist at Cardiff University, and Tony Freeth, a mathematician and filmmaker, who, like Wright and Bromley before them, had come to be dissatisfied with Price's reconstruction and believed that a fresh investigation using newer technology had the potential to advance our knowledge of the Mechanism. In addition to Edmunds and Freeth, the AMRP's academic component comprised two Greek astronomers, John Seiradakis of the University of Thessaloniki and Xenophon Moussas of the University of Athens; a specialist in Greek paleography, Agamemnon Tselikas; and Yanis Bitsakis, a doctoral student in physics at the University of Athens. The museum's contingent included the chemist Eleni Mangou, Mary Zafeiropoulou, curator of antiquities in the bronzes collection, and Yerasimos Makris, the head conservator. Additionally, there were two technical teams: one from Hewlett-Packard, led by Tom Malzbender, and another from X-Tek X-Ray Systems (now a part of Nikon Metrology), led by Roger Hadland. It was not only the number of people involved that made the AMRP campaign different from its predecessors. This was also the first round of investigation in which direct examination of the fragments played no part; because of their delicate condition, they would from now on be handled only by National Archaeological Museum's technicians.

The collection of fragments had again undergone changes in the time since Price's 1958 visit. Besides Fragment D, which had been found again in time for Gears from the Greeks, another previously unknown piece came to light in 1976 and was assigned the letter E. Price saw photographs of Fragment E, which showed some mirror inscription on one side, but it was Wright who determined the correct original location of Fragment E in a gap between Fragments A and B.[71] Then, when Mary Zafeiropoulou went to the museum's storage area in 2005 to find the fragments, other than the three (A, B, and C) that were on public exhibition, for the AMRP research, she found 79 fragments placed in a tray.[72] Among these were most or all of the fragments seen by Price in 1958, Fragments D and E, and several additional fragments not previously known to researchers. Zafeiropoulou assigned the letter *F* to the largest of the new fragments and the letter *G* to Price's "jigsaw" inscribed plate, and she gave the smaller fragments numbers up to 75. This is now the accepted system for identifying the fragments, and since they are mostly flat or roughly slab shaped, the two faces of each fragment have been more or less arbitrarily designated as 1 and 2, extending the notations introduced by Svoronos in 1903.

Malzbender's team carried out a kind of imaging that he and Dan Gelb had developed called polynomial texture mapping; the technology has since been extended and is usually referred to as reflectance transformation imaging (RTI).[73] From a set of conventional digital photographs of an object, taken from a single viewpoint but with flash illumination successively from many different directions, a data file is generated that assigns a "reflectance function" to each pixel. Viewing software allows one to visualize the object in various ways; for example, one can simply simulate lighting from an arbitrary direction, or increase the amplitude of the reflectance functions, or strip out surface coloration. The purpose of RTI is to enhance the visibility of details of the surface shape of an object and allow it to be studied on a computer screen remote from the object itself. It is an easily portable and fairly inexpensive technology; in recent years RTI has found widespread use in many fields of cultural heritage. For the Mechanism, RTI imaging was chiefly intended, and proved to be particularly useful, for studying the inscriptions (figs. M7 and M8).

While RTI was a comparatively novel technology in 2005, X-ray computed tomography (CT) had been around since the early 1970s. While the primary application of CT was medical imaging, it had also been exploited for research on archeological and cultural objects; already in the mid-1980s, casting techniques of Greek bronze statuary had been investigated using CT.[74] As we have seen, the technology had not sufficiently progressed by the end of that decade to be applied to the Mechanism without having the fragments transported to a facility outside the museum, which their condition forbade.

Just in time for the 2005 AMRP campaign, X-Tek had built a microfocus X-ray CT system that was powerful enough to image the fragments and *just* small and transportable enough to bring into the museum.[75] From scans of all the fragments, tomographic volume files were generated in which each voxel (the three-dimensional equivalent of a pixel) recorded the radiodensity of the corresponding microscopic region of the fragment; the finest resolution obtained was 40 microns. These volumes could be manipulated in various ways, but principally by means of CT viewing software allowing the user to create planar slices through any point at arbitrary orientations. One could either work with the viewing software interactively or generate image stacks representing closely spaced parallel slices.

The CT scanning, like the linear tomography of Bromley and Wright, was intended in the first instance to clarify the internal physical and mechanical structure of the fragments. However, Bromley and Wright had noticed in their tomographic radiograms of Fragment C that one could detect the presence of inscribed lettering in the interior of the fragment, where the surface of an inscribed plate lay against another component, though their images were not quite clear enough to allow the text to be read.[76] The AMRP's CT volumes showed such interior inscriptions, which exist also in several other fragments, with great clarity. They even turned out to be helpful with reading text on exposed surfaces, since the letter forms were often better preserved slightly below surface level because of corrosion.

A paper reporting the first outcomes of the AMRP's research was published in *Nature* in 2006.[77] It confirmed the validity and accuracy of many of Wright's findings, including the tooth counts of most gears, the corrected version of Price's train yielding the Moon's mean rate of revolution around the zodiac, and the lunar calendar train leading to the upper back dial. However, a new restoration of the train leading to the lower back dials, substantially the work of Freeth, showed that by positing a single missing gear on one of the axles of the lunar calendar train, driving the platform gear by way of the tier of teeth that Wright had not used, the output of the lower gears could be made to represent cycles known in antiquity for predicting eclipses. The validity of this restored train was confirmed by measurements of the division of the lower spiral dial, showing that it comprised an appropriate number of cells, paralleling Wright's demonstration for the upper spiral dial. Moreover, the platform gear itself now proved to turn at the rate of revolution of the apogee of the Moon's orbit around the Earth, and the epicyclic gearing made sense as a device for introducing a variation of speed in the Moon's zodiacal revolution resulting from the orbit's eccentricity.

With one minor modification, the gearing scheme of the 2006 AMRP paper, consisting as it does of elements contributed by Price, Wright, and the AMRP team, stands as the more or less universally accepted reconstruction of the Mechanism so far as it displayed functions related to the motions of the Sun and Moon.[78] Wright immediately asserted his agreement with it and modified his working model to prove that it actually worked.[79] The basis for this consensus is exceptionally strong, deriving from the physical evidence of the surviving gearwork, the inscribed labels on all the dial scales, and our independent knowledge of ancient astronomical theory. Impressively, it makes use of every surviving gear except the isolated one in Fragment D and requires the restoration of only a few gears, largely on known and visibly damaged axes, in the region of the upper back dials, in the space between Fragments A and B.

The 2006 paper also demonstrated the potential of the RTI and CT imaging for reading the inscriptions, by providing new transcriptions of three of the more extensive texts.[80] These were offered as a "work in progress." The amount of text read was substantially greater than the versions in *Gears from the Greeks* (which we recall were made, chiefly by Stamiris, by direct examination), but there remained many gaps and uncertain or problematic letters, and it was possible to translate only disjointed words and phrases. Nevertheless, these included many significant and suggestive items of Greek astronomical and mechanical vocabulary.

With the appearance of the 2006 paper, the Mechanism achieved an unprecedented level of notice; publication in *Nature* is, after all, an avenue to journalistic as well as scholarly attention, and the theme of cutting-edge technology unlocking ancient secrets has universal appeal. It can be said to have brought to a close the line of questioning that began in earnest with Price: we now know how the surviving gears, except the single one in Fragment D, connected and what was the meaning of the dial displays that they led to.

Paradoxically, the result has been an explosion of new research and a proliferation of the community of researchers. Besides clarifying the structure of the gearwork, the 2006 paper showed the potential of the AMRP data to yield improved readings of the inscribed texts and enhanced knowledge of mechanical and physical details of the Mechanism. Several subsequent publications have presented new and more accurate texts of particular inscriptions, culminating in a series devoted to a comprehensive edition and study of all the inscriptions.[81] Other early-21st-century studies have been devoted to aspects of the construction of the exterior displays and the techniques and tools of construction. Drawing on this new information, more informed proposals have been offered for reconstructing the lost parts of the Mechanism, and its relations to ancient astronomical science, calendrical practices, and the broad cultural context are beginning to be explored. Much of this more recent work will show up in the chapters that follow.

3

Looking at the Mechanism

At the outset of this book I invited the reader to picture a passenger being shown the Mechanism on its ill-fated voyage. It is now time for us to imagine examining it for ourselves, so far as this is possible. Our most important evidence will come from the surviving fragments, but in addition we can sometimes appeal to a verbal witness. This witness is the text inscribed on the so-called back cover, the metal plate that was pressed against the Mechanism's back face during its long time underwater, leaving the mirror-writing impressions that caught the first investigators' attention and baffled them. We can now read parts of more than 50 lines of this so-called back cover inscription (or BCI), and it turns out to have been a systematic description of the exterior features of the Mechanism.[1]

The best place to start is the side of the Mechanism that we conventionally call the rear face (fig. 3.1). About a quarter of it survives in Fragments A, B, E, and F, though it is in large part hidden behind other material. It consisted of a rectangular bronze plate (the back plate), approximately 32 centimeters (cm) in height by 17 cm in width and about a millimeter and a half thick, enclosed in a wooden frame about 4 millimeters (mm) thick on all sides.[2] Most of the plate's surface was taken up by dials, while the leftover spaces around the edges contained a text inscribed in horizontal rows of letters, so there would have been no ambiguity about which way was up.

The upper back dials

Two large spiral dials dominated the top and bottom halves, respectively, of the back plate.[3] Let us consider first the upper dial, about a third of which is extant in Fragment B (figs. M3 and M4). It will be helpful to assign names to the various dials as we introduce them, even if the reasons for the names will not become apparent until later;

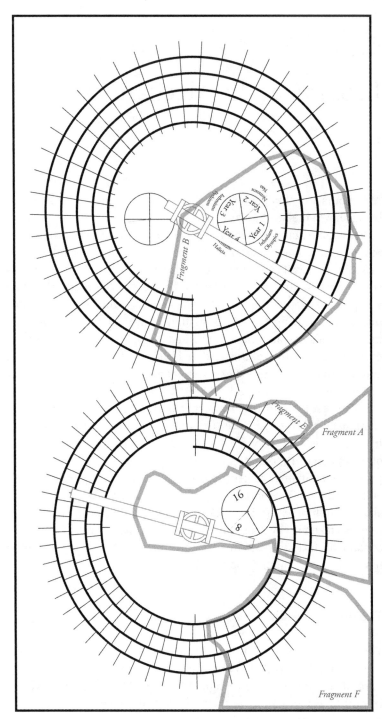

FIG. 3.1. Dial layout of the back plate with its pointers, omitting the inscriptions of the spiral scales, and with the subsidiary dial inscriptions in translation. *Top*, the spiral Metonic dial enclosing the Callippic dial on the left and the Games dial on the right. *Bottom*, the spiral Saros dial enclosing the Exeligmos dial. Gray outlines roughly indicate preserved portions in Fragments B, E, A, and F.

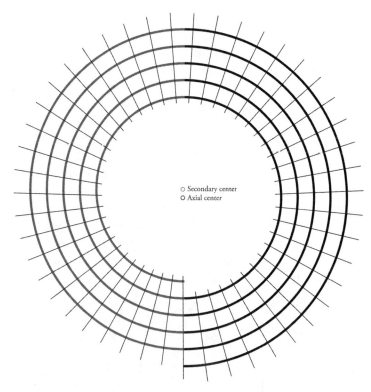

FIG. 3.2. The geometry of the Metonic dial. The black semicircles on the right have the axial center as their center; the center of the gray semicircles on the left is the secondary center, which is situated slightly above the axial center. All the scale divisions are along radii through the axial center.

thus we name the upper dial the Metonic dial (fig. 3.2). Its structure was very unusual, having two distinct centers. We will call one of them the axial center because this was the location of the axle or arbor bearing the dial's pointer. It was halfway between the plate's left and right edges, and about one-quarter of the way down from the top edge. The other was a secondary center about 3 mm directly above the axial center. On the right side of the plate, a series of five concentric semicircular slots, about a millimeter wide and having the axial center as their center, were cut through the plate; their radii ranged from about 44 to about 73 mm. On the left side was another series of five concentric semicircular slots, centered on the secondary center, with radii such that if we traced the innermost semicircle of the left side clockwise from its bottom end, it would continue without break into the innermost semicircle of the right side, and so on until after spiraling through five complete turns it came to an end directly below the starting point. To keep the plate from getting bent out of shape, rows of small U-shaped bridges on its underside connected the plate on either side of the slot along a few radii; one of these rows survives.

Ordinarily, a dial pointer is just that—a long, thin object attached to the axis and functioning like an arrow to indicate a point on the dial's scale. The pointer of the Metonic dial, however, was a rod with rectangular cross section, held by a pair of perforated bearings that flanked a disk mounted on the axle so that the rod could slide back and forth radially, effectively giving it a variable length.[4] At the outer end, it had a pin projecting downward, which rode in the spiral slot. (The pointer survives, though it has come out of its mounting, which is also partially preserved.) A scale was inscribed on the back plate running all the way along the outside edge of the slot. As the axle revolved, the pin followed the slot, and the end of the pointer lay over the corresponding point of the scale. When the pointer reached the end of the slot, the operator had to lift its pin out of the slot and reinsert it at the beginning of the spiral to start the next cycle.

Each round of the scale was divided by engraved radial lines into 47 cells subtending equal angles at the axial center, so that each cell corresponded to an equal interval of revolution of the pointer, though the cells toward the inside end of the spiral were much smaller in area than the outer ones.[5] Since the spiral

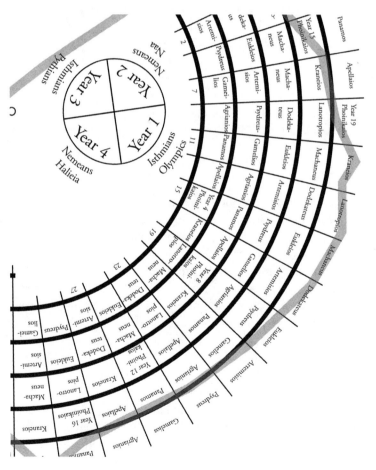

FIG. 3.3. Detail of the Metonic dial with translated calendar inscriptions.

had five turns, the cells totaled 235. Inside every cell was a little bit of inscribed text, just two or three short lines, with the reading direction running clockwise so that up was always away from the axial center (fig. 3.3).[6] Starting with the first cell (at the inner end of the spiral), every 12th or 13th cell's inscription began with an L-shaped symbol meaning "year" and a numeral,[7] counting up from 1 through 19, and then the Greek word *Phoinikaios.* Each of the following 11 or 12 cells in the sequence contained another of a fixed series of 11 Greek words, always in the same order, with each word appearing just once in a sequence of 12 cells, whereas one of the words appeared in two consecutive cells in a sequence of 13 cells.

These words were the names of months in a lunar calendar, and the complete spiral scale was a description of a series of 19 lunar-calendar years forming a repeating cycle. The inscriptions on the back plate provided one further bit of information about this calendar system. Running around the inside edge of the spiral slot, a numeral was written radially below every second or third cell.[8] When the pointer was at one of the months along the radial line outward from one of these numerals, this meant that in counting the days of that month, one was supposed to skip over the indicated number; so, for example, if the pointer was at the cell inscribed "Year 4, *Phoinikaios,*" which was along a radial line having the numeral 15 below it, the days of this month were to be counted 1 through 14 and then 16 through 30, with no day number 15. Hence, every month nominally had 30 days, but in reality nearly half of them were just 29 days long.

All the foregoing can be seen or deduced from the surviving parts of this dial in Fragment B, but it is interesting to compare our description with that of the BCI. At least 14 lines of the BCI (II.2–15) are devoted to the Metonic dial, an exceptionally long treatment of a single feature that probably reflects its unusual and complex nature. We have only short sections of these lines, but the relation of the translatable phrases to the dial is obvious:

> . . . from the divisions . . . in the entire spiral, 235 segments . . . and the days that are to be skipped . . . two bearings around a disk . . . the aforesaid bearings, perforations . . . drawn through the perforations . . .

And after several lines that are too poorly preserved to get much out of,

> "[reinsert?] the pin in the place where it was pulled out. . . ."

The BCI then goes on to describe two other dials:[9]

> . . . two pointers whose tips travel . . . four [sectors?]. One of them shows . . . [the other shows] each 19-year cycle of the 76-year cycle . . .

These dials occupied the more or less circular space enclosed by the spiral, one to the left of the spiral's axle and the other to the right. Only the one on the right survives, but they were probably very similar. They were small circles, the extant one being just over 2 cm in diameter and the lost one probably of the same size, engraved on the plate and divided into four equal sectors by engraved diameters. The pointers, which have not survived, would have been simple ones lying fairly flat against the plate so that they would not obstruct the pointer of the spiral dial.

Inside the four quadrants of the right subsidiary dial were engraved, in counterclockwise order and with up being toward the center, the numerals for 1, 2, 3, and 4, each preceded by the L-shaped "year" symbol.[10] This dial counted years in a repeating four-year cycle. Outside the quadrants, and in the same orientation as the numerals, were engraved the names of various athletic festivals that were regularly held in the corresponding cycle years; we will therefore call this the Games dial.

The left dial, which we call the Callippic dial, would have run clockwise, and, as the BCI says, it counted 19-year cycles in a bigger cycle of 76 years; thus, every time the pointer-follower of the spiral dial traversed its spiral completely, the pointer of the left subsidiary dial would move clockwise one quadrant. We do not know how the quadrants were labeled: possibly with 1, 2, 3, and 4 to show the cycle number, or *empty*, 19, 38, and 57 to show a number of years to be added to the year number indicated on the spiral dial's scale.

The lower back dials

The spiral dial in the lower half of the back plate, called the Saros dial, resembled the upper one rotated 180°, but with only four complete turns to the spiral slot instead of five. Parts of the scales are extant in Fragments A (fig. M2), E, and F, but the pointer, which must have been the same kind as that of the upper dial, is lost. The scale was divided into 223 cells subtending equal angles at the axial center; since this number does not divide evenly by four, the cell divisions did not line up from one turn to the next.[11]

Just as in the Metonic dial, the cells of the Saros dial represented lunar months, but here they were not being related to calendar months and years but to eclipses (fig. 3.4). The majority of the cells contained no inscription. Reading clockwise along the scale from its beginning (at the inside end of the spiral), one would have seen four or five empty cells followed by one or two that contain short, heavily abbreviated inscriptions that indicated that an eclipse of the Moon or of the Sun, or both, *could* occur in this month.[12] A typical inscription might translate as "Moon, hour 6, E." This refers to a possible lunar eclipse. The time means the time when the Sun and Moon were exactly opposite each other (i.e., the middle time of the eclipse), and the letter was a key to finding more information about the eclipse in the back plate inscription (BPI; not to be confused with the BCI), to which we will come presently. The implication of this dial is that lunar months in which eclipses can happen repeat in cycles of 223 lunar months, which is a little longer than 18 solar years.

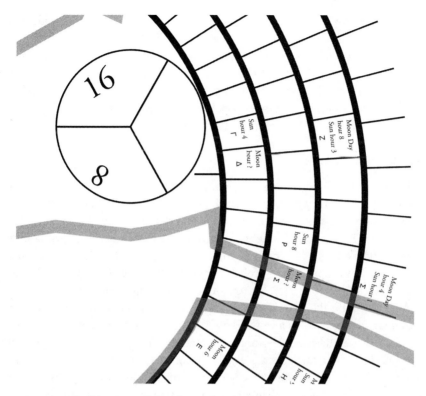

FIG. 3.4. Detail of the Saros dial with translated eclipse inscriptions.

There were no letters or numerals inscribed around the inside of the Saros dial like the "skipped day" numbers of the Metonic dial, but it appears that four short radial lines were engraved just inside the spiral, dividing one round of it into four equal parts[13] (only one of these marks survives). The meaning of the marks seems to have been that when the pointer-follower was lined up with one of them, the Moon would be at its farthest distance from the Earth at full moon.

Inside the spiral and to the right of its axle was a subsidiary dial of the same size as those in the upper spiral, the Exeligmos dial.[14] It was divided into three equal sectors, inscribed (in clockwise order, oriented so that up meant radially outward) *empty*, 8, and 16. This dial's pointer would have revolved clockwise by one sector every time that the pointer-follower of the lower spiral dial completed a full cycle of 223 lunar months. The explanation of this dial is that the mean length of 223 lunar months is close to eight hours more than a whole number of days. Hence, if the pointer-follower of the lower spiral was indicating a cell containing a statement about an eclipse, the subsidiary dial would show what multiple of eight hours, if any, had to be added to the time recorded in the cell.

The BCI's surviving section on the lower back dials (II.20–24) seems to have been much briefer than the section on the upper dials, probably because there was no need to repeat the description of the spiral and pointer. It is also less helpful from our point of view, but we do have the phrase "223 with four[?]," which obviously refers to the scale's 223 cells and perhaps the four turns of the spiral or the four division marks inside it, a mention of something (times?) relating to eclipses; paralleling the "two pointers whose tips travel" in the earlier passage, we here have a pointer whose "tip travels." The singular number seems to be a confirmation that there was no second subsidiary dial.

The back face as a whole

The two spiral dials came close to the four edges of the back plate. It is not absolutely certain how the two spirals came together in the middle of the plate, but measurements suggest that the spiral slots either met end to end or came close to doing so. This would theoretically have caused their scales to overlap, but there would likely not have been a problem arising from that since the topmost cells of the lower spiral were probably vacant. The reconstructions of the rear face shown in this book (e.g., fig. 3.1) show the slots as joining.

The space on the plate not taken up by dials was effectively four triangular regions in the corners and two larger triangular regions halfway down the sides. Of these, the triangle along the middle of the right edge and the one at the bottom right corner are partially extant in Fragments E, A, and F, and they contain parts of the text that we have already mentioned, the Back Plate Inscription (BPI).[15] It is probable that this inscription occupied all six spaces. It was the supplementary text to which the key letters in the inscribed cells of the Saros dial referred, and it presented information relating to the possible eclipses recorded on the spiral that could not have fitted in the cells.

The input drive and the back dials in motion

The top, bottom, and sides of the Mechanism were apparently all wooden and have disappeared except for some traces (less extensive than they were in 1902–1903, before the first conservation). The input drive to the gearwork came in through an axle running through the right side as seen from the front (figs. 3.5 and 3.6). It probably terminated in a simple hand-driven knob or possibly a crank, though cranks are not known to have been in use in ancient Greco-Roman machines.[16] One clockwise revolution of the knob would have represented going forward in time about 78 days, a number that was probably of no special significance; the operator would have measured the change in time not by counting turns of the knob but by watching the dials.

Derek de Solla Price offered an alternative possibility: that the Mechanism was driven not by hand but automatically, say by a water clock apparatus, so that its dials displayed the chronological cycles and astronomical phenomena in real time.[17] In common with many of the present-day scholars who have studied the Mechanism, I think this is unlikely. The traces of the casing suggest

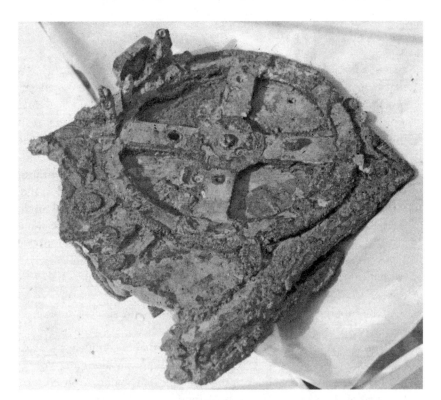

FIG. 3.5. Fragment A-1, oblique view. Projecting up from the far left edge is the contrate gear that drove the large spoked gear and, through it, the entire Mechanism. (Adler Planetarium, © Derek de Solla Price heirs)

FIG. 3.6. Fragment A-2, oblique view. The exterior face of the contrate is at the front; the square socket would have held its axle. The close packing of layered gears mounted on the base plate can also be seen in the center of this image. (Adler Planetarium, © Derek de Solla Price heirs)

a self-contained—indeed, portable—device, and whether its purpose was primarily to calculate or to instruct, its usefulness would have depended on the possibility of showing changes of time at a greatly accelerated pace. Its complex and rather inefficient gearwork would also have almost certainly resulted in intermittent jamming; a human operator would feel this and immediately stop turning the input drive to prevent internal damage.

All the revolving pointers of the back face moved uniformly in proportion to the input motion; that is, turning the knob some fixed amount would always cause a pointer to move in the same direction by the identical angle, or as nearly so as the accuracy of construction of the internal gearwork allowed. On all the dials except the Games dial, moving forward in time was represented by a clockwise motion, and the inscriptions on the dials were deliberately oriented so that the pointers would sweep over them in "reading direction," from left to right.

The motions of the pointers were comparatively slow. It would have taken nearly 19 turns of the knob to make the Games dial's pointer revolve once, nearly 18 turns for the pointer of the Metonic dial to complete a single turn of its spiral, almost 90 turns to make it run all the way along the slot, and over 350 turns to make the pointer of the Callippic dial go once around. A complete traversal of the Saros dial's slot by its pointer would have required more than 84 turns, and a complete revolution of the Exeligmos dial would take more than 250 turns.

The spirals would have compelled the Mechanism's operator to pay close attention to the back face during any prolonged cranking. Suppose, for example, that the pointers had been initially set so that the pointers of the Metonic and Saros dials were simultaneously at the beginnings of their spirals (inside bottom and inside top, respectively). The operator could safely go forward for about 18 years' worth of motion, say 60-some turns of the knob, but then he would have to watch for the moment when the Saros pointer had reached the end of its spiral so he could reset it at the beginning. Another four or so turns would bring the Metonic pointer to the end of *its* spiral; and so forth. Trying to force a pointer beyond the end of the slot (whether running the Mechanism forward or backward in time) could have bent or broken some of the components.

The front dial

While the Mechanism's back face had five dials, each with a single pointer, the front had (so far as we know) only one dial, but with multiple pointers (fig. 3.7). This dial was set in a square plate having approximately the same width as the back plate. The plate's top edge was about 7 cm below the top of the back plate, and its bottom edge was about 8.5 cm above that of the back plate. In the center of the plate there was either a circular opening of about 13 cm diameter or a circular piece of plate filling this space. This was surrounded by two concentric ring-shaped scales, the outermost perimeter of which nearly touched the four sides of the plate. Roughly a quarter of the plate and its dial scales are extant in Fragment C (fig. M5).

The inner of the two scales was divided by engraved radial strokes into 12 sectors, and each sector was divided into 30 subdivisions by shorter strokes. Each sector bore the Greek name of a sign of the zodiac, in order running clockwise and oriented with up being outward; hence the small subdivisions represent single degrees of the ecliptic circle (the circle of the Sun's apparent annual path through the zodiac).[18] In addition, single letters of the Greek alphabet were inscribed at irregular intervals but in alphabetic order, close to the outer ends of certain of the graduation marks. We will call this the Zodiac scale.

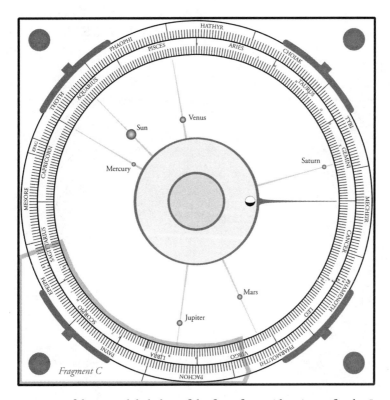

FIG. 3.7. Layout of the central dial plate of the front face, with pointers for the Sun, Moon, and planets. The gray outline shows the part of the plate preserved in Fragment C. The flat cylindrical cap housing the Moon's phase display in the center is also preserved, out of place, in C. The smaller cap at its center is conjectural; it would have concealed the contrate gear driving the phase display, which occupies a window in the larger cap, and could have represented the Earth in the geocentric cosmology. The gray circular features in the corners are the knobs of sliding catches, allowing the plate to be removed from the wooden casing. The four gray arc-shaped features are clips to hold the Egyptian Calendar scale ring in place.

The outer scale was divided in the same manner into 12 equal sectors and a 13th smaller sector subtending one-sixth of the arc subtended by the larger sectors.[19] The large sectors were subdivided by shorter strokes into 30 subdivisions, and the small sector into 5, making a total of 365 for the entire scale, which obviously represent single days in a 365-day year. The sectors were inscribed, in the same way as the sectors of the Zodiac scale, but with the Greek names of the 12 months of the Egyptian calendar year (this calendar will be described in chapter 4). We will call this the Egyptian Calendar scale.

The Egyptian Calendar scale was not an integral part of the front dial plate, but rather a separate ring of plate having about half the thickness of the dial plate, set in a ring-shaped sink in the plate so that its inscribed surface was flush with that of the Zodiac scale and the plate as a whole. The sink was perforated by a ring of 365 drilled holes, and the Egyptian Calendar scale must have had a peg on its back face (probably just one), which could be inserted into any of the holes, thus allowing one to set the Egyptian Calendar scale in any of 365 orientations relative to the Zodiac scale (fig. 3.8).[20]

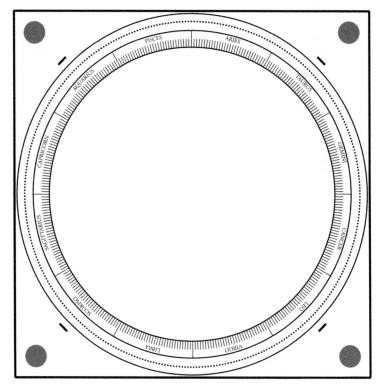

FIG. 3.8. The central dial plate with the Egyptian Calendar scale ring and its clips removed, showing the circle of drilled holes, in one of which a peg on the back of the calendar scale ring would have been inserted. The small black rectangles are perforations of the plate to accommodate the feet of the clips.

The rationale for providing the same dial with two separate scales, one measuring position or motion along the ecliptic in degrees, the other measuring time in days, was that any date in the Egyptian year could be matched up, at least approximately, with the degree of the Sun's position on that date. The Egyptian Calendar scale was made to be adjustable in orientation because, as we shall see, the Egyptian calendar year was not exactly equal to the time in which the Sun revolves once around the ecliptic. There must, therefore, have been a pointer indicating the Sun's position, although no direct physical traces of this pointer survive.

And here we encounter a point of uncertainty. We saw that all the dials of the Mechanism's back face track cycles of time, and their pointers revolved uniformly in proportion to the rotary input. However, Greek astronomers of the time when the Mechanism was constructed knew that the Sun's motion along the ecliptic is not uniform. Was the gearwork designed to make the Sun pointer move with an appropriate variation in speed? If so, it would have been impossible to set the Egyptian Calendar scale so that the Sun's pointer would always show exactly the correct month and day corresponding to the Sun's position; at best, one could keep the errors down to about two days (or 2°) either way. In some reconstructions, therefore, the Mechanism is provided with a Sun pointer moving nonuniformly and a date pointer moving at the same average rate but uniformly.[21] In chapter 5, however, we will consider evidence suggesting that the designer might have solved the problem of displaying nonuniform motion and uniform time on the same dial in a different way, using just one pointer.

A Moon pointer can also be confidently presumed; it would have been attached to the rim of a low cylindrical element, roughly resembling a jar lid, that was mounted at the center of the dial and revolved at a rate representing the Moon's revolution around the zodiac.[22] This element, which has already been mentioned in chapter 2 (p. 27), is now stuck on Fragment C-2 (fig. M6), displaced from its original central location. Near its rim, at the place from which the pointer projected, was a circular hole through which one could see the upper face of a ball composed of white and black hemispheres. As the disk and pointer revolved, the ball would also turn in such a way as to show a likeness of the Moon's phases.

To fill out our picture of the dial, we must turn to the BCI.[23] The first lines of this inscription are very badly preserved, but from line I.15 onward we have a series of partial lines that must be describing the dial and its pointers:

> ... the little sphere travels ... little pointer projecting from it ... arcs, the adjacent [?] ... [the star of Hermes] Gleamer [?], and the [little sphere?] traveling through it ... [the star of] Aphrodite Light-Bearer ... Light-Bearer's arc ... on the pointer lies a little golden sphere ... ray of the Sun, and above the Sun is a circle [?] ... [the star of] Ares Fiery One,

and the [little sphere?] making its way through it . . . [the star of] Zeus
Radiant One, and the [little sphere?] making its way through [it] . . . circle
of [the star of Kronos] Shiner, and the little sphere . . .

In these lines of the BCI we have, in order, Mercury (possibly), Venus, the
Sun, Mars, Jupiter, and Saturn. The planets are named according to two systems that coexisted in Greek astronomy and astrology: one was based on the
names of gods of the Greek pantheon (Hermes = Mercury, Aphrodite = Venus,
Ares = Mars, Zeus = Jupiter, Kronos = Saturn), and the other uses adjectives
describing their visual appearances (Gleamer = Mercury, Light-Bearer = Venus,
Fiery One = Mars, Radiant One = Jupiter, Shiner = Saturn). It is probable that
the first phrases of the passage are referring to the Moon's pointer following
a description of the phase display. What the text appears to be listing is an
assembly of pointers, each carrying somewhere on its length a small sphere
representing the heavenly body whose motion was tracked by the pointer. The
spheres were probably distinguished by having different colors, and it seems
that their distances from the center of the dial also varied so that each would be
seen to revolve over a circular belt belonging to the relevant heavenly body. So
it would appear that there were either eight or seven pointers in all, depending
on whether the Egyptian Calendar scale had a separate date pointer or not. All
the pointers except for the Moon's would have projected from under the phase
display disk.

We know from surviving gearwork that the motion of the Moon's pointer
was nonuniform; that is, turning the input knob by equal amounts would sometimes cause the pointer to shift by a larger arc, and sometimes by a smaller
arc.[24] That the pointers for the planets also moved nonuniformly is practically
certain, as we will see in chapter 7, and in their case the effect would have been
more conspicuous because one would have seen not just variation of speed
but changes in direction. The prevailing sense of all the front dial pointers was
clockwise, corresponding to eastward movement through the zodiac, but each
planet's pointer would alternate between longer intervals of clockwise (direct)
and shorter intervals of counterclockwise (retrograde) motion.

The front dial was in general a faster-paced display than the back dials. One
turn of the knob would have sent the Moon pointer around almost three times,
while the Sun, Mercury, and Venus pointers would take on average less than
five turns to make a circuit of the zodiac. Mercury's pointer would also be seen
to alternate between clockwise and counterclockwise motion about every turn
and a half. The most sluggish motion would have been Saturn's; it would have
appeared to progress by tiny back-and-forth wiggles, needing about 140 turns
of the knob to go once around the dial, but even this would be faster than the
pointers of the Exeligmos and Callippic subsidiary dials on the back.

The fact that the front dial plate was only about half the height of the back
plate raises a question about the appearance of the front and the Mechanism's

overall shape. The earliest known photographs of A-1 show the remains of a wooden frame just tall enough to enclose the gearwork, though it would still have been slightly taller than the front dial plate. If this frame constituted the exterior of the Mechanism, then the back plate would have jutted out above and below this box, while having its own larger but shallow frame. Such a design was suggested by Price in 1959, and more recently Michael Wright has employed it in his models.[25] It has the drawback that one would not have been able to stand the Mechanism upright without an additional prop in the front or some mode of suspension. The alternative is a double frame, with an inner box containing the gearwork and enclosed in a taller frame matching the dimensions of the back plate. In this case, there would have been fairly extensive rectangular areas on the front face above and below the dial plate.

As it happens, remains of two inscribed plates survive stuck on Fragment C (and in some small disconnected fragments) that had about the right dimensions to fill these hypothetical spaces.[26] The text on these plates had a function in relation to the front dial that is analogous to the function of the BPI in relation to the Saros dial. We have mentioned that alphabetic sequences of Greek letters are inscribed at irregular intervals on the Zodiac scale. These letters link the corresponding degree marks to lines of the text on the rectangular plates

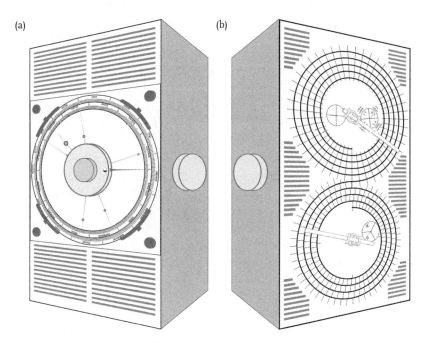

(a)   (b)

FIG. 3.9. Reconstruction of the Mechanism's exterior viewed in perspective. Gray bars indicate where the Parapegma inscription was on the front face, and where the back plate inscription was on the rear. The texts on the spiral dial scales are omitted.

(the so-called Parapegma inscription), which list stars and constellations that become visible for the first or last time in the morning or evening sky when the Sun pointer is indicating the corresponding letter.[27] In 1974 Price reconstructed the front face as incorporating these plates above and below the dial, so that the Mechanism's exterior outline was a simple box. With the exception of Wright's, most of the more recent reconstructions, whether physical or conceptual, have assumed this shape (fig. 3.9). We now have physical evidence that it is correct, in the form of a bearing on the back side of one of the Parapegma inscription plates near its bottom edge that was clearly meant to receive the bolt of one of the sliding catches on the dial plate.[28]

The front-to-back dimension of the Mechanism is uncertain, being dependent on how much gearwork one assumes to have existed in front of the extant Fragment A for the planetary displays, but it can hardly have been less than about 10 cm. Unfortunately it is not known whether Fragment C-2, constituting part of the interior face of the Mechanism's front, was in contact with A-1. Price thought he had found a convincing fit between them, but Wright maintains that there is no visible evidence of a direct join; the cleaning of the surfaces has in any event made it more difficult to be certain.[29]

In reconstructing the exterior of the Mechanism, we have not assigned a place to two inscribed plates, referred to as the "covers." One of these was the plate bearing the BCI; only small parts of the actual plate survive, but the extensive mirror-image offsets of it, covering much of B-1, A-2, and E-1, indicate that it must have been about the same size as the back plate and was lying against it with the inscribed face pointing inward. The other is represented by the extant Fragment G and several small fragments of plate and mirrored offset and bears the so-called front cover inscription (FCI); as found in 1902 it was stuck on the front of C-1 with its inscribed face pointing outward, and its original extent was probably at least equal to the square front dial plate.[30] Price supposed that these plates served as doors hinged to the front and back of the Mechanism.[31] More recent investigators have preferred to refer to them as covers. We have no traces of any means of connection between the plate with the FCI and the Mechanism. Perhaps it is best to admit that we do not know how these plates were meant to be deployed. The texts were evidently meant to help the spectator of the Mechanism to understand what he was seeing, with the BCI identifying the displays and the FCI summarizing the astronomical phenomena simulated by them.

4

Calendars and Games

The meaning of a Greek calendar

Nestled close by the modern Metropolitan Church in the Plaka of Athens, the so-called Little Metropolitan Church is not just a building of distinctive architectural charm in its own right but also a museum of stonework from antiquity through Byzantine times (fig. 4.1). Also known as Ayios Eleftherios and as the Church of Panayia Gorgoepikoos, "the Virgin who is swift to hear," it is often said to date from the 12th or 13th century, though recently discovered evidence suggests that it was actually built between 1436 and 1458, during a period when Athens was under Florentine rule.[1] Its walls are composed of *spolia*, stones reused from older monuments, including many bearing inscriptions or friezes. Of these, one of the most notable is a frieze of pentelic marble above the main entrance, consisting of two blocks that, before one of them was curtailed to fit in its current context, would together have been about 6 meters wide and half a meter tall.[2] Its date is uncertain; estimates have ranged from the Hellenistic period to the second century AD or even later. It may originally have stood above a gate or arch.

The frieze is a disjointed composition of human figures and animals that do not appear to have any connection with each other or that, at most, form little groups sharing an activity. Interspersed among them, however, are the figures of the zodiacal constellations, running from left to right in the order that the Sun passes through the zodiac. Following this clue, the German archeologist and architect Karl Bötticher proposed in 1865 that the frieze was a representation of the ancient calendar of Athens, with the non-zodiacal figures representing the months and various religious festivals.[3] Bötticher's idea is now firmly established, though the interpretations of the individual figures remain less certain.

A segment from the part of the frieze covering late autumn and early winter gives a sense of the whole (fig. 4.2). One is meant to "read"

FIG. 4.1. The Little Metropolitan Church, Athens, early-20th-century photograph. The calendar frieze runs most of the width of the building, immediately below the cornice. (Deutsches Archäologisches Institut, negative D-DAI-ATH-Athen Bauten 133; all rights reserved)

FIG. 4.2. The calendar frieze of the Little Metropolitan Church: the months Poseideon and Gamelion. (photograph: Alexander Jones)

the frieze from left to right, and many of the figures are shown facing or striding rightward. First, then, we have a centaur holding a bow and arrow, which is Sagittarius. A bearded male figure in heavy cloak and boots represents an Athenian month, Poseideon, which roughly coincides with the Sun's passage through Sagittarius (November–December); each calendar month has such a male personification. Next to him is a female figure who stands for a specific religious festival that the ancient spectator would have identified from the following image, a cockfight taking place before three judges seated at a table. (It is not certain what this festival was.) Then comes Capricorn, the fish-tailed goat (December–January), and the personification of the month Gamelion. In front of Gamelion, a boy, the child Dionysus, holds a thyrsus—the god's emblematic staff—while riding a goat, and this is a recognizable emblem of an Athenian festival that was held in Gamelion in honor of Dionysus, the Lenaia.

The Little Metropolitan frieze is a pictorial answer to this question: What did a calendar fundamentally mean to the Greeks? A counterpart in words is offered by the first-century BC writer Geminus, who writes in his book *Introduction to the* (astronomical) *Phenomena* that the Greeks were exhorted by their laws and oracles "to make sacrifices in the manner of their fathers," an injunction that they supposedly interpreted as meaning that they should administer their years according to the Sun and their months according to the Moon.[4] The point of Geminus' fable is that a calendar was before all else the temporal framework of public religion, and this framework was constructed around the cycles of the Sun—made manifest in the frieze through the zodiacal signs—and the Moon.

Pictorial representations of Greek calendars such as the Little Metropolitan frieze are very rare, but the close linkage between calendar and cult is portrayed with a different kind of vividness in a genre of inscription known as "sacrificial calendars," which specify with great precision the offerings to be made during the festivals held in each month of the year. This excerpt concerning sacrifices for a late-summer festival of Demeter called Proerosia ("pre-plowing"), from a fifth-century BC inscription from the community of Thorikos in southern Attica (*Inscriptiones Graecae* [*IG*] I³ 256bis, lines 13–24), is typical:[5]

> Boedromion: the Proerosia; for Zeus Polieus, a select sheep, a select piglet; at Automenai [?], a bought piglet, burnt whole; the priest is to provide lunch for the attendant; for Kephalos, a select sheep; for Prokris, a table; for Thorikos, a select sheep; for the Heroines of Thorikos, a table; at Sounion, for Poseidon a select lamb; for Apollo, a select young billy goat; for Kourotrophos, a select piglet; for Demeter, a full-grown victim; for Zeus Herkeios, a full-grown victim; for Kourotrophos, a piglet; at the salt-works, for Poseidon, a full-grown victim; for Apollo, a piglet.

The chapter in which Geminus writes about these matters, which is titled "On Months," illustrates the curious fact that the Greeks had no actual word corresponding to our "calendar." When we speak of, say, the calendar of Athens, we are grouping together a number of cultural conventions that typically went together in practice but that the Greeks seem not to have conceptualized as a package. These included definitions such as "when does the day begin" or "when does the year begin," as well as the ways that the days, months, and years were named. Superimposed on this structural framework were the various dates assigned to festivals. Close connections often subsisted between the festivals and the calendar's structure: months could be named for festivals that fell within them, and some festivals were associated with seasonal events such as the autumn plowing.[6]

Naturally, a calendar had other roles both in public and private life besides the timing of cult activities. One can distinguish broadly between two ways in which a calendar was used. On the one hand, it had a prescriptive function, establishing the order and timing of *recurring* events. Festivals held on particular days of particular months are an obvious example, and dates could also be fixed for the beginnings of administrative terms of government. Markets might be held on a particular day of every month, and interest on loans could be calculated monthly. In all these cases the important element is orderly repetition, and the specified dates apply to all years or all months. On the other hand, laws, treaties, and private contracts too could be dated according to a calendar. In these contexts a specific day in a specific month and year was meant, and one would want a way of indicating such a date unambiguously, which means that one needed a way of distinguishing or naming individual years as well as the subdivisions of years.

A third, less common use for a calendar was to measure intervals of time. This need would arise in fixed-term agreements and contracts, and in establishing the ages of individuals. For such purposes it would not have been a matter of concern whether the time units were constant or variable in length. In modern life, we do not worry about how many of the years since someone's birth were leap years when calculating the person's age, and we make contracts stipulating constant monthly payments, disregarding the fact that some months are longer than others; and it was much the same in antiquity. The unknown author of the book *Economics*, which has come down to us under Aristotle's name, considered it a fact curious enough to record that the mercenary leader Memnon of Rhodes withheld six days' pay per year from his soldiers on the pretext that half the months had only 29 instead of 30 days.[7]

A calendar was a local institution. Practically every important Greek city had its own calendar, reflecting and regulating the religious and civic institutions of the community. They all had in common the basic principles that months were at least nominally tied to the Moon's cycle of phases, and years, to the cycle of the seasons. But the details varied from place to place. Each calendar had a different set of names for the months, and many systems existed for naming the days of the month.[8] There was no agreement about which season the calendar year should begin in, and years were typically identified by the names of local magistrates or priests who held office during them. The diversity of all these calendars was not purely random; month names shared by different cities were often indicators of real or perceived kinship between their populaces, while in other cases the political or cultural dominance of one city could lead to its calendar being adopted by its neighbors. As a rule, however, a foreigner visiting a city could expect to find that dates were expressed there in unfamiliar ways.

One consequence of this profusion of calendars is that we often have very limited information about the calendars of particular localities. Our main source of evidence consists of dates in archeologically preserved inscriptions. It is a matter of chance whether enough of these survive to give us a complete list of month names or only one or two, and only rarely do we get direct evidence for the order of the months or the time of year to which they corresponded. Our ignorance is still greater when it comes to asking how the day-to-day and month-to-month decisions about running a calendar were made.

The modern Gregorian calendar does not need anyone to make such ongoing decisions. It consists of a set of rules that completely determine the count of days in every month of every year, in such a way that the months will remain closely aligned with the same natural seasons for many centuries; a school-child can learn these rules and use them to project the calendar exactly to any future date. Did Greek calendars ever have this degree of predictability? The Antikythera Mechanism turns out to provide an important part of the evidence that bears on this question, while incidentally also casting light on the place it was made and the person or entity that commissioned it.

Before we come to this evidence, however, it will be helpful to start with some of the well established general properties of the Greek calendars as well as some of the uncertainties. The calendars were of a type known as lunisolar. This means that the succession of days was organized into months whose beginnings were on or close to a certain phase of the Moon, and into years comprising a series of complete months, in such a way that the beginning of the calendar year was always close to the same stage of the natural seasons. Any season was possible for the year beginning of a Greek calendar, while the month beginnings of all calendars appear to have fallen within a few days of the conjunction of the Moon with the Sun; that is, the interval of about two days between the last morning when the waning Moon was visible for the last time and the first evening when the waxing Moon was visible for the first time. It is usually supposed that the appearance of the new-moon crescent—that is, the first sighting of the slender but waxing Moon in the evening just after sunset—which happens a day or so after conjunction, was at least nominally the event defining the beginning of the month for all Greek calendars.

Despite the profusion of different naming practices and starting points, the Greek lunisolar calendars all had—at least in principle—a common structure determined by basic astronomical facts. Consider a hypothetical calendar in which the beginning of each month is the first day following an observation of the new-moon crescent, while the year begins with the first month following an observation of the summer solstice. Putting this calendar into practice would entail designating specific people to make the observations, as well as specific methods of observing and reporting, and the regularity with which the calendar proceeds would be subject to meteorological conditions as well as human error.

To simplify matters, let us imagine that the atmospheric conditions are always ideal and that the observers have consistent visual acuity. In such a situation, every month will have either 29 or 30 days, following an irregular pattern but in the long term averaging about 29.53 days; in other words just slightly more 30-day months (called "full") than 29-day months (called "hollow"). Meanwhile, the time interval between the dates of summer solstices will always be either 365 or 366 days, in the long term averaging about 365.24 days, with a 366-day year practically always following three successive 365-day years. A calendar year consists of all the months beginning with observations of new-moon crescents that fell between one observed summer solstice and the next, and this will sometimes be 12 months and sometimes 13, in the long term averaging approximately 12.368 months per year (365.24/29.53 months). Thus, 13-month years (called "intercalary") will always follow either one or two 12-month years (called "ordinary").

If we turn now to the evidence for the actual Greek calendars, we find that they operated in a manner largely consistent with our hypothetical observational calendar: the months were apparently always either 29 or 30 days long, and the years were either 12 or 13 months long. To be more precise, the days of the month were assigned names that amounted either to counting up to 29 or 30 as the case required, or to assuming a 30-day month as the default and skipping over one of the days if the month was hollow. Twelve names were assigned to the months in a fixed order, with one of the months repeated to make a 13-month year. A repeated month was normally given the same name as its predecessor, with the additional designation "second" or "inserted"; we refer to such months as intercalary months.

When it was necessary to indicate which calendar year some event took place in, the most common practice in Greek cities was to identify it by the name of the person who held a certain annual government office in that year. For example, in Miletus the year was identified by the name of that year's *stephanēphoros* ("crown bearer"; that is, a certain magistrate whose office nominally entitled him to wear a crown), whereas in Athens it was by the name of the *archōn eponymos* (literally, "the magistrate after whom the year is named") alone or with that of the *grammateus* ("secretary"). Obviously this practice could not be applied to years in advance, and it provided no information about the sequence of years. To know how long ago the Athenian year of the archonship of Apseudes was in relation to the current year, or whether it was before or after the archonship of Pythodorus, one would need a chronologically ordered list of archons. Such lists of magistrates existed in antiquity, and sometimes we have the resources to reconstruct parts of them. However, the main function of year naming was not to enable one to know the sequence of events and the intervals between them, but to "date stamp" them. For example, an archon-year designation could be part of the way one specified a particular law or decree.

In Hellenistic kingdoms (and later under the Roman Empire), years were commonly counted numerically from the first regnal year of the current ruler; that is, either the calendar year during which he or she began to rule, or the calendar year that began immediately afterward. The conventions according to which the years were counted could sometimes be counterintuitive. For example, Ptolemy II Philadelphus of Egypt chose to count his regnal years from the year in which he became coregent with his father, Ptolemy I, rather than from the year when he became sole ruler. Compared to the magistrate-year system, it was easier to determine the sequence of events dated by regnal years, though intervals spanning more than one reign could be measured only if one had a king list with lengths of reign. An unbroken count of years starting from a single era, comparable to our AD (or CE) year numbering, is a rarity in antiquity; in Hellenistic times the one example, though an important one, is the Seleucid era, which was a continuous count from the year that Seleucus I Nicator considered to be his first regnal year. Finally, in Elis in the Peloponnese we find dating by sequentially numbered Olympiads, which were intervals of four calendar years beginning with the year in which the Olympic Games were held.

In some cultures that use lunar months, the declaration that a new month has begun is strictly tied to an actual observation of the crescent moon, either following tradition or in obedience to a presumed divine injunction. The Greeks seem to have had a more detached view of the relationship that should subsist between a calendar and the visible cycles of the Moon. One way that this attitude manifested itself was in decisions by a city's magistrates to repeat or skip over certain days of a month—for example, to prevent anticipated military activity from interfering with an upcoming festival—so that the month ended up longer than 30 or shorter than 29 days, and thus the beginnings of the months could get significantly out of synchronization with the phases of the Moon. How widespread this kind of "tampering" with calendars was is not clear, but the practice is well attested for Hellenistic Athens, where inscriptions often gave dates in two forms: "according to the archon," which was the date recognized for civil and cult purposes, and "according to the god" (i.e., apparently, the Moon), which was the date according to the Moon's actual phases.[9] The decision whether to insert an intercalary month in a particular year, and if so, which month was to be repeated, could also be made arbitrarily, with the result that the beginning of the year would get out of its normal synchronization with the seasons.

On the other hand, too close a dependence on observations to regulate the months and years might itself be seen as a source of unwanted irregularity and unpredictability. If the sky was cloudy around the expected appearance of the crescent moon, one might have to choose whether the month coming to an end was to be full or hollow arbitrarily, and if this happened two or three months in a row, a succession of wrong guesses might have to be followed by an anomalously short or long month when the crescent was eventually sighted again. Deciding whether to intercalate or not by observation could also be tricky. If the principle was that the month in which the summer solstice was observed was the last one of the year, for example, the calendar could be thrown off if a solstice that really fell just after a new moon was observed too early or vice versa, and solstice dates were not easy to get exactly right by observation. One method was to look for the date when the Sun's rising point on the eastern horizon was farthest north; another, to watch for when a noon shadow was shortest. Either way, the day-to-day change around the solstice is so small that errors of a day or more would have been frequent. But even the mere reliance on observation to decide what was tomorrow's date or what month was coming next would add an element of uncertainty to planning, say to attend a distant market or religious festival.

The Egyptian calendar

In many ancient calendars, we can see a tendency for rules or calculations to supplant the role originally filled by observation. An extreme case that was familiar to the Greeks was the Egyptian calendar. We have evidence for the existence of some kind of lunar calendar for certain applications from pharaonic through Roman Egypt, and it is plausible that the earliest calendar or calendars in Egypt used lunar months, but from the third millennium BC onward, the principal calendar in use in Egypt—often called the Egyptian "civil" calendar though it was also a framework for religious festivals—had no correlation with the Moon's phases. The Egyptian calendar year comprised three seasons of four months each, with each month having exactly 30 days, plus an additional 5 days at the end of the year that did not belong to any month. The seasons' names refer respectively to the Nile flood, sowing, and harvest, so they ostensibly describe a year tied to nature, beginning in the summer. But because the total number of days in the year was always 365, while the solar year is about 365¼ days, the Egyptian civil year gradually crept backwards relative to the natural seasons. Around 60 BC, the shifting of the Egyptian year had probably gone through nearly two complete cycles since the calendar was set up in this form, and the beginning of the "flood" season according to the calendar was about September 7 in the Julian calendar, which is actually about the point when the Nile had finished rising.

The Egyptians were of course aware that theirs was a wandering year. It was apparently only during the period of Greek rule that someone first saw this as a problem needing to be fixed. In 239/238 BC an assembly of priests held at Canopus, near the western mouth of the Nile, issued a statement in honor of Ptolemy III Euergetes that was recorded in several copies inscribed on stone in Greek and Egyptian, both in Demotic and Hieroglyphic script, like the more famous Rosetta Stone.[10] This "Canobic Decree" covered a wide range of topics relating to the king's involvement in military, political, social, and especially sacerdotal affairs. It pronounces the institution of a great festival in honor of the "Benevolent Gods"—that is, Ptolemy and his queen Berenike, to take place throughout Egypt on the five days beginning with the day when the star Sirius is first seen rising before dawn. In the year of the decree, which was Ptolemy's ninth regnal year, the rising of Sirius is said to have taken place on the first day of the month Payni (July 19, 238 BC, in the Julian calendar), and the festival is to be fixed for all time according to that calendar date. The decree continues:

> And so that the seasons should forever behave appropriately according to the condition of the cosmos that is in effect now, and that it should not happen that some of the public festivals observed in the winter should ever be observed in the summer, because the star shifts one day in every four years, and others observed now in the summer should be observed in the winter in the seasons henceforth, as has occurred in the past and as would occur now too if the year continued to be made up of three hundred sixty days and the five supplementary days that are customarily added following them, from now on one day of festival of the Benevolent Gods is to be supplemented every four years in addition to the five supplementaries preceding the new year, so that everyone will see that the former shortfall regarding the makeup of the seasons and the year and the things that are held to be true concerning the entire orderly arrangement of the heavens has been corrected and completed by the Benevolent Gods.

In other words, from now on, every fourth year was to be, to use the modern expression, a leap year consisting of 366 days instead of 365.

For perhaps several decades after the decree, evidence indicates that this reformed calendar was used by the Ptolemaic administration, but it never quite supplanted the old calendar with its constant years and eventually it was abandoned.[11] Soon after Egypt became a Roman province in 30 BC, leap years were reintroduced in the Egyptian calendar, freezing its alignment with the seasons as it was around that date, and this time the reformed calendar was universally adopted both for civil and religious functions. In modern scholarship the reformed calendar instituted by the Romans is often called the "Alexandrian" calendar, but its usual designation at the time, when anyone saw fit to distinguish it from the old wandering-year calendar, was "according to the Greeks," in contrast to dates "according to the old ones."

Between these two reforming initiatives, however, the Egyptian calendar in its *unreformed* state had become a matter of interest for Greek astronomers outside Egypt. One reason arose out of the needs of astronomical research. Certain theoretical problems (e.g., determining accurate values for periodicities such as the length of the solar year) could be addressed by comparing observations made long ago with recent ones, and for this approach one usually wanted to know the exact number of days between the observations. Old observation records might have been dated according to the Athenian calendar with archon year, or the Babylonian calendar with regnal year of a Babylonian or Persian king or a Seleucid-era year, or the Egyptian calendar with regnal year of the current Ptolemaic king, or some other dating system. Among these systems, only the unreformed Egyptian calendar was based on time units—calendar years—whose length was a constant number of days, so it provided a convenient framework for working with dated observations and generally for expressing the time dimension of astronomical phenomena.

The earliest astronomer who is known to have used the Egyptian calendar in this way is Hipparchus, who was active during the third quarter of the second century BC.[12] But it was not just a resource known to a few advanced specialists: a public inscription concerning calendars erected in Miletus in or soon after 109 BC, *IMilet* inv. 84 (fig. 4.3, *left*), gives Egyptian as well as Athenian

FIG. 4.3. The fragments of the calendar inscription from Miletus, *IMilet* inv. 84 (*left*, excavation drawing, Bayerische Staatsbibliothek Rehmiana Suppl.) and inv. 1604 (*right*). The text in inv. 84 cites the summer solstices of 432 and 109 BC and refers to the 76-year Callippic cycle. The part in inv. 1604 concerns Meton and his 19-year cycle. (both images © Milet-Grabung)

calendar dates for the summer solstices of 432 and 109 BC, evidently because the text's author wanted to say something about the number of days between them and its implications for the length of the solar year, not because these observations (if that is what they were) had anything to do with Egypt.[13] In the Milesian inscription, the years are indicated by the Athenian archons, a convention that a viewer of the inscription might have recognized, though one would not expect that he or she had an archon list handy to check the data. Hipparchus seems to have preferred to designate years in a more mathematically tractable way, either by means of Callippic periods (of which we will hear more presently) or by counting Egyptian years sequentially from the year of the death of Alexander the Great, also called the "Era Philip" because it was the accession year of Alexander's half-brother Philip Arrhidaeus.

A second reason for extra-Egyptian interest in the Egyptian calendar belonged more to the domain of popularization of science, and for this our best witness is again Geminus' chapter "On Months":[14]

> The Egyptians adopted the opposite opinion and purpose to the Greeks. For they neither regulate the [calendar] years according to the Sun, nor the months and days according to the Moon, but they make use of a certain intention all to themselves. For they *want* their sacrifices to the gods not to take place at the same season of the year, but rather to pass through all the stages of the year, and [they want] a summer festival to come to be a winter one and an autumn one and a spring one.

The notion that the Egyptians of yore invented their calendar for the express purpose of having their festivals wander through the seasons is a fanciful one, but the failure of the attempted Ptolemaic reform at least tells us that the Egyptian sacerdotal elites were less bothered by their seasonally shifting festivals than by the prospect of interfering with long-standing calendrical practices. So the Egyptian calendar supplied a textbook example of a system that contrasted in its seeming artificiality with the lunisolar calendars familiar to Geminus' readers, which fulfilled the legendary injunction "to make sacrifices in the manner of their fathers" by keeping the festivals in their proper synchronization with the Sun and Moon.

Hence there are several potential explanations of why the Antikythera Mechanism had a ring scale on its front face whose graduations correspond to the days and months of the Egyptian calendar year. The explanation that might spring to mind first, that the Mechanism was built in Egypt or to be used in Egypt, is the least likely, because, as we shall see, the dials on the back face are inscribed with information relating to a number of localities in the Greek world but not to Egypt. Other possible purposes for the scale are to allow the operator to set the Mechanism to a date according to a chronological system employing the Egyptian calendar (or read off the date according to this system that corresponded to a displayed astronomical configuration), to teach the spectator about the relationship between the Egyptian calendar year and astronomical phenomena, or to allow reading off the time intervals in days between astronomical phenomena simulated on the dials. The designer may have had more than one of these intentions.

Let us recall the details of the Egyptian Calendar scale. It was a ring immediately surrounding the Zodiac scale of the front dial, and like the Zodiac scale it was engraved with graduations radiating out from the center of the dial (fig. 3.7). Although only a part of the dial is extant, we can be confident that there were 13 longer graduations, dividing the scale into 12 larger sectors and 1 smaller one, with the large sectors in turn divided by short graduations into 30 parts, and the small sector into 5, so that the sectors corresponded to the 30-day months of the Egyptian year and the small sector to the additional 5 "epagomenal" days that completed the year. The angular spacing of the day graduations seems to have been made as equal as possible throughout the dial. The Greek names of the Egyptian months were inscribed, in clockwise order, in the middle of their sectors. Only three survive (they are the ones in bold type in table 4.1), but we know the entire set of month names from numerous other sources.

We saw in chapter 3 that the Egyptian Calendar scale was a removable ring of metal that could be mounted in (apparently) 365 orientations around the Zodiac scale, by fitting a small projection or peg—now lost—on the back of the

TABLE 4.1. The Greek names of the months
of the Egyptian calendar.

month number	name
1	Thoth
2	Phaophi
3	Hathyr
4	Choiak
5	Tybi
6	Mecheir
7	Phamenoth
8	Pharmouthi
9	**Pachon**
10	**Payni**
11	**Epeiph**
12	Mesore
	Epagomenai (Epagomenal days)

scale ring into one of a ring of holes drilled through the dial plate at ostensibly equal angular spacing (fig. 3.8). This movability of the scale—it was, incidentally, the only known movable component among the Mechanism's displays that had to be set manually rather than being mechanically driven—proves that the designer was thinking of the "old" Egyptian calendar with its constant, wandering year, not a version with leap years as was prescribed in the Canobic Decree. The existence of the scale makes it probable that there was a pointer on the front dial to indicate a date on it. (Whether this pointer was the same one that indicated the Sun's position in the zodiac is a question we will return to in chapter 5.)

Suppose the operator of the Mechanism wanted to use the scale for the last purpose suggested above; for example, to show how far the Moon moves through the zodiac in 14 days or how many days Venus travels westward (retrograde) through the zodiac between intervals of eastward (direct) motion. For such demonstrations, the scale operates simply as a way of measuring time in days. The ring could be placed in any of its possible orientations since one is interested only in the number of graduations that its pointer moves through as the operator turns the input knob.

How a lesson about the Egyptian calendar and its wandering year might have proceeded we can learn from Geminus, in the continuation of the passage quoted above.[15] He explains that the Egyptian year contains 365 days, leaving out the quarter day that would make the calendar year equal to the solar year because, as he has said, the Egyptians wanted their festivals to regress through the seasons. He points out that this shift should amount to one day every four years, or ten days every forty. And now comes his demonstration:

> This is the cause of the widespread erroneous opinion that has come to be believed among the Greeks, having been given credence through being handed down from long ago down to our times. Most of the Greeks assume that the winter solstice according to Eudoxus takes place simultaneously with the Isia among the Egyptians—which is absolutely false! For the Isia are shifted a whole month relative to the winter solstice.

The Isia that Geminus refers to was a festival of Isis that took place on the four days from the 17th through the 20th of the month Hathyr.[16] Filling out his argument, he is saying that it once *was* true that the Isia approximately coincided with the date assigned to the winter solstice by Eudoxus (this would in fact have been the case during the early second century BC), but in Geminus' own time the Egyptian date of the solstice was a whole month later, say about Choiak 20.

With the Mechanism at hand, a teacher could give visual meaning to Geminus' lesson with little or no operation of the gearwork. He would just have to explain how the Egyptian Calendar scale shows the structure of the Egyptian year with its 365 days, and how, because this is a quarter day short of a solar year, every four years (*perhaps running the Mechanism through four years' worth of motion—about 19 twists of the knob—so the viewer can see the Sun go around the zodiac four times, just to make the point*) the alignment of the calendar with the Sun's motion through the zodiac shifts back by one day (*lifting off the ring and replacing it with the peg shifted one hole counterclockwise*), and every 40 years the alignment shifts by 10 days (*again moving the ring to an orientation ten peg holes counterclockwise*). So (*now moving the ring so that the graduation for Hathyr 17 lines up with the beginning of Capricorn on the zodiac ring*) it was true about a 120 years ago that the Isia festival coincided with the winter solstice, but since then (*lifting the ring off*), because of the accumulated shift (*turning the ring in one's hands about 30° counterclockwise and replacing it*), there is a whole month between the solstice (*pointing out the beginning of Capricorn again*) and the Isia (*pointing out where Hathyr 17 now is*).

Using the Egyptian Calendar scale to set the Mechanism to a date in a specific year, or to read off such a date, would have been a more complicated affair. The main difficulty is that there does not seem to have been any dial on the Mechanism counting Egyptian years directly; the front dial showed only— presuming that the scale was manually set in the correct orientation for the year in question—what Egyptian month and day corresponded to the astronomical and chronological situation displayed on the various dials. This manual setting would not be very difficult; it would suffice to know the alignment for a reference year, correcting this by one peg hole for every four years that the date in question is separated from the reference year.

Derek de Solla Price found the probable means by which this alignment was specified, in the form of what he believed to be an engraved radial line (which he called a "fiducial mark") on the front dial plate on Fragment C, just outside the Egyptian Calendar scale, and approximately lined up with the graduation on the Zodiac scale corresponding to the beginning of the 19th degree in Libra (i.e., Libra 18°);[17] it is visible in figs. M5 and M8 and is drawn in fig. 3.7, slightly left of bottom center. Whether there is a deliberate, engraved line there has been disputed, since the apparent line coincides with a fracture in the plate.[18] If it is a real mark—and from personal inspection and photographs I believe it is real—its role would presumably have been to indicate where the graduation for the first day of the Egyptian calendar year, month Thoth day 1, should have been placed for the reference year. This would fit a reference year around the last decade of the third century BC. In chapter 6 we will meet other evidence that the designer of the Mechanism chose a year in that decade as a kind of "zero" year for the Mechanism's chronology. If the Mechanism was made in the early first century BC, this would have provided sufficient margin for demonstrations of the wandering Egyptian year à la Geminus.

Even with such a reference mark for the alignment of the Egyptian Calendar scale, the scale would not have indicated a precise year number according to the Egyptian calendar, since the precision of its possible positionings was in steps of four years. To read off a complete Egyptian date, therefore, one would have had to make use of the information displayed on the back dials, which pertained to an entirely different calendrical system. It is to this system that we must now turn our attention.

Cyclic calendars

On top of the hill called the Pnyx in Athens, not far from the handsome 19th-century National Observatory, are the remains of a rectangular base cut out of the living rock of the hill, about 4 by 3 meters in dimensions, surrounded by a shallow, level trench that seems to have been intended as a bedding for masonry, now entirely missing (fig. 4.4). A 1932 report by Konstantinos Kourouniotis and Homer Thompson on excavations by the Greek Archaeological Service on the Pnyx suggested that this might be the remains of an astronomical instrument that, according to an ancient annotator of Aristophanes' comedies who was in turn citing the early Hellenistic local historian Philochorus, was erected by the Athenian astronomer Meton:[19]

> Philochorus [says]... that he (*viz*. Meton) placed a *hēliotropion* in the current place of assembly, by the wall on the Pnyx, during the archonship of Apseudes, which preceded that of Pythodorus.

FIG. 4.4. Remains on the Pnyx conjecturally identified as the base of Meton's heliotropion. (photograph: Alexander Jones)

This *hēliotropion* has often been supposed to have been a kind of sundial—a sense the word certainly had at later periods—but another possible interpretation of the word is "solstice instrument," and as Alan Bowen and Bernard Goldstein have pointed out, it could well have been an instrument aligned specifically with the Sun's rising point on the eastern horizon around the summer solstice.[20] Whether the structure whose vestiges survive on the Pnyx was Meton's *hēliotropion* is something we will probably never know for certain—years later, in private correspondence, Thompson expressed doubts about the identification. The *hēliotropion* could simply have consisted of a vertical surface aligned so as to be illuminated at sunrise for just a few days around the solstice, making it easy to estimate the day of solstice itself as the middle day of this interval.

The report from Philochorus is just one of several sources that link Meton to the year of Apseudes' archonship (433/432 BC). Each source gives a particular and incomplete account of what Meton did, and it is a controversial matter how we should reconstruct the story. Thus, while the scholiast on Aristophanes speaks of the erection of an instrument in that year, without providing further details about what Meton did with it and when, Ptolemy tells us that "those about Meton and Euctemon" observed the summer solstice in the archon year of Apseudes as having occurred around daybreak on a specific *Egyptian calendar* date, the 21st of Phamenoth.[21] This is obviously not the form in which the date would have originally been recorded. Ptolemy adds that the observation was "rather crudely recorded." (We shall hear more of Euctemon in chapter 5.) The calendar inscription from Miletus *IMilet* inv. 84, mentioned already, cites this same Egyptian date as the date of a solstice but also gives it an Athenian calendar date, the 13th of Skirophorion. Meton is not named here, but another recently discovered fragment of the same inscription, *IMilet* inv. 1604 (fig. 4.3, *right*), mentions him as having established a 19-year period (*enneakaidekaetēris*). And the historian Diodorus, recounting the events of the archon year of Apseudes, connects the Athenian calendar date with this 19-year period, without telling us that it was a solstice:[22]

> At Athens, Meton the son of Pausanias, who was famed for astronomy, published the so-called *enneakaidekaetēris*, making its beginning from the 13th of the Athenian month Skirophorion. In the stated number of years, the stars make their periodic restitution and receive the cyclic return of some great year, so to speak.

To make sense of this 19-year cycle and its relationship to a summer solstice date, we should look farther east, to Babylonia, where the cycle appears to have first been discovered and used.[23] The Babylonian calendar was lunisolar, with the new-moon crescent defining the start of the month. The alignment of the calendar year with the seasons was maintained by occasional intercalations of the 12th month, Addaru, or (less frequently) the 6th month, Ululu. From

484/483 BC onward, until cuneiform records end in the first century AD, a fixed 19-year cycle of ordinary and intercalary years was followed, with intercalary Addaru in years 3, 6, 9, 11, 14, and 17 of the cycle and intercalary Ululu (replaced by intercalary Addaru in three cycles during the fifth century BC) in year 1. With this cycle, the alignment was locked within a range such that the spring equinox always fell within the first month of the year or just before it.

The 19-year cycle works because 235 lunar months average just two hours over 19 tropical years (that is, years counted from equinox to equinox or from solstice to solstice). Since 19 times 12 is 228, we have to intercalate seven months in 19 calendar years to make up the cycle, and spreading these as evenly as possible, at intervals of two or three years, minimizes the short-term wobble of the year's beginning relative to the seasons. By keeping to the cycle, the Babylonians no longer had to make any astronomical observations to check that the years were maintaining the desired alignment. In fact they *calculated* dates for all the solstices and equinoxes in each year of the cycle, following a simple arithmetical pattern that modern scholars have named the "Uruk scheme." On the other hand, the Babylonian 19-year calendar cycle did not determine which of the 235 months were full and which were hollow. By the third century BC, if not earlier, observation of the new-moon crescent had been supplanted by calculation as the method of determining the beginning of a new month, but the calculation was not based on assuming a simple cycle of repetition; rather, it was an attempt to reproduce the circumstances that determine whether the Moon is far enough from the Sun to be seen in the evening sky.

We come back to Meton, with two questions: How did he find out about the 19-year period (which has come to be named after him, as the Metonic cycle), and what was he attempting to do with it? Meton might have somehow learned about the Babylonian calendar and how it had been regulated by the cycle for the past half century or so. This would have been an exceptionally early instance of the transfer of technical knowledge from Babylonia to Greece, and no obvious channel for the transmission suggests itself. Alternatively, there does seem to have existed a tradition of observing solstices in Athens even before Meton. According to the book *On Signs of Waters and Winds and Storms and Good Weather*, which in modern times has been ascribed (dubiously) to Theophrastus though in the manuscript tradition it is usually either anonymous or attributed (still more dubiously) to Aristotle, we are told:[24]

> At Athens, Phaeinos observed the things concerning the solstices from Mount Lykavettos, and Meton, having learned from him, composed the "year" that is one short of twenty. Phaeinos was a foreign resident at Athens, whereas Meton was an Athenian.

The "things concerning the solstices" could well have included estimates of their dates in the Athenian calendar, and a run of a few decades of records would have sufficed to suggest that the pattern of day numbers was roughly repeating after 19 years.

If Meton's intention was to introduce a cycle of regulation of the Athenian calendar on the pattern of the Babylonian calendar, he does not seem to have been successful. Leaving aside the practice of "tampering," which affected the lengths of the months and their alignment with the Moon's phases but perhaps not the status of years as ordinary or intercalary, we have attestations of four different Athenian months being used on one occasion or another as an intercalary month, apparently at the magistrates' discretion.[25] The sixth month, Poseideon, was the one most frequently doubled. However, from the mid-fourth century onward, it does appear that the pattern of intercalary and ordinary years usually followed a 19-year cycle.[26] This could mean that such a cycle was being consciously consulted—though perhaps only to decide the status of the year, not which month was to be repeated—or that the beginnings of the years were determined through a consistent and competent practice of observing the summer solstices. It must be stressed that a Metonic cycle of intercalation will *automatically* arise if the calendar year is always begun with the first new moon after an accurately determined solstice or equinox. Meton himself may have furnished his city *both* with an instrument that made reasonably accurate solstice observations possible *and* a theoretical cycle that could be used to verify the observations. The particular solstice date from 432 BC might have been mentioned in a dedicatory inscription of the instrument, thus acquiring its special status in the memory of subsequent centuries.

Consistently starting the calendar year with the first month following the summer solstice not only generates a 19-year cycle of intercalations but also determines the specific pattern of ordinary and intercalary years. If we choose to begin the cycle with the year that starts closest to the solstice, the intercalations fall in years 1, 3, 6, 9, 11, 14, and 17 (just as in the Babylonian cycle). In Athens, the pattern of known intercalations from the late fourth through the mid-second century BC conforms to a cycle such that the years beginning in 368 BC, 349 BC, 330 BC, and so forth were year 1.[27] At some point between the mid-second century BC and the mid-first century AD, an adjustment took place, equivalent to assuming that the summer solstice was about a day later than previously supposed. If the old convention had persisted, the years beginning in AD 32, 51, 70, etc., would have been year 1 of the cycle; instead, the years beginning in AD 43, 62, 81, etc., were year 1.

Geminus frames his account of how the Greeks fulfilled the commandment "to make sacrifices in the manner of their fathers" as a historical reconstruction in which they achieved step by step a progressively better reconciliation of their conflicting time units by means of calendar cycles. It is noteworthy that he presents the problem not just as one of fitting whole numbers of months to whole numbers of years, but also as one of fitting days satisfactorily into the scheme by establishing a cyclic pattern of full and hollow months.

With such a scheme, observation has ceased to play any role in the operation of a calendar except in the trivial sense that sunrises and sunsets determine the succession of days. Two problems thus have to be solved: to find a period that is simultaneously a whole number of solar (tropical) years, a whole number of lunar months, and a whole number of days, and to find the best way to distribute the ordinary and intercalary years and the full and hollow months within a cycle whose duration is this period.

The period that best reconciles months and years, according to Geminus, is the 19-year cycle, whose discovery he attributes neither to the Babylonians nor to Meton, but to "those about Euctemon and Philippus and Callippus." Intercalary years are to be spread as evenly as possible within the cycle, probably meaning a pattern such as the one we have just been describing for the Athenian calendar. On the other hand, if, as Geminus assumes, the length of the year is exactly 365¼ days, the 19-year cycle cannot also contain a whole number of days, so "those about Callippus" established a period of 76 years, 4 times 19, which embodied the equation:

76 solar years = 940 lunar months = 27,759 days.

So far as the intercalations and the full and hollow months are concerned, Geminus apparently treats this period as four separate 19-year cycles, the first three comprising 6940 days and the fourth shortened by a day to 6939.

The distribution of full and hollow months is produced by a peculiar rule. Every month is initially supposed to have 30 days, numbered from 1 through 30. However, every 64th day is then skipped over. For example, if we start counting from the 1st day of the 1st month in the cycle, the 63rd day will be the 3rd of the 3rd month, and the next day number is skipped so that the day after the 3rd will be called the 5th, and thus the 3rd month is hollow. Then the next skipped day number will be the 8th of the 5th month, and so forth. Geminus calls these omitted day numbers *exairesimoi*, "days to be removed."

In Ptolemy's *Almagest*, his great treatise on theoretical astronomy written in the middle of the second century AD, there are a number of reports of astronomical observations from the third and second centuries BC whose dates include year numbers in the first, second, or third "period according to Callippus."[28] The astronomers who made these observations include Timocharis, Aristarchus of Samos, and Hipparchus. Other examples of this kind of dating are preserved in a couple of astronomical texts preserved in papyri, where the year numbers are in the fourth and sixth of these Callippic periods. They belonged to a special lunisolar calendar, devised specifically for scientific applications, that used the framework of months and days of the Athenian calendar, but instead of identifying years by the Athenian archons, years were counted in cycles of 76 years beginning with the year following the summer solstice of 330 BC, which was called the first year of the first Callippic period (note that this was also a year 1 of the 19-year cycle as practiced in Athens in the fourth century BC).

Is this "Callippic calendar" what Geminus had in mind in his chapter "On Months"? The 76-year periods were obviously motivated by the reasoning that Geminus summarizes about reconciling days, months, and years. Moreover, the handful of complete dates that we have are compatible with the calendar structure that he describes, though we would need many more to be sure of this. But there is a difficulty: Geminus' narrative takes as its starting point the idea of a calendar as a social and above all a religious institution, but the Callippic calendar was a specialized resource for astronomers. About Callippus himself we know very little. He was born in Cyzicus in northwestern Asia Minor, and his revisions of Eudoxus' planetary theories were described briefly by Aristotle in his *Metaphysics*, so he must have been active in the mid-fourth century BC.[29] His native city honored him with a bronze statue at Delphi, whose base survives.[30] Theon of Alexandria (fourth century AD) asserts, on Hipparchus' authority, that Callippus established that the solar year is 365¼ days long through comparison of his own observations with Babylonian ones, though one would like to know more about what this claim really means.[31] It is not clear whether the Callippic calendar was of Callippus' own devising or merely was named after him because he was associated with the general idea of a 76-year cycle. The calendar, though it used the same nomenclature for months and days as the civil calendar of Athens, was distinct from it, and astronomers used it because, despite its rather complicated structure as a lunisolar calendar, it was governed by rules that were presumably known to the scientific community throughout the Hellenistic world. We do not know why the Athenian calendar was adopted as the model. Callippus had no documented connection with Athens, but the background in Meton's work may have had something to do with it, and in any case the months of the Athenian calendar were probably more widely familiar than those of other cities.

The question of whether the civil calendars of the Greek cities were regulated according to "Metonic" 19-year or "Callippic" 76-year cycles has been a matter of dispute for more than four centuries. Disagreement has been especially bitter concerning the calendar of Athens, for which the evidence is comparatively abundant though far less tractable than our evidence for the Babylonian calendar—the one ancient lunisolar calendar that we really know much about. Even now, unanimity is lacking concerning the Athenian calendar, but a consensus seems to be evolving, as I have described the situation above, that through much of the Hellenistic period and into Roman times the Athenian calendar was subject to at least a weak kind of regulation, with the intercalary years almost always following a 19-year cyclic pattern, while in other respects the administration of the calendar was sometimes arbitrary. The regulation is likely to have become more strict over time.

The larger picture about Greek calendars remains obscure, but a few key items of evidence point to the late second and first centuries BC as a period in which there was heightened interest in cyclic regulation and synchronization as a practicable means of bringing order into the local civil calendars. We have already seen how Geminus motivates the search for a calendrical cycle that will remain synchronized with the Sun and Moon in the perceived requirements for a cult calendar. One might object that he does not close the narrative by saying that any city actually adopted the cycles that he describes in the abstract. His contemporary Diodorus, however, is more explicit in the continuation of the passage already quoted: "Hence down to our time the majority of the Greeks use the *enneakaidekaēteris* and [hence] do not err from the truth." Diodorus' statement is confirmed by attestations of intercalary years in the calendar of Delphi during the second century BC, which conform to the same 19-year pattern tied to the summer solstice as the Athenian calendar, and by attestations of consistent equivalences of months in the Delphic calendar and those of several other cities, which show that these calendars were closely coordinated.[32] The inscription *IMilet* inv. 84 + inv. 1604, erected in Miletus in or not long after 109 BC, is probably also to be understood as a public presentation of the rationale for a reform of the Milesian calendar based on a 76-year cycle. To these witnesses we can now add the Antikythera Mechanism.

The Corinthian calendar on the Mechanism

In chapter 2 we saw how Michael Wright was the first to grasp that the scale of the main upper dial of the Mechanism's rear face was a continuous spiral strip divided by engraved radial lines into 235 cells, making exactly 47 cells for each of the five complete turns of the spiral.[33] According to his reconstruction of the gearwork leading to this dial's pointer, the pointer would have revolved once in the equivalent of 19/5 solar years' worth of motion input through the knob on the Mechanism's side. Obviously the dial represented a 19-year cycle, and each cell represented a lunar month.

Meanwhile, it had been known since Price's work (and in fact Albert Rehm already noted it in his unpublished manuscripts) that Fragment 19 was inscribed with text including notations meaning "19 years" and "76 years."[34] So the Mechanism's designer was aware not just of the Metonic but also of the Callippic cycle. Wright showed how the gear train leading to the Metonic dial could easily have driven the pointer of a subsidiary dial to revolve once in 76 years' worth of motion, and, as we will see presently, he conjectured that an extant subsidiary dial inside the Metonic dial's spiral on Fragment B, which is divided into four equal sectors, was this Callippic dial. This has turned out to be incorrect, but there probably *was* a Callippic dial that counted off a sequence of four Metonic cycles in each revolution of its pointer.

Wright, like Price before him, drew attention to the presence of very tiny inscribed lettering inside the cells of the Metonic dial, but scarcely any letters could be read by direct examination.[35] If anyone had taken bets on what the inscriptions were, the odds would have favored either some system of abstract numerals counting months and years, or the month names of the Athenian calendar because of their association with the Callippic periods. When a group of scholars (of whom I was one) working with the AMRP computed tomography (CT) data succeeded in reading a substantial portion of the cell inscriptions in 2007–2008, the outcome was a considerable surprise.[36]

The inscriptions did show the pattern of repetitions that one would expect for a lunisolar calendar cycle; that is, cells at intervals of 12 or 13 months contained the same text—this was a great help in reading them, since many of the individual cells were only partially legible. Cells corresponding to the first lunar month of a year could be identified by the presence of a symbol known to mean "year" followed by a numeral representing the ordinal number of the year in the Metonic cycle. With this exception, each cell contained only a month name. The names are listed in table 4.2.

This was not the Callippic calendar, nor was it the calendar of any of the localities in the Aegean that had been identified as sources of ceramics, coins, or cargo on the Antikythera wreck. For example, Rhodes had been offered since Price's time as a possible place of origin for the Mechanism, partly because of the Rhodian amphorae recovered from the wreck but above all because of

TABLE 4.2. The month names inscribed on the Metonic dial scale.

Month number	Name
1	Phoinikaios
2	Kraneios
3	Lanotropios
4	Machaneus
5	Dodekateus
6	Eukleios
7	Artemisios
8	Psydreus
9	Gameilios
10	Agrianios
11	Panamos
12	Apellaios

the associations of the island with astronomy (Hipparchus, Posidonius, perhaps Geminus). We know all the Rhodian months, and while among them Panamos and Agrianios are matched exactly with months on the Mechanism, and Karneios and Artamitios are matched except for orthographic variation, the rest are entirely different.

In 1997 Catherine Trümpy had published a book compiling the available information on month names in Greek regional calendars, and a search through this work revealed two areas of interest.[37] Inscriptions from a number of localities in and around the ancient region of Epirus (now in northwestern Greece and southern Albania) attested month names matching almost all the names on the Mechanism exactly or with slight orthographic variants. No single locality provided sufficient names to reconstruct a complete list of 12, but the overlaps suggested that they all shared basically the same calendar. The origin of this calendar, as had been suggested by Trümpy as well as by the French epigrapher Pierre Cabanes, the preeminent specialist in the inscriptions of Epirus, was almost certainly Corinth, which had founded colonies in Epirus in the eighth and seventh centuries BC that had cultural dominance over the region.[38] From Corinth itself only two attestations of months are known, Phoinikaios and Panamos.

The other place of interest was Tauromenion, modern Taormina, in Sicily. A series of Hellenistic inscriptions of civic accounts from Tauromenion preserve not only an almost complete list of the months of the local calendar but also, what is still rarer information, their sequence.[39] Seven of the Tauromenian months match months from the Mechanism, whereas the other five are completely different. But the most striking fact is that the known sequences of the two calendars can be lined up so that the seven matching months are in exactly the same positions. We assumed that the close relationship between the calendars of Tauromenion and Epirus arose through the facts that Tauromenion was settled by Dionysius, the tyrant of Syracuse, with his mercenaries in 392 BC, and that Syracuse was a Corinthian colony dating back to the eighth century. We supposed that Syracuse had also used the Corinthian calendar in essentially the same form as it existed in Epirus, whereas other month names had been introduced in Tauromenion because of the mixed origins of the settled mercenaries.

Thus we identified Corinth, Epirus and environs, and Syracuse as the three candidates for the place for which the Metonic dial of the Mechanism had been designed. Of these, we favored Syracuse. One reason for this was that Rome had devastated much of Epirus following the end of the Third Macedonian War in 168 BC and had destroyed Corinth in 146 BC, and we believed on the basis of the current estimate based on the letter forms of the inscriptions that the Mechanism was probably made later than those dates. Another attraction of Syracuse was the vague possibility that a tradition might have subsisted there of making astronomical mechanisms, tracing itself back to Archimedes in the third century.

To the disappointment of Archimedes enthusiasts, we were mistaken. Only two month names are directly attested for the Syracusan calendar: Karneios, the more common spelling of the Mechanism's Kraneios, which is cited in Plutarch's *Life of Nikias*, and a month beginning with the letters ΑΠΟ- preserved in an inscription from Magnesia on the Maeander (*IMagnes.* 72), conjectured to be Apollonios. None of the Mechanism's month names begin with ΑΠΟ-, but we dismissed this contrary evidence too readily, supposing that the inscription's editor might have misread the last letter, which is near the surviving edge of the stone (which would perhaps make Apellaios possible) or that he may have been mistaken in assuming this was a month name at all. Since 2008 the epigrapher Paul Iversen has confirmed the reading by direct inspection of the stone, as well as its status as a month name.[40] Apollonios is one of the non-Corinthian months in the calendar of Tauromenion, and Iversen has shown that others of these supposedly distinctive Tauromenian months were known in other cities that were under Syracusan influence. The case is compelling that the calendar that we know from Tauromenion was simply the Syracusan calendar, which itself was an amalgam of Corinthian and local months.

It was also a mistake to assume that Epirus and its environs were no longer places where it was plausible that someone might own such a rare and expensive object as the Mechanism after 168 BC. The punitive devastation imposed by the Romans in 168–167 BC was severe but selective; Strabo speaks of the enslavement of 150,000 people and the destruction of 70 cities, but he adds that these were mostly cities of the Molossians, who had sided against Rome in the war.[41] But coastal cities such as Apollonia and Epidamnos, which were along the Adriatic trade routes, flourished under the Romans.

We will come back to the problem of localizing the Mechanism's calendar presently. For the moment let us be content with the recognition that it was a local civil calendar, not an artificial calendar intended for scientific research, like the Callippic calendar or the pre-reform Egyptian calendar as it was used by Greek astronomers outside Egypt (or even within Egypt after the reform took hold). The Metonic dial is thus a practically complete description of a local calendar structured in conformity with Geminus' account of the cycles established by the Greek astronomers.

The links between the Mechanism's calendar and Geminus extend to the treatment of month lengths. Geminus' rule, that all months are nominally assigned 30 days, from which every 64th day is "removed," has met with skepticism on the part of modern historians because of its apparent artificiality. G. J. Toomer has called Geminus' account a "fiction," while Bowen and Goldstein describe it as "obviously a reconstruction and a poor one at that."[42] But inside the innermost turn of the Metonic dial's scale, we find a series of numerals that indicate which day numbers are to be skipped in all the months whose cells line up radially with the numerals. These days are mostly spaced at intervals of 64, though occasionally 65 to obtain slightly more even distribution over the entire cycle, so the scheme is not exactly as Geminus describes it. But the similarity of principle is too close to be accidental. The back cover inscription (BCI) actually mentions these as *exairesimoi* days, the identical rare term found in Geminus to designate the skipped day numbers. Geminus was not making his rules up.

However, I think it would be rash to conclude now that rigorous cyclic structures such as Geminus describes were definitely regulating the Corinthian calendar in actual social practice somewhere where that calendar was used—or to extend this conclusion to late Hellenistic calendars in general. Can we even presume that the designer knew in full detail how the calendar was regulated, especially if we admit the possibility, indeed the likelihood, that the Mechanism was made in a different place? Perhaps we should understand it as something intermediate between a didactic exercise of deducing an ideal calendrical structure and a faithful description of a calendar as it operated in the real world, in effect a proposal for how a real calendar could be perfected.

The games cycles

Around the 130s BC, an athlete named Menodoros, son of Gnaios, an Athenian, had a statue of himself made and erected at Delos.[43] The statue is lost, but inscriptions on its base are extant practically in their entirety. The main inscription, forming the base's front face (fig. 4.5), was a visually striking rectangular grid of stylized wreaths, with each wreath having the name of an athletic festival inscribed above it, and, inside the wreath, the specific competition in which Menodoros had carried the prize for his specialties: wrestling and the pankration (a sort of combination wrestling and boxing). It records 32 prizes from competitions and four specially conferred honors.

Summing up his achievement, Menodoros says that he has won victory in the *periodos* ("circuit") and the "other sacred competitions." The *periodos* meant the complete round of the four venerable Panhellenic competitions: the Olympics, the Nemeans, the Pythians at Delphi, and the Isthmians at Isthmia near Corinth.[44] As for the other competitions, Menodoros kept mostly to the Greek mainland except for one visit to Delos, but within these limits his exploits ranged from the local but high-ranking Panathenaia at Athens and Eleusinia at Eleusis to the distant and relatively minor Naa at Dodona and Nymphaia at Apollonia in Epirus. In all, he won prizes in 14 different places, and allowing for unrecorded losses, he must have been participating in several competitions in each season for many years.

The principle of a Panhellenic religious festival incorporating an athletic competition—some also involved musical competitions—was that all Greeks were open to attend and compete, whether from near or far; preceding them, ambassadors (*theōroi*) were sent out far and wide to give notice of the festival and

(a)

(b)

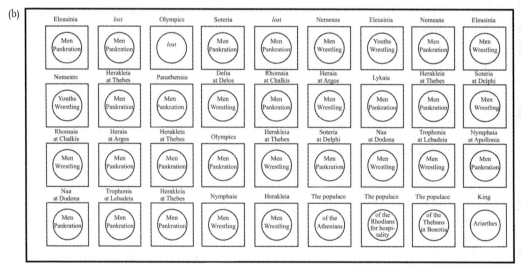

FIG. 4.5. The inscription of Menodoros' athletic victories, from Delos. (photograph: Bizard & Roussel 1907, 434)

of its accompanying sacred truce, functioning as a guarantee that travelers to the festival would have safe passage regardless of wars. Beginning in the fourth century BC and accelerating in the third, there was a great explosion of new festivals modeled on the canonical four of the *periodos*, and with ambitions to equal them in prestige. Like the original Panhellenic competitions, they offered nothing more than a crown as a prize, but victors could expect more material honors from their home cities in recognition of the glory they had won.

Menodoros' career is one reflection of the extensive network of intercity travel and intercity relations fostered by the festivals, comprising ambassadors, athletes, and spectators. Another is a series of inscriptions at Magnesia on the Maeander that records the travels of the city's ambassadors in 208 BC to invite participation in their new festival, the Leukophryeneia, and to seek recognition of the inviolability of their sanctuary and territory.[45] They visited nearly a hundred cities, journeying as far as Sicily—we have already mentioned the inscription recording Syracuse's response for its partial preservation of the month name Apollonios—and Antiocheia in Persis, modern Navahand (Iran). A city's favorable response to the invitation could be followed up by its dispatching its own *theōroi* to attend the festival in an official capacity, in addition to any private citizens who made the journey. If calendars were part of the local, city-oriented aspect of an individual's social place, the Panhellenic festivals were emblematic of the relations between cities as well as the common status of their citizens as Greeks.

The element of time enters into the festivals at two levels. First, there was the cycle of years in which each festival was held. The Olympics and Pythians had a four-year cycle, and such festivals were called "penteteric," meaning literally "five-year" because one thought of the year in which the festival was held as year 1 so its recurrence was in year 5. The Nemeans and Isthmians, on the other hand, took place every second year and so were called "trieteric," literally "three-year." The other Panhellenic festivals were established either as penteteric or trieteric, so that a regular four-year cycle governed them all, with some occurring once and some twice in each cycle.

The Olympics, reputedly the most ancient as well as the most prestigious of the athletic festivals, are commonly taken as the effective starting point of the games cycle. Though the ancient testimony is neither abundant nor free from contradictions, it appears most probable that the Olympic festival was held starting at the full moon of the first lunar month following the summer solstice, and that this was also the first month of the year according to the calendar of Elis (whose territory included Olympia), as it was also according to the calendar of Athens. An "Olympiad" comprised the four calendar years beginning with the year in which the festival fell. Ancient Olympiads were counted sequentially from the legendary first Olympiad beginning in 776 BC, and for purposes of chronology the individual years were numbered from 1 through 4. For example, the summer solstice of Meton in 432 BC, dated according to the Athenians to the archon year of Apseudes, was close to the end of year 4 of the 86th Olympiad. Olympiad numbers and years were employed by some Greek historians to provide a chronological framework for dating events.

The reconstructed cycle of the original Panhellenic athletic festivals according to Olympiad years is as follows:

Year 1: Olympics
Year 2: Nemeans and Isthmians
Year 3: Pythians
Year 4: Nemeans and Isthmians

This list gives a slightly deceptive impression of the cycle, however. While the Olympics, Nemeans, and Pythians took place in the summer following the beginning of the Olympiad year, the Isthmians were held toward the *end* of the Olympiad year, in the late spring. Hence, if one thinks in terms of a competition season running from spring through autumn, the Isthmians preceded the Olympics and Pythians in the same seasons. In any event, no one would have had any difficulty in keeping track of the seasons in which any particular festival would be held.

The timing of the festivals within their seasons presented more challenging problems, both for the cities that hosted them and for those from elsewhere who wished to attend and compete, because they were tied to the local calendars. In the case of a high-ranking festival such as the Olympics, there was no need to accommodate the dates to other festivals, and one could presume that the key dates were widely known—for example, attendees to the Olympics would know that they had to reach Elis by the full moon following the summer solstice; competitors, by the preceding full moon, to satisfy the required minimum of one month's on-site training. For newer, less established festivals, it would have been desirable to avoid having their dates overlap, or even fall too close to, those of the great festivals, and this would not have been a simple matter if their dates were fixed according to local calendars that had different patterns of intercalation. Similarly, an itinerant athlete such as Menodoros had to plan his travels from competition to competition with care, and it would have been an expensive error to arrive a month too late or too soon through ignorance of a calendar's vagaries. By the second century AD, with yet more festivals added to the circuit, their succession through the four-year cycle had become subject to imperial regulation, but we do not know how these matters were handled in the late Hellenistic period, before there was any external authority that could dictate to the cities when they should hold their festivals. Obviously, a trend toward synchronization of intercalations in different calendars, evidence for which has been mentioned above, would have alleviated the difficulties.

On Fragment B-2 of the Mechanism—that is, the side of Fragment B that faced the interior gearwork—one can see within the space inside the remains of the spiral Metonic scale a conspicuous arbor (or axle) bearing a single surviving gear (fig. M4). The corresponding exterior face is hidden behind the layer of accretion matter bearing part of the BCI, but the accretion layer and the dial plate are separated by a gap of a few millimeters, just enough so that Price was able to see in 1958 that the arbor came out at the center of a small circular dial divided into four equal sectors.[46] Wright identified this gear and dial as the output of a gear train branching off the train for the Metonic dial in such a way that the small dial's pointer would revolve once clockwise in the equivalent of four Metonic cycles; that is, a Callippic period of 76 years.[47] This reconstruction made sense of the mention of 76 years in the portion of the BCI on Fragment 19, and so it seemed certain, despite the fact that one had to hypothesize three lost gears beyond those required to complete the Metonic gear train.

When we began to study the inscriptions of the upper back dials by means of CT in 2007, we presumed that any inscriptions found on this dial would relate to the Callippic and Metonic periods. To our surprise, the four sectors turned out instead to be inscribed with notations meaning "year 1," "year 2," "year 3," and "year 4" in *counterclockwise* order (fig. 3.3).[48] And outside each of the sectors, we found the Greek names of the original four Panhellenic competitions of the *periodos*: first NEMEA (Nemeans) outside the sectors for years 2 and 4, then ΙΣΘΜΙΑ (Isthmians) and ΠΥΘΙΑ (Pythians) outside year 3, and finally ΙΣΘΜΙΑ again and ΟΛΥΜΠΙΑ (Olympics) outside year 1. So the dial was not the expected Callippic dial but a four-year dial. Tony Freeth had no difficulty in reconstructing a connection to the Metonic train involving one hypothetical lost gear so that the pointer would revolve once in every four years' worth of input motion.

The dial inscriptions of B-2 as seen in the CT data are rather faint and sometimes hard to distinguish from accidental markings. Nevertheless, it is clear that years 2 and 4 of the Games dial were inscribed with additional names besides that of the Nemean games. In the original 2007 work, the one further name that we read was the second for year 2, NAA. These were the games held at the sanctuary of Zeus at Dodona, often referred to as the Naia but regularly spelled Naa in ancient inscriptions.[49] The Naa was a festival of comparatively local significance to Epirus. Our widely traveled athlete Menodoros lists two victories at the Naa toward the end of his commemorative inscription (that is, among the less prestigious of the competitions in which he took part), and the Naa also figure in a handful of other inscriptions recording athletes' victories, but they evidently ranked well below, say, the Panathenaia at Athens or the Ptolemaia at Alexandria. Their inclusion on the Games dial reinforces the argument favoring Epirus as the region for which the Mechanism was inscribed with the calendar of Corinth.

The Games dial and the calendar are in fact connected by more than the inclusion of the Naa among the more renowned games. While the conventional Olympiad cycle, based on a year beginning after the summer solstice, places the Isthmian games in years 2 and 4, the Games dial has them in years 1 and 3. This must mean that the divisions of the Games dial represent years whose beginnings did not divide the Isthmian games in the spring from the later summer games. This appears to fit the Corinthian calendar. Paul Iversen and John D. Morgan have argued that the month Karneios/Kraneios, which was common to the entire Dorian family of calendars to which the calendar of Corinth belonged, and which was the second month of the Corinthian year according to the Metonic dial, fell around or just after the autumn equinox, so that the year began in the late summer, typically two lunar months later than the Athenian year.[50] It is worth noting that only the very end of the years numbered 1 on the dial overlapped with the very beginning of the years numbered 1 in the conventional Olympiad count.

Though the Games dial's quadrants thus clearly represent the same calendar years as the Metonic dial, the division lines cannot exactly coincide with the beginnings of the years, because the Games dial's pointer traverses each quadrant with a constant amount of input motion, equivalent to one solar year, whereas the calendar years are always either more or less than a solar year. The designer chose to engrave the division lines about 8° counterclockwise of vertical and horizontal, which is approximately the equivalent of one lunar month's motion. Supposing that when the Metonic dial's pointer was at the exact beginning of year 1 of its 19-year cycle, and the Games dial's pointer was exactly oriented horizontally or vertically, this pointer would always have indicated the transition into a new year slightly later than the Metonic dial's pointer. The motivation for this 8° offset may have been to ensure that the pointer was always indicating the correct year of the games cycle toward the end of the calendar year, when the various competitions were held.

Was there an initial "zero" date applying to all the calendrical dials, such that their pointers were simultaneously oriented straight down?[51] This would correspond to the beginning of a Corinthian calendar year that was in the earliest possible position relative to the seasons within the 19-year cycle, and that also had the Olympic Games. These conditions would be met only every 76 years. Let us speculate, for example, that the calendar was synchronized with the Athenian calendar, in such a way that Phoinikaios always coincided with the third Athenian month, Boedromion. If, at the time the Mechanism was made, the Athenian calendar's intercalary years were still following the 19-year cycle such that the year 330/329 BC was in the earliest possible position, extrapolating forward in steps of 19 years, we find that the Corinthian years during which the Olympic Games were held up to the approximate date of the Antikythera shipwreck would have included 273/272 BC, 197/196 BC, and 121/120 BC. If, on the other hand, the Athenian calendar was already following the cycle such that AD 43 was in the earliest possible position, the candidate years would have included 281/280 BC, 205/204 BC, and 129/128 BC. This is as far as we can pursue this speculation for the time being, but in chapter 6 we will find striking confirmation that the beginning of one of these years was indeed an initial date indicated by parallel pointers on the Metonic, Games, and probably also the Callippic dials.

The idea of the Mechanism having a four-year dial has a history preceding the reading of the inscriptions. Price's preferred reconstruction in *Gears from the Greeks* had the main upper back dial, which we now know as the spiral Metonic dial, as a four-year dial, though he had only vague ideas about its purpose.[52] One possible reason for having a four-year dial would be to indicate when, in the process of running the Mechanism through a long span of simulated time, the Egyptian Calendar ring ought to be shifted one peg hole counterclockwise on the front face to correct for the fact that four Egyptian years fall short of four solar years by one day. But the inscribed names of the Panhellenic competitions imply that the dial's primary role was to track the cycle of festivals; that is, a cultural institution having no connection with astronomy. Hence we have called it the Games dial.

There was no practical utility in having the Mechanism indicate which festivals were held in each year of the cycle. The 2008 announcement of the Games dial (under the designation "Olympiad dial") and its inscriptions was greeted by considerable media attention, with sometimes extravagant headlines such as "Ancient Computer Helped Greeks Predict Olympic Games." The Greeks, of course, did not need elaborate and expensive inventions to count to four! As for the calendrical complications involved in knowing the precise dates of the festivals, the Mechanism would have provided no help. The dial's significance was purely symbolic or didactic.

Iversen has made a careful examination of the CT traces of the second name inscribed for year 4, and he argues convincingly that it is to be read ΑΛΙΕΙΑ, "Halieia."[53] This was a penteteric festival held at Rhodes in honor of the Sun (halios in the Doric dialect), and we know from another ancient source that it took place in one of the cycle years that also had the Nemeans.[54] Like the Naa, the Halieia was a rather minor event of local importance. Why might the Halieia have been selected for inclusion on the Games dial?

When we first identified the Metonic dial's calendar as that of Corinth, it was obvious straightaway that this created a problem with respect to the archeological context in which the Mechanism had been found. The location of the Antikythera shipwreck in the passage between Crete and the Peloponnese, as well as the character of the ship's cargo, clearly indicated a voyage heading westward out of the Aegean and into the Ionian Sea; with such a route it is not plausible that the Mechanism was put on board at any of the localities where the Corinthian calendar was used. Since we were under the mistaken impression that the Corinthian calendar would no longer have been in use anywhere after the middle of the second century BC, we were forced to suppose that the device had for some unknown reason been transported from Syracuse, Corinth, or Epirus (i.e., the place for which it was certainly *made*, whether or not it was manufactured there) to somewhere in the East, and then years later it was being transported back west. A far simpler hypothesis, however, is that the Mechanism was made somewhere around the Aegean not long before the shipwreck and was on its way to its intended home by a route that would next have proceeded up the Adriatic toward, say, Brundisium, stopping somewhere along the way to deliver part of the cargo. Occam's razor thus makes it probable that the Mechanism was commissioned by someone who lived in or near Epirus in the first half of the first century BC.[55]

Iversen's suggestion is that the Rhodian Halieia figures on the Games dial because the Mechanism came from Rhodes. Rhodes was where Hipparchus, a native of Nicaea in Bithynia, had settled and made his astronomical observations in the mid-second century BC, and we have other evidence that it was a center of astronomical activity in the late Hellenistic period. Most significantly, we have Cicero's statement in his dialogue *On the Nature of the Gods* that Posidonius of Apamea, another intellectual immigrant to Rhodes, had "made" a mechanical astronomical device that resembled the Mechanism in its functions in the early first century—a claim worthy of trust, since Cicero had met Posidonius around the time he is supposed to have had this object.[56] We do not have to suppose that the famous Stoic philosopher had the craft skills, or the theoretical knowledge of astronomy for that matter, to construct anything like the Antikythera Mechanism himself, but he must have had access to an atelier that specialized in such work. There cannot have been many! Supposing our Mechanism was made by a workshop on Rhodes for a client who lived somewhere in Epirus, it would likely have reproduced a prototype designed for use on Rhodes, while incorporating some customization for Epirus. The retention of the Halieia from the prototype would amount to a discreet label: "Made in Rhodes."

5

Stars, Sun, and Moon

Dating by Sun and stars

Among the oldest surviving documents of Greek science is a collection of books by itinerant physicians of the fifth and fourth centuries BC, in which they recorded their medical observations made during periods they spent in various localities around the Aegean. The identities of the authors are unknown; in due course the books were included in the corpus of medical writings handed down under the name of Hippocrates of Kos, under the title *Epidemics*, which might mean "sojourns among peoples." The records are chiefly in two forms: individual case histories structured in a diary format, and narratives of the general patterns of sickness experienced in the community over one or more successive seasons.

According to one of the prevalent theories in early Greek medicine, expounded in detail in another "Hippocratic" book called *Airs, Waters, Places*, the physical constitutions of the inhabitants of a place were shaped by the local topography, as well as factors such as its orientation with respect to the winds and the quality of the water supply. The authors of the *Epidemics* pay comparatively little attention to these permanent conditions, however. Their interest is more in the conditions of local weather that subsisted during the seasons leading up to and concurrent with the observations. Thus in one of the books we have the following passage introducing an account of health conditions on the island of Thasos in the northern Aegean:[1]

> In Thasos, a little before Arcturus and at Arcturus, many great rains with north winds. About equinox and until Pleiades, a few southerly rains. Winter was northerly, droughts, chills, great winds, snowstorms. About equinox, really big storms. Spring was northerly, droughts, a few rains, chills. About the Sun's summer solstice, a few rains, great chills until Sirius. After Sirius until Arcturus, hot summer. Great heat spells and not intermittent but continuous and violent. There was no rain. The Etesian winds blew. About Arcturus, southerly rains until equinox.

This passage describes the weather in Thasos over a specific interval of time, but the year is not specified and we are given no calendar dates. Instead, time is marked by solstices, equinoxes, and the dates when certain conspicuous stars (such as Sirius and Arcturus, the two brightest stars visible in Greece, and the Pleiades cluster in Taurus) were seen to rise or set for the first or last time before dawn or after dusk. These events, which all take place at about the same stage of the solar year from one year to the next, were so familiar to the author and his expected readers that he could express them in extremely elliptical form. The following list identifies them and provides the approximate Julian calendar dates when they would have taken place for an observer on Thasos around 400 BC:

Arcturus, morning rising	September 17
Autumnal equinox	September 28
Pleiades, morning setting	November 8
Vernal equinox	March 26
Summer solstice	June 28
Sirius, morning rising	July 28

So the interval in question covers a little more than a year, starting in late summer and ending with the autumnal equinox.

Why did the authors of the *Epidemics* use this kind of Sun-and-stars dating instead of a calendar? Galen, the great physician of the second-century AD Roman Empire, tried to explain this in a commentary that he wrote on the first book of the *Epidemics*. According to Galen, Hippocrates (who, as he believed, wrote *Epidemics* Books 1 and 3) avoided using calendar dates because this would inevitably have meant using the months of a specific local calendar. Hippocrates, he maintains, was writing for the benefit of all nations, and none of the Greek calendars were universally familiar.

We nowadays understand the *Epidemics* not as a treatise written for the ages but as physicians' notes worked up and polished for the benefit of their colleagues and pupils, and so Galen's explanation loses much of its force. Besides, it is not only in the Hippocratic Corpus that we find this kind of dating. Aristotle, for example, uses it in his zoological writings, making such statements as "Tuna fish also lurk in the depths in winter and begin to be caught from the rising of the Pleiades to no later than the setting of Arcturus."[2] Yet he also sometimes uses Athenian calendar months in similar remarks about the life cycles of animals. The point seems to be that biological and meteorological phenomena are more appropriately correlated with stages of the solar year than with a lunisolar calendar. Aristotle's occasional references to the calendar of Athens are either concessions to his readers or workarounds for cases when none of the commonly known repertoire of solar and stellar events fell close to some phenomenon that he wanted to date.

Nonscientific authors also sometimes employed dating with reference to solstices, equinoxes, and stellar risings and settings.[3] Already in the Archaic period (ca. 700 BC), they provided the framework for the agricultural year in Hesiod's *Works and Days*. The morning rising of Arcturus was especially well known as an easily observed indicator of the beginning of autumn: the shepherds in Sophocles' *Oedipus the King* herded their flocks on Kithairon "from spring to Arcturus," Thucydides writes that the Peloponnesians completed the siege wall around Plataea in 429 BC "around the rising of Arcturus," and an oration attributed to Demosthenes cites a loan for a commercial voyage to the Black Sea for which the rate of interest was increased if the return voyage was prolonged "after Arcturus," when the weather conditions became more risky.[4]

Dating by solar and stellar phenomena was accessible to ordinary people and for that matter to physicians and philosophers who had no special expertise in astronomy, because the practice was conventionally limited to a small number of annual events involving just a few easily recognized heavenly bodies. Thus, in the *Historia animalium* and the Hippocratic Corpus, only Arcturus, the Pleiades, and Sirius figure as stars whose first and last risings and settings mark stages of the natural year. A rough approximation of the solstices could be obtained by watching where the Sun rises on the horizon; equinoxes are a bit harder to determine, and perhaps for this very reason the morning rising of Arcturus was more commonly cited than the autumnal equinox as the indicator of the change of season. As a supplement to observation, one could easily learn the rough intervals in days from one phenomenon to the next. We must now turn, however, to an extension of the same principles that fell within the province of astronomers in the proper sense.

In the course of the 1902–1903 season of the German excavations at Miletus, four marble fragments of an unusual kind of inscription were discovered at the site of the ancient theater; the following winter a fifth fragment was found in a sheepfold within the territory of the ancient city.[5] These are now referred to as *IMilet* inv. 456A, 456B, 456C, 456D, and 456N. Fragments A, C, D, and N belong to a single inscription, and B to a different but similar one; both appear to belong to the second century BC. The fragments were first published within months of their discovery by Hermann Diels and Albert Rehm (this was less than two years before Rehm began studying the Mechanism).

Let us first look at *IMilet* inv. 456B (fig. 5.1). The block preserves parts of three columns of text; here is a translation of the middle column (with two constellation names restored):

one line of illegible text
 • •

      30
• The Sun in Aquarius.
• Leo begins to set in the morning
  and Lyra sets.

FIG. 5.1. Parapegma inscription from Miletus, *IMilet* inv. 456B. (inv. SK 1606 IV, Antikensammlung, Staatliche Museen zu Berlin Preussischer Kulturbesitz; photograph: Johannes Laurentius)

• •
• Cygnus begins to set at nightfall.
• • • • • • • •
• Andromeda begins to rise in the
  morning.
• •
• Aquarius is at the middle of rising.
• Pegasus begins to rise in the
  morning.
•
• Centaurus entire sets in the morning.
• Hydra entire sets in the morning.
• Cetus begins to set
  at nightfall.
• Sagitta sets. Season of continuous
  Zephyros winds.
• • • •
• Cygnus entire sets at nightfall.
• Arcturus (?) rises at nightfall.

The small black circles represent small holes drilled into the stone, which were evidently intended to accommodate a movable peg. Each hole represents one of the 30 days (the number given in the second preserved line) that the Sun takes to move through the zodiacal sign Aquarius. As the peg was moved each day from one hole to the next, it indicated the days on which the inscribed phenomena were supposed to take place.

FIG. 5.2. Parapegma inscription from Miletus, *IMilet* inv. 456A. (inv. SK 1606 I, Antikensammlung, Staatliche Museen zu Berlin Preussischer Kulturbesitz; photograph: Johannes Laurentius)

Most of the phenomena are first or last risings or settings of part or all of a constellation in the morning or evening sky; the exceptions are the Sun's entry into Aquarius and the beginning of the season of Zephyros (west) winds. The other columns can be seen to have been similar in content and structure. The complete inscription, which must have been about a meter tall and a meter and a half wide, can be reconstructed as having had six columns, each giving the phenomena occurring during the Sun's passage through two consecutive zodiacal signs, beginning with the summer solstice, when the Sun enters Cancer; the three columns in the surviving fragment belong to the sections for Sagittarius, Aquarius, and Aries. In effect, then, we have a quasi-calendar based on a solar year, with about half the days associated with appearances and disappearances of constellations, the Sun's entries into the zodiacal signs, and, very rarely, weather patterns. Just the one section for Aquarius names 11 stars and constellations, so this was a far richer and denser system of Sun-and-star dating than the one used in the *Epidemics* and Aristotle's biology.

Now let us turn to *IMilet* inv. 456A, the best preserved piece of the second inscription (fig. 5.2). It has parts of two columns as follows:

col. i
• Hyades [?] set in the evening according to Eudoxus [?],but according to Kallaneus of the Indians
  Hyades [?] set in the evening,
  a weather change is signified with hailstorm.
•   •   •

- Hyades are hidden in the evening, hailstorms
  follow, and Zephyros blows
  according to Euctemon, but according to
  Kallaneus of the Indians . . .

col. ii
- Capella sets at nightfall
  according to Euctemon.   •
- Capella sets at nightfall according to
  both Philippus and the Egyptians.
- Capella sets in the evening according to
  Kallaneus of the Indians.   •
- Aquila rises in the evening
  according to Euctemon.
- Arcturus sets at dawn and
  a weather change is signified according to Euctemon, and on this day
  Aquila rises in the evening according to
  Philippus.

The format of the inscription consisted of an introductory section at the left end (part of it is preserved in 456C) followed by, apparently, 12 columns corresponding to sections of the solar year defined by the Sun's passage through the zodiacal signs, the whole being about 5 meters wide and perhaps a little under a quarter meter tall. The two columns in 456A belong to Aries and Taurus; the one in 456N, to Gemini; and the two in 456D, to Libra and Scorpio. The principle of the peg holes is the same as before, but this inscription has many more statements about weather, every statement is attributed to an authority, and, because there are multiple authorities, many of the astronomical phenomena appear more than once and are assigned to more than one day. Three of the authorities are Greek astronomers whose names have come up already in chapter 4: Euctemon, Philippus, and Eudoxus. In addition we have a generic nationality, the Egyptians, and most exotic of all, "Kallaneus of the Indians," who is probably supposed to be Kalanos, a "naked sophist" philosopher from Taxila in India who accompanied Alexander the Great from India to Susa, where he immolated himself.

These inscriptions from Hellenistic Miletus were the first examples to come to light containing dates of stellar phenomena and weather changes in the form of an inscription with peg holes.[6] The same kind of material had long been known from other media, however, with the succession of days in the solar year indicated by different means. The most important is a complete document, very similar in character to the second Miletus inscription, that has come down to us appended to Geminus' *Introduction to the Phenomena*. Like the inscription, it attributes all statements to authorities including Euctemon and Eudoxus, has multiple statements of the same stellar phenomena, and contains many weather statements. In place of the peg holes, it divides the solar year into 12 quasi-months associated with the Sun's passage through the zodiacal signs, like the first Miletus inscription, and numbers the days sequentially in each zodiacal "month." Whether it is really a part of Geminus' book has long been a matter of dispute.[7] (My own opinion is that it is an extraneous composition that came to be attached to the book after Geminus' time.)

The peg hole structure of the inscriptions explains the name by which Geminus himself calls such a document: *parapēgma*, literally, "beside pegging." He devotes a very interesting chapter of his book to a discussion of the rationale for correlating dates of stellar phenomena and dates of weather changes in parapegmas.[8] The common opinion in his time among nonexperts, he says, is that the appearances and disappearances of the constellations *cause* the weather changes through a physical process working through the atmosphere. But Geminus argues that this is wrong because the stars are vastly remote from the earthbound level where weather phenomena occur, and the stars' nature lacks the kind of kinship with the elements forming clouds and winds that would make a physical influence possible. He insists that the scientists who made the original observations on which the parapegmas were based did not believe in a causal connection between the astronomical and the meteorological phenomena. They correlated observed weather patterns with stellar dates because they could not date them according to a lunisolar calendar without running into the problem that every city had a different calendar with different ways of naming days and months, and different conventions for the season when the year began (we can recognize in this a version of Galen's explanation of the dating practices of the Hippocratic *Epidemics*). Geminus also remarks that a parapegma based on observations in one locality will not be suitable for another—a fact conspicuously disregarded in the Miletus inscription, with its citations of Egyptians and of a legendary Indian sage! (Geminus has in mind the variability of weather patterns from place to place, but it is also the case that dates of the first and last risings and settings of stars vary with terrestrial latitude, in some cases considerably.)

What the originators of the parapegma tradition really thought about the relation between the annually recurring appearances and disappearances of constellations and annually recurring weather patterns is not at all clear. The notion that stars could affect conditions in the human environment certainly had a place in early Greek thought. Hesiod speaks in the *Works and Days* of

Sirius at its first morning appearance as an agent of parching that makes men weary and women wanton.[9] This, perhaps, could be taken as metaphor. But the author of the Hippocratic text *Airs, Waters, Places* is not speaking figuratively when he warns of the dangers of administering medical treatments at the key dates marking seasonal changes, which include the solstices, equinoxes, and the appearances of the stars, especially Sirius, Arcturus, and the Pleiades.[10]

The earliest of the known compilers of parapegma data was Euctemon. As we saw in chapter 4, Ptolemy associates him with Meton in connection with the summer solstice of 432 BC.[11] We do not know the format in which his records of stellar and meteorological phenomena were originally presented, but he is very frequently cited by name in later parapegmas and related texts, and his influence can be detected elsewhere where no source is explicitly identified. Euctemon established a set of 15 stars and constellations that was adopted by many later parapegmatists, including Eudoxus. This set includes the stars that were well established in lay use (Arcturus, Pleiades, Sirius) as well as an assortment of other stars and constellations, not all of which contained particularly bright stars. The Miletus parapegma inscription to which *IMilet* inv. 456A belongs not only includes phenomena attributed to Euctemon, but in general restricts itself to Euctemon's list of stars. The other inscription, though it has many phenomena involving non-Euctemonian constellations, also appears to incorporate some data dependent on the Euctemon tradition.

The tradition, as represented in the parapegma appended to Geminus' book, also attributes season lengths to Euctemon; that is, the numbers of days separating the solstices and equinoxes:

> Summer solstice to autumnal equinox: 92 days
> Autumnal equinox to winter solstice: 89 days
> Winter solstice to vernal equinox: 89 days
> Vernal equinox to summer solstice: 95 days

On the other hand, the Greek papyrus Louvre inv. N 2325 (also known as *PParis*1), a popularizing text on astronomy from the second century BC, gives a different set of season lengths for Euctemon:[12]

> Summer solstice to autumnal equinox: 90 days
> Autumnal equinox to winter solstice: 90 days
> Winter solstice to vernal equinox: 92 days
> Vernal equinox to summer solstice: 93 days

Whether either of these versions gives us Euctemon's original figures is difficult to say. It is clear, however, that several early Greek astronomers, likely including Euctemon and Meton, assumed unequal season lengths, and the most plausible explanation is that their determinations of the dates of solstices and equinoxes led to this result. By way of contrast, the Babylonian "Uruk scheme" associated with their 19-year calendrical cycle assumed that the intervals were all approximately equal.

The zodiac and ecliptic

A structural feature of Hellenistic parapegmas such as the Miletus inscriptions and the "Geminus" appendix that does *not* go back to Euctemon is the division of the solar year into 12 sections according to the Sun's movement through the zodiacal signs. This partition of the parapegmatic year was based on two foundations. One was the idea of the zodiac as a celestial path of the Sun's apparent motion relative to the stars, divided into 12 *equal* sectors that we call signs of the zodiac. The other was the assumption that the dates of the Sun's entry into the signs Cancer, Libra, Capricorn, and Aries are identical to the dates of the summer solstice, autumnal equinox, winter solstice, and vernal equinox, respectively. The equally divided zodiac was invented in Babylonia not long before 400 BC; the equation of the solstices and equinoxes with the Sun's entries into zodiacal signs was a Greek innovation that followed the transmission of the zodiac as a concept from Babylonia into the Greek world, probably in the course of the fourth century BC, though some scholars prefer a later date in the Hellenistic period.[13]

One obstacle to conceptualizing a "path of the Sun" is that the Sun cannot be seen together with the stars through which it is apparently passing except in the extremely rare situation of a total solar eclipse. What one *can* identify by direct observation is the path of the Moon, and by noticing that the Moon always sets near the same part of the horizon as the Sun at new moon and near a diametrically opposite point at full moon, one can arrive at the realization that their paths must be about the same. In the Babylonian astronomical manual called MUL.APIN, which dates from perhaps about 1000 BC (and certainly before the seventh century BC), we can see that this had already happened and that the path was recognized as a belt of 18 constellations:[14]

> The gods who stand in the path of the Moon, through whose regions the Moon in the course of a month passes and whom he touches: the Stars, the Bull of Heaven, the True Shepherd of Anu, the Old Man, the Crook, the Great Twins, the Crab, the Lion, the Furrow, the Scales,

the Scorpion, Pabilsag, the Goat Fish, the Great One, the Tails, the Swallow, Anunitu, and the Hired Man. All these are the gods who stand in the path of the Moon, through whose regions the Moon in the course of a month passes and whom he touches.

The Sun travels the [same] path the Moon travels. Jupiter travels the [same] path the Moon travels. Venus travels the [same] path the Moon travels. Mars travels the [same] path the Moon travels. Mercury whose name is Ninurta travels the [same] path the Moon travels. Saturn travels the [same] path the Moon travels. Together six gods who have the same positions, [and] who touch the stars of the sky and keep changing their positions.

Records of astronomical observations kept in Babylon from the seventh century BC onward contain many statements such as "Saturn was in front of the Swallow" or "the Moon became visible behind the Bull of Heaven."[15] By about 400 BC, the list of constellation names used for such positional observations had been reduced to 12, and crucially, these 12 names had come to be assigned to intervals of equal length—that is, zodiacal signs—irrespective of the actual sizes of the constellations that bore the same names. The signs of the Babylonian zodiac are listed in the first column of table 5.1.

Most of the signs are named for constellations that have essentially the same imagined picture as our zodiac, which derives from the Greek version.

TABLE 5.1. The signs of the Babylonian zodiac, the zodiac of Eudoxus and Aratus, and their counterparts in modern nomenclature.

Babylonian	Greek	modern counterpart
Hired Man	*Krios* (Ram)	Aries
Bull of Anu	*Tauros* (Bull)	Taurus
Great Twins	*Didymoi* (Twins)	Gemini
Crab	*Karkinos* (Crab)	Cancer
Lion	*Leōn* (Lion)	Leo
Furrow	*Parthenos* (Maiden)	Virgo
Scales	*Chēlai* (Claws)	Libra
Scorpion	*Skorpios* (Scorpion)	Scorpio
Pabilsag	*Toxotēs* (Archer)	Sagittarius
Goat Fish	*Aigokerōs* (Goat-horned one)	Capricorn
Great One	*Hydrochoos* (Water pourer)	Aquarius
Tails	*Ichthyes* (Fishes)	Pisces

This is obvious in the case of, say, the Bull of Anu, the Crab, or the Goat Fish. A few, however, such as the Hired Man and the Great One, are entirely different.

The uniformly divided zodiac provided a ruler-like scale for the "path of the Moon" that made it possible for Babylonian astronomers to develop methods for predicting positions of heavenly bodies according to mathematical theories. For this purpose, each zodiacal sign was divided into 30 equal parts, so that the entire circuit of the zodiac comprised 360 of these units. This was the original context giving rise to our convention of measuring arcs and angles in degrees. It was assumed in the Babylonian theories that the solstices and equinoxes took place when the Sun was at either 8° or 10° in the relevant signs (Crab, Scales, Goat Fish, Hired Man), not at the beginnings of these signs.

We think nowadays of the signs of the zodiac primarily as part of astrology, and this association too originated in Babylonia. Earlier Mesopotamian astrology consisted of the observation and interpretation of phenomena in the sky that were understood as omens or messages from the gods concerning future events involving kings and kingdoms. During the fifth century BC, a new type of astrology emerged that offered predictions about an ordinary individual largely on the basis of the locations of the Sun, Moon, and planets at the date of birth.[16] These locations were specified according to the zodiacal signs, occasionally with the added precision of degrees within the signs. We will look at these astrological developments in more detail in chapter 7.

The methods of Babylonian mathematical astronomy as well as of Babylonian personal astrology were transmitted to the Greco-Roman world in due course—the second century BC appears to be the most likely time for both knowledge transfers—but the zodiac was known to the Greeks well before they needed it for either of these applications. In the early fourth century, Eudoxus wrote two books, called *Mirror* and *Phenomena*, in which he provided the first known detailed descriptions of a system of constellations covering practically the entire part of the sky visible from the latitudes of mainland Greece and the Aegean. These books have not come down to us, but the poem *Phenomena* by Aratus (early third century BC) is largely a versification of Eudoxus' *Phenomena*, and we also have quotations from Eudoxus in Hipparchus' *Commentary on the Phenomena of Aratus and Eudoxus*. How much of Eudoxus' system reflected Mesopotamian sources is not accurately known because our information about the identities of Mesopotamian constellations is very incomplete. Eudoxus certainly described the 12 zodiacal constellations. In Greek these constellations, and the equal signs named after them, acquired the special name *zōdia*, which otherwise means a small figure or statuette, and the term "zodiac" originates from this word. The signs of the Greek zodiac as set out by Eudoxus and Aratus are listed in the second column of table 5.1.

We should take note of one significant difference between the images associated with the Eudoxian zodiac and the ones familiar to us. Instead of the scales of a weighing balance, the constellation corresponding to Libra is

described as the claws of the Scorpion, effectively treating a part of one constellation as another one. The reason for this is not obvious, but it may be
relevant that the constellation Scorpius is the only one of the zodiacal 12 that
figures in Euctemon's list of parapegmatic constellations. Maybe the Scorpion
was already well established as a Greek constellation incorporating the stars
that the Babylonians called the "Scales." The alternative name *Zygos* (Weighing
balance) begins to appear in Greek sources from about the second or first century BC, but *Chēlai* continued in use as the name both for the constellation and
the zodiacal sign as late as the second century AD. The calendar frieze of the
Little Metropolitan Church in Athens, discussed at the beginning of chapter 4,
presents the older convention in a curious visual form by suspending a scorpion deprived of its claws above the representation of the Athenian month
Pyanepsion, while the claws themselves hover over the representation of the
preceding month, Boedromion (fig. 5.3).

The division of the zodiac into 12 equal signs may be found in a Greek geometrical treatise from the third century BC, the *Phenomena* (yet again this title!)
by the famous mathematician Euclid. This book investigates problems relating to the risings and settings of zodiacal signs at an abstract theoretical level,
and the signs are not even named. Here, however, we find for apparently the
first time the characteristically Greek convention that the points of the zodiac
occupied by the Sun at the solstices and equinoxes are at the exact beginnings
of zodiacal signs.

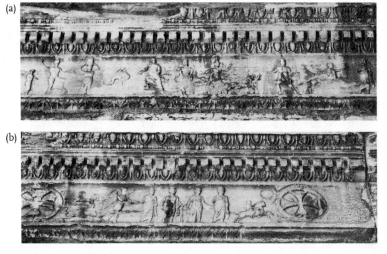

FIG. 5.3. Scorpio and its claws in the calendar frieze of the Little Metropolitan Church.
(photographs: Alexander Jones)

Euclid's book also makes use of the concept of the *ecliptic* circle, a geometrical circle running through the middle of the zodiacal belt; the usual Greek
expression for the ecliptic, the "circle through the middle of the *zōdia*," turns
up already in Aristotle's works in a context referring to Eudoxus' astronomy.[17]
The ecliptic functions as a breadthless idealization of the zodiacal belt, likewise
divided into 12 equal signs; some Greek astronomers, including Hipparchus
and Ptolemy (but not Eudoxus), assumed that the ecliptic was also the apparent
path of the Sun through the zodiac. With the ecliptic as a concept, the apparent positions of the heavenly bodies could be specified by a pair of coordinates:
longitude, measured eastward along the ecliptic, and latitude, measured perpendicularly north or south of the ecliptic.

The earliest surviving parapegma is *PHibeh* 27, a Greek papyrus from
Al-Hibah in Egypt dating from around 300 BC. Its astronomical and meteorological phenomena are structured according to the Egyptian "wandering-
year" calendar (which means that they would have gone out of date after a few
years), and, unusually for a parapegma, it also gives dates of Egyptian religious
festivals. Intermittently this text makes such statements as "in the Maiden" or
"in the Claws of the Scorpion," which refer to the Sun's motion through the
zodiac. The statements appear only on dates of an appearance or disappearance of a star or constellation, so they are not telling us the *first* day when the
Sun is in the stated location; in fact they probably signify just that the Sun was
there in that Egyptian month.[18] Nevertheless, the preserved instances favor
understanding them as references to zodiacal signs, not constellations. The
later parapegmas that we have looked at above use the dates of the Sun's entry
into zodiacal signs to break the solar year up into chunks of variable length,
though always close to 30 days long. Since the solstices and equinoxes are
equated with the Sun's entries into Cancer, Capricorn, Aries, and Libra, each
set of three consecutive chunks beginning with one of these events makes
up an astronomical season, again of varying length though always around
90 days long.

The Sun and Parapegma on the Mechanism

When Albert Rehm had his first brief opportunity to examine the fragments
of the Mechanism in September 1905, it was Fragment C that particularly
attracted his attention.[19] The face of the fragment that we call C-1 had appeared
rather featureless when it was first examined in 1902–1903, but since then
the technicians of the National Archaeological Museum had painstakingly
removed layers of accretion and fused plate, exposing a piece of inscribed plate
that Rehm was apparently the first scholar to examine. He must have been
greatly astonished—and gratified—to discover that the text on this plate was

a parapegma, like the Miletus inscriptions that he had helped interpret and publish a year earlier.

The plate bearing Rehm's Parapegma was stuck on the front of the remains of the Mechanism's front dial, and he was able to see only a small bit of the Egyptian Calendar scale peeking out above it. By the time that Derek de Solla Price examined the fragments in 1958, the Parapegma plate had lost some pieces, probably through wartime damage, exposing part of the Zodiac scale, which was immediately inside the Egyptian Calendar scale. Price was thus enabled to discover how the Parapegma was connected to the Zodiac scale and to make a correct guess about where the Parapegma inscription was originally located on the Mechanism.[20] Research based on the 2005 computed tomography (CT) data and incorporating other surviving fragments of the Parapegma inscription has both confirmed and refined Price's reconstruction.

As we saw in chapter 3, the Zodiac scale was a ring similar to the Egyptian Calendar scale, divided into 12 sectors for the signs of the zodiac, each of which comprised 30° divisions, but unlike the Egyptian Calendar scale it was a fixed part of the front dial plate. A revolving pointer indicated the longitude of the Sun in the zodiac for whatever date was displayed on the Mechanism. The Sun moves through the zodiac from west to east, and on the dial this direction was represented by a clockwise revolution of the Sun's pointer. The beginning of Aries was at the extreme top, that of Libra (labeled as Chelai, "Claws") was at the bottom, and those of Capricorn and Cancer were at the extreme right and left, respectively, of the dial.

Outside the graduation lines marking the individual degrees on the Zodiac scale, letters of the Greek alphabet were inscribed at irregular intervals. For example, the letters alpha, beta, gamma, and delta are inscribed at the 1st-, 11th-, 14th-, and 16th-degree graduations of the sector for the sign Libra, a part of the scale that is exposed to view on C-1. Each index letter signified an astronomical phenomenon that took place whenever the Sun pointer was aligned with the corresponding degree graduation.

To identify the phenomenon, one had to look up the index letter in a list of phenomena that was inscribed on the two rectangular plates that constituted the portions of the Mechanism's front face above and below the dial plate. Each plate had two columns of index letters and descriptions of the phenomena; we refer to the whole text as the Parapegma inscription.[21] If, say, the Sun's pointer was in the upper-right quadrant of the Zodiac dial, somewhere between the beginning of Aries and the end of Gemini, one looked for the index letter in the right column of the upper plate.

As it happens, this upper-right column was almost completely preserved on C-1; this was the text that Rehm transcribed during his first examination of the Mechanism's fragments in 1905, aided by a small wooden stick with which he could follow the engraved letter strokes through the layer of patina covering the inscription. (The patina was subsequently cleaned off, but part of the plate itself has also broken away, so we depend on an early photograph and Rehm's transcription for some of the text.) The index letters run in the order of the Greek alphabet from iota through sigma, probably continuing the series from alpha through theta in the upper-left column of the inscription, of which we have only two fragmentary passages.[22] In the following translation, brackets enclose restored text:

[I   Aries begins to rise. 1]
[Vernal equinox.]
[K   Pleiades set] in the evening. [*nn*]
Λ   Hyades set in the evening. 24
M   Taurus begins to rise. 1
[N] Lyra rises in the evening. 11
Ξ   Pleiad rises in the morning. 17
O   Hyad rises in the morning. 25
Π   Gemini begins to rise. [1]
P   Aquila rises in the evening. [*nn*]
Σ   Arcturus sets in the morning. 10

Most of the statements in the Parapegma inscription concern appearances and disappearances of stars and constellations. For example, the statement indexed with the letter Ξ is the first appearance of the Pleiades near the eastern in the predawn sky. The numeral 17 following this statement either means that this event is supposed to occur on the 17th day counting from the Sun's entry into Taurus, or that it occurs when the Sun's pointer is at the graduation for the 17th degree in Taurus. We are not sure which interpretation is correct, but the day number and the degree number would have generally been the same, or different only by 1.

Statements such as those indexed with M and Π use similar language to the stellar statements, but they actually refer to the Sun's entry into the zodiacal signs. For this reason, they are always followed by the numeral 1, meaning that they happen on the day when the Sun reaches the first degree of the sign. The verb "rise" (*epitellein* or *anatellein*) is used with a different sense when speaking of the zodiacal signs; saying that the Pleiades "rise" means that they are actually visible to an observer, whereas saying that Taurus "begins to rise" means that the first degree of the sign is at the horizon at the moment of sunrise, which is not a phenomenon that one can see. Each of the four columns of the Parapegma inscription began with a two-line statement such as the one indexed with I here, equating the Sun's entry into a zodiacal sign with a solstice or equinox.

The Parapegma inscription resembles the first of our Miletus parapegma inscriptions, *IMilet* inv. 456B, in that it contains no attributed or duplicated

events and no weather statements. On the other hand, it follows Euctemon's
list of stars and constellations. We do not know the source of the specific
data, and whether it was derived from observations or from some kind of
theoretical calculation of the conditions of visibility of stars. The preserved
information seems to fit the latitude of southern Greece or, say, Rhodes
(about 36° N) better than Alexandria (about 31° N) or Epirus (about 41° N).[23]
However, astronomical analysis of ancient parapegmas is always a frustrating exercise yielding limited results. One reason is that stellar visibility is
not a phenomenon for which exact scientific criteria are possible, because it
depends on quality of the observer's eyesight as well as atmospheric conditions near the horizon, both of which are not entirely predictable. Another
source of uncertainty is that we are not always sure which stars in a constellation were considered essential for a constellation to be considered visible.
And on top of these considerations, the Parapegma inscription seems to
reflect influence from the complex tradition of parapegma data inherited
from earlier periods.

Why was the Mechanism provided with a parapegma? As is often the
case, we can try to approach this question from two perspectives: How would
the information yielded by this display have been useful? What didactic or
symbolic value did its presence have? At the practical level, there were a
few—a very few—dates of stellar appearances that had direct significance
in public or private life, such as the first morning appearance of Sirius in
Egypt or that of Arcturus in Greece. Indirectly, dates of stellar phenomena, solstices, and equinoxes had been made broadly familiar through the
parapegma tradition as weather predictors. The absence of weather statements from the Mechanism's Parapegma inscription might seem to limit its
usefulness for forecasting weather changes. Perhaps the designer believed
that there were regular rules for correlating weather to the astronomical
events, or, more plausibly to my mind, he might have limited the inscription
to the astronomical events because the Mechanism was intended for use in a
distant place whose weather patterns could not be assumed to correspond to
those recorded in the available parapegmas—the user would have to conduct
a bit of local research!

If we approach the Mechanism as an instrument for teaching about
astronomy, a parapegma is an obvious thing to provide it with; the compilation and presentation of parapegmatic data was, after all, a central component
of Greek astronomy going back to its beginnings in the fifth century BC.
The Parapegma inscription, with its linkage to the Sun's pointer by way of
the Zodiac dial, also helped render the Mechanism a more comprehensive
reflection of the complete cosmic system by providing a way for the stars to
be shown in relation to the other heavenly bodies. The system of constellations and their arrangement in the sky was a standard elementary topic of
popular expositions of astronomy, and it could be given visual representation

FIG. 5.4. The star globe of the Farnese Atlas, Museo Nazionale Archeologico, Naples. (photograph: Alexander Jones)

in the form of star globes (such as the globe held aloft by the Farnese Atlas; fig. 5.4) or the display dials of mechanized water clocks. It was not something that one could effectively build into the displays of a device such as the Antikythera Mechanism. In a limited way the signs of the zodiac inscribed on the Zodiac dial can be thought of as standing for the stars, but through a parapegma it was possible to relate the annual revolution of the Sun, indicated through the revolving pointer, to a wider range of constellations, even if their representation is verbal rather than visual.

The meaning and length of the solar year

We have been speaking of the "solar year" as if it were a straightforward astronomical time unit, but how did the designer of the Mechanism understand solar years, and how long did he think they were? In a basic operational sense, a solar year on the Mechanism is the time represented by the Sun's pointer going exactly once around the Zodiac scale. The Parapegma inscription offers us two astronomical meanings for this time interval. On the one hand, when the pointer is at the mark for the beginning of, say, the zodiacal sign labeled "Scales" (i.e., Libra), an index letter *alpha* inscribed next to the mark takes us to a part of the inscription that says, "The Scales begin to rise: autumnal equinox." So the time from one equinox or solstice to the next equinox or solstice of the same kind is a solar year. On the other hand, when the pointer is at, say, the 16th-degree mark in the same zodiacal sign, an index letter *delta* links to a statement that "The Crown [i.e., Corona Borealis] rises in the morning." This means that the time from when the Sun is just far enough in the zodiac from a constellation so that the constellation can be seen before sunrise to the next occurrence of this situation is a solar year.

Conceptually, these are two distinct kinds of year. The year defined by solstices and equinoxes is called the "tropical year" (from Greek *tropē*, meaning "solstice"), while that defined by the Sun's passing by stars is the "sidereal year" (from Latin *siderealis*, "starry"). In early Greek astronomy it was assumed, however, that there was no difference between them. Thus, Hesiod puts Arcturus' first evening appearance as 60 days after the summer solstice, and a scheme fixing the numbers of days between stellar phenomena and the solstices and equinoxes appears in the Hippocratic writings.[24] The conventional structure of parapegmas was an elaboration of this principle, and the Mechanism, as we have seen, functioned as an automated parapegma so far as its solar display was concerned.

Through its gearwork, the Mechanism tied its solar years in fixed ratios to the lengths of the mean lunar month and of various planetary periodicities, but not to single days; it is only through the dial scales and inscriptions that we get any information about how many days long the year was supposed to be. When the Sun's pointer goes once around the Zodiac scale, it also goes once around the Egyptian Calendar scale, which is divided into divisions for 365 days, but since this scale was designed so that its alignment with the Zodiac scale could be adjusted, all we learn from this is that the solar year was *approximately* 365 days, subject to some fractional correction. There may have been an instruction in one of the Mechanism's inscribed texts saying how often the Egyptian Calendar scale should be shifted, but if so, it does not survive.

The inscribed numerals inside the Metonic dial's scale imply that in every 47 lunar months, there are 22 "hollow" months of 29 days and 25 "full" months of 30 days, so that a complete 19-year cycle contains 6940 days. This would make a solar year of $365^{5}/_{19}$ days. But this is almost certainly not what the designer believed, because the back cover inscription (BCI) tells us that there was a dial counting the 19-year cycles within a 76-year cycle, and the only motivation for this would have been the assumption of a solar year of exactly $365^{1}/_{4}$ days. There must have been an additional rule, perhaps in a lost part of the BCI, that a particular month of the 19-year cycle was full in three of the cycles but hollow in the fourth to maintain a correct day count over the long term.

Around 128 BC, Hipparchus discovered that the tropical and sidereal years were not exactly equal, finding that the tropical year was approximately 1/300 of a day shorter than $365^{1}/_{4}$ days, whereas the sidereal year was a small fraction of a day longer than $365^{1}/_{4}$ days. Another way of describing this phenomenon, known as "precession of the equinoxes" or simply "precession," is that the stars

have a very slow eastward shift in position relative to the solstitial and equinoctial points (i.e., the points on the ecliptic where the Sun is located at the solstices and equinoxes). Hipparchus also deduced that the stars' relative motion
was a revolution around the poles of the ecliptic, not the equator, so that while
the stars move slowly eastward in longitude, their rising and setting points on
the horizon also gradually change.

A consequence of precession is that the dates of first and last appearances
of constellations are not stable relative to the solstices and equinoxes or even
relative to each other. Since the sidereal year is longer than the tropical year,
dates of these events will fall progressively later if the solar year is considered
to begin with, say, the summer solstice. But the long-term changes in the places
where stars rise and set on the horizon also have complicated effects on the visibility dates. Precession thus implies that the stellar data in parapegmas going
back to centuries-old authorities such as Euctemon and Eudoxus would have
diminishing validity, in addition to the fact that even for their own time the
dates of risings and settings would have been valid only for places at the same
latitudes as they worked.

As an illustration of this twofold variability, we can compare the dates of
Arcturus' first morning rising, and the numbers of days by which the event
preceded the autumnal equinox, as estimated by modern theory for three different latitudes and for 400 BC (roughly the time of Euctemon and Eudoxus)
and 100 BC (closer to the times of Geminus and the Mechanism):[25]

Place	400 BC	100 BC
Alexandria (31° 12′ N)	Sept. 24 (4 days)	Sept. 26 (0 days)
Athens (37° 59′ N)	Sept. 19 (9 days)	Sept. 22 (4 days)
Rome (41° 54′ N)	Sept. 16 (12 days)	Sept. 19 (7 days)

The parapegma appended to Geminus' book places Arcturus' rising 11 days
before the equinox according to Eudoxus and 10 days before according to
Euctemon, which would have been plausible dates for their own times and
for central to northern Greek latitudes. However, for centuries afterward,
the parapegma literature persisted in assigning Arcturus' rising to dates
around 10 or more days before the equinox. Even Galen, writing in the
late second century AD, states that the interval between the two events is
about 12 days.[26] On the Mechanism's Zodiac scale, the last indexed stellar event (omega) preceding the autumnal equinox was almost certainly
the rising of Arcturus, at 20°, which is the approximate equivalent of
Euctemon's date.

With hindsight, we see Hipparchus' discovery of precession as one of his
most important accomplishments, partly because it was a remarkable instance
of scientific analysis of a phenomenon that was just at the threshold of what

could be detected from the observational record available in his time, and also, from a somewhat anachronistic perspective, because the gravitational explanation of precession was a critical issue in the development of Newtonian mechanics. During the period of Greek astronomy between Hipparchus and Ptolemy, however, it had limited impact. Geminus, for example, shows no awareness of precession or of year lengths close to but not exactly 365¼ days, and the same is true of Theon of Smyrna, a Platonist philosopher of the early second century AD who wrote extensively about astronomy in his book *The Mathematics Useful for Reading Plato*. It should not be surprising, then, that the Mechanism also draws no distinction between the sidereal and tropical years, equating both with 365¼ days.

The Sun's varying speed

Of all the ancient writers on astronomy, Geminus is the one whose book has the most points of contact with the Mechanism. We have already seen in chapter 4 how closely his accounts of the calendars of the Greeks and Egyptians parallel the Egyptian Calendar scale and the Metonic dial; now we are about to turn to his treatment of the motions of the Sun and Moon through the zodiac. We would naturally like to know something about him, but the evidence is (alas!) rather thin. Besides the *Introduction to the Phenomena*, he wrote other books that have not survived but that are cited or quoted by later authors: a *Concise Exposition of Posidonius' Meteorology* and a work—or possibly two separate works—on the philosophy of mathematics going by the titles *Philokalia* ("love of beauty") and *On the Classification of Mathematics*.

A rough indication of the date of his career comes from his statement, quoted in chapter 4, that "the Isia are shifted a whole month relative to the winter solstice," which was true for a decade or so around 60 BC.[27] No ancient source associates Geminus with a particular place, but it has often been argued (and sometimes is stated as a fact) that he worked on Rhodes or was born there. The *Introduction to the Phenomena* does, in fact, contain multiple allusions to Rhodes. Many if not most appear to be generic, though; the "parallel through Rhodes" (36° N) was a standard reference latitude in ancient geography and astronomy since it runs more or less through the middle of the Mediterranean. It may be more significant that Mount Attavyros, the highest peak on Rhodes, is one of the examples he cites of a place that is above the level of the clouds when he wishes to demonstrate that the stars are remote from terrestrial weather.[28] Perhaps the strongest sign that Geminus lived on Rhodes is that in his explanation of the Moon's phases (9.12) he calls the 15th day of the calendar month *dichomēnia* ("mid-month") instead of, say, "the 15th," and this is a nomenclature characteristic of the calendars used in

Rhodes and its environs.[29] Posidonius also lived on Rhodes and died in or after 60 BC, so it is quite possible that Geminus was personally acquainted with him.

Geminus was not a researching astronomer but, rather, was a popularizer of the sciences, and he was very good at it. In the very first chapter of the *Introduction to the Phenomena*, he neatly covers in a couple of pages the central topics of this chapter up to the point we have reached, including the zodiac and its division into equal signs of 30°, the placement of the solstitial and equinoctial points of the ecliptic at the beginnings of their signs, and the division of the solar year by the solstices and equinoxes into unequal astronomical seasons.[30] He gives the following as the season lengths:

Summer solstice to autumnal equinox: 92½ days
Autumnal equinox to winter solstice: 88⅛ days
Winter solstice to vernal equinox: 90⅛ days
Vernal equinox to summer solstice: 94½ days

Putting these facts together, we find that the Sun is traversing the four equal quarters of the ecliptic in unequal times; that is, it is slowing down and speeding up. This phenomenon of variable apparent speed was called anomaly (literally, "nonuniformity").

And for the astronomers, anomaly was a problem. A universal principle of the discipline, Geminus says, is that the Sun, Moon, and planets, being eternal and divine beings, must move with uniform speed along circular paths, in contrast to human beings, who are continually slowing down and speeding up because of the daily needs of life.[31] How are we to reconcile this principle with the inequality of the seasons?

To make the nature of the problem clearer and point the way to the solution, Geminus outlines the basic cosmological assumptions.[32] Like most Greek astronomers, he assumes a geocentric cosmology; that is, the Earth (which, as we learn elsewhere in his book, is spherical) stands still at the center of a set of nested spherical shells, the outermost of which is the sphere of the fixed stars.[33] Working our way inward, we come to Saturn, Jupiter, and Mars. Next inward comes what Geminus calls the "space" for the Sun, and below this, Venus, Mercury, and the Moon.

In chapter 7 we will revisit Geminus' cosmology in relation to the Mechanism's portrayal of the motions of the planets. For now, like Geminus, we want to focus just on the sphere of the stars and the Sun. The sphere of the stars is assumed to be spinning at uniform speed around the Earth, and the poles of its axis of rotation are the north and south celestial poles. It is because of this spin that we (presuming we live in the Northern Hemisphere) see stars as revolving counterclockwise on circular paths around the north celestial pole, and if they are far enough from the pole, we see them rise always at the same points on the eastern horizon and set always at the same points on the western horizon.[34] The Sun is carried along with this spinning, but at the same time it is moving more slowly from west to east so that it goes once around the zodiac in a year. Now Geminus argues that if the Sun performed its own annual revolution *on* the sphere of the fixed stars, or even on a smaller circle concentric with it, we would observe the time intervals between the solstices and equinoxes as equal. In reality, however, the Sun revolves along a circle that is off-center with respect to the Earth and the sphere of the fixed stars. (This is probably why Geminus spoke of a "space" for the Sun.) The displacement is such that the arc of the Sun's circle that lies below the quadrant of the ecliptic from the beginning of Aries to the beginning of Cancer (that is, from the vernal equinoctial point to the summer solstitial point) is the largest, and the arc below the quadrant from the beginning of Libra to the beginning of Capricorn (that is, from the autumnal equinoctial point to the winter solstitial point) is the smallest of the four arcs corresponding to the astronomical seasons. As a result, the Sun can travel along its circle with uniform speed while producing unequal seasons, in conformity with the phenomena.

Geminus is the earliest of a series of ancient astronomical authors who present this theory of an eccentric solar orbit as a way of accounting for the phenomenon of unequal astronomical seasons. Theon of Smyrna offers a more detailed geometrical argument to the same effect as Geminus' verbal one, and interestingly, in setting out the problem he gives exactly the same four season lengths in days as Geminus.[35] Ptolemy goes still further by showing how the exact size and displacement of the Sun's eccentric circle can be calculated from just the two season lengths of 94½ days from vernal equinox to summer solstice and 92½ days from summer solstice to autumnal equinox (fig. 5.5).[36] Moreover, he tells us that this calculation had previously been done by Hipparchus, from the same data and with the same results. So it appears that Hipparchus was the ultimate source for all these versions.

Both Theon and Ptolemy also describe an alternative theory (fig. 5.6).[37] We can retain the idea of a circle for the Sun's annual motion concentric with the sphere of the fixed stars, but the Sun does not itself travel uniformly on this circle. What does is the center of a smaller circle, called an "epicycle," while the Sun travels uniformly around the epicycle, in the opposite direction and with the same period of one solar year (as seen from the Earth). This so-called epicyclic hypothesis causes the Sun to travel along exactly the same path in space as the eccentric hypothesis, so there was no observational basis for preferring one over the other. Theon prefers the epicycle because he sees it as more balanced with respect to the symmetries of the cosmos, Ptolemy prefers the eccentric circle because it is simpler, and Geminus does not so much as mention the possibility of an epicycle. From a modern heliocentric perspective, the varying apparent speed of the Sun is a consequence of the Earth's elliptical orbit around the Sun,

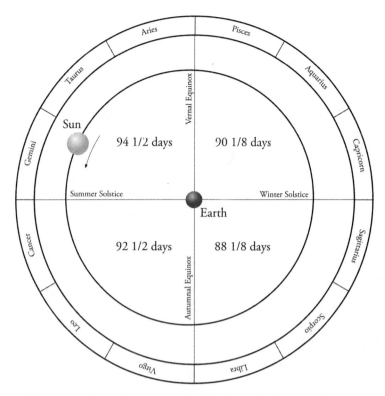

FIG. 5.5. The Hipparchus-Ptolemy eccentric hypothesis for the Sun. The Sun is shown at its apogee.

which, in the frame of reference of an observer on Earth, would translate into an elliptical orbit of the Sun around the Earth. Ptolemy's instinct was thus correct.

The epicyclic hypothesis gives us a way of conceiving the Sun's anomaly as a continuous process. If we imagine the center of the epicycle as a visible body in its own right, it would be observed to travel through the zodiac with uniform speed while the Sun travels along with it but alternately running a bit ahead and lagging behind. We can call the epicycle's center the "mean Sun," and the actual Sun the "true Sun." The gap between the mean Sun and the true Sun never gets larger than about 2°, and the apparent motion of the true Sun in one day is always within 2.5 minutes of arc of its mean daily motion, which is about 59 minutes. This is a rather subtle effect.

We saw in chapter 3 that the Mechanism must have had a pointer indicating the Sun's position on the Zodiac scale. Did this display represent the Sun's motion as varying in speed? The presence of the Egyptian Calendar scale adds a complication to the question because this scale seems to require a pointer moving uniformly with the Sun's mean speed. In Price's reconstruction, according

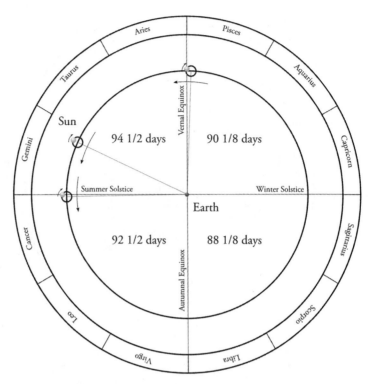

FIG. 5.6. The Hipparchus-Ptolemy epicyclic hypothesis for the Sun. The epicycle and Sun are shown in their locations at the vernal equinox and summer solstice as well as when the Sun is at apogee.

to which the Mechanism displayed only the Sun and Moon and chronological cycles, both the Sun's pointer and the Moon's revolved uniformly relative to the input rotation. After Michael Wright devised his conjectural reconstruction of the Mechanism's front face as a complete planetarium, showing the planets as moving nonuniformly and with periodic reversals of direction, he realized that it would have been feasible to introduce a suitable anomaly into the motion of the Sun's pointer by mechanical means similar to his reconstructions for Venus and Mercury.[38] He therefore posited that there was both a pointer for the true Sun and one for the mean Sun, the latter being the indicator for the Egyptian calendar date.

Then in 2010 James Evans, Christián Carman, and Alan Thorndike published a paper that demonstrated a remarkable and unexpected feature of the front dial scales.[39] Since the Zodiac scale was divided into 360 parts and the Egyptian Calendar scale into 365 parts, the divisions of the Egyptian Calendar scale ought to be slightly smaller in angular measure than those of the Zodiac scale, which of course represent single degrees. Evans, Carman, and Thorndike showed that, over the roughly one-fifth of the scales that survives, the reverse is true: the day divisions are actually larger. The effect is obscured when one compares small arcs on the scales by noise from random errors in the graduations, but on the larger scale it is evident that the day divisions average about 1.6 percent larger than the degree divisions, whereas we would expect them to average about 1.5 percent smaller. Further careful analysis established that the Egyptian Calendar scale was, as expected, divided uniformly into equal divisions, except for the random errors, whereas the ostensible "degrees" of the Zodiac scale are on average about 3 percent smaller than true degrees.

Evans and his colleagues maintain that the tight spacing of the degree graduations on the extant part of the Zodiac scale, which of course must have been compensated for elsewhere on the scale since the total must have remained 360, was intentional, and that its purpose was to enable a uniformly revolving solar pointer—the same pointer that indicated the Egyptian calendar date—to display the position of the true Sun. Up to the present, the community of scholars studying the Mechanism has been reluctant to accept this hypothesis, preferring to assume that the Sun's pointer revolved nonuniformly through mechanical means. For my part, I have come to the conviction that Evans, Carman, and Thorndike are right. The measurements on which their conclusions rest are robust, and the only alternative to intentionally nonuniform graduation of the scale is that it resulted from sloppy division of the dial; however, an accidental error of this magnitude would have been glaringly obvious from the way that the solstitial and equinoctial graduations lined up with dates on the Egyptian dial.

I think the reason that the designer chose an inscriptional rather than a mechanical approach to displaying the Sun's anomaly lies precisely here, in the availability of the Egyptian Calendar scale as a direct way to read off the number of days that the Sun takes to traverse each zodiacal sign or each astronomical season. One would not even need to operate the Mechanism or pay attention to the Sun's pointer. The correspondence of graduations on the two scales would show the pattern immediately. And one could dispense with the inelegance of having a pointer on the front dial that indicated a fictitious, invisible point, the mean Sun, in company with the visible heavenly bodies.

There is a drawback to using nonuniform graduation of the Zodiac scale to display solar anomaly—namely, that the effect of solar anomaly ends up incorporated in the displayed positions of all the other heavenly bodies that have pointers on the dial, at least if their pointers shared the same axis with the Sun's pointer. This would not have been astronomically absurd in the case of the planets, since in reality the planets orbit the true Sun, not the center of the Earth's orbit, but we have no evidence that any astronomer before Johannes Kepler realized this. However, the maximum effect of the nonuniform graduation on a displayed position would have been on the order of only about 2°, and this could have been considered negligible for the purposes for which the Mechanism was designed.

The Moon's variable motion

Like the Earth's orbit around the Sun, the Moon's orbit around the Earth is eccentric, so the Moon also appears to move through the zodiac with varying speed. The Moon's anomaly is more complicated than the Sun's, however, because the Sun's gravity perturbs the Moon's elliptical orbit in various ways. The most important of these is that the major axis of the orbit, called the apsidal line, shifts gradually eastward relative to the stars. Hence, while the Moon goes once around the zodiac on average in about 27⅓ days, it takes slightly more than 27½ days for it to go from its apogee (the farthest point of its orbit from the Earth) back to its apogee. These periods are called the sidereal month and the anomalistic month, respectively.

We know from Ptolemy that Hipparchus at various times worked both with an eccentric hypothesis and an epicyclic hypothesis to explain the Moon's anomaly, as he did for the Sun. In his eccentric hypothesis the direction from the center of the Earth to the center and apogee of the orbit shifted uniformly eastward, while in his epicyclic hypothesis the rate of revolution of the Moon around its epicycle was slightly slower than the rate of revolution of the epicycle's center around the Earth. In this way, the hypotheses could accurately reflect the distinction between the anomalistic and sidereal months.

Geminus takes up the topic of lunar anomaly in the concluding chapter of the *Introduction to the Phenomena*.[40] In contrast to his treatment of the solar anomaly, he shows no interest in *explaining* why the Moon speeds up and slows down, but instead sets about deriving a simple arithmetical pattern for approximating the day-to-day progress of the Moon in degrees. This pattern is what we call a "linear zigzag function." It assumes that the Moon's daily motion increases by a constant amount from one day to the next until a set maximum value is reached, and thereafter it decreases daily by the same constant until a set minimum is reached, and so on. Such patterns were characteristic of Babylonian astronomy, and we know from cuneiform tablets that the specific zigzag function that Geminus derives for the Moon was actually Babylonian in origin.[41]

Geminus connects the zigzag function (in a way that is probably not historically correct) with a period that he calls the *Exeligmos* ("turning of a wheel"), which he says is the shortest time interval that contains exact whole numbers of lunar months, anomalistic months, and days. The *Exeligmos* relation is:

669 lunar months = 717 anomalistic months = 19,756 days

Another author who mentions the *Exeligmos* is Ptolemy.[42] He writes that astronomers in the past had assumed a period relation called *Periodikos* ("periodic"):

223 lunar months = 239 anomalistic months = 6585⅓ days

and that, in order to obtain a period with a whole number of days, they tripled the *Periodikos* to obtain the *Exeligmos*. The *Periodikos* (which is now known as the Saros) and the *Exeligmos*, which express a single period relation in different forms, are actually periods related to eclipses, and we will look at this aspect of them in chapter 6. For the moment, the significant point is what Ptolemy says next; namely, that Hipparchus had *already* shown through analysis of observations that the *Periodikos* and *Exeligmos* were not accurate, and that a much better relation was:

251 lunar months = 269 anomalistic months

We know that both the *Periodikos* (or Saros) and Hipparchus' relation were Babylonian discoveries. Hipparchus was correct in concluding that the 251-month period relation was much more accurate. But Geminus, who shows no awareness of Hipparchus' work on lunar theory, confirms the truth of Ptolemy's statement that people after Hipparchus persisted in trusting the *Exeligmos*.

The revelation that the motion of the Moon's pointer on the Antikythera Mechanism represented lunar anomaly was one of the more remarkable outcomes published by the Antikythera Mechanism Research Project (AMRP) team in 2006 on the basis of their 2005 data gathering.[43] In 2002, Wright had hypothesized geared mechanisms providing anomalistic motion for the planets and also for the Sun and Moon, but these were reconstructions for which the physical and inscriptional evidence at the time was slender.[44] His 2005 gear scheme proposal for the displays relating to the Sun, Moon, and calendar cycles represents the output of lunar motion as uniform.[45] The combination of gears for lunar anomaly that the AMRP team identified was the first proof that the Mechanism had nonuniform outputs of any kind.

We will examine the mechanical means by which a uniform motion of the mean moon was translated into nonuniform motion in chapter 8. Two facts about it deserve attention here. The first is that the contrivance can be understood as a geometrically exact representation either of an epicyclic or eccentric hypothesis of the kind that Hipparchus is known to have assumed in his theoretical work. The second is that the period relation underlying the gearwork is not the Babylonian 251-month relation confirmed by Hipparchus, but rather the Saros (or equivalently, the *Exeligmos*).

The Saros is deeply embedded in the Mechanism's construction, since it also provides the basis for its eclipse prediction functions, as we will see in chapter 6. Like Geminus, the designer seems to have had full confidence in its accuracy. This probably implies that he was not deeply familiar with Hipparchus' researches. (Neither, it would appear, was Geminus, who in his entire book mentions Hipparchus only with respect to two descriptions of constellation figures.) The conformity of the anomaly mechanism to an epicyclic or eccentric hypothesis need not point to even an indirect dependence on Hipparchus, since it is by no means certain that Hipparchus was the first astronomer to apply such hypotheses to the Moon. Evans and Carman have even suggested that the discovery of this way of generating anomalistic motion through gearwork might have led to the idea of epicycles and eccenters rather than the other way around,[46] though such a development of ideas, if it did happen that way, would have had to occur well before Hipparchus, let alone before our Mechanism, if, as I maintain in this book, it dates from the early first century BC.

In many respects the Mechanism had the edge over an author such as Geminus in its ability to give a dynamic, visual representation of astronomical concepts that a book could present only as words and line diagrams. But it was limited to showing simulations of the phenomena. Underlying theories providing the reasons for the phenomena, such as the epicyclic or eccentric hypotheses, were latent in the gearwork, but even if a teacher-operator opened the device up to show the inner workings, few spectators would have been much the wiser. In providing a mechanical simulation of lunar anomaly, the designer was running a risk of creating an effect that the operator might find it challenging to make a convincing display of. The actual variation in the Moon's daily motion is modest; Geminus gives the minimum as between 11° and 12° per day, and the maximum between 15° and 16° per day. The random errors of placement of the graduation marks on the Egyptian Calendar scale, by which the operator would show that he has gone through one day's worth of input motion, would have obscured this range of variation in the Moon pointer's motion. A practical solution, I suggest, would have been to show how far the Moon pointer moves in larger numbers of days, perhaps groups of seven days, which would break the anomalistic month up into sections centering on the slowest, mean, and fastest stages of motion. Lunar anomaly may not have been the subtlest phenomenon shown on the Mechanism, as we shall presently see.

The Moon's phases

Alone among the heavenly bodies visible to the naked eye, the Moon radically changes appearance on a day-to-day basis through phases. In their role as the basis for lunisolar calendars, the cycle of phases was simply a given. Early Greek natural philosophers, on the other hand, saw the phases as a phenomenon in need of explanation. As an example of an early speculative explanation of the Moon's changing appearance, we can take the summary that the third-century AD Christian theologian (and sometime antipope) Hippolytus offers of the cosmology of the early-sixth-century BC Ionian philosopher Anaximander of Miletus.[47] According to Hippolytus, Anaximander believed that the heavenly bodies were celestial fire seen through orifices or vents perforating an otherwise opaque sky. The Moon's apparent changing shape results from a process of blocking and unblocking its orifice, and eclipses too are a blockage either of the Sun's or the Moon's orifice.

About a century after Anaximander, there is good evidence that both Empedocles of Akragas and Anaxagoras of Klazomenai knew the explanation of the phases that became standard in Greek astronomy: that the Moon is a spherical body that gets its light from the Sun, which is also spherical; its originator may have been Parmenides of Elea.[48] The empirical evidence on which this theory rested consisted of the shapes assumed by the Moon through its phases and their correlation with the relative locations of the Moon and Sun in the sky. It also depended on an insight that was part of optics, the Greek science concerned with visual perception; namely, that a circle seen from a direction other than straight on appears as an oval, or as a straight line if the viewer is in the plane of the circle. (Greek artists were fond of exhibiting this phenomenon, for example in the form of highly foreshortened chariot wheels.)[49] If the Moon was a sphere divided into bright and dark hemispheres, the appearance of its phases could be accounted for as a turning-about of the circular boundary between the two halves so that the half of the boundary that is toward us is seen sometimes as a semicircle, sometimes as half an oval, and sometimes as a straight line.

The argument that the division of the Moon into a bright and a dark hemisphere is caused by the Moon's receiving its light from the Sun is that the phases are correlated with the apparent elongation of the Moon from the Sun, in such a way that the Moon waxes as it recedes from the Sun until it is full, when they are diametrically opposite, and then wanes as it approaches the Sun again, and moreover the invisible dark part of the disk is always on the side away from the Sun. When Geminus presents these arguments he adds the refinement that we can see—when the Moon is a waxing or waning crescent and very near the Sun at sunset or sunrise—that an imaginary line bisecting the line through the horns of the crescent points straight toward the point of the horizon where the Sun sets or rises, irrespective of whether it is winter (and this point is south of due east) or summer (and the point is north of due east) (fig. 5.7).[50]

A corollary of this optical theory of the phases is that the Sun must be farther from us than the Moon. If they were at the same distance, or the Moon was farther than the Sun, we would never see a crescent Moon. In the early third century BC, Aristarchus of Samos, more famous now for his hypothesis that the Earth might circle the Sun rather than the other way around, wrote a book titled *On the Sizes and Distances of the Sun and Moon*, which described a mathematical method of determining how many times farther from us the Sun is than the Moon.

Aristarchus realized that at the moment when the Moon is exactly at half-moon phase (i.e., when the boundary between its lit and dark halves is seen as a perfectly straight line), the straight lines from the Moon's center to the Sun

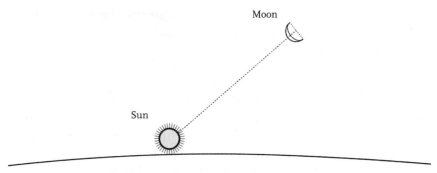

FIG. 5.7. Near sunrise or sunset, an imaginary line bisecting the line joining the horns of a crescent moon points toward the Sun.

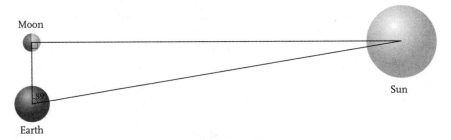

FIG. 5.8. Aristarchus' right-triangle determination of the ratio of the distances of Sun and Moon from the Earth (not to scale).

and to the observer—effectively to the center of the Earth since we are dealing with large distances—have to form a right angle (fig. 5.8). This means that the centers of the Earth, Moon, and Sun are at the vertices of a right-angled triangle, and so the observed angle between the Moon and the Sun is less than a right angle. If we can measure it, we can calculate the ratios of the sides of the triangle, which gives us the ratio of the Sun's distance from the Earth to the Moon's distance from the Earth.

Aristarchus gives this Moon-Earth-Sun angle as 87°, without saying where this figure comes from, whether it was actually measured or is just hypothetical.[51] He proves that, if this angle is assumed, the Sun must be between 18 and 20 times as far as the Moon is from the Earth.[52] If we were to start with an angle closer to 90°, the Sun's distance would come out as farther in proportion to the Moon's. In reality, the Sun is almost 400 times as far as the Moon, so that the theoretical Moon-Earth-Sun angle corresponding to precise half-moon phase is less than one-sixth of a degree short of a right angle. No one in antiquity could have observed such a tiny difference.

Later Greek astronomers did not adopt Aristarchus' method of finding the ratio of distances, but they continued to assume that the ratio was comparatively small, sometimes even smaller than Aristarchus' ratio.[53] Aristarchus' book came to be used as a school text, and astronomers must have been familiar with the simple geometrical argument that the distances that they were assuming for the Sun and Moon meant that half-moon phase was not exactly halfway between conjunction and full moon.

We have already met one of the more enigmatic features visible on the Mechanism's fragments as they were found in 1902, the jar-like cylindrical cap on C-2 (fig. M6). Within this cap, remains of mechanical elements can be seen following a radius line from the cap's center, where there is a small square hole, to a larger circular hole near the projecting cylindrical wall of the cap. In his unpublished notes, Rehm speculated that this might be some kind of apparatus representing an epicyclic hypothesis for the Moon.[54] Price offered two guesses:[55]

> From its position, it might be some part of the dial work for the center of the front dial, possibly a plate indicating the position of the Moon and turned by the inner axle at Axis B. Alternatively, from its construction it is possible that it may be a crank handle . . .

Price's first idea was perspicacious, and entirely correct so far as it went, but he preferred the other one. On the model reconstruction that he donated to the National Archaeological Museum and that was long on display alongside Fragments A, B, and C, the input has a crank handle that is obviously modeled on the cap.

The correct identification of the cap's function is one of Wright's finest contributions to our understanding of the Mechanism.[56] As Price had suggested, the cap was originally at the center of the front dial and turned to represent the Moon's motion through the zodiac by an arbor passing through the square hole; on Fragment C-2 we are seeing the cap from the interior side. There was probably also a pointer, now lost, projecting outward from the wall of the cap to indicate the Moon's location on the Zodiac scale. From his linear tomographic radiographs, Wright established that one component among the mechanical elements in the cap is a broken contrate gear (or crown), through which passes an arbor that originally turned a small sphere that filled the circular hole; the impression of this sphere can still be seen in the accretion matter behind the hole. This sphere represented the Moon and would have been half black, half white (or silvered). Wright showed that if the contrate gear engaged with a lost gear fixed to the arbor representing the Sun's motion, the moon ball would revolve, showing a simulation of the Moon's current phase through the circular window. There was almost certainly a description of this feature in a part of the BCI that is unfortunately preserved only in very short stretches of letters from each text line; the Greek word for "black" survives (BCI, Part I, line 12).

But Wright was aware of a difficulty: the contrate gear is facing the wrong way to engage with a gear mounted on the central axis. He accounted for this by hypothesizing that someone in antiquity had dismantled this part of the Mechanism and reinstalled it with the gear pointing in the incorrect direction. This would not have been a straightforward matter. Because of the way that the contrate gear is fixed to its arbor, it could have been reinstalled backward only if the arbor was *already* broken, and if there was a fixed gear on the central axis that it was supposed to engage with, its teeth would have collided with the back of the contrate when the contrate was inserted the wrong way.

Is there a way to make sense of the contrate gear in its current orientation? In a schematic diagram of the reconstructed gear system of the Mechanism that he published in 2008, Tony Freeth conjectured a pair of coaxial gears mounted inside the moon cap, one of which engaged with the presumed fixed gear on the central axis, while the second engaged with the contrate.[57] This would have produced exactly the same effect as Wright's simpler construction with the contrate pointing inward, and it was hard to see any motive for the additional complication.[58]

Recently, Christián Carman and Marcelo Di Cocco have revisited the problem, reasoning that since the physical evidence seemed to strongly favor the assumption that the contrate was correctly oriented, there had to be an effect that the designer wanted to achieve that Wright's simple engagement did not produce; namely, some kind of nonuniformity in the moon ball's revolution.[59] Carman and Di Cocco's idea is that a device structurally similar to the device that produces the lunar anomaly could have made the moon ball revolve with varying speed so that the half-moon phase is displayed when the Moon is slightly less than 90° away from the Sun.

This new proposal of an anomaly in the phase cycle seems to me to be entirely plausible. Aside from Aristarchus, no ancient author draws attention to the asymmetrical placement of the half-moon phase, but I do not think this is a serious objection, since the surviving astronomical literature is not very abundant.[60] It would require care to demonstrate the phenomenon to a spectator; one would have to view the front face straight on, and the moon ball's orientation would have to be carefully calibrated so that the boundary between the white and black halves is exactly parallel to the Mechanism's face at conjunction and opposition. From a didactic point of view the "Aristarchus effect" could have provided the basis for a discussion of the relative distances of the Moon and Sun, compensating for the fact that they could not be displayed to scale on the front dial because their ratio is too large.

Up to this point our exploration of the Mechanism has revealed two complementary approaches to understanding the motions of the Sun and Moon relative to the stars and to each other: a temporal, and rather abstract, representation of time cycles determined by the Sun's course through the zodiac and the Moon's phases on the upper back dials, and a visual representation of the Sun and Moon in motion on the front dial. It remains to be considered how the Mechanism dealt with the most dramatic phenomena arising from the interactions of the two luminaries: eclipses.

6

Eclipses

Fears and reassurances

A cuneiform tablet from the royal archive of Nineveh preserves a letter from the Babylonian scholar Bel-ušezib to the Assyrian king Esarhaddon (reigned 681–669 BC), advising the king that he need not fear the consequences of a lunar eclipse that had just occurred:[1]

> If an eclipse occurs but is not seen in the capital, that eclipse has passed by. The capital is the city where the king resides. Now there are clouds everywhere; we do not know whether the eclipse took place or not. Let the lord of kings write to Assur and to all the cities, to Babylon, to Nippur, to Uruk and Borsippa; maybe they observed it in these cities. The king should constantly be attentive. Many signs of the eclipse came in [the month] Addaru and in [the month] Nisannu, and I communicated all of them to the king, my lord, and if they perform the apotropaic ritual of the eclipse [*some text lost*], will that do any harm? It is advantageous to perform it; the king should not leave it. The great gods who dwell in the city of the king, my lord, covered the sky and did not show the eclipse, so that the king would know that this eclipse does not concern the king, my lord, and his country. The king can be glad.

Compare this with an anecdote put in the mouth of the Roman general Scipio Aemilianus (185–129 BC) in Cicero's philosophical dialogue *De re publica*, which tells how Gaius Sulpicius Gallus, commanding the Second Legion in the war against Perseus of Macedon in 168 BC, calmed his troops down after an eclipse:[2]

I remember when I was quite young and my father was consul commanding in Macedonia and we were in camp, how our army was deeply troubled with superstition and fear, because on a clear night the brilliant full moon was suddenly eclipsed. Then [Gallus]—for he was our deputy, this being about a year before he was made consul—made no delay the next day in camp in explaining that it was no omen, and that it happened at this time and was always going to happen at fixed occasions, whenever the Sun was positioned in such a way that it could not reach the Moon with its light.

On the surface, two similar situations: someone is scared by an eclipse, thinking it is a portent, and an expert reassures the fearful party that there is nothing to worry about. Yet on a closer look, these turn out to be quite different stories. For Bel-ušezib, there is no questioning that a lunar eclipse in the abstract is an evil omen, a message from the gods signifying the death of a king. This particular eclipse had been expected, and Esarhaddon was understandably impatient to hear from his omen-watching scholars about the details of the observed eclipse, which would allow them to determine whether he was the affected king. But the night of the eclipse was cloudy and the observations could not be made—what should the king do now? Bel-ušezib's response is that this is no crisis: the king can write, if he wants, to scholars in other cities of Assyria and Babylonia to find out if they saw the eclipse; no harm in going through the prescribed rituals for warding off a harmful outcome of the omen, but none of this is really necessary because the cloud cover itself was the gods' way of telling Esarhaddon that the eclipse was not meant for him.

Cicero's story, on the other hand, is a stereotypical one of informed reason overcoming irrational fears. There is no suggestion that the eclipse was being interpreted according to some systematic framework of omen lore; the soldiers' reaction to the eclipse is presented as the primitive, emotional one of ignorant people to a violation of the normal order of nature at a critical moment when battle was imminent—how could the two events not be connected? Gallus offers them an elementary lesson in astronomy. We know *why* eclipses happen, because the Sun's light is briefly blocked from shining on the Moon, and this has nothing to do with the impending battle. Moreover, we know *when* eclipses happen, at regular intervals determined by the Sun's and Moon's revolutions. This eclipse, therefore, has nothing to do with human affairs.

Scipio brings up the tale about Gallus and the eclipse in response to another anecdote involving Gallus that has just been recounted by Lucius Furius Philus.[3] Philus remembers having attended a gathering with Gallus at the house of Marcus Claudius Marcellus in 166 BC, the year that both

Marcellus and Gallus were consuls. Marcellus' grandfather was the Marcellus who had sacked Syracuse in 212 BC, and he had in his private possession an object called a *sphaera* (literally, "sphere") made by the great Archimedes, the only article of booty that the elder Marcellus had kept for himself from the plunder. Philus was not initially impressed by the look of this *sphaera*, comparing it to its detriment to another work of Archimedes, a beautiful star globe—also a *sphaera*—that had been deposited in the Temple of Virtue in Rome.

> But once Gallus began to explain in a most knowledgeable way the principle of this artifact, I judged that there was more intelligence in that Sicilian [i.e., Archimedes] than one would think human nature could contain.... This kind of *sphaera*, in which were present the motions of Sun and Moon and those five stars that are called wanderers and as it were straying, could not be fashioned in that solid *sphaera*, and one had to wonder at the inventiveness of Archimedes in it, that he had figured out how a single revolution could furnish unequal and diverse courses in unlike motions. When Gallus set this *sphaera* in motion, the Moon caught up with the Sun in the same number of turnings in that bronze object as it does in days in the actual heavens, and as a result the same eclipse of the Sun takes place in the *sphaera*, and the Moon falls within that cone that is the shadow of the Earth, when the Sun is situated . . . [*several words or sentences lost*]

We must keep in mind that these are texts of very different genres. Bel-ušezib's letter is an original historical document from an archive. *De re publica* is a philosophical dialogue modeled on Plato's dialogues, using invented conversations among historical figures to explore various themes that Cicero was interested in. In other words, it is a work of fiction, in which one generally cannot distinguish between plausible stories and genuine nuggets of historical fact that Cicero found it convenient to incorporate in the back and forth of made-up speeches. So it is interesting to see how other ancient authors present this eclipse and its consequences.[4] The historian Livy gives a similar story to Cicero's, but he specifically dates Gallus' lecture to the troops to the day preceding the Battle of Pydna (summer of 168 BC) and says that Gallus *predicted* that the Moon would be eclipsed from the second to the fourth hour of night.[5] It is strange that Cicero would have left out these details if he knew them, and there is a certain implausibility in the notion of Gallus carrying about the astronomical resources for making precise eclipse predictions while on campaign. One may reasonably suspect that someone after Cicero embellished his story to heighten its drama, relying on a memory or a retroactive calculation of the eclipse times.

Quite different is the account that the Byzantine encyclopedia called the *Suda* attributes to a lost part of the *Histories* of Polybius (d. after 118 BC), within whose lifetime the war against Perseus took place:[6]

> When the Moon was eclipsed in the time of Perseus of Macedon, the report spread among the masses that it signified an eclipse of a king. And this raised the Romans' morale, while depressing the spirit of the Macedonians.

In this version (which may be abbreviated from Polybius' original narrative), a meaning is attributed to the eclipse that would have made sense to Esarhaddon and his scholars—an "eclipse of a king" must signify his downfall, if not his death. Instead of Gallus teaching the soldiers to regard the eclipse as a harmless natural phenomenon, the soldiers—following an interpretation urged on them by their officers?—are encouraged to take it for an omen, but an omen signifying disaster for their opponents.

There is no reason to suppose that Cicero's story of the gathering at Marcellus' house and of Gallus' disquisition on the mechanical *sphaera* of Archimedes was any more a literal retelling of historical events than his story of Gallus' lecture to the army; they are interconnected pieces of an argument that Cicero is artfully constructing about the orderliness of the cosmos. Cicero's Philus tells us that the *sphaera* of Archimedes showed effigies of the Sun and Moon making simulated eclipses in accordance with the same theory that Gallus is made to expound to the army. Did this description fit any astronomical device that Cicero had seen or knew about? And did the inventors of astronomical devices intend to show the interplay of the Sun, the Moon, and the Earth's shadow as something totally independent of the human world?

Eclipse omens and eclipse observation in Mesopotamia

The earliest texts that we have from ancient Mesopotamia in which phenomena involving the heavenly bodies are treated as omens are cuneiform tablets dating from the Old Babylonian period in the first half of the second millennium BC—possibly from the later 17th century BC, to judge by the style of the script.[7] Among these tablets, four contain omens relating to eclipses of the Moon, and one has omens relating to solar eclipses. From the outset of the Babylonian tradition of astral omens, eclipses—especially lunar eclipses—were regarded as especially important ominous phenomena. The tradition reached its peak in a great series of about 70 tablets that is known, from the opening words of its first tablet, as *Enūma Anu Enlil*; eight of its tablets concern lunar eclipses, and seven concern solar eclipses.[8] The oldest known copies of *Enūma Anu Enlil* were in the so-called Library of Assurbanipal. This was not strictly a single library but it comprises more than one palace collection of tablets from the seventh century BC, excavated at Nineveh by Austen Henry Layard and Hormuzd Rassam in the late 1840s and early 1850s. From the same source we also have an archive of letters and reports from numerous scholars to the Assyrian kings, chiefly Esarhaddon and his son Assurbanipal (reigned 668–627 BC), which give us an intensely vivid picture of the practice of observing and interpreting astral and other varieties of omen.

Belief in omens in Mesopotamia has to be understood in the context of a polytheistic religion, according to which a multitude of gods were personally responsible for various aspects of the world and took great interest in the doings of people, especially kings, who were the gods' representatives on Earth. Prayers and rituals performed on the king's behalf constituted a language of communication from the king to the gods, and reciprocally, the gods communicated their moods and intentions through a language of signs or omens. Omen texts were the key to this language. The typical format of an omen text was an "if . . . then . . ." sentence such as the following examples:[9]

> If Jupiter carries radiance: the king is well; the land will become happy.
>
> If there is an eclipse in [the month] Simānu: there will be a flood, and the water will carry off the land.
>
> If a mongoose passes between the legs of a man, the hand of the god or the hand of the king will seize him.

Omen corpora such as *Enūma Anu Enlil* comprised thousands of such omen texts. It was the business of the expert scholars to observe or collect reports of ominous events, identify which omen texts were pertinent, and advise the king of the meaning of the omens, as well as any actions that ought to be taken in response to them.

The lunar-eclipse omen texts of *Enūma Anu Enlil* have varied outcomes, though for the most part their predictions are dire for some king or country. In practice, as witnessed in the letters and reports from Nineveh, a lunar eclipse was usually understood to declare the imminent death of a king of Assyria, Babylonia, or one of the neighboring lands to the east or west. As a general practice the response to a bad omen was to perform an "apotropaic" ritual; that is, a ritual for warding off the harm threatened by the gods. For eclipses interpreted as signifying the death of the Assyrian king (and also, in Esarhaddon's case, the king of Babylonia's death, since he held both thrones), it was necessary to see to it that the omen was fulfilled in a controlled manner, the substitute-king ritual.[10] A victim, typically a prisoner, was chosen who ritually assumed the personhood of the king for a fixed term, in one known instance a hundred days but usually much briefer, after which he "went to his fate"; that is, he was executed. During this period, the real king lived outside the capital and continued to correspond with his scholars, being addressed as the "farmer." During the reigns of Esarhaddon and Assurbanipal, a substitute-king ritual was performed on average about once every two years.

Observing an eclipse as an ominous event involved paying attention to many circumstances of the eclipse—some of them inherent in the fact of the eclipse itself, some of them (from a modern point of view) incidental. Among the circumstances directly connected with the eclipse itself, time elements were prominent; namely, the calendar month within which it occurred, the day of the month, and the current watch of the night (for lunar eclipses) or the day (for solar eclipses). The appearance of the eclipsed body was also ominously important, especially its color. During the totality phase of a total lunar eclipse, the Moon still receives some light from the Sun refracted through the Earth's atmosphere, so that a dark reddish or grayish disk is visible, depending on the particular atmospheric conditions through which the light passes; even outside totality, meteorological conditions can affect the apparent color of the Moon's or Sun's disk, especially when it is close to the horizon. Directions of obscuration play a large role in the eclipse omens (figs. 6.1–6.2). At the beginning and end of an eclipse, only a small notch of the eclipsed body is obscured, and an observer could take note of the cardinal direction of this notch relative to the center of the disk; for example, "the eclipse began in the south (of the disk) and cleared in the west (of the disk)." In a partial eclipse one could also note the direction of the obscured part of the disk when it was largest, at mid-eclipse. These directions appear to have been reckoned at least roughly with respect to the ecliptic. Incidental circumstances that are invoked in the eclipse omen texts include optical phenomena caused by meteorological conditions such as halos, as well as the direction that the wind is blowing during the eclipse.

Each circumstance taken by itself, as well as sets of them taken together, might match an omen text, including texts that were not specifically about eclipses. For example, following the lunar eclipse of June 11, 669 BC, Issar-šumu-ereš, the king's chief scribe and tutor, sent Esarhaddon a long report in which he quotes 11 eclipse omens that take into account, in various combinations, the calendar month, the day of the month, the watch of the night, the directions on the Moon's disk where the shadow first and last fell, and the direction of the wind; an omen concerning the Moon being "dark" in a particular month; an omen concerning a "star" being darkened in a particular constellation; and three omens concerning Jupiter, which had made its first appearance a few days earlier.[11] From these omens we can reconstruct a complete report of the eclipse as it was observed:

> Month Simanu, day 14, in the morning watch until the end of the watch, the Moon was eclipsed in the constellation Pabilsag [Sagittarius]

(a)

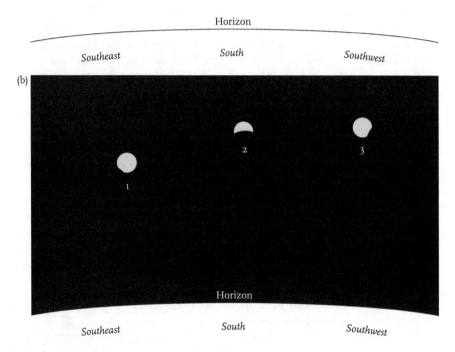

FIG. 6.1. Stages of a partial lunar eclipse, with directions of obscuration at the beginning (1), middle (2), and end (3); (a) Locations of the Moon and the Earth's shadow (darker gray), (b) Appearance to an observer.

beginning in the southeast part of its disk and clearing in the north-west part of its disk, and the north wind blew. Jupiter was visible during the eclipse.

Thus, the structure of the omen texts effectively dictated a routine for observing an eclipse. In later periods, the times and locations relative to the stars were recorded with greater precision, but otherwise the contents of an eclipse observation remained remarkably stable. Here, for example, is a report from Babylon of the lunar eclipse of March 21, 154 BC:[12]

[Month] Addaru, night of the 15th, moonrise to sunset: 3 [time-degrees], measured [despite] clouds. Lunar eclipse; when it began on the south and east side [of the Moon's disk], in 20 [time-degrees] of night 10 fingers were eclipsed; 6 [time-degrees] of night maximal phase. When it began to clear, in 18 [time-degrees] of night it cleared from the north and east [side of the disk] to the south and west [side]. 44 [time-degrees total time for] onset, maximal phase, and clearing. Its eclipse was red, its redness was red brown. In its eclipse, the north wind, which was set to the west side, blew. In the beginning of onset, the south wind

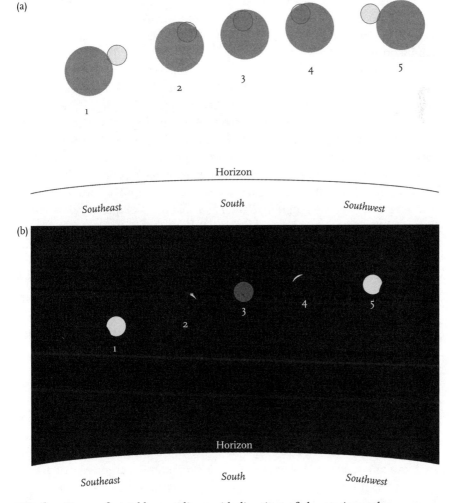

FIG. 6.2. Stages of a total lunar eclipse, with directions of obscuration at the beginning (1), just before the first totality (2), mid-eclipse (3), just after the end of totality (4), and the end of the eclipse (5); (a) Locations of the Moon and the Earth's shadow, (b) Appearance to an observer.

blew [*some text lost*]. In its eclipse, Venus, Mars, and Sirius stood there;
during onset, Jupiter came out; during the end of onset, Venus set;
the remainder of the planets did not stand there. 2 cubits behind the
Bright Star of the Furrow, 1 cubit high to the north, it was eclipsed. At
4 [time-degrees] after sunset.

In this observation, a "time-degree" is a unit of time measured with a water
clock, equivalent to four minutes, a "cubit" is a unit of observed distance
in the sky (approximately equivalent to 2.4°), and a "finger" is 1/12th of the
breadth of the Moon's disk. Note how attention was paid to the color of the
Moon, the directions of the obscuration through the stages of the eclipse,
and the changing wind directions—all factors familiar from the omen texts,
though the report makes no mention of the eclipse as having ominous
significance.

The eclipses described in the letters and reports were provided only with
incomplete dates at best, the month and day number because these were relevant for omen texts, but no year number. Hence, although a large mass of
observations accumulated in the palace at Nineveh, they did not constitute an
astronomical archive that could be easily consulted to review observations from
specific past years or to identify patterns in the occurrence of eclipses. However,
such an archive of eclipse records was already being kept in Babylon, apparently beginning with the lunar eclipse of February 6, 747 BC, during the accession year of the Babylonian king Nabû-nāṣir.[13] The report quoted above comes
from a tablet that belonged to this archive. Eclipse observations were preserved
in a variety of different formats of tablet, including the long-running series
of Astronomical Diaries, which we will encounter in chapter 7. The observers
were probably employed by the Esagila temple complex dedicated to the god
Marduk, and there is no evidence of interaction between them and the "civil
service" scholars reporting to the Assyrian kings, though some of their scholars
were stationed in Babylon too.

A modern perspective

As we learn in school, eclipses of the Moon take place whenever the Moon
passes partly or entirely through the Earth's shadow; eclipses of the Sun,
whenever the Moon's shadow falls on a part of the Earth. So far as we know,
such explanations never played a role in Mesopotamian omen lore or astronomy, but combining them with some basic facts about the solar system
as we understand it today will lead us to some properties of eclipses that
Babylonian and Assyrian scholars discovered empirically and exploited in
their work.

If the Moon's orbit around the Earth was in the same plane as the Earth's orbit around the Sun, lunar eclipses would happen at every full moon, and solar eclipses would occur at every conjunction of the Sun and Moon. In reality, the Moon's orbit has an inclination of about 5° with respect to the plane of the Earth's orbit, which is a small angle, but enough so that the Moon is usually too far north or south of the plane of the Earth's orbit for either kind of eclipse to happen. If we imagine the diameter of the Moon's orbit that is the intersection of its plane with that of the Earth's orbit, called the "nodal line," there can be an eclipse only when the Moon is sufficiently close to this nodal line at the moment when it is also in line with the Earth and Sun. In the short term, the nodal line keeps a roughly fixed direction while the Earth and Moon orbit the Sun. Fig. 6.3 shows four situations where the Earth, Moon, and Sun all are in line. In position (a), the Moon is diametrically opposite the Sun as seen from the Earth, so this is a full moon, but since the Moon is near the southernmost point of its orbit, it passes south of the Earth's shadow and no lunar eclipse takes place. In (b), the Moon is very close to the nodal line, so it will be eclipsed. In (c), the Sun and Moon are in conjunction, but the Moon is again too far south of the plane of the Earth's orbit for its shadow to fall on any part of the Earth. In (d), being close to the nodal line, its shadow will cross the Earth so that a solar eclipse will be seen in some places.

The nodal line does have a slow motion of its own, about a 20th of a degree per day in the clockwise direction as seen from the north side of the solar system. Because of this shift, eclipses do not always happen at the same times of year or against the same background of stars. Also, the orbits of the Earth and Moon are not exactly centered on the Sun and Earth, respectively. The Earth orbits the Sun along a slightly eccentric, near-circular ellipse, and its motion is slower when it is farther from the Sun. Similarly, the Moon travels more slowly on the more distant part of its elliptical orbit—which incidentally is continually changing shape under the influence of the Sun's gravity. The shapes of the orbits affect the precise timing of eclipses, and also the way that they appear to an observer on Earth because the shadows of the Earth and the Moon vary with distance.

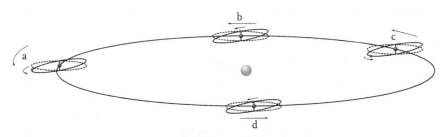

FIG. 6.3. Four alignments of the Earth, Sun, and Moon.

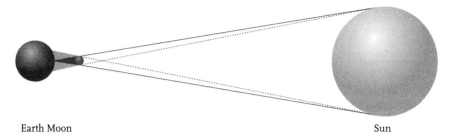

Earth Moon   Sun

FIG. 6.4. Umbra (dark gray) and penumbra (light gray) of the Moon cast on the Earth during a solar eclipse. Sizes and distances are not drawn to scale.

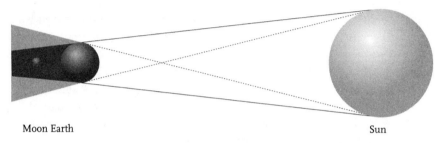

Moon Earth   Sun

FIG. 6.5. Umbra (dark gray) and penumbra (light gray) of the Earth cast on the Moon during a lunar eclipse. Sizes and distances are not drawn to scale.

Both the Earth and the Moon actually cast a complex shadow, because the Sun is not a point source of light but, rather, a sphere larger than either the Earth or the Moon (figs. 6.4–6.5). The "umbra" is the darker shadow inside which an observer cannot see any part of the Sun; it is a conical space that narrows with increasing distance from the body that casts it. Inside the wider "penumbra," an observer can see part of the Sun but not its entire disk; it is also a conical space, but widening with increasing distance.

To a naked-eye observer, the dimming of the Moon when it passes into the Earth's penumbra is very slight. Ancient Mesopotamian and Greek astronomers do not seem to have ever noted a penumbral eclipse (in which the Moon crosses part of the penumbra but does not enter the umbra) or the penumbral stages of a normal eclipse. Since the umbra is a narrowing cone of shadow, if we have two partial eclipses in which the Moon is the same amount north or south of the Earth's orbit but at different distances from the Earth, the one with the greater distance will have a smaller magnitude. Conditions that would make a total eclipse for a smaller distance may make a partial one if the Moon is farther from the Earth. Distance also affects the duration of a lunar eclipse, but in a more complicated way: there is less shadow for the Moon to cross at greater distance, but the Moon also moves more slowly on its orbit.

FIGURE M1. Fragment A-1, facing the Mechanism's front. (photograph: Émile Seraf, Deutsches Archäologisches Institut, negative D-DAI-ATH-Emile 827; all rights reserved)

FIGURE M2. Fragment A-2, facing the Mechanism's rear. Remains of the scales of
the Saros dial, somewhat distorted, are at lower right, partially concealed behind an
accretion layer, which bears offsets of the back cover inscription. The small circular
feature at bottom center marks the location of the dial's axial center. Just to the right
of this, peeking out from beneath the accretion, is the bottom of the subsidiary
Exeligmos dial. Several lines of the back plate inscription survive along the lower right
edge of the fragment. (photograph: Émile Seraf, Deutsches Archäologisches Institut,
negative D-DAI-ATH-Emile 826; all rights reserved)

FIGURE M3. Fragment B-1, facing the Mechanism's rear. The fragment contains a portion of the upper back plate, partly concealed behind an accretion layer. Some of the Metonic dial scale can be seen on the right side with faint traces of the scale inscriptions, while the pointer is visible along the left edge. (photograph: Émile Seraf, Deutsches Archäologisches Institut, negative D-DAI-ATH-Emile 826; all rights reserved)

FIGURE M4. Fragment B-2, facing the Mechanism's interior. The spiral scales can be seen more clearly from this side. U-bridges holding the turns of the scale in position are at the lower left. The main axis was at the slight protuberance along the upper right edge. The better-preserved axis (with a surviving gear) to the left of this is that of the Games dial. (photograph: Émile Seraf, Deutsches Archäologisches Institut, negative D-DAI-ATH-Emile 827; all rights reserved)

FIGURE M5. Fragment C-1, facing the Mechanism's front. Parts of the Zodiac scale, the Egyptian Calendar scale, and the upper edge of the dial plate are visible in the upper left; more is concealed behind the inscribed plate. (photograph: Émile Seraf, Deutsches Archäologisches Institut, negative D-DAI-ATH-Emile 827; all rights reserved)

FIGURE M6. Fragment C-2, facing the Mechanism's interior. The cylindrical feature
is the casing for the Moon phase ball, seen from the back. (photograph: Émile Seraf,
Deutsches Archäologisches Institut, negative D-DAI-ATH-Emile 826; all rights
reserved)

FIGURE M7. Fragment B-1, mirror-reversed image from reflectance transformation imaging file ak42a.ptm with diffuse gain to enhance the legibility of the back cover inscription offsets on the accretion layer. (© Antikythera Mechanism Research Project)

FIGURE M8. Fragment C-1, image from reflectance transformation imaging file ak33a.ptm with specular enhancement. (© Antikythera Mechanism Research Project)

Solar eclipses are very sensitive to the precise situation of the Moon on its orbit. This is because by a curious coincidence of nature, the distances of the Sun and Moon from the Earth are in almost exact proportion to their diameters—hence they look approximately the same size to us. The Moon's umbra therefore diminishes to a point at just about the distance of the Earth from the Moon. If the Earth happens to be a little closer to the Moon than the vertex of the shadow, a small region of the Earth will fall within the umbra, and observers there will see a total eclipse. If the Earth is a little too far, instead of a region of total eclipse, there will be a small region in which one will observe an annular eclipse; that is, the Moon's disk will briefly be seen entirely surrounded by a ring of the Sun's disk (this is different from and much brighter than the solar corona seen around the Moon during a total eclipse).

Lastly, a word about how easy—or in some circumstances, how difficult—it was to observe eclipses in antiquity. A lunar eclipse is a phenomenon of light and shadow on the Moon that has nothing to do with where a person is on the Earth. On average, about one and a half umbral lunar eclipses occur per year.[14] The only issue is whether one is in a position to see the eclipse. Cloudy weather, frequent enough in Mesopotamia, could get in the way of an observation, as was the case with the eclipse that Bel-ušezib wrote about. Presuming a clear sky, an eclipse would have been observable anywhere in the ancient world where it was nighttime. Since a lunar eclipse can last as long as 3 hours 40 minutes, many eclipses would be observable for part of their duration, either rising already eclipsed at sunset or setting still eclipsed at sunrise. An eclipse of very small magnitude might be missed if the observer did not expect it to happen, but it would be easy to detect if one was actually looking. Very roughly speaking, one can estimate that about half of all umbral lunar eclipses ought to have been observed during the centuries of systematic astronomical record keeping in Babylon, something less than one per year on average.

Solar eclipses are even more frequent than lunar eclipses, if we count all occasions when the Moon's umbral or penumbral shadow falls on some part of the Earth. In a typical century, there will be well over 200 solar eclipses. About two-thirds of them will be observable as total or annular *somewhere*, and about a quarter specifically as total. If we restrict consideration to solar eclipses that would have been partial or total for an observer in a particular place—say, Babylon—the number drops to around 40 in a century. More than half of these will be eclipses in which less than half the Sun's disk will be obscured, whereas on average only one total eclipse will be seen in about two centuries.

Whether a partial solar eclipse is likely to be noticed depends very much on whether one is looking for it and has a good idea of when it will happen. A total or near-total eclipse brings about a few minutes of dramatically diminished daylight. If even a 10th of the Sun's disk is left uncovered—which can be the case even in an annular eclipse—the dimming is so inconspicuous that it could easily be taken for the effect of a passing cloud. Nevertheless, we have ancient records of quite small solar eclipses being observed. For example, the Assyrian correspondence includes a report that one Akkullanu saw an eclipse in which the Sun was obscured to only one-sixth of its diameter (this was probably the eclipse of May 27, 669 BC). In this particular instance the eclipse would have been more noticeable because the Sun was rising at the time. Eclipse records from Babylon confirm that a trained observer could expect to notice a solar eclipse of magnitude about one-sixth or higher, but not a smaller eclipse even if it was being watched for.[15] Weather permitting, the Babylonian observers should have been able to see about one solar eclipse every three years or so on average.

Patterns and prediction

Three basic approaches to eclipse prediction can be found in Mesopotamia. Some omen texts have an eclipse as the forecast *outcome*:

> If the Moon at its appearance is very large: there will be an eclipse.[16]

> If the Sun on the day of the Moon's disappearance is surrounded by a halo: there will be an eclipse of Elam.[17]

> If a fog rolls in in [the month] Šabatu: eclipse of the Kassites.[18]

These are astrological forecasts. There is no valid reason why observations of an apparently large Moon or a halo around the Sun or fog in a particular month should be followed by eclipses; here, "there will be an eclipse" is just another possible bad thing to be sent by the gods, like "there will be a flood."

Turning to genuine astronomical methods, patterns in the occurrence of eclipses over time were a powerful tool for anticipating when they were likely to occur and even what they would look like. At the most basic level were the observed facts that eclipses of the Moon occur only at full moon, and eclipses of the Sun occur only during the interval of the Moon's invisibility between its last morning appearance and its first evening appearance. The omen texts in *Enūma Anu Enlil* already reflect this knowledge, since the omens based on the day of the month do not run through every day number from 1 to 30. For lunar eclipses the choices offered are normally 14, 15, and 16, which make sense as dates of full moon, and additionally, for unknown reasons, 20 and 21, which are astronomically nonsensical. It is probable that the Assyrian omen-watching scholars knew how to narrow down the date and time of the moment when the Sun and Moon would be in line or diametrically opposite each other by watching the trend of water-clock measurements of the times between moon-rise and sunrise or between moonrise and sunset on the days leading up to the expected event.

Experience would have shown that two lunar or two solar eclipses never happened in consecutive lunar months. In fact, six months normally pass between consecutive lunar eclipses, though since some eclipses are not observ-able, intervals of twelve months or larger multiples of six months would also be frequent. Occasionally, an interval between observed eclipses would be one less than a multiple of six, implying that a five-month interval has to be injected in the sequence after every seven or eight six-month intervals. We can give the name "lunar-eclipse possibilities" to the series of full moons spread at intervals of six or occasionally five months, which includes all observed lunar eclipses. Solar eclipses occur only either at the conjunction preceding or the conjunc-tion following a lunar-eclipse possibility, a principle that the Assyrian scholars clearly knew.

Once a sufficiently large collection of records of observed eclipses had been built up, longer-term patterns would have been noticeable. For example, there is a very good chance that another lunar eclipse will be observable 47 or 135 lunar months after an observed lunar eclipse. We call such intervals "eclipse periods." An exceptionally useful eclipse period is the one that has acquired the name "Saros" in modern times; we previously encountered it in chapter 5 in its guise as the *Periodikos* period relation for the Moon's anomaly. Its length is 223 lunar months, which is just under 11 days longer than 18 solar years. The Babylonians called it simply "18 years," presumably because an interval of 18 *calendar* years would usually comprise 223 months.

What gives the Saros its special value for predicting eclipses is the fact that if you count 223 lunar months from an observed lunar eclipse, the Moon comes back not only to its nodal line, so that another eclipse will take place, but also to about the same distance from the Earth, so that the eclipses will have similar magnitudes and durations. The fact that a Saros is also fairly close to a whole number of solar years means that certain factors affecting eclipse timing and magnitude that have to do with the Earth's location on its orbit more or less cancel out. This means that one can predict eclipses reasonably reliably and in some detail 18 years in the future, just by assuming that they will repeat the eclipses observed in the current year.

There is a catch, however. A Saros does not contain a whole number of days; the time interval between the exact moments of full moon 223 months apart varies between about 6585 days 6 hours and 6585 days 9 hours, with an average close to 6585 days 8 hours. Because of these extra hours, if one of a pair of lunar eclipses separated by a Saros takes place at night for a particular observer's location, the other one is likely to be a daytime eclipse with the

Moon below the horizon, so that many of the eclipses forecast by the Saros from observed eclipses will not be observable, and many observable eclipses will not be forecastable. Of course there was a workaround: one could go two or even three Saros cycles back in the observational records to find a model eclipse that should have happened at night. When Greek astronomers took over the idea of using the Saros to predict eclipses, they took its length to be exactly 6585 days 8 hours and tripled it to make a cycle a whole number of days long, which, as we saw in chapter 5, they called an *Exeligmos* ("turning of a wheel"). The expectation was that eclipses would repeat after an *Exeligmos* at approximately the same time of night (or day). However, since the Saros is not a perfect eclipse cycle, predictions made using it get less accurate with every repetition.

The Babylonians used the Saros not only to predict eclipses, but also to give a structure to their records of observed and predicted eclipses. We have several fragments of tablets from the Babylon archive that belonged to a series that presented in tabular form every lunar-eclipse possibility over a span of several centuries (fig. 6.6).[19] Each column of the table covered a Saros cycle, and each of the 38 rows represented one of the 38 eclipse possibilities in the cycle, at intervals of six or five lunar months. If an observation record existed, it was written in the appropriate cell; otherwise, a prediction was written, presumably

FIG. 6.6. A fragment from the great Babylonian tablet series of lunar-eclipse observations and predictions (British Museum BM 32234 obverse). Each column of the table contained the eclipse possibilities of one Saros, at six-month and five-month intervals, so that a row of cells read from left to right represents a series of eclipse possibilities at intervals of one Saros. (© The Trustees of the British Museum)

derived from an observation one or more Saros cycles back (i.e., in the same row of an earlier column of the table).

For *solar* eclipses the Saros was of more limited value. Whether one can see a solar eclipse at all, let alone its magnitude and duration, depends on one's geographical location in relation to the Moon's shadow, and the six- to nine-hour shift in time of day between two conjunctions separated by a Saros means that the configuration will be completely different because of the Earth's spinning on its axis. Moreover, the conditions determining the characteristics of solar eclipses are so delicate that even the *Exeligmos* cycle is worthless for predicting them. The best that the Babylonians were able to do was to establish a repeating pattern of 38 solar-eclipse possibilities resembling the lunar pattern, identifying a subset of conjunctions when a solar eclipse of indeterminate magnitude *might* take place.

Alongside the basically empirical method of predicting eclipses cycle-wise from past observations, the Babylonians devised a different, more mathematical approach based on a theoretical understanding of the conditions that make eclipses possible. So far as we know, they did not explain eclipses in terms of light and shadow or, for that matter, in any physical way. But they realized that whether an eclipse happened at a full moon or conjunction depended on how far north or south the Moon was in the zodiacal belt. Their mathematical eclipse predictions involved calculating the dates and positions of the Moon in the zodiac for an entire sequence of consecutive full moons or oppositions, using rules based on simple arithmetical operations (mostly addition and subtraction) that related each event in the sequence to the one before. These calculations were laid out on tablets in a kind of "spreadsheet" table, in which each line represented a successive full moon or conjunction, and the various columns contained calculated quantities involved in determining the date and time of each event, the Moon's position in degrees in a sign of the zodiac, and a measure of the Moon's location in the north–south sense. If this north–south measure was within a certain critical range, it meant that an eclipse was predicted for this date, and in the case of full moons it also indicated the eclipse's magnitude.

Optics and geometry

In his account of the summer of the first year of the Peloponnesian War, the historian Thucydides (ca. 460–ca. 400 BC) mentions the solar eclipse of August 3, 431 BC, describing the Sun as having become crescent shaped while some of the stars became visible.[20] He says that this occurred after noon on the first day of the (lunar) month, and adds that this *seems to be* the only time of month when the Sun can be eclipsed. Knowledge of eclipses and their causes was evidently somewhat limited among educated Athenians of this time! Later, when he recounts how the Athenian general Nikias had followed the advice of diviners to delay the military evacuation of Syracuse until thrice nine days after the total lunar eclipse of August 27, 413 BC, Thucydides comments parenthetically that Nikias was "too much given to superstition and the like."[21] Yet he seems to have thought that eclipses had *some* significance for human affairs, since he includes them among the calamities whose occurrence during the Peloponnesian War appeared to confirm their ominous status:[22]

> And the things that people had formerly said on the basis of hearsay but that had seldom been confirmed by actual events were established as not unworthy of belief, [I mean] regarding earthquakes, which at the same time affected a great part of the Earth and were extremely severe, and eclipses of the Sun, which occurred more frequently than they had been recorded for the time up to then; there were great droughts too in some places, and famines as a result, and the plague caused great harm and destroyed a significant part of the people.

Though this is scarcely reflected in Thucydides' remarks, the fifth century BC marked a crucial innovation in Greek intellectuals' understanding of what an eclipse was. The philosopher Anaxagoras, who was active around the middle of the century, is said by later authors to have assigned the same cause to solar eclipses as we do now; namely, that the Sun is eclipsed because the Moon passes between the Earth and the Sun, and also that the Moon is eclipsed because the Earth passes between it and the Sun.[23] These ideas were obviously bound up with the realization that the Moon derives its illumination from the Sun. From the fourth century onward, most philosophers and, one may presume, all astronomers accepted these explanations of eclipses as fundamental astronomical facts.

At this stage of its development, Greek astronomy was not deeply concerned with forecasting celestial phenomena, and the immediate consequences of the geometrical-optical theory of eclipses were less about time than about space, and specifically about determining the sizes, shapes, and distances of the constituent parts of the cosmos. Foremost, with the darkened part of the Moon's disk in a lunar eclipse identified as the Earth's shadow, its circular outline provided a compelling argument that the Earth is spherical.[24] Other empirical arguments were available to establish that the Earth has a curvature in the north–south direction; for example, as one travels northward, some stars near the southern horizon cease to be visible while more and more stars over the northern horizon are seen never to rise and set.[25] At some point, but this may have been a century or more later, one or two instances of the same lunar eclipses being observed at different local times in different places provided evidence for an east–west curvature.[26] But only the constant curvature of the shadow's boundary seen in all eclipses, no matter where the Moon was in the sky, demonstrated that the Earth's curvature was uniform in all directions.

Another obvious inference was that the Earth's diameter must be more than twice that of the Moon, since the shadow circle, which must be slightly smaller than the Earth, can be seen to be more than twice the Moon's breadth. We saw in chapter 5 how Aristarchus of Samos had arrived at an estimate of the ratio between the distances of the Sun and the Moon from the Earth by considering the triangle formed by the centers of the Earth, Sun, and Moon at half-moon phase; this estimate was much too small but, at least, established a lower bound. In the same book, he demonstrated another relationship that theoretically could be combined with the ratio of distances to obtain actual values for the diameters and distances of the Sun and Moon in terms of the Earth's diameter.[27] Building on Aristarchus' work, later astronomers such as Hipparchus and Ptolemy got the distance from the Earth to the Moon about right (namely, about 30 times the Earth's diameter), though estimates of the distance of the Sun continued to be much too small. The Sun is so distant that no procedure based on naked-eye observations had a hope of establishing even its correct order of magnitude.

The realization that the Moon is comparatively close to the Earth gave Greek astronomers a key element in understanding solar eclipses, ignorance of which was one of the main obstacles preventing the Babylonians from predicting solar eclipses with comparable success to their lunar-eclipse predictions. For the other heavenly bodies, the Greeks relied on the simplifying assumption that the Earth could be treated as if it was a geometrical point; in other words, the Sun, planets, and stars were so far away from us that we effectively see them in the same directions no matter where we stand on the Earth, and so we might as well pretend that we are at the Earth's center for all observations. In the case of the Moon, however, the effect of the observer's location cannot be neglected. The angular difference between the direction in which an observer sees the Moon and the line from the Earth's center to the Moon, called "lunar parallax," depends on how high the Moon is above the observer's horizon. Near the horizon, where the effect is greatest, parallax shifts the Moon's apparent position downward by about a degree; the parallax tends toward zero the closer the Moon is to the zenith. One consequence of this is that observers in the Northern Hemisphere will see the Moon a bit farther south relative to the Sun when they are in conjunction than it would appear from the center of the Earth, the more so the farther north one is on the Earth (fig. 6.7). The parallax is also constantly changing as the Moon crosses the sky through the course of the day, and this affects the times and magnitudes of a solar eclipse as it is seen in different locations. So far as we know, Hipparchus was the first astronomer who worked out

Earth   Moon

FIG. 6.7. Lunar parallax, illustrated for a situation in which the Moon is observed crossing the meridian from a location in the northern hemisphere. The Moon's apparent location is in the direction of the solid line. A theory of the Moon's motion that neglects parallax would predict it to be in the direction of the dotted line, parallel to the true direction of the Moon from the Earth's center (dashed line). From the observer's perspective, the Moon appears to be south, and lower toward the horizon, than its predicted position.

a mathematical theory of parallax that could be exploited for making predictions of how solar eclipses appear in any chosen geographical locality.

Greek predictions of eclipses

Our assertion above, that prediction of astronomical phenomena was not a major concern of early Greek astronomy, may seem to be contradicted by the famous anecdote in Herodotus concerning an event in the wars between the Medes and the Lydians in eastern Asia Minor:[28]

> They were at war with neither side prevailing, and in the sixth year an engagement took place and it happened that, after the battle had begun, the day suddenly became night. Thales of Miletus had forecast to the Ionians that this transformation of the day would take place, giving as a range this very year in which the change happened. The Lydians and the Medes then saw the night falling in place of day, and they stopped the battle and both sides were rather more intent that they should have peace.

Already in antiquity this "turning of the day into night" was interpreted as a solar eclipse, as we know from Pliny the Elder:[29]

> Among the Greeks, Thales of Miletus was the first of all who studied [eclipses]; in the fourth year of the 48th Olympiad he predicted an eclipse of the Sun that happened in the reign of King Alyattes, in the 170th year of the foundation of Rome.

Modern historians have commonly identified this supposed eclipse with the total solar eclipse of May 28, 585 BC, though this does not agree exactly either with Pliny's Olympiad year, which began in the summer of 585 BC, and which he indicates as the year when Thales made the forecast, or his year from the foundation of Rome, which began on April 1, 584 BC, and within which he says that the eclipse actually happened.

Herodotus may well have intended to describe a solar eclipse, but it does not follow that his information was accurate. In a later passage (7.37) he gives a similar account of a disappearance of the Sun in cloudless daytime, seen by Xerxes' army in 480 BC, yet there was no solar eclipse near this date that would have been total or near total for the region in question.[30] In any case, Thales' alleged forecast of the earlier phenomenon makes no sense as an eclipse prediction. Solar-eclipse possibilities are, as we have seen, frequent, and it would have been a pointless exercise to forecast a mere eclipse possibility or even a daytime eclipse of indeterminate magnitude as something that was going to happen sometime or other within a particular year. On the other hand, *no one* in this period, neither in the Greek world nor in Mesopotamia, had the knowledge required to predict a *total* solar eclipse. Herodotus' story must be just part of the aura of legends that accumulated around Thales' name, illustrating his singular wisdom as the "first philosopher."

When did the Greeks (and Romans) really begin to make scientific eclipse predictions? If Livy's version of the story about Sulpicius Gallus and the eclipse of 168 BC is accurate, they were predicting lunar eclipses, including information about the times, by the early second century BC, but as we saw, there are reasons to be skeptical. Immediately after his mention of Thales, Pliny praises Hipparchus extravagantly for his having "foretold the courses of each of the two stars (i.e., the Sun and Moon) for 600 years, taking into account the nations' months and days and hours and the locations of places and the fields of vision [?] of the people."[31] The context makes it clear that this somehow has to do with eclipses, but Pliny's expression is so obscure as to be open to many interpretations, only one of which is that he produced a list of predicted eclipses.

Ironically, it is in Hipparchus' one surviving work, the *Commentary on the Phenomena of Aratus and Eudoxus*, that we encounter a trustworthy contemporaneous reference to eclipse predictions being made around the middle of the second century BC, and he is not referring to himself.[32] Hipparchus wishes to refute the notion, going back to Eudoxus, that the Sun does not travel exactly along the ecliptic in its annual motion around the zodiac, and he does this by an indirect argument. If the Sun had this latitudinal wobble, so would the Earth's shadow cast by the Sun, and this should have a significant effect on the magnitudes of lunar eclipses. But, he says, the "forecasts compiled by the astronomers" generally get the magnitudes accurate to within a sixth of the Moon's diameter (i.e., about a 12th of a degree), which is tiny, and their procedures do not hypothesize a latitudinal wobble of the shadow. One wishes that Hipparchus had said more about these unnamed astronomers, but at least it is evident that he is referring to a practice that he expected his reader to be familiar with, and their methods must have been fairly sophisticated. The description could fit either Babylonian-style arithmetically based methods or methods based on geometrical hypotheses, such as eccenters or epicycles for the motions of the Sun and Moon.

The earliest known example of a list of eclipse predictions originating in the Hellenistic world outside Babylonia is written on a papyrus manuscript from early-first-century BC Abusir el-Meleq in Ptolemaic Egypt, and interestingly, it is in Demotic Egyptian (*PBerol.* 13146+13147).[33] The following is an excerpt from this text, covering two years from the summer of 77 BC through the summer of 75 BC:

Year 26, time 6 months: Moon eclipses [in] Aquarius, [on] III *šmw* 28.

The shift [within] the year named [is] 6 months time: [Moon eclipses in] Leo [at] the ninth hour [of] the night, and the eclipse will occur on the northern face in it, [on] I *prt* 20.

The shift [within] the year named [is] 5 months time: day [?] eclipses, middle [?], [on] II *šmw* 17, [in] Capricorn.

Year 27, time 6 months: Moon eclipses before [?] Cancer, [on] IIII *ȝḫt* 9.

The shift [within] the year named [is] 6 months time: Moon eclipses [in] Aquarius, [on] II *šmw* 7.

These are lunar-eclipse possibilities, at intervals of six lunar months except for the third one, which follows a five-month interval. The year numbers 26 and 27 are according to the Callippic calendar system, an indication that a Greek source probably lies behind our document, while the months and days (e.g., III *šmw* 28) are according to the Egyptian calendar in the original Egyptian form of month number, season name, day number. For each eclipse possibility, the text gives the zodiacal sign occupied by the Moon at the moment of exact full moon. Only the second event in year 26 is provided with further data indicating that an actual eclipse will take place on the date; namely, the time of night and the direction on the Moon's disk where the obscuration will be seen. This was the lunar eclipse of January 28, 76 BC.

A fragment of a similar list of lunar eclipse possibilities, but in Greek this time, survives in a first-century AD papyrus from Oxyrhynchus (*POxy astron.* 4137).[34] The dates are expressed in the full Callippic calendar system, including Athenian month and day, as well as in the Egyptian calendar, and the eclipses are described in greater detail than in the Demotic papyrus. In particular, a measure of the magnitude is given and the directions of the obscuration of the Moon's disk are specified for the beginning, middle, and end of the eclipse.

John Steele has plausibly suggested that the compilations of eclipse predictions in these two papyri were generated using an eclipse period such as the Saros—in the case of the one from Oxyrhynchus it would have had to be the Saros, since other periods are not good for predicting such circumstances as magnitudes and directions of obscuration.[35] By the second century AD, however, Greek mathematical astronomy had progressed to the point where it became possible to make detailed predictions both of lunar and solar eclipses according to a sophisticated theory of the motions of the Sun and Moon that took account of their varying distances from the Earth, including the effects of parallax. Such a theory is presented by Ptolemy in Book 6 of his *Almagest*. Ptolemy's chapters, laying out the method of computing eclipse predictions, runs through a set of circumstances of eclipses that exactly matches the contents of the predictions in the Oxyrhynchus papyrus.

Greek predictions from eclipses

We keep encountering stories of armies and their leaders cast into a state of fear by an eclipse. To some extent this represents a conventional theme in classical literature, but one can hardly doubt that the view was widespread in ancient societies that eclipses were portents, and generally malevolent ones. What made the Mesopotamian tradition of eclipse omens distinctive and attractive was its systematic approach, which claimed to read the precise meaning of an eclipse through rigorous observation and interpretation according to accepted rules. Other cultures of the ancient world readily adopted systematic eclipse interpretation along with other varieties of Mesopotamian omen divination. Already in the second millennium BC we find eclipse omen texts among the Hittites to the northwest, among the Elamites to the east, and in Mari and other cities in Syria.[36]

Systematic astrological interpretation of eclipses came only later to Egypt, perhaps around 500 BC, but once they took hold of it, Egyptian scholars transmuted it into a form adapted to an Egypt-centered regional geography, which eventually offered forecasts, still predominantly grim, for lands all about the Mediterranean and western Asia. Such material survives in several documents both in Egyptian and Greek, dating as we have them from the Roman Empire but clearly harking back to Hellenistic and pre-Hellenistic sources. The most comprehensive version is in an astrological treatise by Hephaestion of Thebes (ca. AD 400), who ascribes the doctrines to the "Egyptians of old."[37]

The treatment both of lunar and solar eclipses in Hephaestion closely resembles parts of *Enūma Anu Enlil*, but it takes the principle of schematic and analogical connections between the ominous aspects of the eclipses in the "if" clauses and the predicted outcomes still further. For example, the directions of the winds blowing at the beginning and end of an eclipse are interpreted in a way reminiscent of the meanings assigned to the directions of obscuration in some *Enūma Anu Enlil* omen texts, but following a more direct scheme of correspondence.[38] If the wind blows from, say, the west at the eclipse's beginning, it foretells harm for whatever country is to the west, and if the wind blows from the south at the end of the eclipse, it foretells benefit for the country to the south.

It seems obvious that the primary purpose of lists of eclipse predictions such as the examples on papyrus that we looked at in the preceding section was some kind of astral prognostication. Many of the characteristics of eclipses cited in the Hephaestion omens could be found in the eclipse predictions— for example, the magnitude or the sign of the zodiac occupied by the Moon. Moreover, Ptolemy's discussion of predictable characteristics of eclipses in Book 6 of the *Almagest* points to the existence of a special application that these characteristics were held to possess. He repeatedly refers to them as having an *episēmasia* ("signification"), the technical term for a weather prediction from astral phenomena such as the risings and settings of stars in parapegmas. This seems to mean a more specifically meteorological system of prediction than we find in texts such as Hephaestion's. Until recently, no example of this kind of system had come to light.

Mechanizing eclipses

Sulpicius Gallus, as he is represented in Cicero's *De re publica*, convinced the Roman soldiers that the eclipse that they had seen was "no omen" because it was a kind of event that regularly recurred on account of physical causes. Supposedly, the mechanical bronze *sphaera* of Archimedes simulated these causes in a graphical, visual manner, showing the Moon entering the shadow of the Earth at the times when the Sun and Moon are diametrically opposite each other in their revolutions around the Earth. Cicero would like us to contemplate the *sphaera* as a teaching tool showing us the orderliness of the heavenly bodies and the consequent falsity of belief in eclipses as portents.

Many ancient intellectuals would have dismissed Gallus' reasoning as a non sequitur. The Assyrian omen-watching scholars knew that occurrences of eclipses were limited to certain widely spaced dates tied to the Moon's phases, and could anticipate their approximate times. Their successors in Ptolemaic and Roman Egypt could consult reliable, detailed predictions of lunar eclipses and saw no inconsistency between this predictability and reading these events as omens. Ptolemy, the preeminent physical scientist of the Roman Empire, was able to predict both lunar and solar eclipses according to a theory based on the optical explanation of eclipses that Gallus invoked, and yet, in his astrological *Tetrabiblos* (2.4), he writes that with respect to the conditions affecting countries and cities, "the foremost and most powerful causation...occurs at the conjunctions and oppositions of the Sun and Moon that are accompanied by eclipses and the courses of the planets at those occasions."[39] Somewhere along the path from the Assyrians to Ptolemy, the rationale of eclipse prognostication had changed from understanding them as communications from the gods to privileging them as configurations of the heavenly bodies that magnified the physical effects that they impart, according to scientifically describable principles, to the world below. A display of the regularity of eclipses through a man-made mechanism would not have necessarily served an agenda such as Cicero's.

Cicero's wording suggests to the reader that Archimedes' *sphaera* showed the Moon falling within the cone of the Earth's shadow when it was set to display the state of the heavens on the date of a lunar eclipse, and notwithstanding the loss of some words in the text as it has come down to us, he probably also said something similar about solar eclipses. Such a literal simulation of eclipses is highly implausible. Leaving aside the question of how an effect resembling the conical shadows of the Earth and Moon could have been produced in a third-century BC device, one would have needed a way of preventing the effigy of the Moon from passing through the Earth's shadow, and preventing the Moon's shadow from falling upon the effigy of the Earth, except at the appropriate oppositions and conjunctions, truly a tour de force of mechanized motion in three dimensions!

The designer of the Antikythera Mechanism chose a different way of incorporating eclipses in the device, one that brought to the fore their patterns and effects rather than their causes. Like the display of first appearances and disappearances of stars on the front face, the display of eclipses on the back face relied heavily on inscribed text to represent the predicted events in words, while a gearwork-driven pointer functioned merely to signal the approximate date for each prediction on a dial that gave visual expression to eclipses' cyclic behavior. To get complete information about an eclipse, someone operating and viewing the Mechanism would have to pay attention both to the front and back faces. From the dials on the lower half of the back face, one would establish that a solar or lunar eclipse was predicted as happening in the currently displayed lunar month, and the identity of this month in the Corinthian calendar was indicated on the Metonic dial. Looking at the front dial, one could find the specific day according to the *Egyptian* calendar—perhaps subject to uncertainty of a day or so—when the Sun and Moon lined up in the right way, as well as their current locations in the zodiac. Finally, the dials and inscriptions of the lower back face would give one the time and other predicted circumstances of the eclipse.

The Saros dial, the lower of the two large spiral dials on the back face, was the main vehicle for eclipse prediction on the Mechanism (see figs. 3.1 and 3.9).[40] Its spiral slot made four complete turns. The pointer tracked through the entire length of the slot, spiraling clockwise from its inner to its outer end, in 223 lunar months' worth of motion; that is, in one Saros eclipse period. The scale running along the slot was divided into cells corresponding to the 223 months of the Saros.

The inscriptions in the cells constituted a cycle of lunar-eclipse possibilities and a cycle of solar-eclipse possibilities. The cells for months within which no eclipse could occur were left blank. If the month represented by a cell had a lunar-eclipse possibility, the cell was inscribed with a text that indicated this and gave a time of day or night associated with the potential eclipse. Because the cells were small, these texts used a highly abbreviated notation, and hence they have acquired the name "eclipse glyphs" (fig. 6.8).[41] The first element in a statement of a lunar possibility was a sigma, Σ, the first letter of *Selēnē* ("Moon"). If the associated time was during the day, this was followed by an abbreviation H̅ formed from the first two Greek letters spelling *hēmeras* ("of day"); otherwise, a nighttime event was implied by default. Next came an abbreviation ⲫ composed of the first letters of *hōra* ("hour"), and lastly a numeral between 1 and 12 for the number of the hour. A solar-eclipse possibility had the same format, except that the first element was an eta, *H*, the first letter of *Hēlios* ("Sun"), and that a nighttime hour was prefixed by the abbreviation N̅ from the first letters of *nyktos* ("of night"), while diurnal events were implied by default.

No dates within the months were indicated, but since the months began with the new moon, lunar-eclipse possibilities would occur about the middle

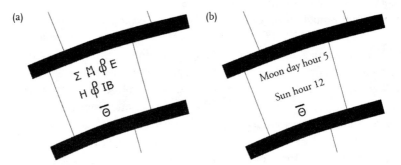

FIG. 6.8. Solar and lunar eclipse glyphs in the cell for month 137 on the Saros dial scale. *Left*, transliteration; *right*, translation. The theta with the horizontal stroke above it is the index letter linking these glyphs to paragraphs of the back plate inscription.

of the month; solar-eclipse possibilities, at the end. As we noted previously, solar-eclipse possibilities tend to fall either on the conjunction preceding or the conjunction following a lunar possibility. In the former case, two consecutive cells would be inscribed with a solar and a lunar glyph, respectively; in the latter case, a single cell would have a double glyph, comprising an inscription for a lunar possibility followed by another inscription for the solar one.

Every cell inscribed with one eclipse possibility or a pair of possibilities also contained an index letter at the bottom of the cell. This served a similar purpose to the index letters on the Zodiac dial, linking the cell to a text inscribed elsewhere on the Mechanism's back face that said more about the predicted events. We will have more to say about these texts later; for the time being we observe just that the letters ran through the 24 letters of the Greek alphabet twice, followed by one or two additional symbols for the last inscribed cells of the Saros cycle (the letters of the second alphabetic sequence are distinguished by a horizontal stroke above the letter). These index letters help us reconstruct the pattern of the eclipse possibilities that were displayed on the dial, since they tell us how many inscribed cells there were in the gaps between preserved parts of the dial scale.

So far as lunar-eclipse possibilities are concerned, the dial's cycle was structured very similarly to the great series of Babylonian tablets that recorded lunar eclipses and eclipse possibilities in tabular format.[42] In the tablets, a column stood for a Saros cycle; on the dial, the spiral strip of 223 cells constituting the scale had this function. The cycles on both media comprised a complete set of 38 eclipse possibilities at intervals of six and intermittently five months.

The solar-eclipse possibilities did not make up a full set of 38; there were likely just 27. The sequence was probably made by starting with a complete sequence of 38 possibilities at six- and five-month intervals, and then removing from the list those conjunctions at which the Moon was calculated to be more than a certain threshold amount south of the ecliptic. The reason for these omissions was parallax. The Mechanism was designed for users in the Northern Hemisphere and specifically in the region of the Mediterranean, and for observers at such latitudes the Moon always appears to be a little south of its position as calculated with respect to the Earth's center. Whoever constructed the sequences of eclipse possibilities assumed that this meant that for some of the 38 eclipse possibilities of the full set, the Moon would always pass south of the Sun's disk, missing it completely. On the other hand, he did not include any additional eclipse possibilities corresponding to conjunctions when the Moon was calculated as passing north of the Sun by a small enough margin for parallax to shift its apparent position so as to overlap the Sun; in other words, the conditions permitting a solar eclipse were assumed to be more restrictive than those permitting a lunar eclipse.

Taking parallax into account in deciding whether a solar eclipse is possible is, as we saw, a contribution of Greek astronomers to the science of
eclipses. However, the framework of the eclipse predictions that a viewer of the
Mechanism would have seen is essentially the Babylonian one based on eclipse
periods, and there is nothing in the Saros dial's inscriptions to draw attention to the "missed" solar-eclipse possibilities and the reason behind them.
Conceivably there might have been some mention of parallax in one of the longer inscribed texts that accompanied the Mechanism—the "front cover inscription" would have been the most suitable place if it had passages discussing the
Sun and Moon in addition to the sections on the planets that are extant—but on
the face of it the Mechanism's designer appears not to have sought to highlight
the physical aspect of eclipses.

Additional information concerning the predicted eclipses was recorded
in the back plate inscription (BCI), a text inscribed on the Mechanism's rear
face in the irregular spaces outside the Metonic and Saros dials.[43] The text
consisted of one set of paragraphs pertaining to the lunar eclipses, and a second set pertaining to the solar eclipses; the lunar paragraphs probably ran
down the left side of the dial plate and the top part of the right side, and the
solar eclipses likely ran along what remained of the right side. The surviving
paragraphs are for solar eclipses. The following is a translation of one of these
paragraphs:[44]

Starting from *thrakias*, they change direction and end up toward
apeliotes. Large [?]. The color is fiery red. Z $\bar{\Theta}$ $\bar{\Sigma}$ P X

The row of letters at the end identifies the solar-eclipse glyphs for which
the paragraph is a supplement; for example, the solar glyph reproduced and
translated in fig. 6.8 is one of this group. What the solar-eclipse possibilities
associated with each paragraph had in common is that the Moon was within
a certain defined range of latitude north or south of the ecliptic for all of
them.[45]

Each of the surviving paragraphs begins with a statement about changing
directions, expressed in terms of Greek names of winds. In the quoted example,
thrakias is the name of a wind blowing from the northwest, and *apeliotes* is a
wind from the east. Two interpretations have been offered for these statements.
They could refer to the directions of obscuration of the predicted eclipse, following the common Greek practice of using wind names to designate cardinal directions according to a standard "wind rose."[46] In this case the quoted
example would describe solar eclipses in which the northwestern part of the
Sun's disk is supposed to be the first to be obscured, and the eastern part is the
last. If this is what the text meant, it was bad astronomy. Directions of obscuration depend not only on the Moon's latitude, but also on whether it is *moving*
northward or southward, and the eclipse possibilities grouped together for the

surviving paragraphs mix up northward-moving and southward-moving cases. Moreover, in solar eclipses the directions have to have a general eastward trend because the Moon is always moving eastward along the ecliptic more swiftly than the Sun, but one of the paragraphs gives a change of direction from northeast to southwest.

According to the other interpretation, the direction statements are predictions of actual winds shifting either in the course of the eclipse or during a subsequent interval, an instance of the kind of systematic meteorological forecasting from eclipses that Ptolemy alluded to in the *Almagest*.[47] In this case, what the Mechanism predicted would have corresponded to a presumed characteristic of eclipses that we know from Hephaestion to have been treated as ominous. The same is true of the third statement in each solar paragraph of the BCI, which predicted the color of the eclipsed disk.[48] Colors of eclipses figure prominently in Hephaestion's astrological forecasts, just as they do in the omen protases ("if" clauses) of *Enūma Anu Enlil*, and they were not restricted to total eclipses as we might expect. No other instance is known from the Greco-Roman world of predictions of eclipse colors, though schemes for this purpose occur in Indian and Islamic astronomy.[49]

Between the direction statements and the color statements, the BCI gives a single word indicating size, such as "small," "intermediate," or "large." This probably was supposed to refer either to the magnitude of the eclipses—that is, the fraction of the disk that would be obscured—or to their durations. At best, however, such a prediction would have served as an upper bound for the magnitude or duration of any actual solar eclipse that might have been observed in any particular locality.

If the BCI's solar-eclipse descriptions seem strange to us, we should remember that the Saros was practically useless for predicting those circumstances of solar eclipses that modern astronomy successfully forecasts. It is a pity that the lunar paragraphs are lost. They might have been quite different, providing quantitative information about magnitudes, durations, and—if they were grouped according to trend of latitudinal motion as well as latitude—directions of obscuration either in place of or in addition to the wind and color forecasts.

The times inscribed in the glyphs are almost certainly meant to be the times of the moment of conjunction or full moon. In the case of a lunar eclipse, this would be the same as the time of mid-eclipse, whereas for a solar eclipse, mid-eclipse can differ from the moment of conjunction by more than an hour because of the effects of parallax. The expressions "hour *n* of day" or "of night" imply that these are *seasonal* hours, which were the conventional divisions of day and night employed in the Greco-Roman world. Seasonal hours were equal 12ths of the time from sunrise to sunset or from sunset to sunrise, so their length varied with the seasons. However, in the glyphs it seems that the seasonal variation was neglected so that the times are effectively counted in *equinoctial* hours—the same as the modern time unit, equal to 1/24th of a mean day and night—from 6 a.m. or 6 p.m. local time.

The idea behind the Saros dial was that the cycle of predicted eclipse possibilities inscribed on the scale would repeat every 223 months. This would not work for the times, however, because, as we saw above, the Saros is not equal to a whole number of days. For this reason, the Exeligmos dial was provided inside the Saros dial to indicate corrections to be added to the predicted times. This dial was divided into three equal sectors, two of which were inscribed with the numerals 8 and 16. The pointer of this subsidiary dial revolved once in every three Saros cycles; that is, in the Exeligmos cycle. When the pointer was in the empty sector, no time correction was needed; when it was in one of the inscribed sectors, the indicated number of equinoctial hours was to be added to the time in the glyph.

The times in the glyphs may have been calculated by a method similar to those used in the Babylonian mathematical "spreadsheet" tablets.[50] A sequence of computed times would have been generated for every conjunction and every full moon in the Saros cycle, but of course only the ones corresponding to eclipse possibilities were recorded on the dial. It is impossible to be certain about the method of calculation because the times are recorded to a precision of only an hour, and a few are affected by errors. It is clear from analysis of the times, however, that a very special assumption was built into the computation of the times: that at the moment of full moon of the first month in the cycle (which incidentally did not correspond to a lunar-eclipse possibility), the Moon was exactly at its apogee, the farthest point of its orbit around the Earth. This alignment was made visible by means of the four radial marks around the inside of the Saros dial's scale (p. 53), which indicated when full moons were aligned most closely with the apogee.

Were these predictions composed to fit real dates, or are they just an artificial sequence constructed to illustrate the patterns of occurrence of eclipses in the abstract? Arguing for real dates is the fact that the cycle's first month does *not* contain an eclipse possibility; we would expect a purely idealized sequence to have the Moon right on its nodal line at the initial full moon. If we look for spans of dates in the last several centuries BC for which the astronomical conditions match both the pattern of distribution of eclipse possibilities on the dial and the pattern of the eclipse times in the glyphs, it turns out that the best (and indeed the only really decent) match has the full moon of the dial's first cell falling on May 12, 205 BC, so that the beginning of the lunar month marking the zero or epoch date of the cycle would have been about April 28.[51] The complete Saros cycle would thus have covered an interval from 205 to 187 BC. This dating was established, according to somewhat different lines of analysis, in recent papers by Christián Carman and James Evans and by Tony Freeth.[52]

Carman, Evans, and Freeth also maintain that the dating of the eclipse times to a series of eclipses that occurred around 200 BC renders it probable that the Mechanism was built around that time or not long afterward. Their principal argument is that the imprecisions inherent in the Saros would have rendered the predictions of the Saros and Exeligmos dials intolerably inaccurate within a small number of Saros cycles of the dates for which the times were computed. This would be a significantly earlier date for the Mechanism's design and construction than has been credibly argued before, bringing it to within a decade of Archimedes' death (212 BC) and about a century and a half before the Antikythera shipwreck. In chapter 4 I argued that the archeological context favors the hypothesis that the Mechanism was new when it was lost in the wreck, because otherwise it becomes difficult to account for the presence of an *antique* object that was manifestly made for a locality west of the Aegean in a cargo originating in the Aegean and destined for points west. Other considerations, too, raise doubts that the 205 BC epoch was chosen for the eclipse prediction cycle because it was close to the date of manufacture.

In the first place, the fact that the eclipse cycle had a definite epoch date makes it more probable that the calendrical cycles of the upper back face (namely, the 19-year cycle of the Metonic dial and the 4-year cycle of the Games dial) also had an epoch date, such that the Metonic pointer indicated the beginning of the calendar year having the earliest possible beginning relative to the seasons, and the Games pointer indicated a Corinthian year during which the Olympic Games took place. This would not have been identical to the epoch date for the eclipses because the Corinthian calendar year began in the late summer, probably about two months after the beginning of the Athenian calendar year (p. 91), but the Corinthian year beginning later in 205 BC would have been a plausible calendrical epoch.[53] In chapter 4 we saw that such coincidences of the 19-year and 4-year cycles happen only every 76 years, and that the year 205/204 BC would have been such a year if the Corinthian calendar was synchronized with the Athenian calendar according to the intercalation pattern attested for Athens from the mid-first century AD onward.

The clinching evidence comes from the way that the Exeligmos dial was laid out on the Mechanism's back face. The division lines of the dial are approximately at the one o'clock, five o'clock, and nine o'clock positions, respectively, marking the beginnings of the Saros cycles in which the eclipse times are to be corrected by adding 0, 8, and 16 equinoctial hours; the one o'clock division is thus obviously where the pointer ought to have been at the eclipse epoch date. This seems a peculiar orientation for which there must have been some reason. If, however, we imagine setting the Saros and Exeligmos pointers to the positions they should have occupied at the eclipse epoch (namely, straight up for the Saros pointer and at the one o'clock mark for the Exeligmos pointer), and then run the Mechanism forward four lunar months to the date we are suggesting for the calendrical epoch (about August 25, 205 BC), the two pointers will end up very nearly parallel at about the one o'clock position, while simultaneously the pointers of the Metonic, Games, and (probably) Callippic dials would be parallel at the six o'clock position (fig. 6.9).[54] It seems clear that this scheme of alignments was an intentional, esthetically motivated element in the design of the back face.

Hence, the Mechanism had *two* epoch dates, one for the calendar functions on or about August 25, 205 BC, and the other for the eclipse cycle four months earlier, on or about April 28, 205 BC. The calendrical epoch must have been the starting point for deciding on these dates because the choice was constrained by the 76-year cycle. Moreover, since the calendrical cycle appears to have been synchronized with the later alignment of the Athenian calendar's intercalation cycle, we can infer that the design of this aspect of the Mechanism originated after the middle of the second century BC, the earliest possible date for the adjustment of the Athenian intercalation cycle. As late as 129 BC, the Corinthian year 205/204 BC would have been the most recent one satisfying the requirements of the two cycles, and even after that year it could have been preferred to the next candidate, 129/128 BC, if the designer wanted to allow for a larger margin of time between the epoch and the present; for example, to facilitate demonstrations of the slow shift of the Egyptian wandering year.[55] The month preceding the calendrical epoch when the full moon fell closest to apogee was then chosen as the epoch of the Saros and Exeligmos cycles, and either the circumstances of the eclipses during the following 223 months were calculated expressly for the Mechanism, or (as I suspect) they were extracted from a preexisting compilation of retrospectively computed eclipses. Finally, the epoch for the Egyptian Calendar ring, indicated by Derek de Solla Price's fiducial mark, was determined by calculating the Sun's longitude on the first day of the Egyptian calendar year (Thoth 1, equivalent to October 13, 205 BC).[56]

Even supposing that the Athenian calendar's intercalation cycle was adjusted as early as about 150 BC and that the Mechanism was made soon afterward, eclipse times read off the Saros dial and corrected from the Exeligmos dial would have shown poor agreement with contemporaneous eclipses, and the discrepancies would have been still worse by the early first century BC. This is an inherent defect of the Saros period; no matter what range of dates was selected for the times on the eclipse glyphs, the numbers would not have stood up to rigorous comparison with observed times except within a narrow window within the span of time—surely a century or more—that the Mechanism's designer had in mind as the range of dates that one might wish to display on its dials. The designer was not alone in having ill-founded confidence in the accuracy of the Saros and Exeligmos dials, even after Hipparchus had demonstrated the superiority of other lunar period relations that formed part of

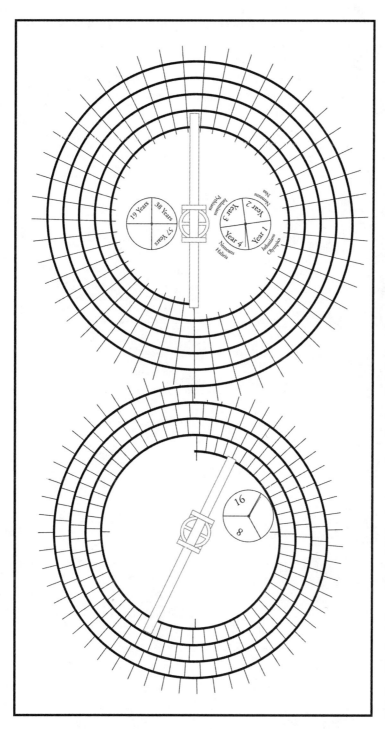

FIG 6.9. The back face with the Mechanism set to its calendrical epoch date, approximately August 25, 205 BC. The pointers of the upper dials all point straight downward, while those of the lower dials are also approximately parallel.

Babylonian mathematical astronomy, as we saw in the cases of Geminus and of Ptolemy's unnamed past astronomers (chapter 5). Greek science, even at its best, was rather patchy when it came to systematic testing of theoretical predictions against observations, and the astronomy of the Mechanism is generally more suggestive of the astronomical knowledge of a Geminus than of a Hipparchus, as befits an instrument intended for the diffusion of science rather than for research.

7

The Wanderers

The planets in Mesopotamian omen lore and observations

Among the handful of Greek letters read on the patina-encrusted fragments of the Mechanism during the first days after it came to light in the National Archaeological Museum, two sequences stood out: ΗΛΙΟΥΑΚΤΙΝ, which spells out the words *Hēliou aktin'*, "ray of the Sun," and ΤΗΣΑΦΡ, apparently the first letters of *tēs Aphroditēs*, "of Aphrodite."[1] Aphrodite was an important deity of the ancient Greek pantheon, but when her name showed up close to a reference to the Sun on what anyone could see to be some kind of scientific instrument, it was only reasonable to conclude that this was an allusion to the "star of Aphrodite," the most common Greek name for the planet Venus. Thankful for a clue linking the mysterious object to astronomy, the experts debating its purpose in 1902 could hardly have guessed that tracking down the exact reference of these inscribed words would be bound up in the last major enigma concerning the Mechanism's functions: What did the Mechanism have to do with the planets?

After the Sun and Moon, Venus is the brightest object in the sky, and it appears in circumstances that draw special attention to itself. For more than eight months in a row, Venus is the "Evening Star," the first starlike object to become visible in the western sky at dusk. During much of that interval it makes its appearance well above the horizon, and the other stars come out before it sets. Just a few days after the Evening Star ceases to be seen, Venus reappears as the "Morning Star" in the eastern sky before sunrise, the last star still visible in the brightening dawn. Another eight months and a few days pass before Venus disappears again, now for about two months, and then the cycle repeats with a new Evening Star.

Venus stands out from ordinary stars in three obvious ways: it is brighter and steadier in its brightness, it has a cycle of appearances and disappearances that is different from an ordinary star's year-long cycle, and it moves relative to the other stars. During its intervals of visibility, Venus gradually traverses the constellations of the zodiac, mostly eastward but reversing into a westward motion a few days before finishing its tour of duty as the Evening Star, and again switching eastward a few days after its morning appearance.

Mesopotamian observers of the third millennium BC knew that Venus as Morning Star and Venus as Evening Star were the same body, and they associated it with the goddess named Inana in Sumerian and Ishtar in Akkadian.[2] By the early second millennium they had recognized five such special stars, designated *bibbu*, "wild sheep," which we can identify as the planets Mercury, Venus, Mars, Jupiter, and Saturn—the only planets that are regularly visible to the naked eye.[3] Though all five have a starlike appearance, Venus and Jupiter are brighter than the others, and Mars tends to have a distinctly ruddy color in contrast to the whitish-yellowish hues of the other planets, but it is not always easy to tell the planets apart by their looks alone. For this, the Mesopotamians came to rely on familiarity with their cyclic appearances and disappearances. For example, an unknown Babylonian scholar of the second millennium BC wrote down a series of dates of disappearances and reappearances of Venus in the Babylonian calendar, beginning as follows:[4]

> On the 15th day of the month Shabatu Venus disappeared in the west; for 3 days it was absent from the sky, and on the 18th day of Shabatu Venus became visible in the east.
> On the 11th day of the month Arahsamna Venus disappeared in the east; for 2 months and 7 days it was absent from the sky, and on the 19th day of Tebetu Venus became visible in the west.
> [and so forth for at least eight years]

Following a hint in the text as it was handed down, these records, which give a very precise description of a possible sequence of Venus's appearances and disappearances, are widely supposed to have been based on observations made during the reign of Ammiṣaduqa, a king of the Old Babylonian period (first half of the second millennium BC). We owe their preservation to the fact that they were included in the 63rd tablet of the Babylonian astral omen compilation *Enūma Anu Enlil* in the form of omen texts; that is, each statement about Venus disappearing and reappearing on stated calendar dates was associated with a forecast such as "springs will open, [the god] Adad will bring his rain, and [the god] Ea will bring his floods, and king will send messages of reconciliation to king." This tablet is informally known as the "Venus Tablet of Ammiṣaduqa," and much effort has been expended on attempting to use the dates in it, along with other evidence, to pin down precisely when Ammiṣaduqa and the other kings of his dynasty reigned—without having achieved a consensus among historians.

Since the oldest surviving copies of *Enūma Anu Enlil*, as well as other tablets recording similar information about the planets, are from the libraries of seventh-century BC Nineveh, we can be certain that by about 700 BC a working knowledge had been established concerning the cycles of visibility not just of Venus but of all the planets, good enough to enable a trained observer to anticipate roughly when and where a planet should make its first appearance in the morning or evening sky. The scholars employed by the Assyrian kings Esarhaddon and Assurbanipal clearly knew when to keep watch for them. When one scholar mistook a sighting of Mercury for a first visibility of Venus, his senior colleagues censured him to their master as "a vile man, an ignoramus, a cheat!"[5]

As the "Venus Tablet" shows, the Mesopotamians regarded the appearances and disappearances of the planets as ominous events. Whether planetary omens pointed to good or bad outcomes depended on the precise circumstances, things such as the apparent color of the planet, which constellation it was in at the time, and the calendar month of the event; as was the case with eclipses, an ostensibly bad outcome, if it turned out to pertain to a rival kingdom, was effectively good. As Mesopotamian astrology evolved, each planet came to be seen as possessing a specific tendency toward good or evil: Venus and Jupiter were benefic planets, Mars and Saturn were malefic, and Mercury was ambivalent.[6] The normal order for listing the planets in late Babylonian astronomical texts was Jupiter, Venus, Mercury, Saturn, Mars, following this astrological principle.

The scholars reporting to the Assyrian kings in Nineveh must have kept records of their observations, at least over the short term, so that they could keep track of the planets over their intervals of invisibility and anticipate their reappearances. No trace of such records survives. In Babylon, however, the same temple archive that preserved eclipse observations from the eighth century BC onward also contained a series of much more comprehensive astronomical records that ran from at least as early as the mid-seventh to the mid-first centuries BC or later. These so-called Astronomical Diaries were tablets reporting observations (and some predictions) of astronomical phenomena and weather on a day-by-day and night-by-night basis over an interval of several months, typically half of a calendar year.[7] Each month's records also included measurements of the level of the Euphrates River, prices of certain commodities, and current events ranging from the extremely local to political and military news: from a break-in at the Esagila temple to the death of Alexander the Great. More than a thousand fragments of Astronomical Diaries are extant, almost all of them now in the British Museum. We do not know the reasons why this grand record-keeping project was instituted and sustained over so many centuries, but it seems likely that the selection of data regularly included in the Astronomical Diaries reflected a belief that patterns connecting various kinds of periodically recurring astronomical events with mundane conditions such as weather and prices could be exploited for making forecasts.

The Astronomical Diaries contain two kinds of observation involving the planets. Whenever a planet was seen to pass by one of a set of about 30 stars adopted as reference stars in the zodiacal belt (modern scholarship calls them "Normal Stars"), a record was usually made on the night of its closest approach, giving its observed distance from the Normal Star in the units called "cubits," equivalent to about 2.4°, which we already encountered in the context of Babylonian eclipse observations. These observations provided a way of keeping track of where each planet was in the zodiac. The other kind of observation was of events that we call "synodic phenomena" connected with the pattern of the planet's observed motion relative to the Sun. The synodic phenomena included first and last appearances as well as stations (when planets appeared to pause in their motion through the zodiac and change direction from eastward to westward or vice versa) and sunset risings (when planets were close to being diametrically opposite to the Sun).

Synodic cycles and recurrence periods

In Mesopotamian cosmology, the planets were believed to change their appearances and travel through the sky according to the will of the gods, and any regularity observed in their behavior was a direct manifestation of divine intention. From the perspective of our modern knowledge of the solar system, however, the synodic phenomena are consequences of the fact that each planet orbits the Sun while we observe it from the Earth, which is also orbiting the Sun at a different distance and speed. A planet's phenomena generally happen in a fixed order, making what we call its "synodic cycle."[8]

To get an understanding of how synodic cycles work, we can think in terms of a simplified solar system in which all the planets orbit the Sun in a single plane, along perfect circles, and with constant speeds. The closer a planet is to the Sun, the faster it travels on its orbit and the shorter its orbital period or "year." Hence, from time to time the Sun will be exactly between the Earth and any of the other planets (fig. 7.1), a situation called "conjunction." To an observer on the Earth, the planet and the Sun will be exactly lined up, and because of the Sun's brightness, the planet will be invisible. The time interval from one such Earth-Sun-planet alignment to the next is a synodic cycle of the planet.

If the planet in question is one of those whose orbits are outside the Earth's orbit (Mars, Jupiter, and Saturn, called "outer" planets), then halfway between two conjunctions, the Earth will pass between the planet and the Sun (fig. 7.2), and to an observer on Earth, the planet will be 180° in longitude from the Sun, a configuration called "opposition." If, however, the planet is one of those whose

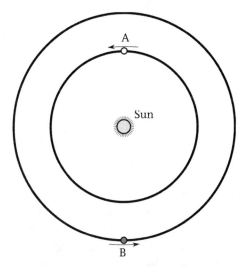

FIG. 7.1. Conjunction of an outer planet (assuming the Earth is A and the planet is B), or superior conjunction of an inner planet (assuming the Earth is B and the planet is A). In this and the following diagrams, the system is viewed from north of the solar system, and the eastward orbital motion of all planets is shown as counterclockwise.

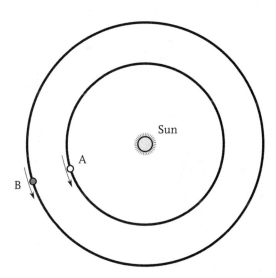

FIG. 7.2. Opposition of an outer planet (assuming the Earth is A and the planet is B), or inferior conjunction of an inner planet (assuming the Earth is B and the planet is A).

orbits are inside the Earth's orbit (Mercury and Venus, called "inner" planets), this situation cannot arise, but instead, halfway between two Earth-Sun-planet alignments, the planet will pass between the Earth and the Sun (fig. 7.2), and it will again be invisible to an observer on Earth. This is also a conjunction, and to distinguish the two situations, the Earth-Sun-planet alignment is called a "superior conjunction" and the Earth-planet-Sun alignment is an "inferior conjunction." Thus, the synodic cycle follows a different pattern for inner and outer planets.

Around the time of an outer planet's conjunction or an inner planet's superior conjunction, the direction from the Earth to the planet is shifting eastward; that is, in the direction of increasing longitude (fig. 7.3). This is called "direct" motion. On the other hand, around an outer planet's opposition or an inner planet's inferior conjunction, the direction from the Earth to the planet is shifting westward, in the direction of decreasing longitude (fig. 7.4). This is called "retrograde" motion. Hence, in every synodic cycle a planet reverses its apparent direction twice, and the dates of these reversals are called "stations."

Since an inner planet has no oppositions (i.e., it can never get as far as 180° away from the Sun as seen from the Earth), its average rate of longitudinal motion is the same as the Sun's, but it appears to be alternately east of the Sun (i.e., at a greater longitude) or west of it (i.e., at a lesser longitude). If it is far enough east of the Sun to be visible, it will appear as an evening star, and conversely if it is far enough west, it will appear as a morning star. Starting a

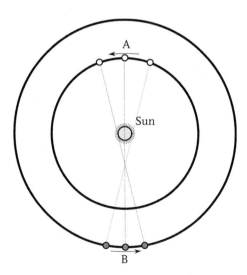

FIG. 7.3. The apparent motion of an outer planet (B) as seen from the Earth (A) around conjunction, or the apparent motion of an inner planet (A) as seen from the Earth (B) around superior conjunction. The lines of sight (broken lines) rotate counterclockwise in the diagram, representing direct apparent motion.

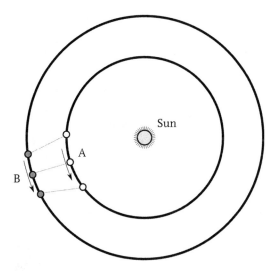

FIG. 7.4. The apparent motion of an outer planet (B) as seen from the Earth
(A) around opposition, or the apparent motion of an inner planet (A) as seen from
the Earth (B) around inferior conjunction. The lines of sight (broken lines) rotate
clockwise in the diagram, representing retrograde motion.

cycle with a superior conjunction, the planet appears to be moving away from
the Sun in the eastward direction, soon making its first evening appearance,
but its apparent speed is continually decreasing until it reaches the stage called
its "greatest evening elongation," after which the Sun begins to catch up with
it. After this comes the planet's evening station, and then—with the planet
now moving retrograde and the Sun, as always, direct—the inferior conjunction. (The evening disappearance comes after the evening station in the case of
Venus, whereas in the case of Mercury it can happen either before or after the
station.) After the inferior conjunction, the planet appears to move away from
the Sun in the westward direction, moving retrograde until the morning station
(again, Venus's first morning appearance always precedes the morning station,
but either order is possible for Mercury). Thereafter, the motion is direct and
accelerating—but still slower than the Sun—until the planet reaches its "greatest morning elongation." For the remainder of the synodic cycle, the planet's
apparent motion is faster than the Sun's, so that it catches up with the Sun at
its next superior conjunction.

Let us take Venus as an example of an inner planet. Starting from superior conjunction, Venus makes its first evening appearance after about 30 days.
Since its apparent motion through the zodiac is direct and faster than the Sun's,
it sets at progressively later times after sunset until, about 221 days after the
superior conjunction, it reaches its greatest evening elongation. From now on,
the time of its setting is progressively earlier in the evening. About 50 days after

the greatest elongation comes the evening station, and henceforth, as observed relative to the stars, it is seen to move retrograde. Its last evening appearance comes a few days before the inferior conjunction, which occurs about 21 days after the station and 292 days after the superior conjunction. This is the half-way point of the synodic cycle. Thereafter, the morning events come in the reverse order to the evening ones: the first morning appearance soon after the inferior conjunction, the morning station about 21 days after the conjunction, the greatest morning elongation about 50 days after the station, and the next superior conjunction (preceded by last morning appearance) about 221 days after the greatest elongation.

The entire cycle has taken about 584 days, which is roughly $1^3/_5$ years and roughly $2^3/_5$ orbital periods of Venus. Since these are not whole numbers, Venus's longitude will be different at each of the synodic phenomena of its next synodic cycle compared to the first cycle. After five complete cycles, however, Venus will be at almost the same position as at the beginning of the first cycle.

An outer planet's direct motion is never as fast as the Sun's, so that relative to the Sun it is always receding in the westward direction. Following conjunction, the planet is moving in direct motion but decelerating. When it is far enough west of the Sun to be visible, it makes its first morning appearance. Thereafter come, in order, its morning station (marking the beginning of the retrogradation), its opposition, and its evening station (marking the return to direct motion). As the Sun overtakes the planet, the planet undergoes its last evening appearance, followed by the next conjunction.

We can use Mars to illustrate the pattern of phenomena in an outer planet's synodic cycle. We begin the cycle with Mars's conjunction, when it is in line with the Sun. First morning appearance occurs after a few days, following which Mars can be observed in direct motion, always falling farther behind the Sun. About 354 days after conjunction comes its morning station and the beginning of the retrograde motion. Opposition follows about 36 days after the station and about 390 days after the conjunction; this is the halfway point of the cycle and is approximately the point when Mars ceases to be above the horizon in the morning right up to dawn and begins to be above the horizon imme-diately after dusk. The evening phenomena are in reverse order: the evening station is about 36 days after opposition, and the next conjunction (preceded by last evening appearance) is about 354 days after the evening station. The entire cycle takes about 780 days, which is roughly $2^1/_7$ years and $1^1/_7$ orbital periods of Mars. Hence, Mars's locations in the zodiac at each phenomenon of the next cycle all will be shifted eastward relative to the first cycle, and only after seven complete cycles will it come back, very roughly, to an alignment with the first cycle.

The two kinds of cycle are summarized in table 7.1, with the phenom-ena that the astronomers at Babylon regularly recorded being indicated in bold type. Since conjunctions are not visible events, the Babylonians did not

TABLE 7.1. Synodic cycles of the planets. Phenomena recorded
by Babylonian astronomers are in bold type.

Inner planet	Outer planet
Superior conjunction	Conjunction
First evening appearance	**First morning appearance**
Greatest evening elongation	**Morning station**
Evening station	**Acronychal rising**
Last evening appearance	Opposition
Inferior conjunction	**Evening station**
First morning appearance	**Last evening appearance**
Morning station	Conjunction
Greatest morning elongation	
Last morning appearance	
Conjunction	

include them among the synodic events that they observed or predicted. They also paid no attention to the greatest elongations of Mercury and Venus, and practically none to these planets' stations. In all the known Astronomical Diaries, there is only a single report of a station of Venus. This is probably because Mercury and Venus have their stations when they are close enough to the Sun as seen from the Earth so that they are usually either not visible, or, at best, visible but without a background of visible stars with reference to which an observer could tell which way the planet is moving. Mercury stays within such a narrow range on either side of the Sun that under some circumstances the Babylonians were unable even to see it make an expected appearance in the morning or evening. Finally, the Babylonians did not consider exact opposition of an outer planet to be a significant event, but rather the event that the Greeks called "acronychal rising" (a synonym for "evening rising"), which was the date slightly before opposition when the planet was last seen to rise after sunset.

Our simplified version of the solar system is good enough if all we care about are the causes of the synodic phenomena and their order in the cycle. However, it suggests a much more uniform pattern in the timing of the phenomena than is actually the case. One reason is that the axis of the Earth's daily rotation is tilted relative to the plane of the Earth's orbit around the Sun; another is that the other planets' orbits are not exactly in the same plane. Both kinds of inclination affect how high a planet is above an observer's horizon, in such a way that the elongation a planet has to have from the Sun in order to be visible varies depending on where the planet is in the zodiac as seen from the Earth. These considerations affect only the dates of first and last appearance. A third cause of irregularity is that the orbits of the planets, including the Earth, are not circles centered on the Sun but ellipses with the Sun at one focus, and a planet's speed on its orbit is not constant but diminishes with increased distance from the Sun. These considerations affect the dates of all the synodic phenomena, again in a way that depends on the planet's apparent location in the zodiac.

What this means is that every synodic cycle of a planet is different in length from the preceding and following cycles, and the number of days between synodic phenomena within a cycle, say from first morning appearance to morning station, also changes from one cycle to the next. This works out differently for each planet. Venus, for example, has a nearly circular orbit, as does the Earth, so Venus's cycles taken as a whole are almost constant, but the tilt of its orbit causes large fluctuations in the duration of its intervals of invisibility. Mars and Mercury have less circular orbits with comparatively large eccentricities, so their synodic cycles are quite variable in length.

Suppose that there is some number of complete synodic cycles that brings both the planet and the Earth back to the exact points of their orbits that they started out from. From this moment onward, everything that the Earth and the planet do will exactly repeat what they did before, so we can use the previous cycles to predict the new ones. Unfortunately, this kind of exact simultaneous return never happens, but given enough time, one can find "recurrence periods" that bring the Earth-Sun-planet configuration to within any desired margin of an exact return. By about 400 BC, the Babylonians knew of recurrence periods shorter than a century, which in modern scholarship are called Goal-Year periods (table 7.2). The errors in the Goal-Year-period equations are on the order of a small number of days. For example, five synodic cycles of Venus are about 2.4 days shorter than eight solar years.

TABLE 7.2. The Babylonian Goal-Year periods.

Jupiter	71 years, containing 65 synodic cycles
	83 years, containing 76 synodic cycles
Venus	8 years, containing 5 synodic cycles
Mercury	46 years, containing 145 synodic cycles
Saturn	59 years, containing 57 synodic cycles
Mars	79 years, containing 37 synodic cycles
	47 years, containing 22 synodic cycles

The Babylonians used the Goal-Year periods to predict both synodic phenomena and passages of the planets by Normal Stars.[9] The first step was to
find a record of an observation one Goal-Year period back by looking in the
Astronomical Diaries for previous years. The date of the old observation would
have to be adjusted by a correction appropriate for the planet, both because
of the errors in the Goal-Year periods themselves and because the dates were
expressed in the Babylonian lunar calendar. The observed locations of the planets relative to Normal Stars would also have to be corrected on account of the
inaccuracies of the Goal-Year periods. It is not known in complete detail how
this was done. What matters for us here is that the Babylonian astronomers
were aware that the Goal-Year periods were inexact, and approximately by how
much.

Alongside the Goal-Year method, the Babylonian astronomers developed
a different, more mathematical approach to predicting the phenomena of the
planets. Instead of obtaining a single prediction from a single observation made
many years before, the mathematical systems provided rules based on ingenious applications of simple arithmetic for obtaining dates and zodiacal positions for a whole series of consecutive occurrences of a particular phenomenon,
as well as other arithmetical rules that connected all the different phenomena
of a planet to each other. Using such rules, they generated spreadsheet-like
tablets containing predictions of all the phenomena of a planet over a span
of many years, all derived in principle from a single observation. Most of the
spreadsheet tablets were published by Otto Neugebauer in a magnificent 1955
edition called *Astronomical Cuneiform Texts*, and from the title's initials the
system of mathematical methods on which they were based have come to be
known as "ACT."

ACT was based on longer and more accurate recurrence periods, on
the order of centuries, which were treated as exact equations of years and
synodic cycles. The Babylonians probably discovered them by combining
shorter periods such as the Goal-Year periods in such a way that their errors
canceled out. The most important ACT periods are given in table 7.3.[10]

TABLE 7.3. The Babylonian ACT periods.

Jupiter	427 years, containing 391 synodic cycles
Venus	1151 years, containing 720 synodic cycles
Mercury	217 years, containing 684 synodic cycles
Saturn	265 years, containing 256 synodic cycles
Mars	284 years, containing 133 synodic cycles

Personal astrology and continuous motion

The transition from the omen-watching associated with *Enūma Anu Enlil* to the later Babylonian observational and predictive routines can be characterized as a shift from emphasis on the irregular aspects of planetary phenomena to their regularities, like thinking of a train trip no longer as a mysterious journey punctuated by interesting events but as a succession of station stops following a timetable. Like a timetable, however, a Diary tablet or ACT spreadsheet did not provide a direct answer to the question of exactly where each of the planets was at any given time *between* its synodic phenomena. At best, a Diary gave intermittent signposts in the form of reports of when planets passed by Normal Stars or, in the latest period, when they crossed from one sign of the zodiac to another.

One reason the Babylonians came to be interested in knowing the locations of the planets during the intervals between their phenomena was the rise of a new form of astrology that was concerned with the fortunes of ordinary individuals rather than kings and kingdoms. This development was perhaps in turn partly motivated by the fact that, after the collapse of Assyria in the late seventh century and the Persian conquest of Babylonia in 539 BC, there were no longer local kings to patronize the practice of omen-based astrology, though other societal changes surely played a part. Whereas at the national level, ominous messages were issued by the gods like a continual stream of bulletins, the astral messages pertinent to an individual consisted of the phenomena occurring close to his or her birthdate and the locations of the heavenly bodies in the zodiac on that date. About 30 examples are known of tablets recording such information for specific individuals born in years ranging from 410 through 69 BC; modern scholars refer to them as "horoscopes."[11] In the majority of the horoscope tablets the astronomical information is not accompanied by any astrological interpretations predicting what kind of life the individual will lead, but a few give brief statements in the manner of the outcomes in omen texts. The tablets come from Babylon, Uruk, and Nippur, all cities where there existed a practice of astronomical observation or prediction.

Most of the horoscope tablets state only the zodiacal signs occupied by those planets that were visible at some time of night around the birthdate; that is, the same imprecise information that one could find in an Astronomical Diary tablet for that month. Some, however, give their zodiacal positions in degrees. The earliest-known horoscope with degrees for the planets is a tablet from Uruk for a child bearing the Greek name Aristokrates, born about June 3, 235 BC.[12] On this date we are told that Jupiter was at Sagittarius 18° (interpretation: "prosperous, at peace, his wealth will be long lasting, long days"), Venus at Taurus 4° ("he will find favor wherever he goes; he will have sons and daughters"), Saturn at Cancer 6°, and Mars at Cancer 24°. Mercury is described as "with the Sun" (i.e., not visible) in Gemini.

We do not know precisely how these locations in degrees were obtained, but the probable source was the mathematical methods of prediction, not tablets such as the Astronomical Diaries. A few tablets of the ACT type show how it could be done. One began by finding the synodic phenomena of the planet that were calculated as having taken place immediately before and after the birthdate. The spreadsheet gave the dates of these phenomena as well as the corresponding positions of the planet in degrees. Thus, one had a known interval of days between the phenomena and a known number of degrees that the planet traveled between them either in the direct or retrograde direction, which could be broken down into a step-by-step motion for each day. The simplest way to do this was by assuming that the planet's speed stayed the same through the interval—in other words, dividing the total degrees by the total days to find the average daily rate of motion. More sophisticated numerical patterns were also sometimes applied to produce an effect of speeding up or slowing down. The key point is that the Babylonians represented the motion of a planet as a series of separate stretches fitted individually to the gaps between the synodic phenomena, not as a continuous process through time that incidentally gave rise to the phenomena. It was a completely different approach from the one we took above in explaining the phenomena as resulting from the planets orbiting the Sun, and also different from the approach that Greek astronomers were going to adopt.

Greek planetary cosmologies

Recollecting in his old age the sayings of his mentor Socrates, the ex-soldier and historian Xenophon tells his readers:[13]

> He advised people to become acquainted with astronomy too, but only as far as being able to recognize the current stage of the night and month and year for the sake of journeying and sailing and watch duty and knowing how to use signs for all the things that are done during the night or month or year by identifying their stages; and he said it was easy to learn these things from nocturnal hunters and steersmen and many others whose business it is to know these things. But as for learning astronomy to the point of also knowing the things that do not take part in the same revolution, the wandering and unsteady stars, wearing oneself out seeking their distances from the Earth and their periods and the causes of these things, he strongly discouraged this, because he said he saw no benefit whatsoever in these things.

Leaving aside Socrates' alleged belief—which has a disturbing resemblance to some present-day views of the value of pure research—that astronomy is worthwhile just so far as it serves the needs of practical life, this passage is one of our earliest testimonies that the planets (*planētes*, "wanderers," a name reminiscent of the Akkadian "wild sheep") had become objects of interest to the Greeks by the end of the fifth century BC. It is not clear when and how the Greeks had become familiar with all five planets, but they were definitely latecomers compared to the Mesopotamians. In the Homeric epics, Venus alone is mentioned, under different names in its roles as Morning Star (*heōsphoros*, "bringer of dawn") and Evening Star (*hesperos*, "evening one"). At the start of the fourth century BC, Plato knew all five, and Aristotle speaks of them by the so-called theophoric names that associated them with gods of the Greek pantheon (table 7.4). Our modern names come from the Greek theophoric names by way of the Roman gods who were traditionally identified with their Greek counterparts. But the Greek names themselves betray Babylonian influence: the Greek gods Aphrodite, Zeus, and Ares have an affinity with Ishtar, Marduk, and Nergal, the divinities that the Babylonians associated respectively with Venus, Jupiter, and Mars.[14] What modes of contact lie behind these linkages, and what other things the Greeks may have learned of Mesopotamian planet lore at this early stage, are unknown.

It was only for the sake of abbreviation that Greek writers sometimes used the god's name directly for its planet, calling Mercury simply "Hermes" and so forth. They generally did not equate the visible objects in the sky with these particular gods, though they commonly spoke of them as "divine" (*theioi*) and sometimes as "gods" (*theoi*). From the early third century BC onward, we also find them using a different set of names, generally descriptive of how each planet appears to the eye, either as alternatives to the theophoric names or alongside them (table 7.5).

TABLE 7.4. Greek theophoric names of the planets.

Mercury	the star of Hermes
Venus	the star of Aphrodite
Mars	the star of Ares
Jupiter	the star of Zeus
Saturn	the star of Kronos

TABLE 7.5. Greek descriptive names of the planets.

Mercury	*Stilbōn* ("gleamer")
Venus	*Phōsphoros* ("light bringer")
Mars	*Pyroeis* ("fiery one")
Jupiter	*Phaethōn* ("radiant one")
Saturn	*Phainōn* ("shiner")

When Xenophon summarizes the planetary investigations that Socrates disparaged as "seeking their distances from the Earth and their periods and the causes of these things," he reveals that early Greek astronomy took a different approach from Babylonian astronomy with respect to the planets, in much the same way as they did with respect to eclipses. An interest in periodicities is a point they had in common, though the evidence that we have for Greek planetary theory before the Hellenistic period, such as it is, suggests that only rather crude values were sought. The planetary periods were not a means of predicting phenomena but aspects of the planets that were connected with their supposed distances from the Earth. For the Mesopotamians, the cosmological framework was a given; for the Greeks it was a goal of astronomical speculation.

The Socrates that Plato portrays in his *Republic* is a far remove from Xenophon's: here it is Socrates who belittles Glaucon's appeal to practicality when Glaucon justifies the teaching of astronomy on the grounds that "being more keenly perceptive of the stages of months and years is appropriate not just for farming and sailing but also at least as much for generalship."[15] Near the end of the work, Socrates tells Glaucon the story of a man named Er who returned to life some days after his death on the battlefield and recounted what he had seen of the journeys and judgments experienced by human souls between death and rebirth.[16] The place where the souls chose the tokens determining their next lives was the "Spindle of Necessity," whose description contains a figurative planetary cosmology:[17]

Its shaft and hook were of steel, and its whorl was a mixture of this and other materials. The nature of the whorl was as follows. Its shape was like that of a whorl here with us. But from what [Er] said, you have to conceive of it as if inside one large whorl that is hollow and scooped out right through, another one like it but smaller is inserted, exactly fitting it, like those jars that fit exactly one inside another; and a third one and a fourth and four more in the same way. You see, there were eight whorls in all, one inserted inside another, showing their upper lips as circles but making a continuous back of a single whorl around the shaft, which passed right through the eighth one.

Now the first and outermost whorl had the thickest circle for its lip; that of the sixth [whorl] came second [in rank of thickness], that of the fourth came third, that of the eighth came fourth, that of the seventh came fifth, that of the fifth came sixth, that of the third came seventh, and that of the second came eighth. And [the lip] of the biggest [whorl] was speckled, that of the seventh was brightest, that of the eighth got its color from the seventh shining upon it, that of the second and fifth were very like each other, being yellower than the others; the third one had the whitest color, the fourth was ruddy, and the sixth came in second place in whiteness.

The entire spindle was turned and spun with one and the same motion, while during the whole thing's revolution the seven interior circles revolved slowly in the opposite direction to the whole. The eighth of them went fastest; in second place and all together the seventh and sixth and fifth; the fourth [circle] went in third place, as it seemed to them, making its round; the third [circle] was in fourth place, and the second in fifth place. And it was turned on the knees of Necessity.

On top of each circle stood a Siren, which was borne around with it, giving forth a single sound, a single pitch, and a single music sounded all together comprising all eight. Three others were seated at equal spacing round about, each on a chair, the daughters of Necessity, the Fates, dressed in white, having garlands on their heads: Lachesis and Klotho and Atropos. They sang to the accompaniment of the music of the Sirens, Lachesis singing the things that had been; Klotho, those that were; Atropos, those that would be. And Klotho touched the spindle with her right hand and gave a spin to its exterior revolution, pausing intermittently, and Atropos gave a spin to the interior [revolutions] with her left hand in the same way, and Lachesis touched both in turn with either hand.

There is not a single explicit astronomical term in this passage, but Plato must have expected his readers to solve at least parts of his riddle and recognize the whorl, or rather the whorls, as an image of an imagined planetary system—not a technical description, but a poeticization. Whorls, rounded weights fixed on the shaft of spindles to increase their angular momentum, existed in various shapes, but when Plato writes that the whorl of the Spindle of Necessity was "like that of a whorl here with us" he likely has in mind the common type shaped like a flaring cone with a flat base that was often decorated with concentric circles and other patterns. But instead of being painted on, the circles of this fatidic spindle were the rims of a series of nested cones that were free to turn relative to each other. Probably no special significance was meant to be attached to the conical shape of the whorl's "back."

The hints suggesting a planetary system are in the number of nested whorls, their motions, their colorations, and the order from outermost to innermost. But to understand the hints, the reader had to be familiar with a cosmology in which the stars, planets, Sun, and Moon revolve at diverse distances and speeds around a stationary Earth at the center of the cosmos. In Plato's metaphors no element corresponds to the Earth, and none to the visible planets, unless the Sirens are intended as sonic manifestations of them; the planets' distinguishing characteristics of color and brightness have been transferred to the circular rims of the whorls.

Fig. 7.5 is a static representation of how the planetary system might have been imagined. The spherical Earth is at the center, surrounded by concentric circular paths belonging, from innermost to outermost, to the Moon, the Sun, the five planets (in the order Venus, Mercury, Mars, Jupiter, Saturn), and the fixed stars. The sizes of the circles have been chosen so that the ring-shaped space immediately inside each circle corresponds in thickness to the rims of Plato's whorls—this may be incorrect, since the information Plato gives about the relative thicknesses of the whorls is a feature of his account whose rationale is lost to us. On the assumption that what Plato says about the color and illumi-nation of each whorl applies in the cosmology to the corresponding spherical heavenly body, we can identify which ones must be the Moon (deriving its light from the next body outward), the Sun (brightest, and illuminating the Moon), Mars (red), and the fixed stars (speckled). The whitest and second-whitest ones are likely to be Venus and Jupiter, and the remaining pair would thus be Mercury and Saturn. The whole system of correspondences is summarized in table 7.6.

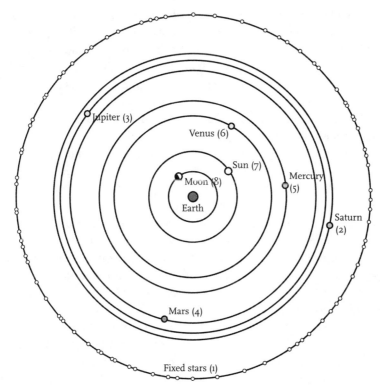

FIG. 7.5. Planetary cosmology corresponding to the whorls of the Spindle of Necessity (cf. table 6).

TABLE 7.6. The whorls of Plato's Myth of Er and their corresponding heavenly bodies.

Whorl number	Rank in Thickness	Coloration	Rank in speed	Heavenly body
1	1	speckled	—	fixed stars
2	8	yellowish	5	Saturn
3	7	whitest	4	Jupiter
4	3	ruddy	3	Mars
5	6	yellowish	2	Mercury
6	2	white	2	Venus
7	5	brightest	2	Sun
8	4	lit by no. 7	1	Moon

The spinning motions of the whorls stand for the heavenly bodies' daily cycles of rising in the East and setting in the West. Greek astronomers and philosophers had two conceptually distinct but interchangeable ways of describing them. One was to say that each of the heavenly bodies—treating the fixed stars as constituting a single body—revolves around the Earth from east to west (i.e., clockwise if one is looking southward) but at slightly different speeds, with the stars being fastest and the Moon being slowest. The other was to say that they all took part in one and the same cosmic revolution, which is directly observable in the risings and settings of the stars, but that the Sun, Moon, and planets combine this rapid motion with a slower one in the opposite direction, from west to east, which we can observe as their more gradual motion relative to the background of the stars. According to this point of view, the Moon is fastest and Saturn is slowest, while the stars have no independent movement at all. This is how Plato specifies the motions of the whorls.

Separating the apparent cycles of rising and setting into a rapid revolution of the whole cosmos around the Earth and a slow individual revolution of each heavenly body lends itself to an easy transformation into the modern perspective of the solar system. The cosmic revolution is how we perceive the rotation of the Earth on its axis, if we think of the Earth as stationary. A complete revolution takes place in approximately 23 hours 56 minutes (this being the interval between two successive risings of the same star). The Moon's motion relative to the stars is its orbit around the Earth, completed in approximately 27 days 8 hours, and the Sun's motion is how we perceive the Earth's orbit around the Sun if we again think of the Earth as stationary. As was the case with their synodic cycles, the planets' revolutions relative to the stars behave differently for the inner and the outer planets. We see an outer planet's orbit roughly as if we were standing on the Sun, except that the Earth is making its own orbital wobble around the Sun that is small relative to the planet's orbit. Hence, an outer planet's revolution is, on average, the same as its orbital period: about 30 years for Saturn, 12 for Jupiter, and a little over 2 for Mars. On the other hand, we see an inner planet's orbit as a wobbling motion going alternately faster and slower than the Sun but never getting more than a certain limiting elongation from it. Hence, an inner planet's average revolution is the same as the Sun's (namely, a solar year). Plato's ancient readers were not thinking in terms of the modern solar system, but they must have known the basic observable facts, and so they would have recognized how the speeds of Plato's whorls match up with the heavenly bodies: the whorl for the Moon spins fastest in its contrary motion, those for the Sun, Venus, and Mercury all have equal rates of motion, and the remaining three planets are slower, in the order Mars, Jupiter, and Saturn.

The synodic cycles are conspicuously absent from Er's account of the Spindle of Necessity. The whorls corresponding to the planets, like those of the Sun and Moon, are simply said to turn "in the opposite direction to the whole," as if there was no such thing as a station or retrograde motion. It is possible that Plato meant to suggest some variation in speed in his description of how the Fates set the whorls in motion by an on-again-off-again action of their right or left hands, but if so, he chose a singularly obscure way of carrying out this intention.

The idea that the heavenly bodies are all at different distances from the Earth is characteristic of Greek cosmology. There was obvious empirical evidence that the Moon is closer to us than the other bodies: it frequently passes in front of stars, much more rarely in front of planets, and by Plato's time the explanation of solar eclipses as caused by the Moon's passing between the Earth and Sun was well established. Beyond this placement of the Moon, the ordering of distances implied by Plato's whorls followed a nonempirical assumption that was shared by most Greek planetary cosmologies, that the longer a heavenly body's period of revolution relative to the stars, the farther it was from the Earth. Another way of putting this is that the closer a heavenly body was to the fixed stars, the slower its independent motion. This principle determined the sequence stars-Saturn-Jupiter-Mars going from outermost inward and was consistent with having the Moon innermost. But it did not give a straightforward criterion for the relative distances of the Sun, Venus, and Mercury, and turning from one ancient author to another one finds these three in different permutations. Plato evidently accepted the sequence Mercury-Venus-Sun going inward, perhaps because this placed them in increasing order of brightness.

In later sources the orders Venus-Mercury-Sun and, especially, Sun-Venus-Mercury came to be more commonly preferred. Whereas in Babylonian texts the planets tended to be listed in an order based on their presumed astrological tendencies, Greek texts usually adhere to one of these orders on the basis of presumed distance, even when the context is astrology. One interesting and unobvious manifestation of this is the association of the Sun, Moon, and planets with a seven-day cycle, from which many modern languages derived their names for the days of the week—including English, though this is partially obscured by substitution of Germanic gods for Greco-Roman ones. The underlying principle was that each hour of each night and day was considered to have one of the seven heavenly bodies as its astrological ruler, in the sequence Saturn-Jupiter-Mars-Sun-Venus-Mercury-Moon. The day as a whole was governed by the ruler of its first hour, giving rise to the sequence Saturn-Sun-Moon-Mars-Mercury-Jupiter-Venus for the planetary week. Evaluating days by their planetary lords came to be a popular practice in Rome and the Latin West as early as the first century BC.[18] The eventual syncretism of the astrological cycle with the Judeo-Christian week in later antiquity was a natural development, though it was predictably deplored by some religious figures.

The narrative of the journey of Er's soul does not lend itself to a literal understanding of just where the Spindle of Necessity is situated in relation to our world, but it seems clear that Plato did not mean the Spindle and its whorls to be identified with our cosmos, beheld as it were from outside. Rather, it is a idealized *model* of our cosmos, by which the destinies of the cosmos and its inhabitants are controlled by the Fates. The relationship between a model of the cosmos and the cosmos itself has a powerful ambiguity: a man-made model would be an imperfect imitation of the observable cosmos, but in this mythologizing context it is *our* cosmos that mimics the model. The same idea can be seen in certain Roman sarcophagi on which sculpted Fates are equipped with a sundial and a celestial sphere, which here are metaphorical instruments not for observation but for controlling the individual's destiny and time of death.[19]

Later students of the *Republic* were alert to the potential for relating Plato's account to tangible man-made constructions. Theon of Smyrna, the Platonist philosopher of the early second century AD whom we met in passing in chapter 5, tells us that he built a physical model (*sphairopoiia*) of the Spindle of Necessity as a teaching tool.[20] Cicero's *De re publica* concludes with the Dream of Scipio, a deliberate echo of Plato's Myth of Er, in which Scipio Aemilianus is allowed to behold the spheres of the *actual* cosmos in a dream, but this tale is artfully balanced at the work's beginning by the story (see chapter 6) of how Archimedes' wonderful mechanical *sphaera* was demonstrated at the house of Marcellus.

The Dream of Scipio (*Somnium Scipionis*) acquired a life of its own as an independent text with a commentary by Macrobius (fifth century AD), and in fact it was the only part of Cicero's *De re publica* known in modern times until Angelo Mai discovered a palimpsest codex containing most of the dialogue in the Vatican Library in 1819. In some medieval manuscripts the Dream's account of the heavenly spheres is accompanied by a diagram showing a cross section of Cicero's cosmology, with the Earth at the center surrounded by seven rings for the Sun, Moon, and planets and an outermost ring containing the names of the 12 signs of the zodiac (fig. 7.6). Similar diagrams are found in various Byzantine

dcduob' orbib' alta diametros duplo altam umet. illu
orbe cui diametros dupla e orbe alto octies ee maiore.
Gc erbis dicendu e sole octies tra ee maiore. h de sot mag
nitudine tiuc demultis excerpta libruum'. S; qm vii
spas eglo duum' ee subiectas extiore qq quas interius'
ccmet ambie. longeq. nacelo ouis nase single recesser.
ric querena cu rodiac' uni sie ri is coster eglo sictib'
isms. que amodu inferio spar stelle insignas rodiaci
meare dicant. Nec longu e inuenire roem que iapso
uestibulo excubat questions. Veru ite. neq. sole luna ue
neq. deuagis ulla ita insignis rodiaci fieri ut cor sictibus
misceant. s; millo signo ee unaqq pibet qd habuerit sup
itnee mea qils subiecta e circti sui regioe discurrens qt
singlar spar curtos in xii partes aq ut rodiacu tu diuisit.
Gt que mea parte circuli sui uenerit que sub parte rodia
ci e arieti depurat' ipsu ariete uenise cocedit simitq. obser
uatio i sigtas partes migrantib' stell tenet. Et quia facilior
ad intellactu poctos uia e idqd sermo descipsit uis adsignet. •

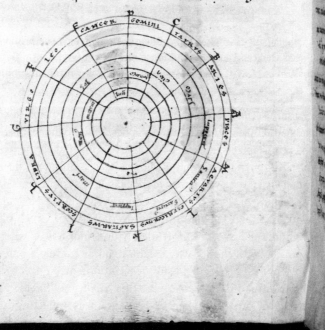

FIG. 7.6. Cosmological diagram accompanying Macrobius' *Commentary on Cicero's*
Dream of Scipio, Walters Art Museum MS W.22 (12th century), f. 43v. (© The Walters
Art Museum, licensed under Creative Commons: http://www.thedigitalwalters.org)

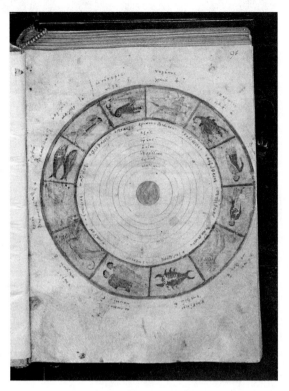

FIG. 7.7. "Pagan" cosmology from Kosmas Indikopleustes, *Christian Topography*, Biblioteca Medicea Laurenziana Plut. 9.28 (11th century), f. 96r. (reproduced with permission of MiBACT; further reproduction by any means is prohibited)

Greek manuscripts; for example, to illustrate the ostensibly false cosmology of the "pagans" in copies of the *Christian Topography* by the sixth-century AD traveler Cosmas Indicopleustes—one of the few genuine flat earthers of the Middle Ages (fig. 7.7). Although no example is known that certainly dates from before late antiquity, such visual representations of the planetary system must have been common in the teaching of elementary astronomy already in the Hellenistic period.

Did there exist *mechanical* representations of Greek planetary cosmologies? Theon of Smyrna unfortunately does not tell us whether his model of the Spindle of Necessity was mechanized or merely an assemblage of parts movable by hand. Cicero's brief descriptions of the *sphaerae* of Archimedes and Posidonius in *On the Nature of the Gods*, the *Tusculan Disputations*, and *De re publica* can be trusted up to a point as reflecting what was possible in an astronomical mechanism in his own time, though with respect to Archimedes their testamentary value is more questionable. In each passage he is explicit that these devices showed the motions of the five planets as well as the Sun and Moon. Thus, in *On the Nature of the Gods*, his Stoic interlocutor Balbus says:[21]

If someone took to Scythia or Britain this *sphaera* that our Posidonius has made recently, each turning of which produces the same behavior for the Sun and Moon and five wandering stars that is produced in each day and night, who in those barbarian lands would question that this *sphaera* was fashioned by reason?

In the *Tusculan Disputations*, speaking in his own voice, he writes:[22]

For when Archimedes bound the motions of the Moon and Sun and five wanderers in a *sphaera*, he achieved the same thing as that god of Plato did who built the world in the *Timaeus*; namely, that a single revolution should govern motions that are dissimilar in slowness and speed.

And we have already quoted the words given to Philus in *De re publica*:[23]

This kind of *sphaera*, in which were present the motions of Sun and Moon and those five stars that are called wanderers and as it were straying, could not be accomplished in that solid *sphaera*, and one had to wonder at the inventiveness of Archimedes in it, that he had figured out how a single revolution could furnish unequal and diverse courses in unlike motions.

But *how* the motions of the planets were shown, and whether there was any representation of their spatial relations relative to each other and to the Earth, we are not told. Even the term *sphaera* leaves the form of these devices an open question. Literally, of course, it means a sphere, but does this mean that the mechanical *sphaerae* were globe shaped, or is its application metaphorical, indicating that they were *representations* of the cosmic sphere?

One might imagine that *sphaera* could only have been metaphorical, because constructing a globe-shaped planetarium display would have been technically difficult if not impossible. Michael Wright, however, has refuted this by constructing an ingenious model mechanism encased in a spherical metal shell representing the celestial sphere with its constellations, such that by manually rotating the sphere to simulate its daily revolution around the Earth, one drives the hidden gearwork, and a system of pointers flush with the surface and radiating outward from one of the poles of the ecliptic simulate the motions of the Sun, Moon, and planets through the zodiac.[24] One might question whether such a device was likely to have been invented at an early stage in the evolution of astronomical mechanisms in antiquity, but it *could* have been done.

In the *De re publica* passage, Cicero contrasts Archimedes' mechanical *sphaera* to his more speciously beautiful but less intellectually impressive *sphaera*, which had been deposited in the Temple of Virtue and was apparently a star globe with no moving parts. The key word by which Cicero distinguishes the star globe from the mechanism, *solida*, has the same ambiguity that the translation "solid" has in English—does it mean that the star globe was not hollow, or that it was three-dimensional? I think that the latter sense may be what Cicero had in mind. Just previously, Cicero has spoken of the star globe as "solid and replete" (*solidae atque plenae*), possibly repeating the same idea in different words for emphasis, but if they were intended to convey complementary ideas, they would signify a literal, three-dimensional globe that moreover was not hollow.[25] This would make sense if Cicero visualized—or remembered, from his acquaintance with Posidonius—the mechanical *sphaera* as having a two-dimensional display standing in place of the spherical heavens, opening up the possibility that it portrayed the planets as elements in a cosmos in cross section.

The first person to offer a well-articulated argument that the Antikythera Mechanism showed the motions of the heavenly bodies was Albert Rehm. In his 1906 "Athens lecture" on the Mechanism, Rehm began by listing a few of the isolated words that had been identified in the Mechanism's inscriptions.[26] *Hēlios* ("Sun") and *ho tēs Aphroditēs astēr* ("the star of Aphrodite"), which were already known from the 1902–1903 transcriptions of Adolf Wilhelm and Ioannis Svoronos, showed that the Mechanism was somehow astronomical, as had already been realized. But Rehm had discovered a new word on a small bit of detached plate: *stērigmos*, the technical term for a planet's station, proof that the Mechanism had to do with the *motions* of the planets. This, and the remains of complicated gearwork, ruled out the standing hypothesis that the Mechanism was some sort of astrolabe, leaving just one possibility:

> It must have displayed the motion of the stars; it must have shown how, through the round of the year, the Sun's course causes the fixed stars to rise above the horizon or set below it at ever different hours of day, and how the planets travel through the starry heavens, now ahead of the Sun, now behind it.

Such devices, Rehm continued, exist in our own day, where they are used for teaching, and the term for them is *planetaria*. A modern planetarium shows the Earth circling the Sun along with the other planets, but an ancient planetarium would naturally show a geocentric system with the Sun circling the Earth. We knew from Cicero's reports that Archimedes and Posidonius had constructed planetaria, made of bronze and reproducing the various celestial motions through a single driving motion. Until now, however, we had no idea what such a device would have looked like.

Rehm made a bold effort to make sense of the visible features of Fragments A, B, and C in terms of his planetarium hypothesis, but this was doomed by his ignorance of how the fragments originally fitted together, together with a too superficial knowledge of the physical details, derived from Periklis Rediadis's published descriptions and only a few hours of direct inspection of the fragments. Rehm mistook the surviving parts of the spiral scales of the Metonic and Saros dials in Fragments A and B for a set of five concentric rings that he thought would have been turned by gearwork at rates appropriate for the five planets; a marker on each ring would have stood for the planet itself. He supposed that the Sun's motion was indicated by a pointer revolving above the rings.

Although Derek de Solla Price related the Mechanism in a general way to the Greco-Roman tradition of planetaria as witnessed by Cicero and other ancient authors, and he knew that the inscriptions contained references to Venus and to planetary stations and retrogradations, the planets played only a slight part in his attempts to reconstruct the Mechanism's functions. At one stage he thought that the upper back dial (the Metonic dial) might have indicated the occurrences of synodic phenomena of the planets.[27] By the time that he wrote *Gears from the Greeks*, he had given up on this notion, but he suggested, very tentatively, that a lost system of gears in the space between Fragments A and C might have driven pointers showing the motions of the five planets on the front dial.[28]

At the beginning of the 21st century, several proposals were offered for reconstructing a system of pointers for some or all of the planets on the front dial.[29] Among the originators of these proposals, only Wright adduced substantial new arguments that a planetary display of this kind existed. In particular, Wright showed that vestigial features on the large gear with four spokes known as b1, exposed on the front face of Fragment A, were likely to be from the mountings of gears that could plausibly have driven pointers for the motions of Mercury and Venus. Beyond this physical evidence, the main reason that people were exploring the viability of planetary pointers on the front dial seems to have been the ancient literary testimony that mechanical astronomical devices such as Archimedes' *sphaera* showed the planets.

A different kind of reconstruction was suggested more recently by James Evans, Christián Carman, and Alan Thorndike: instead of a single dial on the front with pointers showing the motions through the zodiac of the planets as well as the Sun and Moon, a set of five smaller dials inside the ring of the Zodiac scale, each showing the current stage of one of the planets' synodic cycle.[30] This proposal, which does without gearwork devices for producing nonuniform motion of pointers, has some resemblance to Price's initial idea for the function of the upper back dial. However, it seems less attractive now that the references to the planets in the Mechanism's inscriptions have been more fully read.

The letters on Fragment B spelling "star of Aphrodite," which were the starting point for this chapter, belong to the back cover inscription (BCI). The partial reconstruction of this text from parts surviving on Fragments B, A, and 19 was among the most impressive outcomes of Price and Georgios Stamiris's work on the Mechanism's inscriptions, and the Antikythera Mechanism Research Project team's 2006 paper in *Nature* marked another big step forward by incorporating readings that Price and Stamiris had missed on Fragment B and elsewhere (in addition to the text in Fragment E, which Price had not had access to).[31] Further work was needed to clear away the noise of misidentified letters that continued to obscure the inscription's meaning, but by 2012 the larger context of the reference to Venus had become clear.[32] It belonged to a systematic description of the Mechanism's front dial as a planetarium.

The BCI was written as a single wide column of text on a plate approximately as wide as the Mechanism itself, with about 75 letters in a typical line. In the part we are speaking of (quoted in chapter 3), we have less than half of each line, starting at or close to the line's beginning. Fortunately, the structure of the text is somewhat repetitive, so that we can often get a good idea of what was in the missing patches of text by comparing with other lines. The basic pattern is a series of sentences more or less along these lines: "Above this is the circle of such and such a planet, and the little sphere that travels through it is such and such a color." The planets were specified both by their theophoric and their descriptive names; for example, "the star of Ares, Pyroeis (fiery one)." They are listed in the order Mercury (almost certainly—most of its name is lost), Venus, Mars, Jupiter, Saturn. Between Venus and Mars, however, there is the description of a pointer for the Sun, bearing on it a little golden sphere.

Thus, we have the most common Greek ordering of the heavenly bodies from the Moon outward (see fig. 3.7). Behind the pointers of the front dial, there may have been a plate engraved with concentric circles like those in the diagram from Kosmas Indikopleustes's book, with the cylindrical casing for the Moon's display constituting the smallest of the circles. Each planet was represented by a pointer bearing a small spherical or disk-shaped marker at an appropriate distance from the central axis so that it was above the appropriate "circle" on the engraved plate. Unfortunately, words giving the colors of all the spheres except the Sun's are lost, but one can make plausible guesses, such as red for Mars. This combination of pointers and spheres made it possible for the front dial to be both a diagram in motion of a planetary cosmology and a device from which one could read off the approximate positions of the heavenly bodies in the zodiac. Even the Zodiac scale itself would have served such a double function, both as the scale for reading the planetary positions and as a representation of the outermost sphere of the fixed stars. Just below its inventory of the planetary pointers, the inscription actually has the word "cosmos," though regrettably in a rather broken verbal context.

Modeling the planetary phenomena

Rehm's conviction that the Mechanism was a planetarium arose in part because he had found the Greek word *stērigmos*, signifying a planetary station, on a small fragment of inscribed plate. Price would later find both the beginning of this word and another that meant moving retrograde, *proēgeitai*, on a different fragment, but unlike Rehm, he made nothing of it.[33] However, even Rehm missed the full implication of his discovery. The manuscript sketches in which he conjectured ways of driving a planetary display by gears show that he was aiming at a uniform rate of motion through the zodiac for each planet. But references to stations show that the Mechanism's designer was aware of synodic phenomena and the variations of the planets' speeds, and that he sought to reproduce them on his device.

The characteristic approach to synodic phenomena and synodic cycles in Greek astronomy was the reverse of the Babylonian approach. The Babylonians took the phenomena as the primary facts, constituting a series of discrete events with associated dates and positions, and obtained a description of a planet's continuous course of motion, when they needed it, by interpolating stretchwise between one phenomenon and the next. These methods were transmitted to the Greek-speaking world at some time during the Hellenistic period. But Greek astronomers had already developed ways of explaining the synodic phenomena as *consequences* of a continuous, mathematically definable pattern of planetary motion that could be projected indefinitely into the past and future.

An early and very interesting theory of planetary motion involving synodic cycles was developed by the mathematician and philosopher Eudoxus of Cnidos around the middle of the fourth century BC. Our earliest report of it, unfortunately very terse, is in Aristotle's *Metaphysics*, Book 12.[34] The fundamental idea was that a heavenly body's motion could be broken down into a combination of circular revolutions performed at constant speed, all centered on the Earth though in different planes. A more physical way of visualizing this theory was to suppose that the visible heavenly body was lodged on a transparent spherical shell centered on the Earth, and that this shell revolved on an axis whose poles are lodged on another spinning spherical shell immediately outside the first one, and so forth for as many spheres as necessary to explain the observed pattern of motion in the sky.

Aristotle tells us that in Eudoxus' system the outermost sphere, whose axis of rotation has a fixed position, is the same for all the heavenly bodies and functions like the sphere on which the fixed stars lie. It corresponds to the outermost of the whorls in Plato's Myth of Er and causes the daily risings and settings of the stars and, indirectly, the other heavenly bodies. Each of the five planets had three further spheres. The next one inward from the sphere of the fixed stars is "along the circle through the middles of the zodiacal signs," which means that the points where its poles are lodged on the sphere of the fixed stars do not coincide with the poles of that sphere, since the ecliptic circle ("the circle through the middles of the zodiacal signs") is inclined with respect to the celestial equator. This second sphere accounts for a planet's general eastward trend around the zodiac and thus corresponds to the planet's whorl in Plato's myth, though Plato's whorls have all their rims in the same plane so that there is no attempt there to represent the obliquity of the ecliptic.

The third sphere of a planet, according to Aristotle, has its poles lodged at two diametrically opposite points of the ecliptic circle on the second sphere, while the fourth sphere's axis is inclined with respect to the axis of the third sphere. The only way of making astronomical sense of this pair of spheres in relation to actual planetary motion is to attribute to them equal but opposite rates of revolution, so that the visible planet, lodged on the fourth sphere, never gets farther than a certain distance from the ecliptic because the two rotations cancel each other out in the long term. In the short term, the planet will oscillate slightly north and south of the ecliptic, and in coordination with this cycle it will appear to travel along the ecliptic with speed alternately faster and slower than its mean speed—and depending on the specific rates of revolution and angle of inclination between the poles, it may perform periodic retrogradations. This is in fact how a much later author, Simplicius (sixth century AD), described the motions of the third and fourth spheres.[35] Simplicius claimed to derive his more detailed information about Eudoxus' astronomy ultimately from a book on the subject by Eudoxus himself, by way of intermediaries. Modern scholars are not in agreement about the general historical reliability of his account, but at least in this point concerning the motions of the third and fourth spheres of the planets, what he says makes good astronomical sense.[36] It can scarcely be doubted that Eudoxus devised this planetary hypothesis in order to produce synodic cycles, though it has been disputed whether he was attempting to obtain stations and retrogradations or just variations of apparent speed. Neither Aristotle nor Simplicius mentions retrogradations in connection with Eudoxus' hypothesis.

In planetary theories based on combinations of circular motions that all are centered on the Earth, the distance of the planet from the Earth never changes, and if we imagine the circular motions as produced by spherical shells, the shells can be as thin and closely packed one inside another as we please. Simplicius says that astronomers eventually gave up on Eudoxus-style hypotheses because variations in the planets' observed brightnesses (he specifically mentions Venus and Mars) seem to indicate that they are sometimes nearer to the Earth and sometimes farther.[37] This may be a supposition that Simplicius, or one of his sources, made in hindsight. There are many reasons why such hypotheses might have lost favor; for example, because of perceived discrepancies between the apparent motions that they predicted and more detailed observational experience, or because their three-dimensional geometry made mathematical analysis of their behavior cumbersome. It would definitely have been a very challenging task to construct a mechanism simulating them.

With respect to our knowledge of Greek planetary astronomy, the interval from the time of Plato and Eudoxus to that of Ptolemy in the second century AD is a half millennium of darkness intermittently illuminated by flashes of evidence, and these flashes are sometimes seen reflected only in the possibly distorting mirrors of later writers' testimony. We cannot tell a connected story, but we *can* point to certain key developments and try to understand how and why they happened, even if the chronology is much less clear than we would like.

One such development was the appearance in the Greek world of systematic programs of recording dated astronomical observations, which we can situate in Ptolemaic Egypt around the beginning of the third century BC. The first of these was associated with an astronomer named Timocharis, who worked at Alexandria between 295 and 272 BC. Another early program was carried out by a different group of observers somewhere in Egypt, perhaps Alexandria, between 272 and 241 BC; we do not know their names, but they used a special astronomical system for dating their observations that was ascribed to a certain Dionysius. The handful of observations of planets that we know of from these programs survived because they were quoted by Ptolemy in his *Almagest* and, in one case, by another astronomical author of the generation before Ptolemy, a scrap of whose work survives on a papyrus (*POxy astron.* 4133).[38]

The Greek observational programs may have been inspired by some knowledge of the observational practice in Babylon that produced the Astronomical Diaries. But the way that they recorded planets' positions relative to stars, though apparently carried out without measuring instruments, seems to have aimed at a greater accuracy than the reports in the Astronomical Diaries, and observations were recorded of the same planet on closely spaced dates so that one could determine the rate of its motion. It is noteworthy that one of the "Dionysian" reports that Ptolemy cites (from 265 BC) is of Mercury at its morning station, an event that was very challenging to observe because it falls close to, or more often within, the interval of the planet's invisibility around inferior conjunction. In contrast to the situation in Babylon, none of the Greek observational programs seem to have had an institutional base that allowed it to run for more than a few decades. Nevertheless, their existence meant that a patchwork body of empirical data began to accumulate that could be used to test and calibrate theories of planetary motion.

The rise of Greek horoscopic astrology was another stimulus to the development of planetary astronomy. The origins of Greek astrology lie in the spread both of the practices and the practitioners of Babylonian astrology from Mesopotamia west into the Mediterranean civilizations during the Hellenistic period. One of the first names frequently associated with the transmission of

Babylonian science to the Greeks is Berossus, a priest of Marduk from Babylon who moved to Kos in the first half of the third century BC and composed a history of Babylon in Greek, known to us (alas!) only from quotations and secondhand reports. Whether Berossus' reputation in later antiquity as an astrologer and writer on astrology was founded in fact has been a topic of intense controversy in modern scholarship.[39] Similar uncertainties adhere to a certain Sudines, a "Chaldean" who, we are told, interpreted omens from the organs of sacrificed animals for King Attalus I of Pergamon in the 230s BC, and whom later writers identified as an astronomer. We are on firmer ground when we come to the second century BC. From an inscription in his honor we know of a "Chaldean *astrologos*" named Antipatros, who made his abode in Larissa in Thessaly and was even granted citizenship by the nearby city of Homolion around the middle of the second century.[40] What is particularly interesting about this Antipatros is that he was not originally from Babylonia but from Hierapolis in Syria, which shows that expertise in Babylonian astronomy and astrology was to be found in more centers in the Near East than we would know about from our cuneiform sources.

"Chaldeans" had even penetrated as far west as Italy by this time, though their reception among the Romans was not wholly friendly: Cato the Elder advised against allowing farm administrators to consult them—or haruspices, augurs, and soothsayers for that matter—and in 139 BC Gnaeus Cornelius Hispanus, the *praetor peregrinus* (magistrate responsible for legal affairs involving foreigners), reportedly issued an edict expelling them from Italy on the pretext that they were making money from foolish people by selling lies about the stars.[41]

Greek astrology took over from the Babylonian tradition the idea that one could make predictions about the life of an individual by interpreting the state of the heavens on and around the date of the individual's birth. But the rationale justifying such predictions was radically different. Babylonian horoscopy developed out of the earlier practice of interpreting astral omens, and the shift to a kind of omen relating to ordinary people instead of king and kingdom did not entail giving up the belief that the observable behavior of the heavenly bodies constituted messages from the gods. In Greek astrology, the heavenly bodies were understood as material (though divine) objects that, in their revolutions around the Earth, *cause* changes in our environment and in ourselves through a transmission of physical agency from the heavens to the world below. In other words, it presumed a cosmology that was loosely of the Plato-Aristotle kind, with a spherical mundane world made up of material bodies behaving in complex ways, enclosed by *and controlled by* a spherical celestial region made up of material bodies behaving in regular and predictable ways.

In a Greek horoscope, the place on Earth where a person is born plays a prominent role. The zodiac, including the invisible half of it below the Earth, is thought of as divided by the horizon and the meridian (i.e., the north–south vertical plane) into regions of varying astrological significance, of which the most important is the one that is currently rising at the eastern horizon, called the *horoskopos* or "hour watcher" (our word "horoscope" comes from this term). How the Sun, Moon, and planets affect a person at his or her birth depends on the inherent natures of each heavenly body, on their locations with respect to the signs of the zodiac and the stars, and on their locations with respect to the horizon and meridian. Thus, the conditions determining the lives and characters of people at their birth are constantly and rapidly changing as the celestial sphere revolves around the Earth. Whereas a Babylonian horoscope was about events and ongoing states of the heavenly bodies around a particular date, a Greek horoscope was a snapshot of an entity that is in continuous motion.

The construction of Greek astrology out of elements coming from ancient Near Eastern divination and from Greek philosophical cosmology and astronomy probably dates to some time in the second century BC, or at the very latest early in the first century BC, and Ptolemaic Egypt is the most likely place where it happened.[42] The authors of later astrological writings ascribed the origins of their knowledge primarily to legendary Egyptian sages of the remote past, including a certain King Nechepsos and Petosiris and occasionally also Hermes (the Egyptian god Thoth) and Imouthes (Imhotep); the "Chaldeans" or Babylonians occupy a decidedly subordinate place in this story of origins. In reality, few concepts in Greek astrology derived from pharaonic Egypt. But as we saw in connection with eclipses, a distinctively Egyptian flavor of the Mesopotamian astral omen tradition had existed since about the fifth century BC, and the horoscopic astrology appears to have emerged from some interaction between Egyptian temple-based scholars and Greek-speaking intellectuals.

The new horoscopy demanded astronomical resources; in particular, methods for determining where all the heavenly bodies were in the zodiac and how the zodiac was positioned in relation to the horizon for arbitrary past dates and times. Greek astrology was not at all observational; astrologers were wholly dependent on almanacs and numerical tables for their astronomical data. When the practice of Babylonian astrology had spread into the Greek world, it must have been accompanied by the more portable parts of Babylonian predictive astronomy—that is, the mathematical methods. Greek astrology took these over, and this explains how we find fragments of astronomical tables on Egyptian papyri of the first through the fourth centuries AD that are in all essentials Babylonian mathematical astronomy, except that they are written in Greek and employ the Egyptian calendar.[43] However, the argument could be made that astrologers should use astronomical data that were obtained by methods consistent with the same cosmology of circular motions in the spherical heavens that provided astrology's conceptual underpinnings. In this way, the huge success that Greek astrology had in displacing the Babylonian traditions would have been a spur to developing increasingly precise and quantitative theories of planetary motion based on combinations of circles.

Epicycles and eccenters

The specific form that these theories took was the epicyclic and eccentric hypotheses, with which we are already acquainted from their application to the varying speed of the Sun and Moon (see chapter 5). Ptolemy's testimony gave us Hipparchus as the earliest known astronomer who studied the Moon's motions in relation to epicycles and eccenters, and it is again from Ptolemy that we have the earliest indication of a mathematical analysis of the planets' motions according to one or the other of these hypothesis types.[44] This takes the form of a sophisticated geometrical theorem that shows how one can determine exactly where a planet must be on its epicycle or eccenter at one of its stations; Ptolemy tells us that he adapted the theorem from a version "by various mathematicians, in particular Apollonius of Perge." Apollonius is very well known to us as one of the most important Greek mathematicians of the Hellenistic period, ranking with Euclid and Archimedes, and his career fell somewhere within the late third and the first half of the second centuries BC, so we are now speaking of developments dating to, at a minimum, a generation before Hipparchus.

It is not clear from Ptolemy whether Apollonius was working with epicycles or eccenters, but he does say that in its original form Apollonius' theorem was applied on the assumption that all synodic cycles of a planet were identical. In other words, Apollonius' hypothesis consisted of just two uniform circular motions, a primary one centered on the Earth and a secondary one of the planet around the point that is revolving around the Earth, just as in Hipparchus' two hypotheses for the Moon. The rates of the two circular motions would be directly obtained from whatever recurrence period was assumed for the planet's synodic cycles. The other important quantity determining the hypothesis's behavior is the ratio between the radii of the two circular motions.

Apollonius' theorem showed that if one had values for these three parameters, one could calculate the lengths of the time intervals between a planet's conjunctions, stations, and (in the case of outer planets) oppositions to the Sun. For the inner planets there was also a straightforward geometrical way to calculate the dates of the greatest elongations. Dates of first and last appearance and acronychal risings, on the other hand, cannot be determined from just the hypothesis and its parameters, since optical factors come into play. Hence, in describing a planet's synodic cycle with reference to an epicyclic or eccentric hypothesis, one would naturally pay primary attention to a different set of synodic phenomena from the ones that were important in Babylonian astronomy.

Unlike Eudoxus' hypotheses, which were composed only of concentric spherical motions, epicyclic and eccentric hypotheses can provide very satisfactory first approximations of the actual paths of the planets if one treats the Earth as the fixed point of reference for the planetary system. Consider first an inner planet such as Venus, and again let us imagine the orbits of Venus and the Earth as perfect circles centered on the Sun (fig. 7.8a). If we replace the Sun with the Earth as the fixed point of the system of relative motions, the Sun now appears to orbit the Earth while Venus orbits the Sun (fig. 7.8b), and the radius of Venus's orbit has the same ratio to that of the Sun's orbit in this geocentric system as it had to the Earth's orbit in the heliocentric system. Since a naked-eye observer can determine only directions to heavenly bodies, not distances, we can separate Venus's motion from the Sun's by scaling down the absolute sizes of the two circles involved in Venus's motion so that they are entirely inside the Sun's orbit, resulting in a simple epicyclic hypothesis (fig. 7.8c). This shows the special requirements of an epicyclic hypothesis for an inner planet: the center of the epicycle has to revolve around the Earth at the same rate as and in line with the Sun, and the planet has to revolve on its epicycle in the same sense (counterclockwise as seen from the north).

In fig. 7.9a–c, we see the same transformations applied to an outer planet, Mars. Since Mars's orbit is larger than the Earth's, instead of an epicycle we now get an eccenter whose center revolves around the Earth in line with the Sun. We can make a further transformation, using the principle of equivalence of epicyclic and eccentric hypotheses that we previously encountered when looking at Hipparchus' investigations of the Moon, that the two circular motions can exchange places without affecting the path that the planet travels. This gives us an epicyclic hypothesis (fig. 7.9d), but with different requirements: the center of the epicycle has to revolve around the Earth with the period of the planet's mean revolution around the zodiac, and the planet has to revolve on its epicycle in the same sense and in such a way that the line from the center of the epicycle to the planet is always parallel to the direction from the Earth to the Sun.

Since the simple epicyclic and eccentric hypotheses are exact translations of our simplified solar system into a geocentric frame of reference, they cannot reproduce any effects that arise from the fact that the real orbits of the planets around the Sun are off-center and elliptical. A remarkable passage in Book 9 of Ptolemy's *Almagest* shows us that Greek astronomers had not gotten further than the simple hypotheses by the second half of the second century BC.[45]

In this passage, Ptolemy explains that satisfactory hypotheses for the motions of the planets are very difficult to deduce, partly because of the inherently complex character of their motions, since two different periodic variations are entangled in them, and partly because it was only comparatively recently that large numbers of observations of the right kind began to be recorded. So, he continues, it is not surprising that Hipparchus, great theorist though he was, produced (so far as Ptolemy knew) no planetary hypotheses of his own; the only book by him on the subject was a demonstration that the hypotheses for the planets that had been proposed up to his time were not correct. Specifically, they presumed that all the synodic cycles of a planet were identical, so that, for example, every interval of retrogradation took the same time and covered the

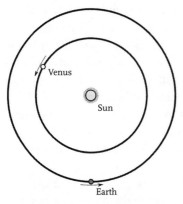

a. Orbits of Venus and Earth in heliocentric frame of reference.

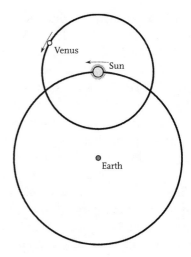

b. Orbits of Venus and Sun in geocentric frame of reference.

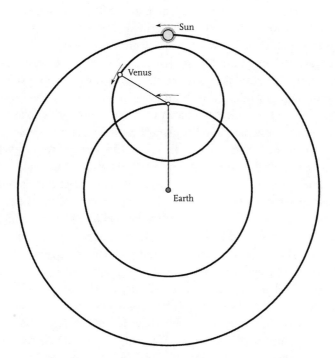

c. Epicycle model for Venus.

FIG. 7.8. Transforming Venus's orbit from a heliocentric perspective to an epicyclic hypothesis.

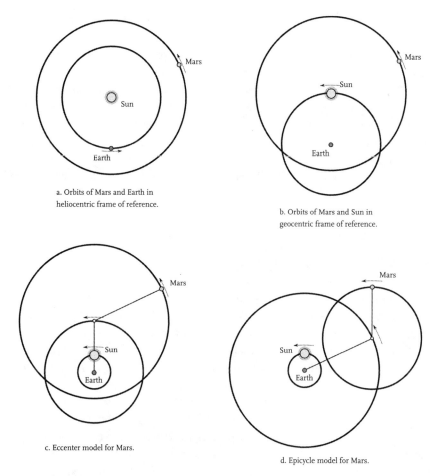

a. Orbits of Mars and Earth in
heliocentric frame of reference.

b. Orbits of Mars and Sun in
geocentric frame of reference.

c. Eccenter model for Mars.

d. Epicycle model for Mars.

FIG. 7.9. Transforming Mars's orbit from a heliocentric perspective to an epicyclic hypothesis.

same number of degrees of the ecliptic as every other, whereas, as Hipparchus showed from observations, they are in reality variable.

If Ptolemy's terse report is accurate, Greek astronomers before Hipparchus were not aware of the so-called zodiacal anomaly, the variation in planets' synodic cycles that depends on the planet's location in the zodiac. This suggests that the Babylonian mathematical methods of predicting planetary phenomena were not yet well known in the Greek world, since according to those methods the intervals of time and motion between synodic phenomena are very obviously variable. The Babylonian algorithms were based on arithmetical sequences fitted to empirically recognized patterns of dates and positions, and could not have readily been "translated" into hypotheses built up out of circular motions. Ptolemy tells us that some people after Hipparchus—he does not offer any names—attempted to build geometrical planetary theories that accounted for the zodiacal anomaly; for example, by introducing an eccentricity into an epicyclic hypothesis. But the pace of these developments is unknown; the three centuries of astronomical research between Hipparchus and Ptolemy are an almost complete blank for us. The hypotheses presented in the *Almagest*, which were as far as we know the culmination of ancient Greek planetary theory, essentially solve the problems of planetary motion, so far as it was then understood, through an economical combination of epicycles, eccenters, and a subtle redefinition of uniform circular motion that gave a close approximation of Kepler's second law of planetary motion: that the revolving radius from the Sun to any planet sweeps out equal areas in equal times.[46]

The Mechanism's planetary theory

We have rather good knowledge about the assumptions relating to the Sun and Moon around which the Antikythera Mechanism was designed, through an interplay between the physical evidence of the surviving gears and other mechanical features and the textual evidence of the dial scales and the other inscribed texts. When it comes to the planets, physical features contribute to the argument that a planetary display once existed, but these features tell us little about the astronomical underpinnings of that display. Fortunately, the Mechanism came accompanied by texts that were manifestly intended to help the viewer understand the meaning of what he or she observed on its dials. We have already seen how the BCI describes the static look of the front dial with its miniature planetary cosmology. Now we must turn to the front cover inscription (FCI), which brings in the temporal dimension.[47]

The FCI was inscribed on a metal plate, possibly serving as a protective cover, that lay in front of the Mechanism's front face while it was under the sea, so that a large piece of it was stuck on the front of Fragment C when it was first discovered in 1902. As part of the first round of conservation of the fragments in 1905, the layer of accreted matter covering this "front cover" plate as well as the remains of the plate itself were separated from Fragment C bit by bit. Most of the plate was eventually reassembled as the current Fragment G, and in addition we have two detached bits of the plate and many bits of the accretion layer, which preserve mirror-image impressions of the lettering. The words referring to stations and retrogradations that Rehm and Price discovered were on some of these fragments. But for the most part, the remains of the FCI are much more corroded than the other inscriptions of the Mechanism, and the recovery of its text—with frustrating gaps—has been especially challenging.

What has emerged is a description of the planets' synodic cycles, the most technically detailed document relating to Greek planetary theory that we have from the entire interval between Eudoxus and Ptolemy. It is likely that the complete inscription also discussed the Sun and Moon, but the 42 incomplete lines of text that survive belong to a series of sections taking up the five planets in turn, in the order Mercury-Venus-Mars-Jupiter-Saturn—the same order as that in which they appear in the BCI, but without the Sun intervening between Venus and Mars. What the inscription says about each planet is obviously meant to describe what a viewer would see happening as the Mechanism was operated, since it would hardly do to lead the spectator to expect things that the Mechanism failed to deliver. Hence, despite the fact that the inscription says nothing directly about the internal construction of the Mechanism, it provides evidence simultaneously for what the designer believed about the motions of the planets and for the mechanical contrivances by which he tried to reproduce these motions on the front dial.

Each section began with the descriptive name of the planet (apparently omitting its theophoric name); a statement of a period relation equating whole numbers of synodic periods, solar years, and revolutions of the planet around the zodiac; and a statement of the approximate length of the synodic period in days. None of the numerals for the lengths of the synodic periods survive complete; in fact, we can read only the first digit (representing 500) of the one for Venus. But this is not a great loss because these figures would have been derived from the period relation and were rounded to the nearest whole number, sometimes prefaced by "a little more than" or "a little less than"; any decent period relation, even a fairly crude one such as one of the Babylonian Goal-Year periods, will give the same number. So we can be confident that the numbers in the inscription were the ones in table 7.7. It is worth remarking that the text presents these periods as if they were constants.

From the period relations, only two numerals are legible: 462 in the section for Venus, and 442 in that for Saturn. Fortunately, these numbers are enough to enable us to identify the complete period relations for these planets:

289 synodic periods of Venus = 462 solar years = 462 zodiacal revolutions
427 synodic periods of Saturn = 442 solar years = 15 zodiacal revolutions

TABLE 7.7. Restored synodic periods of the FCI.

Planet	Accurate value	Value as given in the inscription
Mercury	115.88 days	a little less than? 116 days
Venus	583.92 days	584 days
Mars	779.94 days	a little less than 780 days
Jupiter	398.88 days	a little less than 399 days
Saturn	378.09 days	a little more than? 378 days

These relations, which have never been found previously in an ancient text, are very accurate, comparable in quality to the Babylonian ACT periods or the periodicities that Ptolemy used in the *Almagest*. Where did they come from? In the case of the Venus relation, a conceivable explanation is that the Mechanism's designer knew the Babylonian ACT period relation, but because the ACT relation cannot be exactly represented by gearwork, he found a different relation that was almost equivalent but was mechanically feasible. Obviously this presumes that the ACT period relations were known to Greek scientists by the early first century BC; we have no other evidence that they were, though it is possible. However, the Saturn relation cannot be accounted for in this way, because the ACT relation for Saturn is already suited for representation through gearwork. So the inscription attests to independent Greek research on refining the planetary periodicities that we would otherwise know nothing about. Building period relations of this kind of accuracy into the Mechanism meant that its representations of planets' cycles of motion would have kept in correct alignment over a span of several centuries, whatever short-term inaccuracies there may have been.

The rest of each section of the FCI consists of a description of the planet's synodic cycle. Specific durations in days are stated for the intervals between synodic phenomena—again, these are treated as constants—along with the direction that the planet travels in each interval and, for an inner planet, whether it is approaching or receding from the Sun. The phenomena listed for the inner planets include the conjunctions, greatest elongations, and stations; those for the outer planets include the conjunction, stations, and oppositions. First and last appearances are not mentioned anywhere in the surviving text. All in all, the treatment of the synodic cycles is quite different from what we find in Babylonian astronomy, and it is strongly suggestive of simple epicyclic or eccentric hypotheses.

Several of the numerals giving the numbers of days between synodic phenomena are legible, and they agree very well with the intervals one would derive from epicyclic or eccentric hypotheses, assuming an astronomically appropriate ratio of radii for the constituent circular motions. For Venus, the inscription gives 224 days for the intervals between the superior conjunction and the greatest elongations, and 68 days for the remaining intervals between the greatest elongations and the inferior conjunction; computation using an accurate ratio from modern theory yields 221 days and 71 days, respectively (cf. p. 167). For Mars, the inscription's 349 days between conjunction and the stations and 82 days for the retrogradation between the stations agrees well with the accurate values, 354 and 72 days (cf. p. 168). For Jupiter, the inscription's 139 days between conjunction and the stations agrees to the day with accurate computation. The inscription breaks the interval of Jupiter's retrogradation up into three parts: 8 days effectively stationary, 104 days of retrograde motion, and 8 days effectively stationary, for a total of 120 days, which is again approximately correct. (Because of neglect of fractions of days, adding all of Jupiter's intervals together gives a synodic period of just 398 days instead of the correct 399.) The numbers look too good to have been obtained just by watching the Mechanism in action; they were probably calculated mathematically from the assumed hypotheses.

All the indications, then, are that the planetary mechanism was an embodiment of a system of simple epicyclic or eccentric hypotheses, on the basis of very accurate period relations and good values for the ratios of the circular motions. It was a Greek geometrically based theory, only remotely dependent on Babylonian astronomy. Was it state-of-the-art astronomy for the early first century BC? In one important respect, it was not: it did not take account of zodiacal anomaly and thus had the defect that Hipparchus had exposed several decades earlier. In our current state of knowledge, we cannot say whether this was because more successful planetary hypotheses had not yet been devised, or because the designer was not conversant with new developments, or because implementing them mechanically would have been beyond his resources.

In one of his last works, the *Planetary Hypotheses*, Ptolemy castigated the "usual way" of making astronomical mechanisms for two faults: they did not get the theoretical hypotheses right, and they showed the appearances instead of the reality. From his point of view, the Antikythera Mechanism had both faults, since the planetary hypotheses on which it was based were too simple, and the front dial attempted to display only the directions of the planets from the Earth and their relative distances.[48] Ptolemy's remark that a mechanism such as this constitutes an exhibition of technical skill rather than astronomical truth seems rather uncharitable, since he offers no practical guidance with respect to how one could construct a device to his liking. It would hardly have been possible to show all the heavenly bodies simultaneously traveling on their epicycles and eccenters in a unified cosmology. The Mechanism's designer could not even have preserved the relative scales of the hypotheses by making the distances of their markers from the center of the dial reflect the mean distances of the heavenly bodies from the Earth, because the principle of nesting epicyclic or eccentric hypotheses one inside another results in a quasi-exponential growth from the inner to the outer "spheres" of a complete planetary system—Saturn would have to be about 75 times as far from the center as Mercury! With respect to the planets, the Antikythera Mechanism was approaching the limit to which ancient technology could keep up with contemporaneous astronomy in a single device.

8

Hidden Workings

Secrets in the box

The earliest allusion to something resembling a geared device in ancient literature appears in a book titled *Mechanics* (or *Mechanical Problems*) that has come down to us under Aristotle's name, though it is now widely believed to be a composition by an unknown philosopher of the late fourth or early third century BC. The author would have it that circles and circular motion are the foundations of practically all mechanical devices, including balances and levers, and one fact about circular motion that he sees as particularly important is that there are motions in opposite directions at the two ends of any of the circle's diameters, a principle that he says has been exploited by inventors:[1]

> Some people arrange it so that out of one motion many circles move simultaneously in opposite senses, like the little bronze and iron wheels that they make and set up in temples. For if there is some other circle *CD* in contact with circle *AB*, and the diameter of circle *AB* moves in the forward sense, diameter *CD* will move in the opposite sense to circle *AB*, so long as this diameter moves around the same point. Hence, circle *CD* will move in the opposite sense to circle *AB*. And again this circle will move the next one, *EF*, in the opposite sense to itself for the same reason. In the same way, even if there are many circles, they will do this though only one circle is set in motion. So the craftsmen, taking this nature that resides in the circle, construct an instrument while concealing the principle, so that only the astonishing character of the contrivance is visible, but the cause is not apparent.

As it is transmitted to us, the *Mechanics* is missing its diagrams, but the author had in mind a situation such as is shown in fig. 8.1, with three

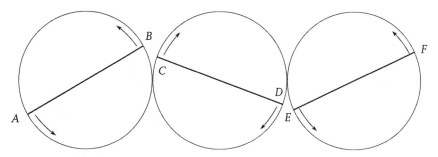

FIG. 8.1. Diagram for the touching wheels in pseudo-Aristotle, *Mechanics* 848a.

wheels mounted on axles and having their circumferences touching each other, so that turning the leftmost wheel, say, counterclockwise will cause the middle wheel to turn clockwise and the rightmost wheel to turn counterclockwise. The ideas that he wants to bring out are the transmission of rotational motion and the alternation of senses of motion. For us, however, his "real world" example is of special interest: devices found in temples that produced an astonishing effect by means of wheel-to-wheel contacts that were hidden from the spectator.

What sort of device is he speaking of? There are references to wheels in temples, especially in Egypt, in a few other authors' works. Most signifi- cantly, the late Hellenistic or early Roman period writer on mechanics, Heron of Alexandria, refers to a wheel called a *hagnisterion* ("sanctifier") that he says could be found in the entrance areas of temples; giving the wheel a spin was supposed to purify the visitor.[2] He describes two ways that such wheels could be connected to a mechanism to produce an astonishing effect: in one, turning the wheel caused sanctifying water to flow out of a pipe in its axle, while the other caused a toy bird (apparently a blackcap) to spin about and sing by means of a mechanism that included two cogged wheels engaging each other at right angles. The devices known to the author of the *Mechanics* were likely much simpler affairs, but the concept was the same: a contrivance that did some- thing unexpected and apparently magical, whose connection with the original impulse provided by the hand was out of sight.

The ancient Greek technical literature on mechanical devices is divided between descriptions of instruments of practical utility (artillery, surveying instruments) and wonder-working devices, which apparently existed in great variety both for entertainment and for more solemn purposes. The wonder- working devices employed hydraulic, pneumatic, and other mechanical ele- ments such as pistons, floats, strings, weights and pulleys, and, occasionally, gearwork, which were invariably hidden inside a casing that could be a simple box or something more decorative, say an urn or an imitation architectural column. The reader of books such as Heron's was initiated into the mysteries of how these things worked, but keeping the broader public mystified was part of the game. Concealing the mechanism meant giving emphasis to the effect rather than to the means by which it was achieved, and it also protected the exclusivity both of the possessor and the makers of an original device from imitators.

The Antikythera Mechanism's two faces constituted two distinct kinds of device from the point of view of what they displayed. The dials of the rear face were abstract spatial representations of time measured off according to various cycles, justifying Derek de Solla Price's expression "calendar computer." Their closest analogs in the ancient mechanical literature are the odometers described by Vitruvius and Heron, which represented traveled distances abstractly by the readings of pointers on dials or by an accumulating heap of pebbles.[3] The Mechanism's front dial, on the other hand, was a visual portrayal of the cosmos in motion. The representation was a hybrid, partly "realist" to the extent that it showed the heavenly bodies revolving around the Earth in what was believed to be their correct order of relative distances, and partly "phenomenological" since it showed the directions in which the heavenly bodies would be seen from the Earth but not their presumed motions in three dimensions. Making allowance for this compromise, the planetarium display was an imitation of nature, and from this point of view it deserves to be grouped with the many ancient wonder-working inventions, such as Heron's singing blackcap, that astounded the spectator by imitating living nature. In seriousness of purpose, of course, there is no comparison—one could hardly teach a lesson in zoology using Heron's twittering birds and hissing dragons!

When ancient authors allude to astronomical mechanisms, they are always described as planetaria.[4] This does not prove that the devices that they had seen, or more often that they had heard or read about, lacked chronological dials; in an object that had both kinds of display, the moving image of the cosmos would have most strongly provoked the imagination. Our present-day curiosity and admiration regarding the Antikythera Mechanism and other ancient mechanical *sphairai* tend to center on the technological aspect: How did these things work? How were they invented? These questions would also have interested ancient craftsmen professionally, but the users of the *sphairai* had other concerns. Someone utilizing a *sphaira* as a kind of astronomical calculator—supposing that this was an envisioned application, which is open to dispute—would care only about the data read off the dials. A teacher of elementary astronomy demonstrating lessons upon it would want the student to focus on the displays as a kind of accelerated simulation of the heavens, not on the gears that effect that simulation. For a philosopher such as Cicero, deriving arguments for a craftsman divinity or for a divine element of ingenuity in the human inventor from the mere existence of *sphairai*, what mattered was the idea of a complexity of coordinated movements driven by a single input motion by the forethought of an intellect, not the means by which it was accomplished. For all these users, it was preferable to keep the box shut, literally or figuratively.

Up to this point, we have approached the Antikythera Mechanism primarily from this ancient users' perspective, concentrating on the displays and their context in Hellenistic science and culture. In this chapter we will open the box and see how the Mechanism's functions were performed through a creative combination of astronomical, mathematical, and mechanical principles.

The arithmetic of rotating gears

Much of the operation of the Antikythera Mechanism depended on two basic ways of connecting two or more wheels or gears: fixing them to the same axle, or "arbor" to use the term used in mechanical clockwork, and placing them side by side in the same plane but on separate arbors so that the revolving periphery of one sets the adjacent periphery of the other in motion through the engagement of their teeth.

When gears are fixed to a common arbor, turning one will obviously cause the others to turn in the same sense and with the same rate of rotation. Gears mounted on a single arbor obviously have the same axis of rotation, but the converse is not necessarily true. In some circumstances it may be desirable to have two or more gears rotating on a single geometrical axis but having distinct rates of motion; for example, to drive pointers representing the motions of different heavenly bodies on a common dial. To effect this, an arbor may take the form of a hollow cylinder or "pipe" through which another arbor passes freely (fig. 8.2). The design of the Mechanism involved several such arrangements of pipes.

Gears engaging each other by their teeth are an extension of the idea in the Aristotelian *Mechanics* of touching wheels. Given a pair of touching wheels, and assuming that no slippage occurs between their surfaces, the speeds with which any points on the two wheels' peripheries are moving, considered in

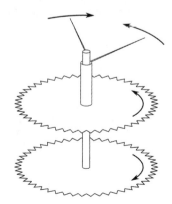

FIG. 8.2. A pipe enables arbors to have a common axis but separate motions.

terms of distance traveled per time unit, will be equal. If the wheels have identical radii, their periods of rotation will be identical (though the rotations are in opposite senses). If the radii are unequal, the periods of rotation will be proportionate to their circumferences; that is, to their radii. For example, a wheel of radius 12 units revolving once in three seconds will cause a touching wheel of radius 8 units to revolve once in two seconds. The radii can be in any ratio one wishes, even an irrational one such as the ratio of the square root of 2 to 1.

In any real situation, however, there will be slippage. Modest slippage might not have mattered if all that one wanted to accomplish was an unexpected motion in a place remote from the sacred wheel that the visitor to a temple was spinning. However, the craftsman making such devices would soon have realized that by giving the wheels rough surfaces, one could reduce the slippage, and this would soon lead to the idea of providing the wheels with spokes or teeth so that slippage is effectively eliminated (fig. 8.3).

A special case of engagement through teeth is where one of the gears is a contrate (or "crown"), whose teeth project at right angles to the plane of the circular disk along its periphery. A contrate's axis of rotation is at right angles to the axis of the conventional gearwheel that it drives or is driven by (fig. 8.4). While almost all the Mechanism's gearwork revolves in planes parallel to the front and rear faces, it also had two contrates: one to introduce the input motion from the side of the Mechanism, and the other to turn the little ball representing the Moon in its cycle of phases on the front dial.

The teeth of the Antikythera Mechanism's gears are triangular, approximating equilateral triangles. Those of the few surviving geared mechanisms from late antiquity (e.g., the Byzantine geared portable sundial in the London Science Museum, fifth or sixth century AD, see p. 241) and the Islamic Middle Ages (e.g., the geared astrolabe of Muhammad b. Abi Bakr in the Oxford Museum of the History of Science, AD 1221/1222) have similar teeth, and diagrams of ancient mechanical texts in medieval manuscripts also represent the teeth of gearwheels as triangular.[5] This is far from an optimal shape, since if engaged gears are too close together then jamming takes place, while too-generous

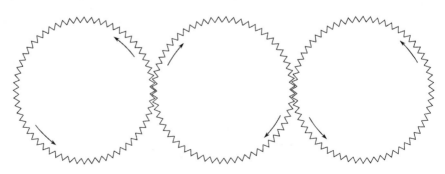

FIG. 8.3. Three gears engaged by their teeth.

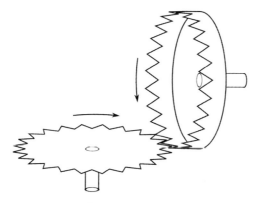

FIG. 8.4. Contrate (crown) engaged with conventional planar gear.

spacing results in jumpy performance and inefficient contact for transmission of motive power.

When toothed gears engage, the ratio of their periods of rotation is no longer determined by their radii but instead equals the ratio of their tooth counts, which is necessarily a ratio of whole numbers. Since the teeth on both gears need to be about the same size for smooth interlocking, this ratio will be close to that of the radii, but with some leeway. Applying gearwork to astronomical problems thus becomes a question of finding combinations of whole-number ratios that, when multiplied together, represent the ratios embedded in astronomical phenomena either exactly or as closely as possible. The numbers also have to result in gears of reasonable size. If a gear has too few teeth it will not engage properly; if it has too many it will be too large relative to the other components and the device as a whole. In the Mechanism the smallest gear had just 12 teeth, while the largest is estimated to have had either 223 or 224.

A succession of gear-to-gear engagements all in a single plane, such as the three touching wheels in the example of the *Mechanics*, will not multiply the ratios, because the contributions of the intermediate gears cancel out. For example, in fig. 8.5 a gear of 60 teeth rotating with a period of 8 seconds turns a gear of 30 teeth so that its period is 4 seconds, and this gear turns a third gear of 90 teeth so that its period is 12 seconds. This is exactly the same period that would be obtained if the first and third gears were directly engaged without the intermediary, except that the sense of rotation of the final gear is reversed. In general, any series of intermediate gears (called "idlers") will have no effect on the ratio of periods between the first and last gears in this kind of train, but if there is an even number of idlers, the first and last gears will turn in opposite senses whereas an odd number of idlers will make the sense of rotation of the last gear the same as the first.

Multiplication is obtained by having a *compound* gear train comprising engagements alternating with transfers of motion through arbors. A simple

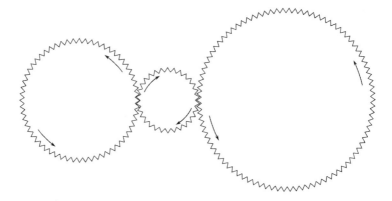

FIG. 8.5. Gear train composed only of engagements by teeth.

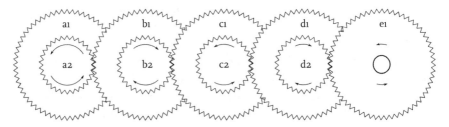

FIG. 8.6. Gear train of the *baroulkos*.

mechanism employing this principle—really a textbook example rather than a device that could have functioned well in the "real world" with ancient materials—is the *baroulkos* ("weight hauler") described in various texts by Heron and Pappus of Alexandria.[6] The basic structure of the *baroulkos* is shown schematically in fig. 8.6. (In this and subsequent discussions, gears on the same axis will be assigned the same letter followed by a distinguishing number.) Each pair of gears (a1 and a2, b1 and b2, and so forth) is mounted on a common arbor so that their periods of rotation are equal. Gear a2 engages with b1, b2 engages with c1, and so forth. Instead of a small gear, the right-most arbor just has a shaft around which winds a rope attached to whatever object one wishes to haul. In this example, all the larger gears have 60 teeth and all the smaller gears have 30 teeth. If gear a1 is set in rotation by an external agent, a2 will turn b1 so its period is double that of a1, and so on along the train until e1 and its hauling shaft rotate with a period 16 times that of a1. The point of the device was not the exponential slowing down of the rates of rotation, however, but the concurrent increase in power: the load attached to the rope can be hauled by exerting a force equivalent to little more than a 16th of its weight, though it will take many turns of a1 to move the load a short distance.

The arrangement in the *baroulkos* is called "gearing down"; that is, motion is transferred from smaller gears to larger gears in each engagement. If the device was operated in reverse, with gear e1 as the driving gear, we would have a situation of "gearing up." A train involving successive gearings up, such as the reversed *baroulkos*, converts a slow input rotation into a faster output rotation. It requires significantly greater effort to set in motion, and the gearwork may be strained or jammed. In an astronomical mechanism, operation will be smoothest if the outputs are designed to be slower, or not much faster, than the input rotary motion.

The idea of using gearwork as a way of doing analog computations is present, in a very simple way, in the odometers described by Vitruvius and Heron. The most straightforward version is Heron's land odometer. Instead of engagements of geared wheels in a single plane, Heron employs engagements of a helical screw gear ("worm") with a toothed wheel (fig. 8.7). Rotating a worm once causes the engaged gear to turn the interval corresponding to one tooth, so each engagement multiplies the period of rotation by the tooth count, making possible a more extreme gearing down than with pairs of toothed wheels. In the odometer, the arbor of each toothed wheel also bears a worm, which engages with the next toothed wheel, and so forth. Each arbor also projects outside the box containing the mechanism, so that an attached pointer can indicate its revolutions on a dial graduated with the same number of divisions as the toothed wheel has teeth. Since each engagement involves a 90° turn in the orientation of the rotations, the dials have to be on different faces of the box. Supposing there were three dials with gears having a tooth count of 60, the last dial would measure the distance traveled in units equivalent to 3600 rotations of the input worm up to a maximum of 216,000; the middle dial, in units of 60 up to 3600; and the first dial, in units of single rotations up to 60.

Heron's worm-and-gear engagements are suited to a device intended to count extremely large numbers of input rotations. The same displays could,

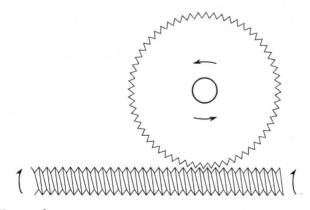

FIG. 8.7. Worm-and-gear engagement.

in principle, be driven by a *baroulkos* type of compound gear mechanism, but each stage of gearing down by a factor of 60 in our example would have to be accomplished through two or three gear pairings, say with 1:3, 1:4, and 1:5 ratios of tooth counts. In the Antikythera Mechanism, the maximum gearing down from the input rotation was by a factor of only a little more than 350, and it employed no worms.

Uniform motions in the Mechanism

The arbors of most of the Mechanism's gears were mounted on a metal plate, called the "base plate," situated between the front and rear faces and parallel to them. There were, apparently, 14 axes connected to the base plate, which in the established reconstruction are designated by the letters *b* through *i* and *l* through *q*.[7] Most were simple arbors, but axis *e* had a pipe arbor enclosing a second arbor, while axis *b*, though represented by a simple arbor where it is mounted on the base plate, had several nested pipes farther toward the front face. Axis *b* was the center of the zodiac dial, and the various arbors on it represented the geocentric apparent motions of the Sun, Moon, and planets.

An impression of the complexity of the gearwork can be obtained from fig. 8.8, which shows the reconstructed gearwork for the solar, lunar, and calendrical functions of the Mechanism, and figs. 8.9, 8.10, and 8.17, which show the gears surviving—in some cases just as fragments—in front of and behind the base plate in Fragment A, projected into a single plane. For consistency, all these diagrams show the arrangement as if seen from the rear. Shades of gray indicate the distinct levels of gears, with fainter shades for gears closer to the base plate. These diagrams are, however, not especially helpful for understanding what the gears are doing. In the following, I will explain the individual trains using schematic diagrams that represent the connections among the gears but not their spatial relationships.

With respect to a large part of its functionings, including all the time-cycle displays on its back face, the Mechanism was essentially a more elaborate cousin of an odometer or *baroulkos*. What distinguishes it from those devices was, first, the use of branching gear trains leading from the single input to multiple outputs—the several dials on Heron's odometer, by contrast, are just stages along a single train—and the requirement that each output has to conform to exact whole-number ratios to the other outputs that are determined by their astronomical or chronological meaning.

To get some sense of what this involved for the designer, let us imagine what might have gone into the design of a simplified version having the same set of back dials as the Antikythera Mechanism but, on the front, just pointers showing the mean motions of the Sun and Moon, with no mechanical representation of their anomalies. All the astronomical theory required for these

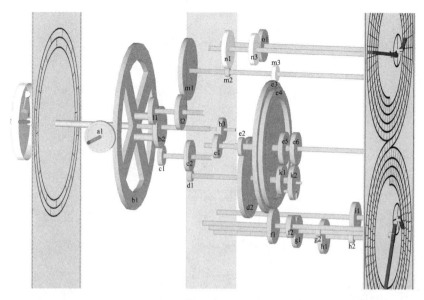

FIG. 8.8. Exploded view of the gearwork driving the solar, lunar, and calendrical outputs of the Mechanism. The base plate is represented by the transparent rectangle in the middle. Gears shown in dark gray are at least partly extant, while those in pale gray are restored completions of the trains; the conjectured Callippic dial and the four conjectural gears that would have driven it are omitted. (image by and copyright of M. G. Edmunds)

functions is contained in the following two period relations, which come from the Metonic 19-year cycle and the Saros eclipse cycle:

19 solar years = 235 lunar months = 254 lunar revolutions of the zodiac
223 lunar months = 1 Saros = ⅓ Exeligmos = 239 anomalistic months

We can also assume that a fundamental design decision was made early on: that the primary driving rotation in the Mechanism would be a gear—or gears fixed to a common arbor—representing the Sun's annual revolution around the zodiac. In the Mechanism, this is performed by a gear designated b_1. This is the large gear shaped as a ring with two perpendicular spokes that is so conspicuous on Fragment A-1 (see fig. M1). It was driven by a smaller contrate gear transmitting the input motion from the knob or crank on the Mechanism's side (see figs. 3.5 and 3.6).

Taking a single complete rotation of b_1 in the clockwise sense as seen from the Mechanism's front as a solar year, the problem was to devise gear trains leading off from b_1's arbor that would convert solar years into the time units of the assorted dials. The sense of rotation of the pointers was a further constraint: the lunar pointer on the front face had to revolve clockwise, like the

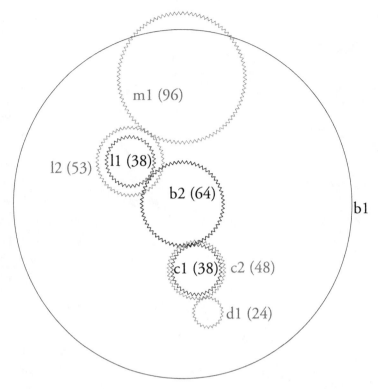

FIG. 8.9. Gears of Fragment A in front of the base plate, as if seen from the rear. Gears closer to the base plate are in lighter shades of gray.

solar pointer, and the designer evidently had a strong preference for clockwise rotation on the rear dials. This meant that a train leading to a pointer on the front face had to have an even number of engagements, whereas clockwise rotation of a rear face pointer needed an odd number of engagements.

We may now turn to the specific requirements for each display, and their implementation.

Mean-sun pointer on the zodiac dial. This is trivial: the pointer is fixed to b_1's arbor.

Mean-moon pointer on the zodiac dial. The pointer has to revolve 254 times clockwise around the dial in the same time as b_1 rotates 19 times; hence the desired ratio of periods is 19:254. A gear with 254 teeth would probably have been considered undesirably large (b_1, the largest gear, had either 223 or 224 teeth). The prime factors of 254 are 2 and 127, so a gear with 127 teeth was unavoidable as the driving gear in an engaged pair. A gear with 19 or a small multiple of 19 will be necessary as a driven gear; since 19 is an uncomfortably small number of teeth for a gear, we can tentatively choose 38 as the smallest viable multiple. If we just had a gear pair with tooth counts 38 and 127, the

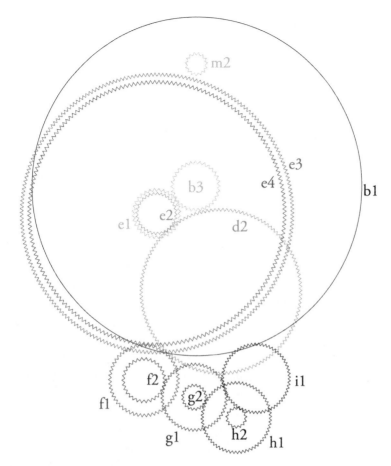

FIG. 8.10. Gears of Fragment A behind the base plate, as seen from the rear. This diagram omits e5, e6, k1, and k2, for which see fig. 8.16. Gears closer to the base plate are in lighter shades of gray.

resulting ratio would be four times what we want, so additional gears must be provided that collectively amount to a ratio of 1:4. The choice of specific tooth counts for these additional gears is arbitrary.

The solution that the designer adopted, minus the additional components producing the lunar anomaly (which come between gears e2 and e1), is illustrated schematically in fig. 8.11. In this and subsequent gear train diagrams, vertical strokes indicate gears fixed to a common arbor, and the driving gear is at the top left. Gear b2 is fixed to the same arbor as b1 (not shown), while b3's arbor would drive the mean-moon pointer in our simplified mechanism. The final pair of engaged 32-tooth gears is required so that the Moon's pointer revolves clockwise. It is worth remarking that this scheme involves considerable gearing up, necessarily so since the Moon's mean rate of motion is more

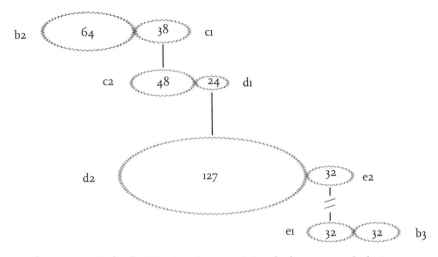

FIG. 8.11. Gear train for the Moon's pointer, omitting the lunar anomaly device between e2 and e1.

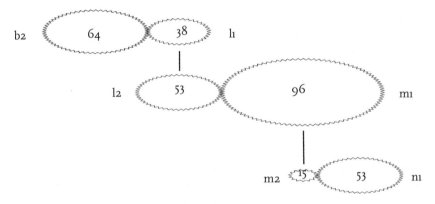

FIG. 8.12. Gear train for the Metonic dial's pointer.

than 13 times that of the Sun, and that a scheme with fewer gears could be devised, for example using just two gear pairs with tooth counts of 96 and 38 or of 127 and 24. The strain would have been mitigated to some extent by the gearing down from the input contrate to b1, which effectively prevented the operator from running the Mechanism very fast.

Metonic dial. The Metonic dial deliberately divides the 19-year cycle into 5 subcycles of 47 months so that the same pattern of full and hollow months can occur in each subcycle. So the pointer has to revolve, preferably clockwise as seen from the Mechanism's rear (since the designer evidently liked to have the pointers revolve in that sense) once for every 19/5 times that b1 rotates. This is an easy ratio to obtain. A single gear pair with tooth counts of 95 and 25 would do it. The designer used three pairs, as illustrated in fig. 8.12. The train begins with the same gear b2 as that of the Moon's pointer, and the gear with which it engages, l1, has the same tooth count (38) as the corresponding gear in the other train, c1, because the factor 19 is again required. The gears l2 and n1 (the latter of which is no longer extant but was conjectured by Michael Wright) cancel out except for reversing the sense of rotation, so their tooth counts could have been chosen to be any reasonable number. The apparently curious choice of 53 will explain itself later on.

Games and Callippic dials. The Games dial's pointer, with its period of four solar years, could have been driven directly by the annual rotation of b2's arbor, but since the dial is inside the Metonic dial, the designer chose a simple two-gear train branching off the Metonic dial pointer's arbor (fig. 8.13, as conjecturally restored by Tony Freeth, to link to o1, which is extant on Fragment B-1), even though this results in the only counterclockwise revolution displayed on the rear face. Two gear pairs having rather extreme ratios branch off the same arbor to yield the slow Callippic dial's revolution (fig. 8.13, with n2, p1, p2, and q1, as restored by Wright).

Saros dial. The Saros dial divides the 223-month Saros cycle into four sub-cycles, apparently to highlight a periodicity of lunar anomaly latent in the Saros. The pointer thus has to revolve clockwise (as seen from the rear) with a period equal to 223/4 lunar months; that is, $(223/4)\times(19/235)$ solar years, combining the two period relations. In this ratio, 223 is a prime number, so there is no way to avoid having a rather large gear with 223 teeth. The correct period and sense could have been obtained by a train of three gear pairs with ratios such as 38:64, 64:40, and 223:47. Since this train employs the same initial pair as in both the mean-moon and Metonic trains, it might have been possible for the rest of the train to branch off from the arbor of either l1 or c1.

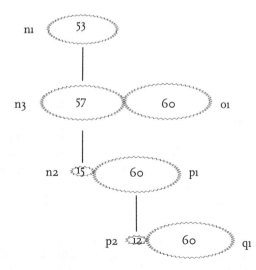

FIG. 8.13. Gear train for the pointers of the Games and Callippic dials.

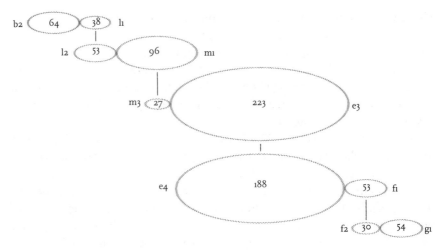

FIG. 8.14. Gear train for the Saros dial's pointer.

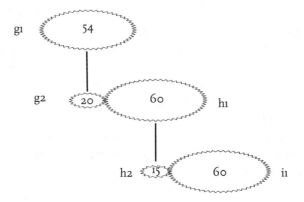

FIG. 8.15. Gear train for the Exeligmos dial's pointer.

The designer chose a more complicated solution (fig. 8.14), which branches off from the arbor of m1 and involves a total of five pairs (Freeth conjectured the linking gear m3). We note again that the two 53-toothed gears l2 and f1 cancel out, and as was the case for the Metonic dial train, another tooth count could have served equally well. But there is a purpose behind this seemingly inefficient train and the 53-toothed gears. The period of rotation that it yields for the 223-toothed gear is $(19\times223)/(9\times53)$ solar years. Assuming an eccentric hypothesis to explain the Moon's anomaly, this is precisely the period of revolution of the eccenter's apogee around the zodiac that is implied by the equations of 235 lunar months with 19 solar years and of 223 lunar months with 269 anomalistic months. As we will see, the 223-toothed gear plays a crucial role in converting the Moon's mean motion into its nonuniform motion. If we modify our original design requirements so that they include not only the outputs of the back dials and uniformly revolving Sun and Moon pointers on the front dial but also a large gear that turns with the period of revolution of the Moon's apogee, the system of trains of the Mechanism proves to be a tour de force of mathematically guided design, though it was risky because the additional load could have been too much for smooth operation.

Exeligmos dial. The period of the Exeligmos dial's pointer is just 1/12th that of the Saros dial. This gearing-down is accomplished easily by two gear pairs driven by the arbor of the Saros dial's output (fig. 8.15).

Differential gearing

Two rates of rotation in a geared mechanism can be added together, or one can be subtracted from the other, by an apparatus called "differential gearing," but this resource does not appear in the surviving ancient mechanical literature. Price believed that he had discovered a differential apparatus in a system of gears mounted on the conjoined gears e3-e4.[8] According to his reconstruction, the apparatus had as its two inputs the rotations representing the Sun's and the Moon's mean motions through the zodiac, and its output was their difference; namely, the Moon's motion relative to the Sun, which measures the current stage of the lunar month. Subsequently, however, Wright showed that Price's reconstruction was mistaken.[9]

There *was*, however, a differential apparatus in the Mechanism, and its function was indeed to subtract the Sun's motion from the Moon's. By a further twist of fortune, it was Wright who first identified it.[10] This device is the means by which the ball displaying the Moon's phases on the front face, discussed in chapter 5, was made to rotate. As we saw in chapter 5, there are two standing proposals for reconstructing the phase display: Wright's economical one, which, however, requires one to assume that a key component (the contrate) is the wrong way around in its current position in Fragment C, and Christián Carman's more complex gearwork, which aims to account for the remains as they are. For simplicity, we will follow Wright's version here.

The moon ball was mounted in a circular window near the periphery of a circular disk that was situated at the center of the Zodiac dial and rotated clockwise at the rate of the Moon's motion around the zodiac (fig. 8.16). An arbor connected the ball to a contrate that, as Wright has it, faced the center of the disk so that it engaged with a gear bo that was fixed to the arbor representing the Sun's clockwise motion through the zodiac.

The easiest way to understand this apparatus is to visualize it in the frame of reference of the disk, so to speak from the point of view of an insect standing on the revolving disk's surface. In this frame of reference, bo rotates *counterclockwise* at a rate that is the difference between the lunar and solar motions. Since the contrate has the same tooth count as bo, it too rotates at this

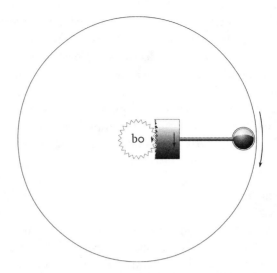

FIG. 8.16. The lunar differential gearwork for the lunar phase display as reconstructed by Wright, with directions of rotation shown in the stationary frame of reference of the Mechanism as a whole.

differential rate, clockwise as seen from the center of the disk, so that the moon ball rotates appropriately with the lunar month as its period while it revolves around the zodiac.

Mechanizing nonuniform motion

The surviving ancient literature on mechanical technology offers no example of a device that employed gearwork to generate a nonuniform revolving output motion driven by an ostensibly uniformly revolving input. When Wright undertook to reconstruct a conjectural planetarium mechanism, he drew on his knowledge of European clockwork mechanisms of the late Middle Ages and after, in which one finds practical solutions to the same problem.[11]

In chapter 7 we saw that one way Hellenistic astronomers accounted for the apparent direct and retrograde motions of the planets was by an epicyclic hypothesis. This can be represented mechanically by having a gear standing in place of the epicycle (*e* in fig. 8.17), with its arbor mounted on a gear or platform (*d*) that revolves around the central axis of the Zodiac dial at the same rate that the epicycle's center theoretically revolves around the Earth. The epicyclic gear must itself be made to revolve at the appropriate rate too, and a pin fixed off center on the epicyclic gear stands for the planet revolving around the epicycle. Finally, a slotted arm is mounted freely on the central axis so that the pin rides

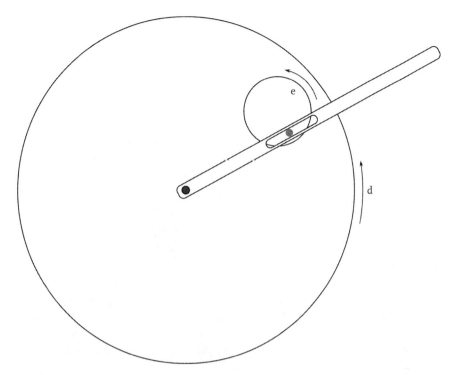

FIG. 8.17. Representation of an epicyclic hypothesis by epicyclic gearing and a slotted arm.

along the slot; the arm thus always points in the direction of the planet, and a pointer attached to it indicates the planet's position in the zodiac.

A slotted-arm implementation of an epicyclic hypothesis would have been easy to implement for Mercury and Venus.[12] The centers of their epicycles revolve around the Earth at the same rate as the mean sun, so the large gear b_1 can serve as the platform carrying the epicyclic gears. Suppose that the assumed period relation for the planet can be expressed as:

Π synodic periods = Y solar years

where Π and Y are whole numbers small enough so that either they themselves or multiples of them could be practicable tooth counts of gears. Then there is a simple way to make the epicyclic gear turn at the appropriate rate. A gear with Π teeth (or $k\Pi$ teeth where k is some whole number) is mounted in fixed position to the central axis, and an epicyclic gear having Y (or kY) teeth engages with it while being carried around by b_1. Freeth has proposed such simple two-gear mechanisms for Mercury and Venus, assuming rather short period relations that are not particularly accurate in the long term.[13]

However, we now know from the front cover inscription (FCI; see chapter 7) that the assumed period relation for Venus was:

289 synodic periods of Venus = 462 solar years

and it is plausible that a period relation of comparable time scale was attributed to Mercury. To implement such relations with gears would have required a gear train with an odd number of intermediate engagements between the fixed gear on the central axis and the epicyclic gear. For example, an engaged pair of gears with tooth counts in the ratio 51:66, with the second of these gears sharing its axle with the first gear of an engaged pair with the ratio 51:63, would produce the desired rate of rotation for Venus's epicycle but turning in the wrong direction; this could be fixed by inserting an idler in the compound train (fig. 8.18). Wright's conjectural reconstructions of all the planetary mechanisms involve compound gear trains to obtain long, high-accuracy period relations.[14]

Slotted-arm mechanisms to represent epicyclic hypotheses for Mars, Jupiter, and Saturn could not use gear b1 as the platform for their epicyclic gears, because the periods of zodiacal revolution of their epicycles are longer than the solar year. Wright therefore provided each of these planets with a separate platform revolving around the central axis at the appropriate rate, carrying a gear train leading to an epicyclic gear.[15]

While there is no direct physical evidence that slotted arms were used to obtain nonuniform motion in the Mechanism, a different but related device for

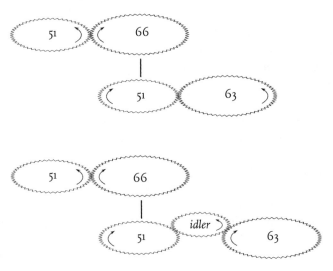

FIG. 8.18. *Top*, a compound gear train yielding the 289:462 input-to-output ratio appropriate for simulating Venus's epicycle, but with the wrong sense of rotation. *Bottom*, inserting an idler gear reverses the ouput direction without changing the rate of rotation.

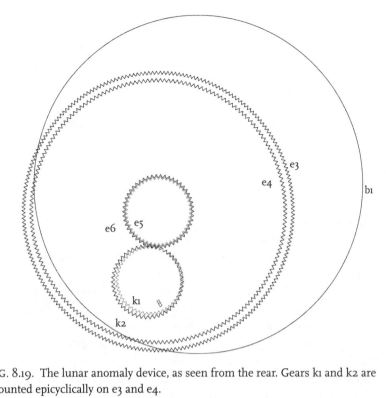

FIG. 8.19. The lunar anomaly device, as seen from the rear. Gears k1 and k2 are
mounted epicyclically on e3 and e4.

the same purpose survives in the gearwork for the motion of the Moon. This
device is a pin-and-slot engagement of gears on slightly displaced axes.

The large pair of gears e3 and e4 (fig. 8.19) are actually a single component
having a ring of 188 teeth (e4) inset like a circular ridge on one face of a 223-
toothed gear (e3). This component carries a system of epicyclic gears whose
physical interrelationship was worked out partly by Wright in 2005 and partly
by the Antikythera Mechanism Research Project (AMRP) team in the following
year.[16] As we saw above, the train leading from b1 to the Moon's pointer on the
Zodiac dial causes e2 to revolve with the period of the Moon's mean zodiacal
revolution. If this gear was on the same arbor as e1, the Moon's pointer would
revolve with uniform speed. However, the connection between e2 and e1 is not
so direct.

The arbor of e2 passes through the center of the double gear e3-e4 and
also carries a 50-toothed gear e5 adjacent to the other face of e3-e4. This gear
engages with k1, another 50-toothed gear mounted epicyclically on e3. Gear k1
has a pin near its circumference that passes through a radial slot in k2, which
is still another 50-toothed gear that is also epicyclically mounted on e3 but with
its center slightly displaced from that of k1. (The slot, now broken at its exterior end, is the tiny notch that Periklis Rediadis observed in 1903; see p. 21.)

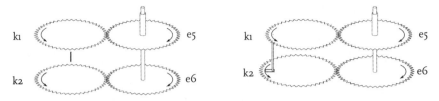

FIG. 8.20. Conventional coupling by arbor (*left*) and pin-and-slot coupling (*right*).

Finally, k2 engages with e6, a fourth 50-toothed gear whose arbor runs back up through the center of e3-e4 and also bears e1.

The effect of this apparatus becomes clearer if we start by considering an imaginary simpler version, in which e3-e4 has no motion of its own so that it is just a stationary platform for gears k1 and k2, while k1 and k2 share the same arbor (fig. 8.20, *left*). This arrangement of gears would simply transfer the motion of e2 (via e5 with a pipe arbor) to e1 (via e6 with an arbor enclosed in the pipe) exactly as if they were on the same arbor. Gear e5 would turn k1 at the same rate but in the opposite sense, k1 would turn k2 at the same rate and in the same sense (i.e., opposite to that of e5), and finally k2 would turn e6 at the same rate but in the opposite sense (i.e., back in the same sense as e5). Obviously this would serve no purpose at all.

But k1 and k2 are actually on slightly different axes, and k1 drives k2 by means of the pin-and-slot coupling (fig. 8.20, *right*). The effect of this is that, while k2 turns exactly once in every turn of k1, the rate of k2's revolution is non-uniform, slower when the pin is near the outer end of its slot, and faster when it is near the inner end. Thus, an anomaly is introduced into the Moon's rate of motion. If we still imagine the platform e3-e4 to be standing still, the Moon's pointer will always move most slowly in a particular part of the zodiac, and fast-est in the diametrically opposite part; that is, the pointer would behave as if the apogee of the Moon's orbit around the Earth has a fixed position.

However, when we were examining the train leading to the Saros dial, we saw that the designer had contrived it so that e3-e4 rotates slowly with the zodiacal period of the Moon's apogee. It actually rotates in the wrong sense for the apogee relative to b1; but e5, whose motion is modified by the epicyclic apparatus, is also rotating in the wrong sense for the Moon's zodiacal motion, so the two reversals cancel out. Thus, the complete arrangement results in a lunar anomaly having the astronomically correct period as implied by the Saros period relation.

If the epicyclic gear plus slotted-arm device physically imitates an epicy-clic hypothesis, the pin-and-slot coupling has a closer relation to an eccentric hypothesis. A uniformly revolving driving gear can be interpreted as the uni-form motion of a heavenly body along its eccentric orbit, with the gear's axis representing the center of the orbit and the pin representing the heavenly body itself. The axis of the second gear with the slot functions as the observer's view-point on Earth, and the direction from this axis toward the slot and its pin represents the nonuniformly changing direction in which the observer sees the body revolve.[17]

According to Ptolemy, Hipparchus estimated that the eccentricity of the Moon's presumed circular orbit was approximately 0.104 times the orbit's radius, on the basis of an analysis of three Babylonian reports of observations of lunar eclipses, though in a separate analysis of a different set of Alexandrian eclipse observation reports, now assuming an epicyclic hypothesis, Hipparchus obtained the equivalent of a significantly smaller eccentricity, approximately 0.079.[18] The measurements of the AMRP group from computed tomography (CT) data led to an estimate that the Mechanism's pin-and-slot device for the lunar anomaly was equivalent to an eccentricity of approximately 0.115.[19] Hipparchus' larger estimate is likely within the error range implied by the AMRP measurements, so it is possible (though by no means certain) that the Mechanism was intended to reflect Hipparchus' eccentric hypothesis so far as the eccentricity is concerned, though the periodicities built into the Mechanism, derived from the Saros, are different from and cruder than the periodicities from Babylonian mathematical astronomy that Ptolemy tells us Hipparchus considered to be accurate.

Freeth and Carman (the latter collaborating with Alan Thorndike and James Evans) independently realized that similar pin-and-slot devices could have represented the anomalistic motions of Mars, Jupiter, and Saturn.[20] The hypothetical reconstructions proposed in their respective papers assume that the planetary mechanisms were based on period relations involving comparatively small whole numbers, such as the Babylonian Goal-Year relation for Saturn (cf. table 7.2):

59 solar years = 57 synodic cycles = 2 revolutions of Saturn around the zodiac.

Carman, Thorndike, and Evans point out that an arrangement of epicyclic gears similar to the one shown on the left in fig. 8.20 could economically translate the mean solar motion of gear b_1's arbor into the mean motion of a planet on an arbor sharing the same axis (fig. 8.21, *left*).

It helps to visualize the apparatus in b_1's frame of reference, according to which gear b' rotates *counterclockwise* at the rate of the Sun's mean motion around the zodiac; that is, with the solar year as its period. Gears s' and s'' therefore rotate clockwise with a period of 59/57 solar years, which is Saturn's synodic period according to the assumed period relation, and b'' revolves with this period too but counterclockwise. This rotation is slightly slower than the Sun's mean motion, and in the stationary frame of reference of the Mechanism as a whole, the rotation of s'', being this rotation subtracted from the Sun's mean motion, is Saturn's slow rate of mean motion, with a period of 59/2 years.

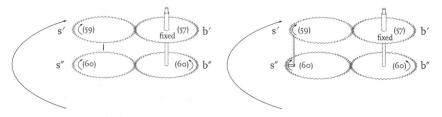

FIG. 8.21. *Left*, epicyclic gearing with conventional arbor coupling, yielding Saturn's mean motion through the zodiac. *Right*, epicyclic gearing with pin-and-slot coupling, yielding Saturn's nonuniform motion. Gears b′ and b″ are coaxial with b₁, while s′ and s″ are mounted epicyclically on b₁.

Since the gear pair s′-s″ rotates (in the frame of reference of b₁) with Saturn's synodic period, if they are coupled by a pin on s′ riding in a slot on s″ instead of by a common arbor (fig. 8.21, *right*), an anomaly will be introduced into the rotations of s″ and b″, mimicking the behavior of an eccentric or epicyclic hypothesis. The effect is large enough that, in b₁'s frame of reference, the rate of the counterclockwise rotation of b″ is periodically a little faster than the clockwise rotation of the Sun's mean motion, so that in the stationary frame of reference it rotates alternately clockwise and counterclockwise to represent Saturn's alternating direct and retrograde motion through the zodiac.

We now know from the FCI (see chapter 7) that the period relation for Saturn assumed in the Mechanism was:

442 solar years = 427 synodic cycles = 15 revolutions of Saturn around the zodiac

and it is probable that Mars and Jupiter also had comparably long period relations. Implementing the planets' motions by means of pin-and-slot couplings according to such period relations would have necessitated compound gear trains. For example, for Saturn a fixed gear b′ of 61 teeth could have engaged with an intermediate gear t′ of 68 teeth, and on the same arbor as t′, a gear t″ of 56 teeth could have engaged with s′ of 52 teeth, which thus had a counterclockwise motion with a period of 442/427 years, Saturn's synodic period according to the assumed period relation. Between s″ and b″, a single idler gear would give b″ the correct sense for the planet's motion through the zodiac.

Would these hypothetical devices for planetary anomaly have worked in practice? Wright's physical reconstructions of the Mechanism demonstrated that slotted-arm constructions with compound gear trains are indeed viable for all the planets. His speculative working re-creation of an "Archimedean *sphaira*" in the form of a bronze globe (see chapter 7) successfully employs planetary gearwork based on pin-and-slot couplings and short Goal-Year-type period relations for Mars, Jupiter, and Saturn.[21] Pin-and-slot couplings are also, in principle, possible for the inner planets Venus and Mercury.[22] Whether pin-and-slot constructions are physically practicable with compound gear trains remains to be tested.

Summing up, the gearwork of the Mechanism embodied a powerful repertoire of means for transferring and transforming rotary motions: arbors and tooth engagements of gearwheels and contrates, differential and epicyclic gearing, and devices for generating periodic nonuniform motions that included pin-and-slot coupling and likely also slotted arms. With these resources the designer succeeded in mechanizing a profusion of distinct chronological cycles as well as a planetarium that portrayed the simultaneous nonuniform motions of the Sun, Moon, and planets through the zodiac. Although some elements of the Mechanism's gearwork can be found in much less sophisticated inventions described in the Greek and Latin mechanical literature, the differential moon phase device and the contrivances for anomalistic motion that enabled the Mechanism to provide a reasonably faithful reflection of late Hellenistic astronomical theory have no known counterparts in other ancient artifacts or technical treatises.

Materials and craft

We have so far been looking at the Mechanism's gearwork in a rather abstract way, as an ancient mechanical theorist might have explained its operation. If we now wish to turn to the practical question of how it was made, we run into an obstacle: the fragmentary and corroded condition of its remains. Of the original materials, only tiny bits of the wooden frame survive, while the metal constituting what is left of the mechanical parts and the inscribed plates has almost entirely turned into corrosion products. Some detail has also been lost as a consequence of early conservation and cleaning of the fragments. On the other hand, surviving examples of metalworking tools as well as evidence of metalworking derived from better preserved artifacts give us some sense of the resources that were available in a late Hellenistic or Roman-period workshop. Wright has made a convincing case, both through such evidence and his experience in building working models, that it was well within the normal capabilities of an ancient workshop to fashion and assemble the Mechanism's components.[23]

The gears, the front and rear faces, the frame plate on which the gearwork was mounted, the inscribed so-called cover plates, and various other static components all were made from sheet metal, which Wright estimates as having been about 1.5 millimeters thick except for the frame plate, which was significantly thicker.[24] Other components such as arbors may have been cast or cut from larger pieces of metal. Price was allowed in 1958 to take small samples for analysis from a quantity of crumbled bits of metallic corrosion products in one of the cardboard boxes that were used at that time to store the fragments; these are likely to have come chiefly from the plates.[25] Chemical analyses by Earle Caley of Ohio State University and spectrographic analysis by Cyril Smith of the Institute for the Study of Metals at the University of Chicago determined that the metallic composition of the samples was primarily copper with a small amount of tin (probably less than 10%) and negligible other metals; in other words, a low-tin bronze.[26] Caley suggested that the absence of significant lead in the alloy indicates manufacture much earlier than the first century BC, since leaded bronzes became prevalent in later Hellenistic and Roman times. However, the principal motive for including lead was to improve bronze's casting properties, and objects made from sheet metal continued to be made in later antiquity primarily from unleaded bronze, which was less brittle and thus more suited to hammering. The composition of the metal sheet from which the Mechanism's plate-like components were produced was probably chosen deliberately for its mechanical durability and workability.

A few components within the larger fragments show in radiographs and CT as much more radiodense than the rest, indicative of a different and apparently less corroded metal. It is also possible that not all the inscribed plates were composed of low-tin bronze but of a softer alloy. A recent nondestructive chemical analysis of the surface composition of 25 of the smaller fragments, conducted by Panagiotis Mitropoulos in the electron microscopy and microanalysis facilities of the University of Athens, found in addition to unleaded tin bronze two further, pewter-like alloys in which tin was the predominant element, with smaller quantities of copper and lead.[27] The remarkably high apparent proportion of tin in these alloys may be partly due to a corrosion process that drew tin content toward the surface, but it does appear probable that diverse materials were chosen with care in accordance with their suitability for various roles in the Mechanism.

A lathe is likely to have been used for components such as arbors; otherwise, Wright maintains that hand tools would have sufficed for making the Mechanism.[28] The shape and somewhat irregular spacing of the triangular gear teeth indicate that they were cut by using a handheld file or a similar tool. The workman could have divided the metal disk's circumference into an arbitrary number of parts for the locations of the teeth by using a process of approximate adjustment following an initial division by means of dividers, though Wright has also suggested that a template ("division plate") could have been employed.[29] A typical gear of around 60 teeth could have been cut in less than an hour.

The entire process of building a copy of the Mechanism, once a successful prototype had been achieved, might have taken a single workman one or two months, less time if there was a small team. The engraving of the inscriptions would have been a job for a specialist, who was not necessarily experienced in stone letter cutting (since the technique would have been different) but was familiar with the letter forms of stone inscriptions.

Though a workshop that had succeeded in making a device such as the Antikythera Mechanism would surely not have limited the production to a single specimen, it is unlikely that sufficient demand would have existed to have encouraged a shop to specialize exclusively in astronomical gearwork. There were more common spheres of activity, however, that called for small-scale precision working in bronze and other nonprecious metals; for example, surgical instruments—vaginal dilators, for instance, typically incorporated a screw mechanism to adjust the opening—and parts of musical instruments such as organs and auloi. The Mechanism was probably just an exceptionally large and intricate job for versatile master craftsmen whose production was quite wide ranging.

Imperfections and inaccuracies

When we ask how accurate the Mechanism was as an astronomical calculator, we are really bundling together several questions: What errors would have arisen from imperfections in the physical manufacture of the device? How closely did the design of the device, disregarding such imperfections, represent contemporaneous astronomical knowledge? How well did contemporaneous knowledge correspond to the actual celestial phenomena?

The most significant kind of imperfection in the manufacture would have consisted of the inaccurate division of circles into equal fractional arcs, whether for the division marks on the dial scales or for the teeth on the gears. We can take as an illustration the division of the Egyptian Calendar scale into 365 ostensibly equal arcs representing the single days comprising the Egyptian calendar year. Even though we have only about a fifth of the complete scale ring in Fragment C, we can safely assume that the builder of the Mechanism made sure that there was indeed a total of 365 scale markings; in other words, there was no systematic error in division placement over the entire circle. However, there could have been systematic errors over large portions of the scale, arising for example from errors in an initial geometrical division of the circle into halves or quarters or sixths. Such errors are difficult for us to assess because of the incomplete and distorted condition of the fragments, though they probably would have been small since these large divisions of a circle are easy to establish and verify.

The size of random errors in the individual divisions can, however, be estimated. In the case of the Egyptian Calendar scale (and likewise of the Zodiac scale), the standard deviation of the arcs between consecutive marks is about 1/10th of a degree, so that the date indicated by the pointer will typically be randomly off by about 1/10th of a day one way or the other—sometimes by as much as a quarter of a day. This means that the Mechanism was not capable of measuring out single days with much precision. For demonstrations involving most of the heavenly bodies, this would not have mattered, but it would have been an inconvenience if one wished to measure the Moon's exact position or its speed on a given day, since misreading the date by 1/10th of a day would result in an error on the order of a degree in the Moon's position.

M. G. Edmunds has investigated the errors of placement of the teeth of the Mechanism's gears, and their consequences for the outputs of the gear trains.[30] He found little evidence for systematic errors over large arcs of the gears' peripheries, while for the random errors he found standard deviations generally in the range of 0.04 to 0.08 of the average tooth spacing, which is a bit better than the accuracy of the graduations of the Egyptian Calendar and Zodiac scales. Random errors propagate in compound gear trains, but for most of the outputs the effect would have been negligibly small relative to the spacing of the scale divisions. For example, on the Metonic dial the error arising from the gear train would typically have been well under a degree, whereas the scale divisions are about 7.7°, and in doubtful cases one could determine which cell of the scale was indicated by consulting the Sun and Moon pointers on the front face. In the case of the Moon's pointer itself, however, the long train with its gearing up should have resulted, according to Edmunds's estimations, to typical errors of *at least* 4° and intermittent errors of three times that much—in other words, about a full day's motion.

Because of the triangular shape of the teeth, the Mechanism would also have been subject to an effect called "backlash." Engaged pairs of gears with triangular teeth must be placed so that there is a slight space between the tips of one gear's teeth and the V-shaped indents of the other, since otherwise the gears jam. With such a space, however, there will be a small arc within which one gear can turn back and forth freely without moving the other gear at all (fig. 8.22). In a compound train each engagement will have this little margin of free movement.

Suppose that the Mechanism's gearwork has been set up so that all the pointers are in their astronomically and chronologically correct alignments when the input drive is being turned in the forward direction. If the input is now reversed, each engagement along each train will experience a pause until the driving gear begins moving and then turns through its free margin before coming into contact again with the driven gear. Initially, none of the pointers will move, but then they will begin turning in reverse in stages, starting with those that have the shortest gear trains. The Moon pointer, because of its exceptionally long train, will start moving last of all, and so long as the Mechanism is driven backward in time, this pointer will be several degrees out of synchronization with any of the other displays. To restore synchronization, the operator would have to go a bit further back in time than the intended date and then run the Mechanism forward to undo the backlash effect.

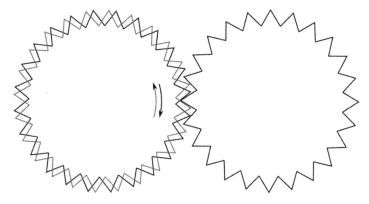

FIG. 8.22. Backlash in a gear engagement. The black outline of the gear on the left shows its position when driving the right gear clockwise; the gray outline shows its position when driving the right gear counterclockwise. The gear can turn freely between the two positions without moving the right gear at all.

And what of inaccuracies inherent in the underlying astronomical theories built into the Mechanism? The theories can be thought of as falling into two parts: the period relations, which determine how well the displays would stay in line with nature over the long term, and the representation of nonuniform motions. The Mechanism embodied seven period relations: the Saros and the 19-year cycle, which together account for all periodicities involved in the lunar displays on the front face and in the chronological displays of the rear face dials, and one period relation for each of the five planets. Of these seven, we do not know what the relations for Mercury, Mars, and Jupiter were. A measure of the quality of the others can be obtained from the values that they give rise to for the mean synodic periods and periods of zodiacal revolution and for the Moon's anomalistic month. In tables 8.1 and 8.2 these are expressed in terms of solar years and are compared with values from Babylonian mathematical astronomy (*Astronomical Cuneiform Texts*, or ACT), Ptolemy's *Almagest*, and modern astronomical theory.[31]

The Mechanism's two known planetary period relations both have a duration of more than four centuries and are quite accurate by ancient standards. The error in Saturn's zodiacal period amounts to about a degree in 125 years, and the errors in the synodic periods of Saturn and Venus would have led to a noticeable phase error in their phenomena only after running the Mechanism forward more than a century. It seems plausible that all the planetary period relations were of comparable quality.

The only other set of comparably good planetary period relations that are known to have been available by the first century BC are the Babylonian ACT relations. They are first definitely attested in Greek in astronomical tables preserved in papyri of the first or second century AD; that is, not long before or

TABLE 8.1. Comparison of ancient values for mean synodic periods and the anomalistic month, expressed in solar years. The values from Ptolemy and from modern theory (valid for AD 2000) are in sidereal years.

	Mechanism	ACT	Ptolemy	Modern
Synodic month	0.0808511	0.0808480	0.0808489	0.0808489
Anomalistic month	0.0754384	0.0754381	0.0754389	0.0754389
Venus	1.59861	1.59861	1.59869	1.59873
Saturn	1.03513	1.03516	1.03514	1.03515

TABLE 8.2. Comparison of ancient values for mean periods of zodiacal revolution, expressed in solar years. The values from Ptolemy and from modern theory (valid for AD 2000) are in sidereal years. Venus's mean zodiacal period, being exactly one solar year, is not tabulated.

	Mechanism	ACT	Ptolemy	Modern
Moon	0.0748031	0.0748005	0.0748013	0.0748013
Moon's apogee	8.8826	8.8505	8.8497	8.8502
Saturn	29.46667	29.44444	29.45528	29.44750

contemporaneous with Ptolemy, though the transmission likely took place already in the late Hellenistic period.[32] On the other hand, the fact that Ptolemy associates the much-shorter Goal-Year period relations with Hipparchus suggests that Hipparchus did not know the ACT relations.[33] The Mechanism's relation for Venus is almost equivalent to the ACT relation and could be accounted for as the nearest approximation to it that could be represented conveniently by gearwork; the Saturn relation, however, is slightly inferior to its ACT counterpart.

The Mechanism's periodicities relating to the Moon are poorer, reflecting the comparative brevity of the underlying period relations. The longitudinal period's excess, which follows from the 19-year period relation, is equivalent to a shortfall of a degree of mean lunar motion in less than nine years. This systematic deviation would have taken several decades of operation to become conspicuous because of the large random errors in the Moon's displayed position caused by irregular tooth spacing.

The period of longitudinal motion of the Moon's apogee, derived from the Saros together with the 19-year relation, is also too long and would have produced a shortfall of a degree in less than seven years. The apogee was not displayed on the Mechanism's dials, but its revolution was represented by the platform gear e3-e4 bearing the epicyclic gear device for the lunar anomaly. However, the errors in the rates of motion of the mean moon and its apogee largely cancel each other so far as the anomaly is concerned, so that it would require many decades for a noticeable phase error in the Moon's varying speed to arise.

Already in the second half of the second century BC, according to Ptolemy's testimony, Hipparchus had lunar periodicities superior in accuracy to those implied by the 19-year cycle and the Saros, and these were largely derived from Babylonian ACT astronomy.[34] As we saw in chapter 6, however, Ptolemy also indicates that some astronomers after Hipparchus continued to assume that the Saros was correct. While the designer of the Mechanism may have devised its lunisolar gearwork in full awareness that the period relations on which it was based, though convenient for representation by gears, were not the best available, I think that he may in fact have had little or no direct knowledge of Hipparchus' work. The absence of any reflection of Hipparchus' researches on the length of the solar year and precession could likewise be due to either ignorance or an intentional simplification.

In its handling of nonuniform motion, the Mechanism may have been a reasonably faithful physical representation of the contemporaneous state of geometrically based Greek astronomical theory. The pin-and-slot device for the Moon's anomaly provided a gearwork analog to the simple epicyclic and eccentric hypotheses that Hipparchus worked with, and the range of variation of speed that it generated was in the neighborhood of the optimum for a single-anomaly theory, with resulting errors of position on the order of 1°. The descriptions of the planets' synodic cycles in the FCI, since they make no allowance for variations in the cycles, also imply that the gearwork for each planet was equivalent to a simple epicyclic or eccentric hypothesis. Ptolemy tells us that Hipparchus demonstrated that single-anomaly hypotheses were insufficient to account for the planets' observable patterns of motion, without, however, offering a resolution of the problems. The highly successful planetary theories in the *Almagest* depend on combining the eccenter and epicycle principles and on a sophisticated new definition of the uniform circular motions that were supposed to be the building blocks of the hypotheses, but these innovations are likely to date from well after Hipparchus' time. The Mechanism's displays of the planets' locations in the zodiac would inevitably have been subject to significant errors, especially for Mercury and Mars, which have the least circular orbits around the Sun. In the case of Mars, errors would frequently have been of the order of 30°.[35]

As a qualitative simulator of the celestial motions, the Mechanism would have been highly impressive; as a calculator of quantitative positions and phenomena, it was hampered by the limitations both of the gearing technology and the mathematical astronomy of its time. In contrast to contemporaneous Babylonia, astronomy in the Hellenistic world was only sporadically an observational science, and perhaps only a few researching astronomers would have known how poorly at times some of the displays corresponded to reality.

Designing the Mechanism

Ancient writers on mechanical technology were conscious of the tension between its theoretical and practical aspects. As the mathematician Pappus of Alexandria (ca. AD 300) puts it:[36]

> One part of mechanics is about theory and another is about craft. The theoretical part consists of geometry and number theory and astronomy and reasonings about nature, whereas the craft part consists of bronzeworking and building construction and carpentry and painting and manual training in these things. A person who is versed in the aforesaid sciences from youth and who has acquired ability in the aforesaid skills and who, in addition, has an agile character will be the most outstanding inventor and artificer of mechanical works. But it is impossible for a single person to excel in so many branches of learning and at the same time to learn the aforesaid skills . . .

There was a notorious exception, of course: Archimedes. But even Archimedes did not entirely escape the dichotomy between theoretical pursuits and hands-dirty practical skills. It might almost be said that there was not one Archimedes but two. One was the subject of the anecdotes told by historians and biographers about his amazing inventions, such as the contrivance of pulleys by which he hauled by himself out of dock one of King Hieron's great freighters laden with passengers and cargo, as well as the "claw" that could upend a besieging vessel or the mirrors that set the Roman ships aflame. Some of these tales are manifestly fabricated, and perhaps none are entirely free from elaboration. The other Archimedes was the author of the brilliant, difficult, and abstract treatises on mathematics and mathematical physics that were preserved through the Middle Ages.

In his *Life of Marcellus*, Plutarch asserts that Archimedes regarded his inventions as trifles to which he condescended at Hieron's behest, while according to Pappus it was said that he wrote only one book on mechanical technology.[37] This book, incidentally, was supposed to have been about *sphairopoiia*, the construction of "an image of the heavens by means of uniform and circular motion." The mathematical treatises attributed to Archimedes that have come down to us in Greek are clearly authentic, though some were modified in various ways after Archimedes' time; his reputation made his name an attractive one to attach to anonymous or spurious texts, and caution is due when it comes to a book that is alluded to only by a single witness (and that at second hand and with no details about its contents).

Many of the wonder-working inventions described in the mechanical literature were thought up in the first instance by the experts in practical mechanics as eye-catching applications of their repertoire of basic devices— variations on a theme, as it were. Such an origin is hardly imaginable for the Antikythera Mechanism. It must have been designed through a true col- laboration between someone possessing a degree of astronomical knowl- edge and someone with outstanding mechanical skill and creativity; between them, some facility was also required in mathematics, especially the manip- ulation of ratios of whole numbers. The balance of expertise was not neces- sarily symmetrical. Whereas the mechanician must have been first rate, the scientific input could have derived from intelligent secondhand familiarity with the astronomical literature. From the scientific adviser came the origi- nal agenda specifying what displays were desired, the theoretical parame- ters (period relations, measures of anomaly, etc.), and the information to be inscribed on the scales and in the supplementary texts. But there must have been much back and forth between him and the "master mechanic" (to use Wright's phrase), who would have been the final arbiter of what was techni- cally feasible and who may sometimes have suggested functions that the scientist had not imagined.

Or is this account of the Mechanism's origins oversimplified? Should we not suppose that the object whose fragments we chance to possess was the outcome of a long history of gear-driven astronomical mechanisms of progres- sively increasing complexity? Common sense tells us that the Mechanism was not a prototype without antecedents. It is too complex, too miniaturized, too polished a production to be the very first of its kind. But once all the key ideas behind the Mechanism's workings had been discovered, an intense program of experimentation might have led quite rapidly to the device as we have it, perhaps within a generation and in a single workshop.

The first astronomical mechanisms driven by gears would likely have employed only the principle of branching compound gear trains to translate an ostensibly uniform input motion into diverse but uniform outputs on separate dials, such as the rear face displays of the Antikythera Mechanism. A device showing the Sun and Moon revolving around the Earth with uni- form rates of motion in a suitable ratio would have constituted a significant advance from schematic, odometer-style display of motions toward visual realism; the prerequisites would have included pipes and, if the Moon's phases were shown, contrates. Adding planets to such a display would have been a more problematic and unsatisfying exercise. Perhaps it would have seemed worthwhile for Mars, Jupiter, and Saturn to be seen circling the zodiac more slowly than the Sun, albeit without their characteristic retrogradations, but to show Mercury and Venus revolving with a period identical to the Sun's, without showing them alternately ahead of and behind the Sun, would have been absurd. Devices employing epicyclic gearing and slotted elements to convert uniform rotations into nonuniform motion opened the way to planetaria, and these innovations might not have been much older than our Mechanism.

9

Afterword: The Meaning of the Mechanism

While spending a few days in Athens in June 1980, Richard Feynman wrote a letter to his family in which he described his visit to the National Archaeological Museum, an experience that on the whole he says he found wearisome and boring.[1] The one object that truly caught the physicist's eye was the Antikythera Mechanism, a thing "so entirely different and strange that it is nearly impossible." He lamented what he saw as a lack of awareness of or interest in the fragments on the part of the Greek archeologists, one of whom he portrays as wondering aloud why, of all the wonderful pieces in the museum, the American professor wanted to know more about *this* one.

Feynman's position seems inconsistent, though: he faults modern Greeks for overrating the ancients' scientific and intellectual achievements, a symptom, he thought, of a disproportionate preoccupation of the Greeks with their past, but at the same time he complains that they did not appreciate what a remarkable achievement *this* artifact had to be—so remarkable that he wonders whether it might be "some kind of fake." But the truth is that in 1980, soon after the appearance of *Gears from the Greeks*, it would have been difficult for *anyone* to find many points of connection between the Mechanism and the civilization that gave rise to the other artworks and artifacts in the museum. If this is now possible, it is due to the enormous progress in our understanding of the gearwork and dials since that time, and, still more, to our greatly enhanced reading of the inscribed texts.

In the central chapters of this book, I have tried to show how each one of the Mechanism's astronomical and chronological functions had a rich context in ancient Greek life and thought. It is probably just a matter of chance whether one of these functions closely resembles what we know from other sources or tells us something substantially new. With respect to calendars, the motions of the Sun and Moon through the zodiac, and the Parapegma, the Mechanism has very close relations to Geminus, Hipparchus, and various inscriptions and papyri. Its eclipse predictions and planetary theory correspond to areas where our knowledge for the period is otherwise profoundly defective. In the future it will be impossible to write on the history of these aspects of ancient astronomy without referring to the Mechanism.

Starting already with Derek de Solla Price, some scholars have made much of links between the Mechanism and Babylonian astronomy, perhaps more than the case warrants. That Greek astronomy was heavily indebted to the ancient Near East is indisputable, and some specific elements incorporated in the Mechanism can indeed be traced to Babylonia. These include the signs of the zodiac, the division of the zodiac into 360 degrees, the Saros eclipse cycle, and arguably the 19-year calendar cycle—all concepts that were fully integrated into Greek astronomical practice by the late Hellenistic period to the extent that it is doubtful whether Greek astronomers thought of them as importations. It is also possible, though by no means certain, that the arithmetical methods characteristic of Babylonian mathematical astronomy are reflected in the eclipse times inscribed on the Saros dial and in the nonuniform division of the Zodiac scale. On the other hand, the mechanical treatment of the Moon's varying speed as well as everything that we know about the planetary displays are referable to characteristically Greek hypotheses based on uniform circular motion. All in all, the Mechanism's astronomy does not seem to me to be more "Babylonian" than that of Hipparchus or Geminus.

As a work of technology, the Mechanism again can be set in a context of Greco-Roman complex mechanical inventions, but the specific parallels for its gearwork, as we have seen, are limited to a few technical descriptions of much simpler devices and to vague, nontechnical allusions to planetaria. Despite the much more advanced repertory of gearing methods found in the Mechanism, there can be no doubt that its makers belonged to the artisanal tradition that was responsible for the surviving ancient mechanical literature, whose vocabulary and expressions are shared with the Mechanism's back cover inscription.

Price's brilliant title *Gears from the Greeks*, in short, is entirely vindicated. The Mechanism was thoroughly characteristic of its cultural setting; no other civilization would have produced anything quite like it. Its technological sophistication, moreover, appears as that of a young and rapidly developing craft tradition in which innovative ideas are found side by side with less than optimal means—the triangular gear teeth in particular—and questionable design choices such as the spiral dial slots. With respect to its astronomy, too, it seems to have been an uneven performance, in some respects scientifically accurate in relation to contemporaneous theory, in others less so. It was truly a remarkable creation, but not a miracle of perfection.

And what was it made for? The reader will already have gathered that I do not believe that its purpose was to compute data or make predictions to be applied in some practical context. Now that we are familiar with all its known functions, I can explain more fully why.

Many of the early investigators of the Mechanism supposed that it was an instrument of navigation, in the first instance, of course, because it was found on a ship. The principal way in which astronomical knowledge could be useful for mariners in antiquity was in establishing directions and, to a more limited extent, locations. Directions could be determined at night by a few easily recognized constellations, in particular Ursa Major and Ursa Minor, which throughout the Greco-Roman world were always above the horizon and near the north celestial pole; during the day, directions could be determined by the Sun's position in the sky, and especially its rising and setting points on the horizon. Ancient texts on marine geography frequently specify eastward and westward directions as being toward sunrise and sunset on the equinoxes or solstices. This kind of directional navigation needed no written resources or equipment, and none of the Mechanism's displays would have been relevant to it.

We have no evidence for shipboard determination of geographical latitude or longitude in antiquity. Latitude could have been measured, if someone wanted to, by the angle of elevation above the horizon of familiar stars or of the Sun at noon, with the aid of a couple of reference tables, but again, the Mechanism did not provide this kind of information. In principle, predicted times of lunar eclipses such the hours inscribed on the Saros dial can be compared with observations of the same eclipses to establish the interval of longitude between one's location and the meridian for which the predictions were computed. But a navigator could hardly have waited months on end for a suitable eclipse, and anyway the Saros dial's times are given only to the nearest hour, so that even if one (unwisely) trusted them to be correct, they would yield one's longitude only within a margin of 15°; that is, about half the breadth of the Mediterranean.

The Mechanism could have supplied mariners with weather forecasts according to ancient meteorological theories. The predictions of first and last appearances of constellations in the Parapegma inscription would have had to be translated into predictions of weather changes according to a scheme not provided explicitly by the Mechanism. Additionally, the directional statements associated with predicted eclipses in the back plate inscription, if they refer to winds and are meant to be applicable to an extended time interval following each eclipse, might have been seen as useful for navigation. The same information, however, could have been provided more compactly, more securely, and much more cheaply in written form, and it is hard to imagine why mariners would have wanted the Mechanism's other functions, such as the planetarium.

The difficulty in understanding the Mechanism as a practical tool, whether at sea or on land, comes down to two questions: Who needed the full range of its displays? What advantage did mechanization offer to outweigh the cost?

One immediately thinks of the Games dial, a feature whose predictions would have been relevant for athletes and civic officials—people, in other words, who had little use for the Mechanism's other displays and were surely capable of counting years in twos and fours without the aid of gearwork.

The one practical context in which knowledge of the locations of the planets in the zodiac was essential was astrology. A high-class astrologer who could afford a device such as the Mechanism might have used its planetarium as an alternative to astronomical tables for calculating the positions of the heavenly bodies for his clients' horoscopes. However, the Mechanism was clearly not designed with an astrologer's needs in mind. On the one hand, the Parapegma inscription and the Games dial were irrelevant for astrology. On the other, a device intended specifically for horoscopic astrology—or for pure astronomical research, for that matter—should have had a coherent way of setting and reading off the exact year and date according to a standard chronological system such as the Egyptian calendar (counting years from a recognized era) or the Callippic-period system. The only year counts displayed on the Mechanism were the nonstandard numbering of Corinthian calendar years within the 19-year cycle on the Metonic dial and within the 4-year cycle on the Games dial, whereas the only display of individual days was on the Egyptian Calendar scale. Moreover, the gearwork was not really precise enough to indicate single days accurately.

A somewhat better fit is with the variety of astrology connected with a popular kind of astronomical almanac called an "ephemeris." If a person wanted astrological guidance concerning whether this was a good-luck or bad-luck day to do something important, he or she could look it up in one of these tables, with no need to consult a professional astrologer. Thus, in his sixth *Satire*, Juvenal mocks a certain type of woman who will not set out to meet her husband if the ephemeris says the day is not auspicious for the journey, and Pliny the Elder writes of a fashionable physician from Massilia named Crinas who took an ephemeris into account when prescribing to his Roman patients.[2] We have many fragments of such ephemerides in Greek papyri from Roman Egypt (fig. 9.1). They tabulate the day-by-day positions of the Moon as well as the motions of the planets through the zodiac, so that the user of the ephemeris can see on which days the Moon is within a certain range of degrees of a benefic or malefic planet, resulting in favorable or unlucky conditions for one's activities. Perhaps a very affluent individual might have wanted a sort of mechanized ephemeris as a prestige object, and, for such an amateur, features indicating weather changes and Panhellenic festivals could have been an attractive additional frill.

But what the Mechanism was really suited for is instruction—not so much the training of astronomers, for whom a grasp of the technical and mathematical literature was the sine qua non, but the diffusion of the basics of astronomy among students of philosophy and the educated elite. Geminus' *Introduction*

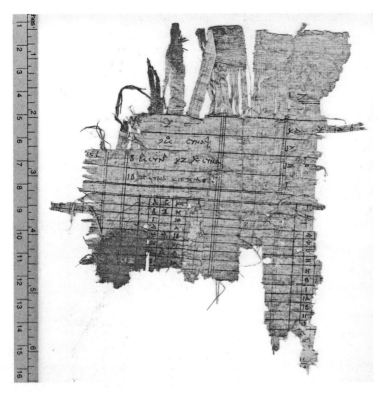

FIG. 9.1. *POxy astron.* 4175, the oldest known fragment of a Greek ephemeris, from 24 BC. The upper part of the table summarizes the motions and phenomena of the five planets, while the lower part gives daily positions of the Moon, with dates expressed according to the Egyptian and Roman calendars. (© The Egypt Exploration Society and Imaging Papyri Project, Oxford)

to the Phenomena shows us what these basics were taken to be in the late Hellenistic period, and I have already remarked on how intellectually close he was to the scientific designer of the Mechanism. Practically every function of the Mechanism, in fact, has a counterpart somewhere in Geminus' work (table 9.1).[3]

Obviously, the Mechanism does not illustrate everything that Geminus covers. It is limited to the aspects of astronomy that relate to time and temporal cycles on a scale of days, months, and years, but not fractions of a day. Topics such as the figures of the constellations, the seasonally varying lengths of days and nights, astronomical geography, and astrological relations of the zodiacal signs fall outside its scope. But the Mechanism reflects in common with Geminus a conception of astronomy as being about not just the motions and phenomena of the heavenly bodies, but their impact both on the terrestrial environment and on human society. The Mechanism was too small to

TABLE 9.1. The Mechanism and Geminus' *Introduction to the Phenomena* compared.

Feature on the Mechanism	Chapter in Geminus
Zodiac scale	1. On the circle of the zodiacal signs.
Egyptian Calendar scale	8. On months.
Motions of the Sun, Moon, and planets	1. On the circle of the zodiacal signs. 12. That the planets make a movement contrary to that of the cosmos. 18. On the Exeligmos.
Moon phase display	9. On the phases of the Moon.
Parapegma inscription	13. On risings and settings. 17. On weather signs from the stars.
Metonic and Callippic dials	8. On months.
Games dial	*no corresponding chapter*
Saros and Exeligmos dials	10. On the eclipse of the Sun. 11. On the eclipse of the Moon. 18. On the Exeligmos.

have been effective in demonstrations for large groups, but as a resource to accompany tutorials, its didactic impact would have been tremendous because it provided a visual and mobile representation of abstract chronological structures alongside simulated celestial motions in a greatly accelerated scale of time.

But the Mechanism was much more than an assemblage of displays relating to diverse topics in astronomy. As a moving image of the cosmos, it showed the coordination and counterpoint of celestial and mundane phenomena, all governed by the flow of time while obeying deep principles of regularity. This was, after all, what Hellenistic philosophers saw as the crucial challenge for astronomy, to reduce the apparent complexity of the phenomena to the constant and regular fundamental motions that were suited to divine beings. A man-made artifact that exhibited such behavior provoked questions about how the cosmos itself worked and why.

At this point we are really talking not just about the individual Mechanism whose fragments are extant in the National Archaeological Museum—and which, after all, might never have been seen or operated by anyone except the craftsmen who made it—but about the whole class of ancient mechanized models of the cosmos. How extensive was this class, and how many people had direct experience of examples? M. G. Edmunds has assembled a list—which is not exhaustive—of (by my count) 18 Greek and Latin texts that allude plausibly or unambiguously to astronomical mechanisms, a respectable number that shows that the *idea* of such devices had wide currency.[4] However, in none of these texts does the author assert, in his own voice, that he has seen one. In the majority of the passages it is difficult to tell whether what is said about the mechanisms comes from personal experience or from reading about them, and a few are obvious fictions or literary tropes.

We need to be careful to distinguish mechanized planetaria from certain other concepts and categories of object that may be described in similar language. The Greek word *sphaira* (or Latin *sphaera*) may refer to an astronomical mechanism but was also appropriate for a simple globe, so that for example the *sphaira* of one Billaros that, according to Strabo, was plundered from Sinope by Lucullus about 71 BC is more likely to have been a terrestrial or celestial globe than a mechanism.[5] *Sphairopoiia* can designate a complex of heavenly spheres as part of astronomical theory, as well as a mechanical model or the practice of constructing such models. Models for illustrating cosmology could consist of independently mobile parts without gearwork or other mechanical connection. This is probably what Plato had in mind when he wrote in the *Timaeus* that the complexities of the celestial motions can be fully understood only by looking at "imitations," and nothing in a fragmentarily preserved passage of the philosopher Epicurus' *On Nature* (ca. 300 BC), in which he criticizes the astronomers of Cyzicus for their reliance on "instruments" (*organa*) to visualize astronomical phenomena, implies that they were mechanized.[6] Lastly, descriptions of devices that showed the revolving heavens sometimes are referring to display dials of water-driven clocks on which the constellations were represented in a stereographic projection (see chapter 2).

Cicero's mentions of mechanical *sphaerae* (see chapters 6 and 7) not only are among the most important, but also the earliest that we have. They deserve to be considered in relation to two episodes of his early life: his sojourn in the Greek east in 79–77 BC and his term as quaestor in Sicily in 75 BC. During his travels in Athens, Asia Minor, and Rhodes he met or studied under several teachers of philosophy and rhetoric, among them the Stoic Posidonius of Apamea, whose school was in Rhodes.[7] Although we do not know the specific circumstances of his acquaintance with Posidonius, it clearly made a powerful impression on Cicero, who subsequently referred to him both as a friend (*familiaris*) and as a teacher (*magister*).[8] As for his quaestorship, the relevant incident, recounted in his *Tusculan Disputations*, is his successful search for the tomb of Archimedes, which had fallen into neglect and become overgrown with vegetation.[9] Cicero was fascinated by the stories of Archimedes, and in his speeches and writings the mathematician's name is a frequent byword for intellectual brilliance.

The *sphaera* passages appear in philosophical works from later in Cicero's career, the *De re publica* of 54–51 BC and *On the Nature of the Gods* and *Tusculan Disputations*, composed around 45 BC. *On the Nature of the Gods* recounts a fictitious conversation among three elder acquaintances of Cicero's that must be supposed to have taken place soon after Cicero's return to Rome in 77 BC, with the young Cicero himself as an all-but-mute witness. So when he makes the Stoic Balbus imagine the barbarous people of Scythia or Britain encountering "this *sphaera* that our Posidonius has made recently," it is hard not to see this as referring to something that Cicero himself saw in Rhodes. It may have been a close cousin of the Antikythera Mechanism.

The case of Cicero's accounts of the *sphaera* of Archimedes in *De re publica* and the *Tusculan Disputations* is less straightforward. The description in *De re publica* is the most extensive, but its presentation, as part of a retrospective narrative within a dialogue that itself is set in the remote past, relieves the reader of any duty to receive it as any more a historically true story than, say, Socrates' tale of his youthful interlocution with the wise woman Diotima in Plato's *Symposium*. But in the *Tusculan Disputations*, though the work is also formally a dialogue, Cicero is speaking in his own contemporaneous voice when he likens Archimedes' "binding" the disparate motions of the seven heavenly bodies in a *sphaera* to the *Timaeus*' Craftsman shaping the cosmos. He surely believed, then, that Archimedes made an astronomical mechanism, and there was probably some truth behind that belief.

How much did he know about Archimedes' device? Perhaps little more than that it had existed. What impressed Cicero primarily about Posidonius' *sphaera* was that a single turning motion imparted to it resulted in an imitation of the distinct motions of the Sun, Moon, and planets just like their actual motions in the heavens, and this same characterization, which would fit the Antikythera Mechanism so well, reappears in both the Archimedes passages. In *De re publica* Cicero attributes another feature to Archimedes' *sphaera*, the apparently realistic representation of the Sun-Moon-shadow conditions causing eclipses, but it is difficult to conceive of how this could have been mechanically implemented. One may well suspect that he invented it to provide a connection to the ensuing story of Sulpicius Gallus' lecture to the Roman troops on the causes of eclipses.

In any case, the obvious implication of Cicero's invoking *specific* mechanisms associated with Archimedes and Posidonius to make his philosophical points is that these were rare objects, not to be found in every schoolroom or in every rich man's collection. We hear no more of mechanical *sphairai* or *sphaerae* until the second century AD, when astronomical mechanisms resurface as a topic of discussion among several scientific and philosophical writers, including Theon of Smyrna, Ptolemy, Galen, and Sextus Empiricus. Significantly, they speak of the mechanisms as if they expect their readers to be familiar with such things, even to have seen them. Perhaps the true heyday of the technology was not the Hellenistic period but Antonine Rome.

The third century AD is again a blank, as it is for most scientific activity in the Greco-Roman world, and one runs across only a few knowledgeable allusions to astronomical mechanisms afterward, but these include the only references we have to a technical literature on *sphairopoiia*. The fifth-century

Neoplatonist philosopher Proclus cites an "astronomical treatise" (*astrologikē pragmateia*) by a certain Carpus of Antioch, whom he further describes as a mechanician, for certain basic definitional issues in mathematics, the relevance of which to the subject of Carpus' book was, Proclus insinuates, rather tenuous.[10] What the subject was can be inferred not just from the author's profession, but also from the fact that Pappus of Alexandria (ca. AD 300) ascribes to this same Carpus the statement that the only book that Archimedes wrote on a mechanical topic was on *sphairopoiia* (see chapter 8). This is unfortunately *all* that the ancient sources tell us about Carpus' or Archimedes' books.

From Proclus we also learn that the tradition of making astronomical mechanisms had not wholly died out in his time. Toward the end of a short book, *On Providence*, that he addressed to a certain Theodorus the Mechanician, Proclus mentions that Theodorus had constructed a device, "employing disks and lathes," that he called a "parapegma."[11] If the name made any sense, Theodorus' mechanism was not a full planetarium but rather a simpler display of time cycles, a mobile counterpart not so much of the stars-and-weather parapegmata that we met in chapter 4 but rather of a genre of peg hole inscriptions from the western Roman Empire that allowed the user to track the current date simultaneously according to cycles including the lunar month and the seven-day astrological week (fig. 9.2).[12]

And as chance would have it, the one other surviving example of astronomical gearwork from antiquity is just such a mobile parapegma and is roughly contemporaneous with, or a little later than, Theodorus and Proclus. It is a portable sundial of unknown provenance (doubtless from somewhere in the eastern Mediterranean region), now in the collection of the London Science Museum (fig 9.3).[13] The sundial is of a type common in late antiquity, designed for telling the time of day at a wide range of latitudes, but in addition to this time-telling function it had an internal system of gearing. As reconstructed by Michael Wright, this was driven by a manual input that one was supposed to advance by one day's worth of motion, and it led to dials on the front and back faces showing the current day of the lunar month, the phase of the Moon, the day according to the astrological week, and possibly also the Sun's and Moon's locations in the zodiac. (Unfortunately, the rear face and part of the gearwork are lost, so that the reconstruction is partly speculative.) The ratios underlying the gearwork are rather simple and crude affairs—in particular, two lunar months are equated to exactly 59 days—and nonuniform motion is not attempted. Knowledge of a simple variety of geared mechanism, but so far as we know not the refined technology of the Antikythera Mechanism, survived into the Middle Ages and resurfaced centuries later in the Islamic world (fig. 9.4).[14] I am inclined to believe that the appearance of astronomically sophisticated planetarium clocks in 14th-century Europe reflects a reinvention of contrivances for achieving nonuniform motion rather than a resurfacing of ancient Greek ideas that had been lurking in a millennium of sources unknown to us.[15]

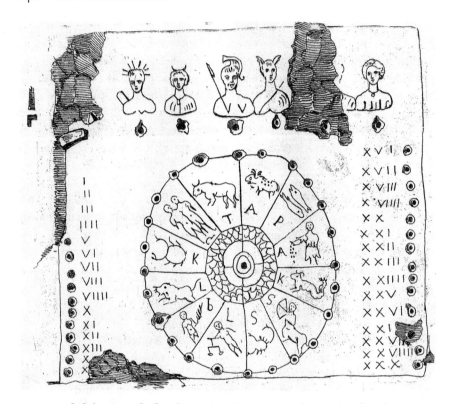

FIG. 9.2. 1816 drawing of a fourth-century AD parapegma inscription found near the Baths of Trajan, Rome; the original is no longer extant. Peg holes tracked the astrological week (*top row*, with busts of the planetary gods), the lunar month (*left and right columns*), and the Sun's or Moon's progress through the zodiac (*lower center*). (Guattani 1817, plate XXII)

We are obviously a long way from being able to put together a coherent story of the evolution and eventual degeneration of the ancient tradition of astronomical mechanisms, but there is enough evidence to suggest that complex and scientifically ambitious mechanisms were being made at least through the three centuries from about 100 BC to AD 200, and that the people who were most likely to encounter them were mechanicians, philosophers, and scientists. Among these three groups, the existence and nature of the mechanisms aroused strikingly diverse responses.

Vitruvius is a representative of the practical professionals who understood how mechanical devices worked and how they were made. He makes no explicit mention of man-made astronomical mechanisms of the planetarium variety in his *On Architecture*, but he must have known something about them because he speaks of the heavens themselves as a mechanism: if, he says, the Sun, Moon, and planets were not spun about mechanically (*machinata*), we would have neither light nor the fruits of the seasons, and from this observation our

(a) (b)

FIG 9.3. The London geared portable sundial. *Left*, the front exterior face, with the dial for the astrological week at the upper left, engraved with busts of the weekday gods. *Right*, interior of the front face with the surviving gears. The largest gear, with 59 teeth, has engraved numerals for the days of the lunar month, which would have been visible in turn through a window in the lost rear face. (Science Museum/Science & Society Picture Library)

ancestors were inspired to invent devices to deliver benefits to mankind.[16] The idea that the revolutions of the heavenly bodies keep the elements of the world below in the continual flux that makes life possible is straight out of Plato's *Timaeus* and Aristotle's *On Generation and Corruption*, but that word *machinata* inserts something new, a vision of those revolutions themselves as caused by a system of invisible, interlocking parts.

Proclus' mechanician acquaintance Theodorus pursued the conception of the cosmos as gearwork to the limit, applying it not only to the heavens but also to the world below and to ourselves, as Proclus paraphrases him:[17]

> [You hold], if I may express it following your words, that there is a certain mechanically acting and ineluctable cause that moves all things, that this cosmos encloses and has within itself; that the universe is like a single mechanism, and all the spheres are analogous to engaged wheels, while those things that are moved by [the spheres], animals and their souls and everything, depend on a single entity that sets them in motion.

Being thus driven by mechanical connections, Theodorus asserted, all components of the cosmos, including "all the varieties of tragic and comedic and other interactions of human affairs," were governed by fate—here he also seems to be thinking of something like the automatic miniature theater described by

FIG. 9.4. The interior gearwork of the astrolabe of Abu Bakr of Isfahan (see fig. 2.3), driving displays on the astrolabe's rear face of the Sun's and Moon's motions through the zodiac and the Moon's phases. (Museum of the History of Science, University of Oxford)

Heron of Alexandria, which presented the story of the god Dionysus through figures moved by strings and pulleys[18]—and so we have no responsibility for our actions.

Theodorus' ideas had something in common with the cosmic determinism of Stoic philosophy, but the Stoics equated fate with the providential plan of the Stoic God who extends throughout the cosmos and governs it, and they also believed that they could reconcile this fate with individual human responsibility. Proclus, who as a Platonist did not hold to complete determinism, nevertheless leveled an argument against Theodorus' dismissal of providence that could almost have come from a Stoic: before Theodorus' gearwork parapegma existed as a physical object, the behavior of whose parts was locked into a fate-like condition by mechanical connections, did it not exist in his mind as a plan? So even if the cosmos was similarly locked into a destined course of evolution, would this not reflect the forethought of the divine Craftsman who conceived it?[19]

Scientific writers seem to have been wary of drawing analogies between man-made mechanisms and the workings of nature. Galen does it on one occasion, in a discussion of the coordinated changes in the breasts and uterus during pregnancy. Do such phenomena, he asks, show that the organs know what they are supposed to do through some process of reasoning? But then they would not be organs—the basic sense of the Greek word *organa*, after all, is instruments or tools—but rational beings in their own right. Or do they act under compulsion arising from the physical construction of the body?

> For just as people who imitate the revolutions of the wandering stars by means of certain instruments [*organa*] instill a principle of motion in them and then go away, while [the devices] operate just as if the craftsman was there and overseeing them in everything, I think in the same way each of the parts in the body operates by some succession and reception of motion from the first principle to every [part], needing no overseer.[20]

But he certainly did not mean to suggest that the connection between these organs was literally mechanical; when he gets around to explaining how the breasts respond to changes in the uterus, he attributes the apparent action at a distance to certain vessels that he believed joined the uterus to the breasts, conveying nutriment to both.[21] Like Cicero, Galen does not want us to look inside the astronomical mechanism to see how it works.

We saw in chapter 7 that Ptolemy complained in his late book *Planetary Hypotheses* about the "usual way of doing *sphairopoiia*," which failed to make visible the hypotheses underlying the appearances of planetary motion and, anyway, got those hypotheses wrong.[22] One of his purposes in writing the book was to provide the designers of mechanisms with a complete and accurate set of astronomical specifications to follow. The legitimate purpose of astronomical mechanisms, in his view, was to instruct the spectator in scientific truths, not to show off the mechanical art, and this meant somehow showing the epicycles and eccenters in action.

Previously, Ptolemy had warned that it could be misleading to liken the motions of the Sun, Moon, and planets too closely to the operation of man-made mechanisms, and in particular to judge that an astronomical hypothesis was false because one could not make a working model of it in the workshop.[23] The materials from which we build our models are the mutable four elements, and the mechanical parts rub against each other and resist being set in motion; the ethereal matter of the heavens, by contrast, is divine and free of all hindrance in its motions. Combinations of motions that seem impossibly complex to us may be simple for the heavenly bodies and the spheres that carry them.

Ptolemy's cosmology stands as a repudiation of the idea of the cosmos as mechanism, whether purposeless as Theodorus imagined it or crafted by the Platonists' master Craftsman. The physical nature of the ethereal bodies in the heavens gives them the freedom to revolve effortlessly, but what makes them move is the rational impulse of souls that govern each individual planet's system, as our souls govern our limbs and organs.[24] We are to liken them not to the workings of invisible gears, but to "a circle of hands joined in a dance, or a ring of people performing a weapon dance: one supports another in the interchange, and they join forces with each other without their bodies coming together, so that they do not obstruct their actions, nor are they hampered by them."[25]

The Antikythera Mechanism and its ancient mechanical siblings made few converts to the idea of a clockwork universe, thus failing to accelerate the Enlightenment by a couple of millennia; nor were they the advance guard of an ancient Industrial Revolution. The science writer Arthur C. Clarke envisioned the missed potential in sensational terms: "If the insight of the Greeks had matched their ingenuity...we would not merely be puttering around on the Moon, we would have reached the nearer stars."[26] Well, perhaps! At least, however, these wonders of ancient science brought the stars down to the Greco-Roman world.

Glossary

anomaly: The technical term in astronomy for **nonuniform motion**.

apogee: The farthest point from the Earth in a heavenly body's orbit or in a component of its motion, according to a geometrical **hypothesis**.

apparent motion: Motion of a heavenly body as seen by an observer on the Earth.

appearance, first: The date when a star or planet is visible in the night sky after an interval when it cannot be seen. For a star or outer planet, the first appearance is the **morning rising**. An inner planet has both a first morning appearance (which is its morning rising) and a first evening appearance.

appearance, last (or **disappearance**): The date when a star or planet ceases to be visible in the night sky. For a star or outer planet, the last appearance is the **evening setting**. An inner planet has both a last morning appearance and a last evening appearance (which is its evening setting).

arbor: A stationary or revolving axle to which gears or pointers are attached.

axis: A center of rotation. In gearwork, one or more **arbors** may share a single axis through the use of **pipes**.

calendar: A set of practices or rules determining the number and names of days within calendar months and of calendar months within calendar years, usually existing for religious, governmental, and private purposes in a community but sometimes for astronomical chronology.

calendar, Callippic: A calendar devised for astronomical applications, regulated by a **76-year cycle** and taking its names for the months from the calendar of Athens. Callippic calendar years were counted within 76-year Callippic periods, the first of which began immediately after the summer solstice of 330 BC.

calendar, Egyptian: The civil **calendar** in Egypt from pharaonic through Roman times. The Egyptian calendar year comprised 12 months of 30 days followed by some days called "epagomenal days" that did not belong to any month. In the original, unreformed version of the calendar, all years had five epagomenal days so that the Egyptian year was a constant 365 days. Soon after Egypt came under Roman rule, a reformed calendar was instituted in which every fourth year had six epagomenal days.

calendar, lunar: A **calendar** in which the months always begin near the same phase of the Moon, usually the new-moon crescent. Lunar months normally have either 29 days ("hollow") or 30 days ("full").

calendar, lunisolar: A **lunar calendar** in which the years always begin at roughly the same season of the natural year. Lunisolar calendar years normally have either 12 months ("ordinary") or 13 months ("intercalary"). Greek calendars, as well as the Babylonian calendar, were lunisolar.

Callippic cycle: See **cycle, 76-year.**

celestial sphere: An imaginary spherical surface with the center of the Earth as its center, used as a frame of reference for apparent positions of heavenly bodies. In Greek astronomy the celestial sphere was usually imagined as rotating on a fixed axis to account for the daily risings and settings of the stars, Sun, Moon, and planets.

conjunction: Date when two heavenly bodies (one of which is usually the Sun) have the same **longitude** as measured along the **ecliptic.**

conjunction, inferior: Conjunction of Venus or Mercury with the Sun, such that the planet is nearer to the Earth than the Sun; occurs during the planet's **retrograde motion.**

conjunction, superior: Conjunction of Venus or Mercury with the Sun, such that the planet is farther from the Earth than the Sun; occurs during the planet's **direct motion.**

contrate: A gear whose teeth project at right angles from the plane of the gear, allowing transfer of motion to an **axis** at right angles to the gear's axis.

crown gear: See **contrate.**

cycle, 19-year: A cycle determining which years of a **lunisolar calendar** are intercalary, on the basis of the approximate equality of 19 solar years with 235 lunar months; often called a Metonic cycle.

cycle, 76-year: A cycle for regulating a **lunisolar calendar**, comprising four **19-year cycles** and assumed to total 27,759 days, on the basis of a solar year of $365\frac{1}{4}$ days.

differential gearing: An arrangement of gears that receives two input rotatory motions and yields a motion representing the difference of their rates, or some other linear combination of the inputs.

direct motion: Apparent motion of a heavenly body in the direction of increasing **longitude** (i.e., eastward along the **ecliptic**).

directions of obscuration: At the beginning, end, and other stages of an eclipse, the parts of the disk of the eclipsed body that are obscured, specified according to the cardinal directions north, south, east, and west.

eccenter: A circular orbit whose center is not the center of the Earth.

eclipse period: An interval comprising a constant whole number of **synodic months** at which eclipses or **eclipse possibilities** have a tendency to recur.

eclipse possibility: A **full moon** or **conjunction** of the Sun and Moon at which the Moon's **latitude** is relatively small so that an eclipse may occur; for example, a lunar eclipse possibility may be defined as a full moon such that the Moon's latitude is less than at the preceding and following full moons.

ecliptic: The apparent circular path of the Sun through the middle of the zodiac on the **celestial sphere**.

elongation: The interval of **longitude** between two heavenly bodies.

elongation, greatest: The date when Venus or Mercury reaches its maximum **elongation** in either direction from the Sun.

epicycle: In Greek astronomy, a heavenly body's hypothetical circular path of motion, the center of which revolves along a larger circular path around the Earth.

epicyclic gearing: Arrangement of gears whose arbors are fixed to off-center points on a base gear.

equator, celestial: The circle on the **celestial sphere** that is equidistant from the poles of its rotation. Exactly half the celestial equator is always above the horizon, so that the dates when the Sun is on the celestial equator are **equinoxes**.

equinoctial point: One of two points where the **ecliptic** intersects the **celestial equator**, and where the Sun is located at the **equinoxes**.

equinox: Date of the year when the Sun rises (approximately) due east and sets due west on the horizon, and the interval of daylight is approximately equal to the interval of night.

Exeligmos: A 669-lunar-month cycle for predicting eclipses, comprising three 223-month **Saros** cycles and assumed to total exactly 19,756 days.

fiducial mark: A reference mark on a scale or dial.

gear train: A series of mechanically connected gears.

gearing down: A gear train whose input motion is faster than its output.

gearing up: A gear train whose input motion is slower than its output.

geocentric: The normal frame of reference assumed in Greek astronomy, according to which the center of the Earth is assumed to be the stationary center of the cosmos.

heliocentric: Frame of reference according to which the Sun is assumed to be the stationary center of the cosmos or of the planets' systems of motion.

horoscope: An astrological document recording the configuration of apparent positions of the heavenly bodies on or about a particular date (e.g., a birthdate of an individual). In a Greek horoscope, both the zodiac and the horizon function as frames of reference, and particular significance adheres to the point of the zodiac rising on the eastern horizon (called "ascendant" or *hōroskopos*).

hour, equinoctial: A constant unit of time equal to $1/24$ of a mean day and night (i.e., our modern hour).

hour, seasonal: A seasonally varying unit of time equal to $1/12$ of the interval from sunrise to sunset or from sunset to sunrise; in the Greco-Roman world, times of day or night were most commonly expressed in seasonal hours.

hypothesis: In Greek astronomy, an astronomical theory or model. Hypotheses to account for the apparent motions of the heavenly bodies typically comprised uniform circular motions such as **eccenters** and **epicycles**.

idler: An intermediate gear in a gear train that has no effect on the ratio of input to output rates of motion, though the inclusion of idlers may reverse the sense of rotation.

latitude, celestial: Coordinate of the apparent position or motion of a heavenly body measured perpendicularly north or south of the **ecliptic**.

longitude, celestial: Coordinate of the apparent position or motion of a heavenly body measured eastward along the **ecliptic**.

Metonic cycle: See **cycle, 19-year.**

month, calendar: A month as defined by the rules of a **calendar**; for example, in a **lunisolar calendar**, a **lunar month**.

month, full: A **lunar month**, in particular a **calendar month** in a **lunisolar calendar**, comprising 30 days.

month, hollow: A **lunar month**, in particular a **calendar month** in a **lunisolar calendar**, comprising 29 days.

month, intercalary: In a **lunisolar calendar**, a 13th **calendar month** added to a **calendar year**. In most ancient lunisolar calendars, the intercalary month was a repetition of the preceding month.

month, lunar: The interval, in whole days, between two successive occurrences of the same **phase of the Moon** (e.g., between two **new moons**).

month, sidereal: The period, or mean period, of return of the Moon to the same position along the **ecliptic** relative to the fixed stars.

month, synodic: The interval in which the Moon first returns to its initial **elongation** from the Sun (e.g., between two successive **conjunctions**).

new moon: The date when the Moon is first visible as a waxing crescent near the western **horizon** after sunset. (An alternate sense, equivalent to **conjunction**, is avoided in this book.)

nonuniform motion: **Apparent motion** of a heavenly body at a variable rate.

opposition: Date when the Moon or a planet is diametrically opposite the Sun in **longitude** (i.e., at 180° **elongation**).

parallax: The difference in apparent position of a body as observed from different points; in particular, lunar parallax is the difference between the apparent position of the Moon (as reflected in its longitude and latitude) as observed from a point on the Earth's surface and as it would be observed from the center of the Earth.

parapegma: A document or object for tracking one or more chronological cycles (e.g., a cycle of annually repeating **risings** and **settings** of constellations or the **astrological week**).

period relation: An approximate equation of numbers of different astronomical cycles (e.g., **solar years** and **synodic periods** of a planet).

pin-and-slot: A device by which one planar gear drives or is driven by another planar gear by means of a pin projecting perpendicularly from the first gear into a radial slot in the second gear.

pipe: A tube-shaped mechanical part; for example, a hollow **arbor** that may enclose another arbor sharing the same **axis**.

planetarium: A mechanical device displaying images of the Sun, Moon, and planets in their motions around the **zodiac**.

planets: The five planets that are visible to the naked eye and were known to ancient astronomy are Saturn, Jupiter, Mars, Venus, and Mercury. Mars, Jupiter, and Saturn are called "outer planets," while Mercury and Venus are "inner planets." The Sun and Moon are also sometimes spoken of as planets (see **wandering stars**).

planets, descriptive names: Conventional Greek adjectival names for the five planets, relating to their supposed visual aspects (e.g., Mercury = "Gleamer" [*Stilbon*]).

planets, theophoric names: Conventional Greek phrases identifying the five planets by associated divinities (e.g., Mercury = "the star of Hermes").

precession: The gradual shift in apparent positions of the stars relative to the **solstitial** and **equinoctial points**.

retrograde motion: Apparent motion of a heavenly body in the direction of decreasing **longitude** (i.e., westward along the **ecliptic**).

rising: The term "rising" often applies to a date when a star or planet is observed to rise for the first or last time before sunrise or after sunset.

rising, evening or acronychal: The date when a star or outer planet is last seen to rise after sunset.

rising, morning: The date when a star or planet is first seen to rise before sunrise.

Saros: A 223-lunar-month cycle for predicting eclipses. In Greek astronomy its duration was sometimes assumed to be a constant $6585^{1/3}$ days.

setting: The term "setting" often applies to a date when a star or planet is observed to set for the first or last time before sunrise or after sunset.

setting, evening: The date when a star or planet is last seen to set after sunset.

setting, morning: The date when a star or outer planet is first seen to set before sunrise.

solstice: Date of the year when the Sun's rising and setting points on the horizon and its noon altitude are farthest north or south, resulting in the longest or shortest interval of daylight.

solstitial point: One of two points of the **ecliptic**, at 90° **elongation** from the equinoctial points, where the Sun is located at the **solstices**.

sphaira (sphaera): Term used in Greek and Latin texts for a **planetarium**.

station: A date when a planet changes from **direct motion** to **retrograde motion** or vice versa.

synodic cycle: A cycle of phenomena of the Moon or one of the planets, tied to its **apparent motion** relative to the Sun (e.g., the cycle of phases of the Moon).

synodic period: The time interval associated with a **synodic cycle**.

tooth count: The number of teeth on a gear.

uniform motion: In Greek astronomy, motion along a circular path at a constant rate.

wandering stars: Visible heavenly bodies that are seen to change position relative to the fixed stars; namely, the Sun, Moon, and the five **planets**.

week, astrological: A repeating seven-day cycle according to which each day in turn is ruled astrologically by one of the heavenly bodies in the sequence Kronos (Saturn), Sun, Moon, Ares (Mars), Hermes (Mercury), Zeus (Jupiter), Aphrodite (Venus).

year, calendar: A year as defined by a **calendar**, as opposed to a **solar year**.

year, sidereal: The mean period of the Sun's revolution around the **ecliptic** relative to fixed stars.

year, solar: A year as defined by the Sun's revolution around the **ecliptic** or by phenomena dependent on the Sun's revolution.

year, tropical: The mean **solar year** as defined by successive **solstices** or **equinoxes** of the same kind.

zodiac: The circular belt among the stars, constituting the path of **apparent motion** of the Sun, Moon, and planets; divided into the twelve zodiacal signs.

zodiacal signs: Equal 30° sectors of the **zodiac**, named after the constellations that approximately coincided with them in antiquity.

Notes

Preface

1. Cassiodorus, *Variae* 1.45.
2. Price, "An Ancient Greek Computer," 60.

Chapter 1

1. The authoritative study of the Antikythera shipwreck and its cargo is Kaltsas et al. 2012 (also published in a Greek-language edition). Among earlier publications, the following are noteworthy: Anonymous 1902, Svoronos 1903, Weinberg et al. 1965, Throckmorton 1970, 113–68.
2. Bouyia 2012. Isotopic analysis of lead from anchor stocks, hull sheeting, and other artifacts from the ship indicates an origin in Chalkidiki, suggesting that the ship was of Greek, not Italian, origin: Foley 2016.
3. Tselekas 2012.
4. See especially chapter 4.
5. For the history and archeology of the island, see Bevan & Conolly 2013, esp. 133–5 and 187–96; Tsaravopoulos 2004–2009.
6. The destructive processes affecting various materials in marine environments are surveyed in Pearson 1987.
7. Accounts of the discovery and salvage operations in Svoronos 1903, 1–14; Throckmorton 1970, 113–68; Tsipopoulou et al. 2012; and contemporaneous reports in Athenian newspapers of 1900–1901, accessible in digitizations through the websites of the Library of the Hellenic Parliament (http://catalog.parliament.gr/hipres/help/null/horizon/microfilms2.html) and the National Library of Greece (http://

efimeris.nlg.gr/ns/main.html) and in transcriptions through the website of the Aristotle University of Thessaloniki (http://digital.lib.auth.gr). On Greek sponge divers, see Bernard 1967.

8. Zahariadis 2008.

9. The Julian calendar was used in Greece until 1923, and dates from Greek sources of this time will be given here in their original Julian form; to obtain the Gregorian equivalent, add 13 days. Orthodox Easter in 1900 fell on April 9 (Julian).

10. Seiradakis (forthcoming), on the authority of Lykoudis 1957. Unfortunately, no records relating to this incident can be found in the Historical Archive of Antiquities and Monuments (personal communication from Dr. Stavroula Masouridi).

11. Throckmorton 1970, 124–6. Aspects of Throckmorton's account were disputed by one of the divers' descendants in a letter to the newspaper *Kathimerini* in the 1970s, according to Eleni Kladaki-Vratsanou in Stikas 2014, 69.

12. *The Standard* of London alone printed at least a dozen notices about the salvage operations between November 1900 and July 1901.

13. Tsipopoulou et al. 2012, 22.

14. *To Asty*, July 13, 1901. The autumn 2015 campaign of the new excavations of the wreck confirmed that the site had been fairly thoroughly disturbed down to a depth of the better part of a meter: Foley 2016.

15. Theofanidis 1929, 83.

16. In addition to the government's compensation, the Archaeological Society at Athens awarded 500 drachmas to each diver (Svoronos 1903a, 14). The estimated dollar equivalent assumes that the payment was in gold drachmas; the paper drachma's value fluctuated around two-thirds of a gold drachma. In any case the payment was substantial, roughly 8 percent of the Greek government's total annual expenditures (around 120 million drachmas in 1902; Colby 1903, 315).

17. Tsipopoulou et al. 2012, 23.

18. The 1905 campaign was extensively reported in the Athenian newspapers but was subsequently forgotten.

19. Dumas 1972, 67–82; Kolonas 2012.

20. Vyzantinos 1901a, Vyzantinos 1901b.

21. The dispute can be followed in contemporaneous newspaper reports, many of them indexed in Svoronos 1903.

22. Tsipopoulou et al. 2012, 24–8.

23. His father, Athanasios Rousopoulos (1823–1898), had been a noteworthy archeologist whose reputation was tarnished by accusations of illegal trafficking in antiquities.

Chapter 2

1. *To Asty*, May 21, 1902. Much of the following narrative is based on the contemporaneous newspaper reports, for which see chapter 1, note 7.

2. Tracy 2009.

3. *Skrip*, May 21, 1902.

4. *Skrip*, May 22, 1902; *Neon Asty*, May 22, 1902.
5. *Neon Asty*, May 22, 1902; *Hestia*, May 22, 1902; *Skrip*, May 23, 1902; *To Asty*, May 23, 1902; *Neon Asty*, May 23, 1902.
6. *Neon Asty*, May 23, 1902.
7. *To Asty*, May 24, 1902; *Neon Asty*, May 25, 1902.
8. *To Asty*, May 29, 1902.
9. *To Asty*, May 30, 1902.
10. Anonymous 1902; in Svoronos 1903, 16, the authors are identified as Valerios Stais, Hristos Tsountas, and Konstantinos Kourouniotis, writing under Kavvadias's supervision.
11. Svoronos 1903.
12. Svoronos 1903, 44–52. Rediadis had already given a provisional description of Fragments A, B, and C in *To Asty*, June 23 and 24, 1902. *The Standard* (London), June 7, 1902 (corresponding to May 25 in Greece), had printed a brief notice of the discovery among the bronze fragments from Antikythera of an "astronomical instrument ... which appears to have been used as an astrolabe." The Mechanism is also mentioned, for its bearing on the date of the shipwreck, in Vicars 1903, 562, which apparently got its information from Kavvadias.
13. For a fuller explanation of the astrolabe and its functions, see Evans 1998, 141–61.
14. Announced (for December 16, 1906) in *Mitteilungen des Kaiserlich Deutschen Archäologischen Instituts, Athenische Abteilung* 31 (1906): 569. For brief reports of the lecture, see the publications cited in note 20.
15. The principal sources for the following narrative are unpublished documents in the Rehm *Nachlass* in the Bayerische Staatsbibliothek, Munich, especially Rehm 1905, Rehm 1906a, and Rehm 1906b.
16. Rousopoulos 1905, 253.
17. Stais 1905, 18–23.
18. Diels & Rehm 1904.
19. Karo seems to have been chiefly interested in its bearing on the date of the shipwreck.
20. Rados 1910, 34–6; Rediadis 1910, 157–9.
21. Theofanidis was the first of three generations of distinguished admirals in the Greek navy; his wife was the great-granddaughter of Kolokotronis, the hero of the War of Independence.
22. Theofanidis 1929.
23. Theofanidis, 1934; Magou 2012, 235.
24. Beaver 1985; Falk 2014.
25. Petrakos 1994.
26. Vlachogianni 2012; *Eleftheria*, January 11, 1959: 11.
27. The most important is Price 1955–1956.
28. Price 1955–1956, 33.
29. Price 1959b; personal communications (July 7–8, 2014) from Charles B. Greifenstein, American Philosophical Society Library.
30. Price's collection of photographs is in the collection of the Adler Planetarium, Chicago.

31. Fragment D was not locatable at this time. On the chemical and spectroscopic analyses made of samples from the "crumb box," see chapter 8.
32. Price 1974, 12.
33. *The Science News-Letter*, 75.3 (January 17, 1959): 36.
34. *Washington Post*, December 31, 1958: A6.
35. *Eleftheria*, January 8, 1958: 1; *Baltimore Sun*, January 7, 1959: 3.
36. *Eleftheria*, January 11, 1959: 11.
37. Clarke 1975.
38. Price, unpublished notes on the Mechanism's inscriptions, Adler Planetarium collection.
39. Price 1959a, 66.
40. Price 1959a, 61; Price 1974, 48.
41. Price 1959a, 65; in Price 1974, 19–20, Price modifies the argument and shifts the date back to about 87 BC. See also chapter 4.
42. Price 1975, 376.
43. Price 1974, 12.
44. Price 1964, 15.
45. An excellent survey of radiography applied in archeology and cultural heritage is Lang & Middleton 2005.
46. In 1964 Edwin Battison, mechanical engineering curator at the Smithsonian Institution, applied to the Museum and the Antiquities and Restoration of Monuments Service to X-ray the fragments, but this initiative too came to nothing; see Tsipopoulou et al. 2012, 31, note 92, and correspondence in Smithsonian Institution Archives Collection 397, Box 20, Folder "Misc., Computer, Astronomical, Antikythera." It is not clear whether Price had any connection with it.
47. Toishi 1965; Miller et al. 1970.
48. Price 1974, 12–3.
49. For Karakalos's report describing his radiography of the Mechanism, see Price 1974, 66–8.
50. Parts of the object closer to the focus have larger projections on the film. Moving the X-ray source closer to the object exaggerates this effect.
51. Price 1974, 41.
52. Price 1974, 32.
53. Wright 2003a, 275.
54. Price 1974, 41–2. See also chapter 8.
55. Zeeman 1986, 150–1.
56. Wright et al. 1995. For a narrative of the collaboration of Wright and Bromley derived from interviews with Wright, see Marchant 2008, 171–93; criticisms of aspects of this account by friends and family of Bromley are at http://www.connectives.com/decoding-the-heavens-bromley-comments.html.
57. Littleton & Littleton 1996.
58. Wright 2005a.
59. Price 1959a, 64–5.
60. Price (Price 1974, 44) had suggested a gear train that would have produced a 3.8-year period for the upper back dial, but several tooth counts in this proposed

train were incorrect. The train that Price favored gave a longer period of exactly four years.

61. Wright 2003a, 279; Wright 2005b, 57–9 and 61–2.
62. Price 1974, 34–5; Wright 2005b, 54, note 34.
63. Wright 2005c.
64. Much later in his career, in 1943, Rehm corresponded with the historian of astronomy Ernst Zinner about the possibility of constructing a model, but nothing came of the idea because accurate measurements of the fragments could not be obtained (unpublished correspondence in Bayerische Staatsbibliothek, Rehmiana IV).
65. Price 1959a, 66.
66. Price 1974, 21.
67. Price 1974, 59.
68. Wright 2002a.
69. Wright 2011.
70. Edmunds et al. 2006; Antikythera Mechanism Research Project 2012.
71. Unpublished correspondence between Price and Petros Kalligas in Adler Planetarium collection; Wright 2004.
72. Zafeiropoulou 2006; Zafeiropoulou 2012, 242.
73. Explanations with references at http://www.hpl.hp.com/research/ptm/ and http://culturalheritageimaging.org/Technologies/RTI/.
74. Heilmeyer 1985; Goebbels et al. 1985.
75. Seabrook 2007.
76. Wright et al. 1995, 542.
77. Freeth et al. 2006.
78. The modification resulted from the identification of the extant subsidiary dial of the upper back face as displaying a 4-year cycle instead of a 76-year cycle as previously assumed; see Freeth et al. 2008, supplementary notes 22.
79. Wright 2007, 27, note.
80. Freeth et al. 2006, supplementary information 5–14.
81. Allen et al. 2016, Jones 2016c, Bitsakis & Jones 2016a, Bitsakis & Jones 2016b, Anastasiou et al. 2016a, and Anastasiou et al. 2016b.

Chapter 3

1. Bitsakis & Jones 2016b (text and translation 232–8).
2. The exact dimensions are difficult to determine; for details see Allen et al. 2016, 24–32.
3. Price 1959a, 64, with the diagram on 62–3, gave the general layout of the back plate, with the crucial correction in Wright 2004, 10, that the slots of the large dials are spirals, not concentric circles.
4. Anastasiou et al. 2014, 3–7, refining a previous description in Freeth et al. 2006, 589, fig. 3.
5. Wright 2005a, 10.

6. Freeth et al. 2008, supplementary notes 7–11; Anastasiou et al. 2016b, 155–7 and 169–75.
7. The numerals inscribed on the Mechanism were in the so-called Ionic notation, which used the 24 letters of the standard Greek alphabet, plus three special symbols, to represent 1 through 9, 10 through 90, and 100 through 900.
8. Freeth et al. 2008, supplementary notes 12–4; Anastasiou et al. 2016b, 157–8 and 170–1.
9. This is the passage preserved on Fragment 19 that, as we saw in chapter 2, helped Price in his correct partial reconstruction of one of the Mechanism's gear trains.
10. Freeth et al. 2008, supplementary notes 19–21; Anastasiou et al. 2016b, 158 and 174–5.
11. Freeth et al. 2006, 589.
12. Freeth et al. 2006, 589, and supplementary information 5; Freeth et al. 2008, supplementary notes 24–9; Anastasiou et al. 2016b, 158–62 and 179–91.
13. Freeth et al. 2008, supplementary notes 39–40.
14. Freeth et al. 2006, 589; Freeth et al. 2008, supplementary notes 40–41; Anastasiou et al. 2016b, 163.
15. Anastasiou et al. 2016b, 163–8 and 192–209.
16. Wright 2011, 12–3.
17. Price 1959a, 66; Price 1974, 22.
18. Price 1959a, 64; Price 1974, 17–8; Bitsakis & Jones 2016a, 83–4.
19. Price 1959a, 64; Price 1974, 18–9; Bitsakis & Jones 2016a, 85. The Egyptian Calendar scale was first described in Rehm 1905 and Rehm 1906b.
20. Wright 2003b, 20. The holes were first seen by Price from radiographs, but their location is inexactly described in Price 1974, 17.
21. Wright 2002b; Freeth & Jones 2012, section 3.3.3.
22. Wright 2006.
23. Freeth & Jones 2012, section 2.3.2. See also Wright 2002 and chapter 7 for Wright's arguments, antedating the reading of this passage of the BCI, for reconstructing a system of planetary pointers along similar lines to what is described here.
24. Freeth et al. 2006, 590–1. See also chapter 5.
25. Price 1959a, 62, figure; Wright 2012. There are differences in structural detail between Price's and Wright's reconstructions of the frame.
26. Price 1974, 16; Bitsakis & Jones 2016a, 85–9.
27. Price 1959a, 64; Price 1974, 18 and 49.
28. Bitsakis & Jones 2016a, 76–7 and 103–4.
29. Price 1974, 12; Wright 2006, 323.
30. Anastasiou et al. 2016a.
31. Price 1959a, 60 and 65; Price 1974, 20–2.

Chapter 4

1. Kiilerich 2005.
2. Palagia 2008.

3. Bötticher 1865.
4. Geminus, *Introduction to the Phenomena* 8.6–15.
5. Translation (with some editorial elements removed) from Attic Inscriptions Online, https://www.atticinscriptions.com/inscription/LupuNGSL/1, Creative Commons license http://creativecommons.org/licenses/by-sa/3.0/deed.en_GB.
6. For further reading on ancient calendars, see Hannah 2005, Steele 2007, Steele 2010, Ben-Dov et al. 2012, and Stern 2012.
7. Aristotle, *Economics* 1351b12–6.
8. Samuel 1972; Trümpy 1997.
9. Pritchett & Neugebauer 1974.
10. *Orientis graeci inscriptiones selectae (OGIS)* 56.
11. Bennett 2011, 49–50.
12. Observation reports in Ptolemy, *Almagest*, e.g., 3.1.
13. Jones 2016b.
14. Geminus, *Introduction to the Phenomena* 8.16–7.
15. Geminus, *Introduction to the Phenomena* 8.18–20.
16. Jones 1999b.
17. Price 1959a, 65.
18. Bromley 1990, 651–2. In Carman & Evans 2014, 760–3, the authors cautiously argue for the genuineness of Price's fiducial mark.
19. Kourouniotes & Thompson 1932, 207–11; *Scholia on Aristophanes' Birds* 997.
20. Bowen & Goldstein 1988, 72–3.
21. Ptolemy, *Almagest* 3.1.
22. Diodorus, *Bibliotheca historica* 12.36.
23. Britton 2007.
24. [Theophrastus], *On Signs* 4.
25. Stern 2012, 31, note 25.
26. Morgan 1996.
27. I owe the information on Athenian intercalation patterns in this paragraph to John D. Morgan (personal communication).
28. Jones 2000.
29. Aristotle, *Metaphysics* 12.8, 1073b32.
30. Bousquet 1991, 180–3.
31. Theon, *Commentary on Ptolemy's Almagest*, ed. Rome, 839.
32. Cavaignac 1938, 282–8; Mommsen 1901; Nikitsky 1895. I am grateful to John D. Morgan for alerting me to these works.
33. Wright 2005a.
34. Price 1959a, 65; Rehm's unpublished notes in Bayerische Staatsbibliothek, Rehmiana III, 7 and 9.
35. Price 1959a, 64–5 with diagram on 64; Wright 2005a, 10.
36. Freeth et al. 2008.
37. Trümpy 1997.
38. Cabanes 2007.
39. *Inscriptiones graecae (IG)* XIV 423–31; Manganaro 1964, 38–68.
40. Iversen 2013a.
41. Strabo, *Geography* 7.7.3.

42. Toomer 1984, 12–3; Bowen & Goldstein 1988, 43.
43. *Inscriptions de Délos* 1957, published in Bizard & Roussel 1907, 432–5. Fragments of a similar monument erected by the same Menodoros at Athens are extant: Geagan 2011, text *Agora* XVIII C-196.
44. In fact none of Menodoros' legible victories were at the Isthmians, perhaps reflecting a temporary loss of prestige of that festival during the years after the Roman destruction of Corinth, when Sikyon assumed their administration.
45. Parker 2004.
46. Price 1959a, 64, diagram.
47. Wright 2005a, 10–1.
48. Freeth et al. 2008, supplementary notes 19–21.
49. Cabanes 1976, 336–41, and Cabanes 1988.
50. Iversen 2013a.
51. For an exploration of this idea, see Iversen 2017.
52. Price 1974, 44.
53. Iversen 2013b. The Halieia had previously been conjectured for the dial inscription by M. Zafeiropoulou; see Zafeiropoulou 2012, 247. The original publication of the Games dial inscriptions indicated the possibility that there might have been third names listed for years 2 and 4. We no longer believe that there are any convincing traces of third festivals in the CT data.
54. *Scholia on Pindar, Olympians* 7, 147c.
55. Jones 2012.
56. Cicero, *On the Nature of the Gods* 2.288.

Chapter 5

1. [Hippocrates], *Epidemics* 1.2.7.
2. Aristotle, *Historia animalium* 599b8.
3. Jones 2007.
4. Sophocles, *Oedipus the King* 1133–7; Thucydides 2.78; [Demosthenes] *Against Lakritos* 10.
5. Diels & Rehm 1903, Rehm 1904, Lehoux 2005.
6. The only close parallel that I know of is a small fragment of a Latin inscription (Naples, Museo Nazionale Archeologico inv. 144808) preserving a peg hole accompanying a statement "Delphinus sets in the evening, storm"; see Lehoux 2007, 158–60.
7. Evans & Berggren 2006, 275–6.
8. Geminus, *Introduction to the Phenomena* 17.
9. Hesiod, *Works and Days* 586–7.
10. [Hippocrates], *Airs, Waters, Places* 11.
11. Ptolemy, *Almagest* 3.1.
12. Blass 1887.
13. Britton 2010.
14. Hunger & Pingree 1989, 67–71.
15. Texts and translations in Sachs & Hunger 1988–.

16. Rochberg 1998.
17. Aristotle, *Metaphysics* 1073b20–8.
18. Jones 2007, 161–2.
19. Rehm 1905.
20. Price 1974, 16–17.
21. Bitsakis & Jones 2016a.
22. The conjectural index letters of the upper left column are Freeth's proposal; see his illustration of the reconstructed front face of the Mechanism in Freeth & Jones 2012, fig. 4.
23. Anastasiou et al. 2013; Bitsakis & Jones 2016a, 117–9.
24. Hesiod, *Works and Days* 564–7; [Hippocrates], *Regimen*, Book 3, section 68.
25. Computed by the software Alcyone *Planetary, Lunar and Stellar Visibility*, version 3.1.0.
26. Galen, *Commentary on Hippocrates Epidemics Book 1*, ed. Kühn, 17a.17.
27. In Neugebauer 1975, Vol. 2, 579–81, the author argues for a dating in the first century AD, identifying Geminus' "Isia" with a different Egyptian festival. But it is highly improbable that he would not have mentioned the Roman reform of the Egyptian calendar if he had written later than the 20s BC. For further discussion, see Evans & Berggren 2006, 15–22.
28. Geminus, *Introduction to the Phenomena* 17.4.
29. Geminus, *Introduction to the Phenomena* 9.12; Samuel 1972, 110–3.
30. Geminus, *Introduction to the Phenomena* 1.1–17.
31. Geminus, *Introduction to the Phenomena* 1.19–21.
32. Geminus, *Introduction to the Phenomena* 1.23–30.
33. Geminus declares the sphericity of the Earth at *Introduction to the Phenomena* 15.1.
34. On a scale of centuries, the rising and setting points do have a noticeable shift because of precession.
35. Theon, ed. Hiller, 151–8.
36. Ptolemy, *Almagest* 3.4.
37. Theon, ed. Hiller, 158–66; Ptolemy, *Almagest* 3.3.
38. Wright 2002b.
39. Evans et al. 2010.
40. Geminus, *Introduction to the Phenomena* 18.
41. Jones 1983.
42. Ptolemy, *Almagest* 4.2.
43. Freeth et al. 2006, 590–1.
44. Wright 2002a, 170.
45. Wright 2005c, 3, fig. 2.
46. Evans & Carman 2014.
47. Hippolytus, *Refutation of All Heresies* 1.6; Graham 2006, 8.
48. Graham 2006, 179–80.
49. See for example the fourth-century BC fresco of the abduction of Persephone in Tomb I at Vergina.
50. Geminus, *Introduction to the Phenomena* 9.3–4.
51. Aristarchus, *On Sizes and Distances*, hypothesis 4.
52. Aristarchus, *On Sizes and Distances*, proposition 7.

53. On the history of attempts to measure these cosmic distances see van Helden 1985, chapters 2–4.
54. Rehm 1905, Rehm 1906a, and Rehm 1906b.
55. Price 1974, 20.
56. Wright 2006. In Wright 2004, 10–1, Wright had already suggested the idea more tentatively, with acknowledgment that Price had anticipated it.
57. Freeth et al. 2008, supplementary notes 22, fig. 14.
58. Freeth subsequently abandoned this proposal and accepted Wright's hypothetical misinstalled contrate, albeit with misgivings: Carman & Di Cocco 2016, reporting personal communication from Freeth.
59. Carman & Di Cocco 2016.
60. Geminus, *Introduction to the Phenomena* 9.8 misses an opportunity to mention it, writing that the half-moon phase occurs when the Moon is a quarter of the zodiac away from the Sun.

Chapter 6

1. British Museum K 772, translation from Parpola 1993, text 114.
2. Cicero, *De re publica* 1.23.
3. The gap between where the anecdote about Archimedes' *sphaera* cuts off and the lead-in to the anecdote about Sulpicius Gallus and the eclipse resulted from a loss of either one or (less likely) three leaves of the manuscript from which the palimpsest *Vaticanus latinus* 5757, the unique transmitter of *De re publica*, was composed: Ziegler 1969, ix–xv. A typical leaf corresponds to about 15 lines in Ziegler's edition.
4. See also Bowen 2002.
5. Livy 44.37.
6. Polybius 29.16 = *Suda*, article Π 1867.
7. Rochberg 2010, 303–15.
8. The lunar-eclipse tablets are edited in Rochberg-Halton 1988.
9. Hunger 1992, texts 115 (British Museum K 742) and 4 (K 750); Parpola 1993, text 33 (British Museum Rm II 6).
10. Parpola 1970–1983, Vol. 2, xxii–xxxii.
11. Hunger 1992, text 4 (K 750).
12. British Museum BM 41129, translation from Sachs & Hunger 1988–, Vol. 5, text 20.
13. Steele 2000a, 432.
14. The statistics on eclipse frequencies in this and the following paragraph are derived from data obtained from the NASA eclipse website, http://eclipse.gsfc.nasa.gov.
15. Parpola 1993, text 148 (British Museum 80-7-19, 36); Huber & De Meis 2004, 34–7.
16. Hunger 1992, text 251.
17. Hunger 1992, text 382.
18. Hunger 1992, text 417.

19. Steele 2000a, 432, and Steele 2011, 455–7.
20. Thucydides 2.28.
21. Thucydides 7.50.
22. Thucydides 1.23.
23. Graham 2006, 221.
24. The first appearance of this argument is in Aristotle, *On the Heavens* 297b24.
25. Aristotle, *On the Heavens* 297b30.
26. For Hipparchus' familiarity with this argument, see Strabo, *Geography* 1.1.12.
27. Aristarchus, *On Sizes and Distances*, propositions 15 and 17.
28. Herodotus, *Histories* 1.74. On this supposed eclipse see Stephenson 1997, 342–4.
29. Pliny, *Natural History* 2.53.
30. Herodotus, *Histories* 7.37; Stephenson 1997, 342–3.
31. Pliny, *Natural History* 2.53.
32. Hipparchus, ed. Manitius, 90.
33. PBerol. 13146+13147, translation from the edition in Neugebauer et al. 1981; see also Jones 2000, 147–8.
34. *POxy astron.* 4137, in Jones 1999a.
35. Steele 2000b, 86–91.
36. Rochberg 2010, 306.
37. Hephaestion, *Apotelesmatika* 1.21–2.
38. Montelle 2011, 152–5.
39. Ptolemy, *Tetrabiblos*, ed. Hübner, 2.5 = ed. Robbins, 2.4.
40. Freeth et al. 2006, 589 and supplementary information 5; Freeth et al. 2008, supplementary notes 24–41; Anastasiou et al. 2016b, sections 6–12.
41. Freeth et al. 2006, supplementary information 5.
42. In Steele 2011, 461–5, the author points out the relation to the Babylonian tablets, while drawing contrasts in the manner of presentation.
43. Anastasiou et al. 2016b, sections 4vi and 9–12; Freeth 2014, note S2.
44. The index letters are given following the reconstruction in Freeth 2014, note S2; see also Anastasiou et al. 2016b, section 10. The translation "large" follows Charles Crowther's conjectural reading *megalēn* as reported by Freeth, which is plausible in sense but grammatically problematic in its context.
45. Freeth 2014, note S2.
46. Freeth 2014, note S2.
47. Anastasiou et al. 2016b, section 11.
48. Anastasiou et al. 2016b, section 12.
49. Montelle 2011, 219 and 241–2; Goldstein 2005.
50. Carman & Evans 2014, 741–6; Freeth 2014, note S4.
51. Inferior but perhaps acceptable fits would be obtained for the full moons on May 23, 187 BC, and June 3, 169 BC, but only if the pointer of the Exeligmos dial was set to indicate a correction of 8 or 16 hours, respectively. However, it is hard to see the sense in prescribing a time correction for the *initial* cycle represented by the Saros dial.
52. Carman & Evans 2014; Freeth 2014.
53. Iversen 2017. Iversen's arguments are partly different from what follows here, because he assumes that the Corinthian year was regulated by the principle that

either the autumnal equinox or (less likely in his view) the rising of Arcturus always fell in Phoinikaios.

54. If the division lines were exactly at 30°, 150°, and 270° clockwise from vertical, which is difficult to establish on the extant Fragment A, the Saros pointer would have been at approximately 26° and the Exeligmos pointer approximately at 32°. The tininess of the Exeligmos pointer would have concealed a 6° discrepancy. Agreement would be even closer for the next month, at 32° and 33° respectively, and this *might* be an indication that the design was originally for a calendar, such as that of Rhodes, whose years began one month later than the Corinthian year.

55. Ancient astronomical tables typically employed epochs centuries before the time of their composition; for example, the Era Nabonassar (February 26, 747 BC) for Ptolemy's *Almagest*, the Era Philip (November 12, 324 BC) for his *Handy Tables*, and the almost incredibly remote June 2, 37,633 BC for the tables used by the author of the late-second-century AD papyrus *P.Fouad* 267 A, for which see Fournet & Tihon 2014 and Jones 2016a. For an astronomical mechanism, one would not want an epoch so distant as to necessitate excruciating amounts of cranking of the input knob.

56. On October 13, 205 BC, the Sun's longitude was about Libra 17° according to modern theory (and also according to the tables of Ptolemy's *Almagest*). The fiducial mark is at Libra 18°.

Chapter 7

1. *To Asty*, May 23, 1902.
2. Koch-Westenholz 1995, 125.
3. Under certain circumstances, Uranus can be seen by unaided vision, but if it was ever sighted in antiquity, it would have been taken for a dim star.
4. Translations adapted from Reiner & Pingree 1975.
5. Parpola 1993, texts 72 (British Museum 83-1-18,126) and 65 (British Museum K 13104).
6. Rochberg 2010, 135–42.
7. The dated Astronomical Diaries are edited in Sachs & Hunger 1988–, Vols. 1–3.
8. This general rule that a planet's synodic phenomena follow a fixed order does not apply to Mercury's first and last appearances. One irregularity, the occasional omission of an appearance (and subsequent disappearance) of Mercury from the alternation of morning and evening intervals of visibility, is mentioned below. Additionally, Mercury's stations may fall within the intervals of the planet's invisibility or visibility.
9. Gray & Steele 2008, Gray & Steele 2009.
10. The period relation listed here for Mercury is only the shortest of four attested ACT relations for that planet.
11. Rochberg 1998. Some modern scholars have preferred to call them "proto-horoscopes" because they do not make reference to the rising point of the ecliptic, the Greek term for which (*hōroskopos*) gave rise to the word "horoscope."
12. Yale Babylonian Collection MLC 2190, text 10, in Rochberg 1998.

13. Xenophon, *Memorabilia* 4.7.4.
14. Koch-Westenholz 1995, 115–30. The gods usually associated with Saturn (Ninurta) and Mercury (Nabû) have less obvious affinities with the Greek Kronos and Hermes. Except in the case of Venus-Ishtar, the planets are seldom *named* according to the associated divinities in cuneiform texts.
15. Plato, *Republic* 527d1.
16. Plato, *Republic* 614b2–621d3.
17. Plato, *Republic* 616c5–617d1.
18. The earliest-known instance seems to be Tibullus, *Elegiae* 1.3.18, an ironic allusion to the day of Saturn.
19. Robert 1897–1919, Vol. 3, 436–49.
20. Theon, ed. Hiller, 146.
21. Cicero, *On the Nature of the Gods* 2.88.
22. Cicero, *Tusculan Disputations* 1.63.
23. Cicero, *De re publica* 1.22.
24. Marchant 2015.
25. Cicero most commonly employs *solidus* in the sense "firm" or "substantial" (either literally or metaphorically). The geometrical sense "three-dimensional" occurs in *On the Nature of the Gods* 2.47 and *Timaeus* 15.1; the sense "not hollow," in *On Divination* 1.48. The ambiguity of the Latin adjective mirrors that of the Greek *stereos*.
26. Rehm 1906b.
27. Price 1959a, 65.
28. Price 1974, 21.
29. Wright 2002a, Edmunds & Morgan 2000, Freeth 2002a, Freeth 2002b.
30. Evans et al. 2010, 22–35.
31. Price 1974, 47, fig. 36; Freeth et al. 2006, supplementary information 8–9.
32. Freeth & Jones 2012, section 2.3.2. See Bitsakis & Jones 2016b.
33. Price 1974, 48 and fig. 37, *right* (transcription of the fragment now designated Fragment 21).
34. Aristotle, *Metaphysics* 12 (Λ), 1073b17–32.
35. Simplicius, *Commentary on Aristotle, On the Heavens*, ed. Heiberg, *Commentaria in Aristotelem graecae* (*CAG*), Vol. 7, 495–7.
36. Diverse views in Bowen 2013, Mendell 2000, Yavetz 1998, and Yavetz 2001.
37. Simplicius, *Commentary on Aristotle, On the Heavens*, ed. Heiberg, *CAG*, Vol. 7, 504–5.
38. Jones 2006; *P.Oxy astr.* 4133, in Jones 1999a.
39. Steele 2013.
40. Gallis 1980.
41. Cato, *De agri cultura* 5.4.5; Valerius Maximus, 1.3.3; Livy, *A.U.C. Periochae ex POxy 668*, 191–2.
42. Pingree 1997, 21–9; Greenbaum & Ross 2010.
43. Jones 1998.
44. Ptolemy, *Almagest* 12.1.
45. Ptolemy, *Almagest* 9.2.
46. Aaboe 2001, 135–70.

47. Anastasiou et al. 2016a.
48. Ptolemy, *Planetary Hypotheses* 1.1.

Chapter 8

1. [Aristotle], *Mechanics* 848a19.
2. Heron, *Pneumatics* 1.32 and 2.32.
3. Vitruvius 10.9; Heron, *Dioptra* 34 and 38.
4. A useful list of passages in Greek and Latin literature referring to astronomical mechanisms is provided in Edmunds 2014, 13–4.
5. Field & Wright 1985, 116–25. A fragment of a gear, found in 2006 at Olbia, Sardinia, and accompanied by no related mechanical remains but in an archeological context reportedly dating to about 200 BC, has been claimed as part of the original planetarium of Archimedes; see Pastore 2006 and Pastore 2013. Its material is brass, and its teeth have rounded, roughly cycloidal shape. Contamination of the archeological context by an artifact of much more modern date is the most probable explanation of the fragment.
6. Heron, *Dioptra* 37; Heron, *Mechanics* 1; Pappus, *Collection* 8.19–24.
7. For the notations, I follow the version of the gear train diagram in Freeth et al. 2008, supplementary notes 22, fig. 14.
8. Price 1974, 41–2.
9. Wright 2003a, 279; Wright 2005b, 57–9 and 61–2.
10. Wright 2006.
11. Wright 2002a.
12. As Wright 2002b has shown, it can also be used to represent solar anomaly according to an epicyclic hypothesis if, notwithstanding the arguments of Evans, Carman, and Thorndike, distinct pointers for the mean sun and true sun revolved around a uniformly graduated Zodiac dial.
13. Freeth & Jones 2012, section 3.3.1.
14. Wright 2013b.
15. Wright 2002a, 171–2.
16. Wright 2005b; Freeth et al. 2006, 590.
17. The correspondence between motions in an eccentric hypothesis and in a pin-and-slot coupling is less straightforward if the pin-and-slot gears are mounted epicyclically as in the lunar-anomaly apparatus, because the engagements with the gears on the central axis reverse the sense of their revolution relative to the astronomical theory. The mathematically adept designer of such mechanisms would have had no difficulty in perceiving their relation to the theoretical models, but it would have been obscure to a layman even if the gearwork had been exposed to view.
18. Ptolemy, *Almagest* 4.11.
19. Freeth et al. 2006, 590.
20. Carman, et al. 2012, Freeth & Jones 2012. In Wright 2012, 290, the author points out that Venus and Mercury could also have been modeled by pin-and-slot devices instead of the slotted-arm devices described earlier.

21. Wright 2013a and personal communication with the author.
22. Evans & Carman 2014, 164–6; Wright 2012, 291.
23. Wright 2011.
24. Wright 2011, 9.
25. Price 1974, 47.
26. Price 1974, 63–6.
27. Zafeiropoulou 2012, 243.
28. Wright 2011, 14–6.
29. Wright 1990, 83–7; Wright 2011, 15.
30. Edmunds 2011.
31. "Mechanism" lunar periodicities are derived from the reconstructed gearwork; planetary periodicities, from the relations recovered from the FCI. "ACT" planetary periodicities are from the relations in table 7.3, and lunar periodicities are from the common ACT equation of one year with 12;22,8 synodic months and the System B relation equating 251 synodic months with 269 anomalistic months. "Ptolemy" periodicities are from the daily mean motions in *Almagest* 4.3 and 9.3 and his precessional rate of 1° in 100 years.
32. Jones 1999a, texts 4152–61. The oldest of these planetary tables is probably *P.Oxy astr.* 4160a, which contains ACT computations of phenomena of Jupiter for AD 6 through 13.
33. Ptolemy, *Almagest* 9.2. Unfortunately Ptolemy's presentation leaves it unclear whether Hipparchus' version of the Goal-Year periods incorporated correction terms and, if so, what they were.
34. Ptolemy, *Almagest* 4.2.
35. Freeth & Jones 2012, section 3.10.
36. Pappus, *Collection* 8.1.
37. Plutarch, *Life of Marcellus* 14; Pappus, *Collection* 8.2–3.

Chapter 9

1. Feynman 1988, 93–7.
2. Juvenal, *Satires* 6.572–6; Pliny, *Natural History* 29.9.
3. Geminus' discussion of the planets is rather cursory, but at 1.22 he makes an unfulfilled promise to treat them in detail "elsewhere." Is the work as we have it incomplete?
4. Edmunds 2014, 275–6. Edmunds counts 19 texts plus another 6 "less direct or doubtful" ones, but his first, Archimedes' reported book on *sphairopoiia*, is not extant.
5. Strabo, *Geography* 12.3.11; Mastrocinque 2009 speculates that the Antikythera Mechanism *was* Billaros' *sphaira*.
6. Plato, *Timaeus* 40d2; Epicurus, *On Nature*, Book 11, in Sedley 1976, 31–7 (Sedley maintains that the *organa* were indeed gearwork).
7. Plutarch, *Cicero* 4.5.
8. Cicero, *De fato* 5.7 and *De finibus* 1.6.11. For a later exchange of correspondence between Cicero and Posidonius see Cicero, *Letters to Atticus* 2.1.

9. Cicero, *Tusculan Disputations* 5.64–6.
10. Proclus, *Commentary on Book I of Euclid's Elements*, ed. Friedlein, 125, 241, and 243.
11. Proclus, *On Providence* 65.
12. Lehoux 2007, 168–79.
13. London Science Museum inv. 1983–1393. See Field & Wright 1985 and, on portable sundials in general, Talbert 2016.
14. Field & Wright 1985, 88 and 116–21.
15. For a contrasting view, see Edmunds 2014.
16. Vitruvius, *On Architecture* 10.1.4.
17. Proclus, *On Providence* 2.
18. Heron, *De automatis.*
19. Proclus, *On Providence* 65.
20. Galen, *On the Use of the Parts* 12.5.
21. Galen, *On the Use of the Parts* 12.8.
22. Ptolemy, *Planetary Hypotheses* 1.1.
23. Ptolemy, *Almagest* 13.2.
24. Ptolemy, *Planetary Hypotheses* 2.3.
25. Ptolemy, *Planetary Hypotheses* 2.8.
26. Clarke 1975, 116.

Bibliography

Aaboe, A. 2001. *Episodes from the Early History of Astronomy.*
New York: Springer.

Allen, M., W. Ambrisco, M. Anastasiou, D. Bate, Y. Bitsakis, A. Crawley,
M. G. Edmunds, et al. 2016. "General Preface to the Publication of
the Inscriptions." In *Special Issue: The Inscriptions of the Antikythera
Mechanism. Almagest* 7.1: 5–35.

Anastasiou, M., Y. Bitsakis, A. Jones, X. Moussas, A. Tselikas, and
M. Zafeiropoulou. 2016a. "The Front Cover Inscription." In *Special
Issue: The Inscriptions of the Antikythera Mechanism. Almagest* 7.1: 250–97.

Anastasiou, M., Y. Bitsakis, A. Jones, J. M. Steele, and M. Zafeiropoulou.
2016. "The Back Dial and Back Plate Inscriptions." In *Special Issue: The
Inscriptions of the Antikythera Mechanism. Almagest* 7.1: 138–215.

Anastasiou, M., J. H. Seiradakis, C. C. Carman, and K. Efstathiou. 2014. "The
Antikythera Mechanism: The Construction of the Metonic Pointer and
the Back Plate Spirals." *Journal for the History of Astronomy* 45.4: 418–41.

Anastasiou, M., J. H. Seiradakis, J. C. Evans, S. Drougou, and K. Efstathiou.
2013. "The Astronomical Events of the Parapegma of the Antikythera
Mechanism." *Journal for the History of Astronomy* 44.2: 173–86.

Anonymous. 1902. "Τὰ εὑρήματα τοῦ ναυαγίου τῶν Ἀντικυθήρων." Ἐφημερὶς
Ἀρχαιολογικὴ 1902:145–72 and plates 7–17.

Antikythera Mechanism Research Project. 2012. "Functions and Models of
the Antikythera Mechanism." In *The Antikythera Shipwreck: The Ship, the
Treasures, the Mechanism; Exhibition Catalogue, National Archaeological
Museum April 2012–April 2013.* Edited by N. Kaltsas, E. Vlachogianni, and
P. Bouyia, 256–72. Athens, Greece: Kapon.

Beaver, D. 1985. "Eloge: Derek John de Solla Price." *Isis* 76:371–74.

Ben-Dov, J., W. Horowitz, and J. M. Steele, eds. 2012. *Living the Lunar
Calendar.* Oxford: Oxbow.

Bennett, C. 2011. *Alexandria and the Moon: An Investigation into the Lunar Macedonian Calendar of Ptolemaic Egypt*. Studia Hellenistica 52. Leuven, Belgium: Peeters.

Bernard, H. R. 1967. "Kalymnian Sponge Diving." *Human Biology* 39.2: 103–30.

Bevan, A., and J. Conolly. 2013. *Mediterranean Islands, Fragile Communities and Persistent Landscapes: Antikythera in Long-Term Perspective*. Cambridge, UK: Cambridge University Press.

Bitsakis, Y., and A. Jones. 2016a. "The Front Dial and Parapegma Inscriptions." In *Special Issue: The Inscriptions of the Antikythera Mechanism. Almagest* 7.1: 68–137.

Bitsakis, Y., and A. Jones. 2016b. "The Back Cover Inscription." In *Special Issue: The Inscriptions of the Antikythera Mechanism. Almagest* 7.1: 216–48.

Bizard, L., and P. Roussel. 1907. "Fouilles de Délos, exécutées aux frais de M. le Duc de Loubat (1904): Inscriptions (1)." *Bulletin de Correspondance Hellénique* 31.1: 421–70.

Blass, F. 1887. "Eudoxi ars astronomica qualis in charta Aegyptiaca superest." Kiel Universität, Universitätsprogramm Sommersemester 1887. Reprinted in *Zeitschrift für Papyrologie und Epigraphik* 115 (1997): 79–101.

Bötticher, C. 1865. "Der antike Festkalender an der Panagia Gorgopico zu Athen." *Philologus* 22.3: 385–436.

Bousquet, J. 1991. "Inscriptions de Delphes." *Bulletin de Correspondance Hellénique* 115.1: 167–81.

Bouyia, P. 2012. "Maritime Commerce and Luxury in the Age of Cicero: The Evidence of the Antikythera Shipwreck." In *The Antikythera Shipwreck: The Ship, the Treasures, the Mechanism; Exhibition Catalogue, National Archaeological Museum April 2012–April 2013*. Edited by N. Kaltsas, E. Vlachogianni, and P. Bouyia, 287–92. Athens, Greece: Kapon.

Bowen, A. C. 2002. "The Art of the Commander and the Emergence of Predictive Astronomy." In *Science and Mathematics in Ancient Greek Culture*. Edited by C. J. Tuplin and T. E. Rihll, 76–111. Oxford: Oxford University Press.

Bowen, A. C. 2013. *Simplicius on the Planets and Their Motions: In Defense of a Heresy*. Philosophia Antiqua 133. Leiden, The Netherlands: Brill.

Bowen, A. C., and B. R. Goldstein. 1988. "Meton of Athens and Astronomy in the Late Fifth Century B.C." In *A Scientific Humanist: Studies in Memory of Abraham Sachs*. Edited by E. Leichty, M. de J. Ellis, and P. Gerardi, 39–92. Occasional Publications of the Samuel Noah Kramer Fund 9. Philadelphia: University of Pennsylvania Museum.

Britton, J. P. 2007. "Calendars, Intercalations and Year-Lengths in Mesopotamian Astronomy." In *Calendars and Years: Astronomy and Time in the Ancient Near East*. Edited by J. M. Steele, 115–32. Oxford: Oxbow.

Britton, J. P. 2010. "Studies in Babylonian Lunar Theory: Part III; The Introduction of the Uniform Zodiac." *Archive for History of Exact Sciences* 64.6: 617–63.

Bromley, A. G. 1990. "Observations of the Antikythera Mechanism." *Antiquarian Horology* 18.6: 641–52.

Cabanes, P. 1976. *L'Épire de la mort de Pyrrhos à la conquête romaine (272–167 av. J.C.)*. Paris: Les Belles Lettres.

Cabanes, P. 1988. "Les concours des Naia de Dodone." *Nikephoros* 1:49–84.

Cabanes, P. 2007. "Recherches sur le calendrier corinthien en Épire et dans les régions voisines." In *Corpus des inscriptions grecques de l'Illyrie méridionale et d'Épire*. Vol.

2, *Inscriptions de Bouthrôtos*. Edited by P. Cabanes and F. Drini, 275–88. Études Épigraphiques 2. Athens, Greece: École Française d'Athènes.

CAG = Commentaria in Aristotelem graecae.

Carman, C. C., and M. Di Cocco. 2016. "The Moon Phase Anomaly in the Antikythera Mechanism." *ISAW Papers* 11. http://dlib.nyu.edu/awdl/isaw/isaw-papers/11/.

Carman, C. C., and J. Evans. 2014. "On the Epoch of the Antikythera Mechanism and Its Eclipse Predictor." *Archive for History of Exact Sciences* 68.6: 693–774.

Carman, C. C., A. Thorndike, and J. Evans. 2012. "On the Pin-and-Slot Device of the Antikythera Mechanism, with a New Application to the Superior Planets." *Journal for the History of Astronomy* 43.1: 93–116.

Cavaignac, E. 1938. "La date de l'archontat d'Eukleidas à Delphes." *Revue des Études Grecques* 51.240: 282–8.

Clarke, A. C. 1975. "Technology and the Limits of Knowledge." In *Technology and the Frontiers of Knowledge*. By S. Bellow, D. Bell, E. O'Gorman, Sir P. Madawan, and A. C. Clarke, 111–34. Frank Nelson Doubleday Lectures 1972–1973. New York: Doubleday.

Colby, F. M., ed. 1903. *The International Year Book: A Compendium of the World's Progress during the Year 1902*. New York: Dodd, Mead.

Cumont, F. 1935. "Les noms des planètes et l'astrolatrie chez les Grecs." *L'Antiquité Classique* 4.1: 5–43.

Diels, H., and A. Rehm. 1904. "Parapegmenfragmente aus Milet." *Sitzungsberichte der Königlich Preußischen Akademie der Wissenschaften* 1904.3: 92–111.

Dumas, F. 1972. *Trente siècles sous la mer*. Paris: Éditions France-Empire.

Edmunds, M. G. 2011. "An Initial Assessment of the Accuracy of the Gear Trains in the Antikythera Mechanism." *Journal for the History of Astronomy* 42.3: 307–20, 423.

Edmunds, M. G. 2014. "The Antikythera Mechanism and the Mechanical Universe." *Contemporary Physics* 55.4: 263–85.

Edmunds, M. G., A. Freeth, Y. Bitsakis, X. Moussas, J. Seiradakis, E. Magkou, M. Zafeiropoulou, et al. 2006. "The Antikythera Mechanism: Real Progress through Greek/UK/US Research." In *Recent Advances in Astronomy and Astrophysics: 7th International Conference of the Hellenic Astronomical Society, Lixourion, Kefallinia Island, Greece, 8–11 September 2005*. Edited by N. H. Solomos, 913–8. AIP Conference Proceedings 848. Melville, NY: American Institute of Physics.

Edmunds, M. G., and P. Morgan. 2000. "The Antikythera Mechanism: Still a Mystery of Greek Astronomy?" *Astronomy & Geophysics* 41.6: 10–7.

Evans, J. 1998. *The History and Practice of Ancient Astronomy*. New York: Oxford University Press.

Evans, J., and J. L. Berggren. 2006. *Geminos's Introduction to the Phenomena: A Translation and Study of a Hellenistic Survey of Astronomy*. Princeton, NJ: Princeton University Press.

Evans, J., and C. C. Carman. 2014. "Mechanical Astronomy: A Route to the Ancient Discovery of Epicycles and Eccentrics." In *From Alexandria, through Baghdad: Surveys and Studies in the Ancient Greek and Medieval Islamic Mathematical Sciences in Honor of J. L. Berggren*. Edited by N. Sidoli and G. Van Brummelen, 145–74. Berlin: Springer.

Evans, J., C. C. Carman, and A. S. Thorndike. 2010. "Solar Anomaly and Planetary Displays in the Antikythera Mechanism." *Journal for the History of Astronomy* 41.1: 1–39.

Falk, S. 2014. "The Scholar as Craftsman: Derek de Solla Price and the Reconstruction of a Medieval Instrument." *Notes and Records of the Royal Society of London* 68.2: 111–34.

Feynman, R. P. 1988. *"What Do You Care What Other People Think?": Further Adventures of a Curious Character.* New York: Norton.

Field, J. V., & M. T. Wright. 1985. "Gears from the Byzantines: A Portable Sundial with Calendrical Gearing." *Annals of Science* 42.2: 87–138.

Foley, B. 2016. "New Underwater Research at Antikythera." Lecture, American School of Classical Studies at Athens, February 19, 2016. http://www.ascsa.edu.gr/index. php/news/newsDetails/videocast-new-underwater-research-at-antikythera

Fournet, J.-L., and A. Tihon. 2014. *Conformément aux observations d'Hipparque: Le Papyrus Fouad inv. 267 A.* Publications de l'Institut Orientaliste de Louvain 67. Louvain-la-Neuve, Belgium: Université Catholique de Louvain, Institut Orientaliste.

Freeth, T. 2002a. "The Antikythera Mechanism: Challenging the Classic Research." *Mediterranean Archaeology and Archaeometry* 2.1: 21–35.

Freeth, T. 2002b. "The Antikythera Mechanism 2: Is It Posidonius' Orrery?" *Mediterranean Archaeology and Archaeometry* 2.2: 45–58.

Freeth, T. 2014. "Eclipse Prediction on the Ancient Greek Astronomical Calculating Machine Known as the Antikythera Mechanism." *PLoS ONE* 9.7: e103275. http://www.plosone.org/article/info%3Adoi%2F10.1371%2Fjournal.pone.0103275

Freeth, T., Y. Bitsakis, X. Moussas, J. H. Seiradakis, A. Tselikas, H. Mangou, M. Zafeiropoulou, et al. 2006. "Decoding the Ancient Greek Astronomical Calculator Known as the Antikythera Mechanism." *Nature* 444.7119: 587–91. Supplementary information, http://www.nature.com/nature/journal/v444/n7119/suppinfo/nature05357.html

Freeth, T., and A. Jones. 2012. "The Cosmos in the Antikythera Mechanism." *ISAW Papers* 4. http://dlib.nyu.edu/awdl/isaw/isaw-papers/4/

Freeth, T., A. Jones, J. M. Steele, and Y. Bitsakis. 2008. "Calendars with Olympiad Display and Eclipse Prediction on the Antikythera Mechanism." *Nature* 454.7204: 614–7. Supplementary notes (amended June 2, 2011), http://www.nature.com/nature/journal/v454/n7204/extref/nature07130-s1.pdf.

Gallis, K. I. [Κ. Ι. ΓΑΛΛΗΣ]. 1980. "Νέα επιγραφικά ευρήματα από τή Λάρισα." Αρχαιολογικά Ανάλεκτα εξ Αθηνών 13.2: 246–61.

Geagan, D. J. 2011. *The Athenian Agora.* Vol. XVIII, *Inscriptions: The Dedicatory Monuments.* Princeton, NJ: American School of Classical Studies at Athens.

Goebbels, J., H. Heidt, A. Kettschau, and P. Reimers. 1985. "Fortgeschrittene Durchstrahlungstechniken zur Dokumentation antiker Bronzen." In *Archäologische Bronzen, antike Kunst, moderne Technik.* Edited by H. Born, 126–31. Berlin: D. Reimers Verlag.

Goldstein, B. R. 2005. "Colors of Eclipses in Medieval Hebrew Astronomical Tables." *Aleph: Historical Studies in Science and Judaism* 5:11–34.

Graham, D. W. 2006. *Explaining the Cosmos: The Ionian Tradition of Scientific Philosophy.* Princeton, NJ: Princeton University Press.

Gray, J. M. K., and J. M. Steele. 2008. "Studies on Babylonian Goal-Year Astronomy I: A Comparison between Planetary Data in Goal-Year Texts, Almanacs and Normal Star Almanacs." *Archive for History of Exact Sciences* 62.5: 553–600.

Gray, J. M. K., and J. M. Steele. 2009. "Studies on Babylonian Goal-Year Astronomy II: The Babylonian Calendar and Goal-Year Methods of Prediction." *Archive for History of Exact Sciences* 63.6: 611–33.

Greenbaum, D. G., and M. T. Ross. 2010. "The Role of Egypt in the Development of the Horoscope." In *Egypt in Transition: Social and Religious Development of Egypt in the First Millennium BCE; Proceedings of an International Conference, Prague, September 1–4, 2009.* Edited by L. Bareš, F. Coppens, and K. Smoláriková, 146–82. Prague: Czech Institute of Egyptology, Faculty of Arts, Charles University in Prague.

Guattani, G. A. 1817. *Memorie enciclopediche sulle antichità e belle arti di Roma per il MDCCCXVI.* Rome: De Romanis.

Hannah, R. 2005. *Greek and Roman Calendars: Constructions of Time in the Classical World.* London: Duckworth.

Heilmeyer, W. D. 1985. "Neue Untersuchungen am Jüngling von Salamis am Antikenmuseum Berlin." In *Archäologische Bronzen, antike Kunst, moderne Technik.* Edited by H. Born, 132–8. Berlin: D. Reimers Verlag.

Huber, P. J., and S. De Meis. 2004. *Babylonian Eclipse Observations from 750 BC to 1 BC.* Milan: Associazione Culturale Mimesis.

Hunger, H., ed. 1992. *Astrological Reports to Assyrian Kings.* State Archives of Assyria 8. Helsinki: University of Helsinki Press.

Hunger, H., and D. Pingree. 1989. *MUL.APIN: An Astronomical Compendium in Cuneiform.* Archiv für Orientforschung 24. Horn, Austria: Verlag Ferdinand Berger & Söhne.

IG = Inscriptiones graecae.

Iversen, P. 2013a. "The Antikythera Mechanism and the Corinthian Family of Calendars." Paper presented at the 144th Annual Meeting of the American Philological Association, Seattle, WA, January 3–6, 2013. https://classicalstudies .org/annual-meeting/151iversen

Iversen, P. 2013b. "The Antikythera Mechanism and Rhodes." Paper presented at a workshop titled "The Antikythera Mechanism: Science and Innovation in the Ancient World," Lorentz Center, Leiden, The Netherlands, June 17–21, 2013. http://www.lorentzcenter.nl/lc/web/2013/570/abstracts.php3?wsid=570&type=pre sentations&venue=Oort

Iversen, P. 2017. "The Calendar on the Antikythera Mechanism and the Corinthian Family of Calendars." *Hesperia* 86 (forthcoming).

Jones, A. 1983. "The Development and Transmission of 248-Day Schemes for Lunar Motion in Ancient Astronomy." *Archive for History of Exact Sciences* 29.1: 1–36.

Jones, A. 1998. "Studies in the Astronomy of the Roman Period: III; Planetary Epoch Tables." *Centaurus* 40.1: 1–41.

Jones, A. 1999a. *Astronomical Papyri from Oxyrhynchus.* 2 vols. in 1. Memoirs of the American Philosophical Society 233. Philadelphia: American Philosophical Society.

Jones, A. 1999b. "Geminus and the Isia." *Harvard Studies in Classical Philology* 99:255–67.

Jones, A. 2000. "Calendrica I: New Callippic Dates." *Zeitschrift für Papyrologie und Epigraphik* 129:141–58.

Jones, A. 2006. "Ptolemy's Ancient Planetary Observations." *Annals of Science* 63.3: 255–90.

Jones, A. 2007. "On Greek Stellar and Zodiacal Date Reckoning." In *Calendars and Years: Astronomy and Time in the Ancient World.* Edited by J. M. Steele, 149–67. Oxford: Oxbow Books, 2007.

Jones, A. 2012. "The Antikythera Mechanism and the Public Face of Greek Science." Paper presented at a workshop titled "From Antikythera to the Square Kilometre Array: Lessons from the Ancients," held 12–15 June 2012 in Kerastari, Greece. *Proceedings of Science* 038. http://pos.sissa.it/cgi-bin/reader/conf.cgi?confid=170

Jones, A. 2016a. "Unruly Sun: Solar Tables and Calculations in the Papyrus P. Fouad 267 A." *Journal for the History of Astronomy* 47.1: 76–99.

Jones, A. 2016b. "The Miletos Inscription on Calendar Cycles: IMilet Inv. 84 + Inv. 1604." *Zeitschrift für Papyrologie und Epigraphik* 198: 113–27.

Jones, A. 2016c. "Historical Background and General Observations." In *Special Issue: The Inscriptions of the Antikythera Mechanism. Almagest* 7.1: 36–66.

Kabbadias [Kavvadias], P. 1901. "The Recent Finds off Cythera." *Journal of Hellenic Studies* 21:205–8.

Kaltsas, N., E. Vlachogianni, and P. Bouyia, eds. 2012. *The Antikythera Shipwreck: The Ship, the Treasures, the Mechanism; Exhibition Catalogue, National Archaeological Museum April 2012–April 2013.* Athens, Greece: Kapon.

Kiilerich, B. 2005. "Making Sense of the *Spolia* in the Little Metropolis in Athens." *Arte Medievale*, n.s. 4.2: 95–114.

Koch-Westenholz, U. 1995. *Mesopotamian Astrology: An Introduction to Babylonian and Assyrian Celestial Divination.* Carsten Niebuhr Institute of Near Eastern Studies (CNI) Publications 19. Copenhagen: Museum Tusculanum Press.

Kolonas, L. 2012. "The 1976 Investigations." In *The Antikythera Shipwreck: The Ship, the Treasures, the Mechanism; Exhibition Catalogue, National Archaeological Museum April 2012–April 2013.* Edited by N. Kaltsas, E. Vlachogianni, and P. Bouyia, 32–4. Athens, Greece: Kapon.

Kourouniotes, K., and H. A. Thompson. 1932. "The Pnyx in Athens." *Hesperia* 1:90–217.

Lang, J., and A. Middleton, eds. 2005. *Radiography of Cultural Material.* 2nd edition. Oxford: Butterworth-Heinemann.

Lehoux, D. 2005. "The Parapegma Fragments from Miletus." *Zeitschrift für Papyrologie und Epigraphik* 152:125–40.

Lehoux, D. 2007. *Astronomy, Weather, and Calendars in the Ancient World: Parapegmata and Related Texts in Classical and Near Eastern Societies.* Cambridge, UK: Cambridge University Press.

Littleton, J. T., and M. L. D. Littleton. 1996. "Conventional Tomography." In *A History of the Radiological Sciences: Diagnosis.* Edited by R. A. Gagliardi and B. L. McClennan, 369–402. Reston, VA: Radiology Centennial.

Lykoudis, E. 1901. "Τὰ ἀγάλματα τῶν Ἀντικυθήρων." *Παναθήναια* 1: 390–392.

Lykoudis, S. 1957. "Ο περίφημος θησαυρός της νήσου των Ἀντικυθήρων." *Ἥλιος* 345: 563.

Magou, E. 2012. "Archaeometric Research of the Antikythera Mechanism during the Century Following Its Recovery." In *The Antikythera Shipwreck: The Ship, the*

Treasures, the Mechanism; Exhibition Catalogue, National Archaeological Museum April 2012–April 2013. Edited by N. Kaltsas, E. Vlachogianni, and P. Bouyia, 232–40. Athens, Greece: Kapon.

Manganaro, G. 1964. "Iscrizioni latine e greche dal nuovo edificio termale di Taormina." *Cronache di Archeologia e di Storia dell'Arte* 3:38–68.

Marchant, J. 2008. *Decoding the Heavens: Solving the Mystery of the World's First Computer.* London: William Heinemann.

Marchant, J. 2015. "Archimedes' Legendary Sphere Brought to Life." *Nature* 526.7571: 19.

Mastrocinque, A. 2009. "The Antikythera Shipwreck and Sinope's Culture during the Mithridatic Wars." In *Mithridates VI and the Pontic Kingdom.* Edited by J. M. Højte, 311–20. Black Sea Studies. Aarhus, Denmark: Aarhus University Press.

Mendell, H. 2000. "The Trouble with Eudoxus." In *Ancient and Medieval Traditions in the Exact Sciences: Essays in Memory of Wilbur Knorr.* Edited by P. Suppes, J. M. Moravcsik, and H. Mendell, 59–138. CSLI Lecture Notes. Stanford, CA: Center for the Study of Language and Information.

Miller, F. J., E. V. Sayre, and B. Keisch. 1970. *Isotopic Methods of Examination and Authentication of Art and Archaeology.* Oak Ridge National Laboratory IIC-21. Oak Ridge, TN: Oak Ridge National Laboratory.

Mommsen, A. 1901. "Zur Orientierung über die delphische Chronologie." *Philologus* 60.1–4: 25–80.

Montelle, C. 2011. *Chasing Shadows: Mathematics, Astronomy, and the Early History of Eclipse Reckoning.* Johns Hopkins Studies in the History of Mathematics. Baltimore: Johns Hopkins University Press.

Morgan, J. D. 1996. "The Calendar and the Chronology of Athens." Paper presented at the 97th Annual Meeting of the Archaeological Institute of America. *American Journal of Archaeology* 100.2: 395.

Neugebauer, O. 1975. *A History of Ancient Mathematical Astronomy.* 3 vols. Studies in the History of Mathematics and Physical Sciences 1. Berlin: Springer.

Neugebauer, O., ed. 1955. *Astronomical Cuneiform Texts: Babylonian Ephemerides of the Seleucid Period for the Motion of the Sun, the Moon, and the Planets.* 3 vols. London: Lund Humphries.

Neugebauer, O., R. A. Parker, and K.-T. Zauzich. 1981. "A Demotic Lunar Eclipse Text of the First Century, B.C." *Proceedings of the American Philosophical Society* 125.4: 312–27.

Nikitsky, A. 1895. *Delfiskiye Epigraficheskiye Etyudi.* Odessa, Russia.

OGIS = Orientis graeci inscriptiones selectae.

Palagia, O. 2008. "The Date and Iconography of the Calendar Frieze on the Little Metropolis, Athens." *Jahrbuch des Deutschen Archäologischen Instituts* 123:215–37.

Parker, R. 2004. "New 'Panhellenic' Festivals in Hellenistic Greece." In *Mobility and Travel in the Mediterranean from Antiquity to the Middle Ages.* Edited by R. Schlesier and U. Zellmann, 9–22. Reiseliteratur und Kulturanthropologie 1. Münster, Germany: Lit Verlag.

Parpola, S., ed. 1970–1983. *Letters from Assyrian Scholars to the Kings Esarhaddon and Assurbanipal.* 2 vols. Alter Orient und Altes Testament 5.1–5.2. Kevelaer, Germany: Verlag Butzon & Bercker.

Parpola, S., ed. 1993. *Letters from Assyrian and Babylonian Scholars.* State Archives of Assyria 10. Helsinki: University of Helsinki Press.

Pastore, G. 2006. *Antikythera e i regoli calcolatori*. Policoro, Italy: Giovanni Pastore.

Pastore, G. 2013. *The Recovered Archimedes Planetarium*. Policoro, Italy: Giovanni Pastore.

Pearson, C., ed. 1987. *Conservation of Marine Archaeological Objects*. Butterworths Series in Conservation and Museology. London: Butterworths.

Petrakos, V. 1994. "Τα Αρχαία της Ελλάδος κατά τον πόλεμο 1940–1944." *Ο Μέντωρ* 7.31: 69–185.

Pingree, D. 1997. *From Astral Omens to Astrology: From Babylon to Bīkāner*. Serie Orientale Roma 78. Rome: Istituto Italiano per l'Africa e l'Oriente.

Price, D. de S. 1955–1956. "Clockwork before the Clock." *Horological Journal* 97 (December 1955): 810–4; *Horological Journal* 98 (January 1956): 31–5.

Price, D. de S. 1959a. "An Ancient Greek Computer." *Scientific American* 200.6: 60–7.

Price, D. de S. 1959b. "Grant No. 2379 (1958) $460: The Antikythera Mechanism, an Ancient Greek Computer." *American Philosophical Society Yearbook* 1959:618–20.

Price, D. de S. 1964. "Automata and the Origins of Mechanism and Mechanistic Philosophy." *Technology and Culture* 5.1: 9–23.

Price, D. de S. 1974. *Gears from the Greeks: The Antikythera Mechanism, a Calendar Computer from ca. 80 B.C.* Transactions of the American Philosophical Society, n.s. 64.7. Philadelphia: American Philosophical Society.

Price, D. de S. 1975. "Clockwork before the Clock and Timekeepers before Timekeeping." In *The Study of Time II: Proceedings of the Second Conference of the International Society for the Study of Time, Lake Yamanaka–Japan*. Edited by J. T. Fraser and N. Lawrence, 367–80. New York: Springer.

Pritchett, W. K., and O. Neugebauer. 1947. *The Calendars of Athens*. Cambridge, MA: Harvard University Press.

Rados, K. 1910. *Ναυτικαὶ καὶ Ἀρχαιολογικαὶ Σελίδες: Περὶ τῶν Θησαυρῶν τῶν Ἀντικυθήρων*. Athens, Greece: En Typois Panelleniou Kratous.

Rediadis, P. 1910. "Τὸ ἐξ Ἀντικυθήρων ἀστρολάβον." *Ἀρχαιολογική* 10:158–72.

Rehm, A. 1904. "Weiteres zu den milesischen Parapegmen." *Sitzungsberichte der Königlich-Preussischen Akademie der Wissenschaften: Philosophische-historische Klasse* 23:752–9.

Rehm, A. 1905. "Meteorologische Instrumente der Alten." (unpublished manuscript). Bayerische Staatsbibliothek, Rehmiana III.7.

Rehm, A. 1906a. "Notizbuch" (unpublished notebook). Bayerische Staatsbibliothek, Rehmiana III.7.

Rehm, A. 1906b. "Athener Vortrag" (unpublished paper). Bayerische Staatsbibliothek, Rehmiana III.9.

Reiner E., and D. Pingree. 1975. *Enūma Anu Enlil Tablet 63: The Venus Tablet of Ammiṣaduqa*. Bibliotheca Mesopotamica 2.1. Malibu, CA: Undena.

Robert, C. 1897–1919. *Die antiken Sarkophag-Reliefs: Dritter Band, Einzelmythen*. 3 vols. Antiken Sarkophagreleifs 3. Berlin: G. Grote'sche Verlagsbuchhandlung.

Rochberg, F. 1998. *Babylonian Horoscopes*. Transactions of the American Philosophical Society 88.1. Philadelphia: American Philosophical Society.

Rochberg, F. 2010. *In the Path of the Moon: Babylonian Celestial Divination and Its Legacy*. Ancient Magic and Divination 6. Leiden, The Netherlands: Brill.

Rochberg-Halton, F. 1988. *Aspects of Babylonian Celestial Divination: The Lunar Eclipse Tablets of Enūma Anu Enlil.* Archiv für Orientforschung 22. Horn, Austria: Verlag F. Berger.

Rousopoulos, O. 1905. "Über die Reinigung und Conservierung der Antiquitäten." In *Comptes rendus du Congrès international d'archéologie: 1re session, Athènes 1905.* Edited by Internationaler Kongreß für Archäologie, 250–5. Athens, Greece: Imprimerie "Hestia," C. Meissner & N. Kargadouris.

Sachs, A. J., and H. Hunger, eds. 1988–. *Astronomical Diaries and Related Texts from Babylonia.* 9 vols. Oesterreichische Akademie der Wissenschaften, Denkschriften der Philosophisch-historische Klasse 195, 210, 247, 299, 346, and 466. Vienna: Verlag der Oesterreichische Akademie der Wissenschaften.

Samuel, A. E. 1972. *Greek and Roman Chronology: Calendars and Years in Classical Antiquity.* Handbuch der Altertumswissenschaft 1.7. Munich: Beck.

Seabrook, J. 2007. "Fragmentary Knowledge: Was the Antikythera Mechanism the World's First Computer?" *The New Yorker,* May 14, 2007: 94–102.

Sedley, D. 1976. "Epicurus and the Mathematicians of Cyzicus." *Cronache Ercolanesi* 6:23–54.

Seiradakis, J. H. (forthcoming). "Is There a Connection between the 1897 Cretan Revolt and the Discovery of the Antikythera Shipwreck?" In *Instruments—Observations—Theories: Studies in the History of Early Astronomy in Honor of James Evans.* Edited by C. Carman and A. Jones, (forthcoming.)

Stais, V. 1905. *Τὰ ἐξ Ἀντικυθήρων Εὑρήματα.* Athens, Greece: Sakellarios.

Steele, J. M. 2000a. "Eclipse Prediction in Mesopotamia." *Archive for History of Exact Sciences* 54.5: 421–54.

Steele, J. M. 2000b. *Observations and Predictions of Eclipse Times by Early Astronomers.* Archimedes 4. Dordrecht, The Netherlands: Kluwer.

Steele, J. M. 2011. "Visual Aspects of the Transmission of Babylonian Astronomy and Its Reception into Greek Astronomy." In *Special Issue: Between Orient and Occident: Transformation of Knowledge. Annals of Science* 68.4: 453–65.

Steele, J. M. 2013. "The 'Astronomical Fragments' of Berossos in Context." In *The World of Berossos: Proceedings of the 4th International Colloquium on "The Ancient Near East between Classical and Ancient Oriental Traditions," Hatfield College, Durham 7th–9th July 2010.* Edited by J. Haubold, G. B. Lanfranchi, R. Rollinger, and J. M. Steele, 99–113. Classica et Orientalia 5. Wiesbaden, Germany: Harrassowitz.

Steele, J. M., ed. 2007. *Calendars and Years: Astronomy and Time in the Ancient Near East.* Oxford: Oxbow.

Steele, J. M., ed. 2010. *Calendars and Years II: Astronomy and Time in the Ancient and Medieval World.* Oxford: Oxbow Books.

Stephenson, F. R. 1997. *Historical Eclipses and Earth's Rotation.* Cambridge, UK: Cambridge University Press.

Stern, S. 2012. *Calendars in Antiquity: Empires, States, and Societies.* Oxford: Oxford University Press.

Stikas, C. 2014. *Antikythera Mechanism: The Book; Unwinding the History of Science and Technology.* Athens, Greece: Constantin Stikas.

Svoronos, I. N. 1903a. Ὁ Θησαυρὸς τῶν Ἀντικυθήρων. Athens, Greece: Beck & Barth. Republished in Svoronos, Τὸ ἐν Ἀθήναις Ἐθνικὸν Μουσεῖον, Athens, Greece: Beck & Barth, 1908.

Svoronos, I. N. 1903b. Die Funde von Antikythera. Athens, Greece: Beck & Barth. Republished in Svoronos, Das Athener Nationalmuseum, Vol. 1, Athens, Greece: Beck & Barth, 1908.

Talbert, R. J. A. 2016. Roman Portable Sundials: The Empire in Your Hand. New York: Oxford University Press.

Theofanidis, I. 1929. "Ἁγίου Παύλου (πλοῦς)." Μεγάλη Στρατιωτικὴ καὶ Ναυτικὴ Ἐγκυκλοπαίδεια 1:83–96. (pp. 89–96 are misnumbered as 97–104)

Theofanidis, I. [Jean Théophanidis] 1934. "Sur l'instrument en cuivre dont des fragments se trouvent au Musée Archéologique d'Athènes et qui fut retiré du fond de la mer d'Anticythère en 1902." Πρακτικὰ τῆς Ἀκαδημίας Ἀθηνῶν 9:140–9.

Throckmorton, P. 1970. Shipwrecks and Archaeology: The Unharvested Sea. Boston: Little, Brown.

Toishi, K. 1965. "Radiography of the Great Buddha at Kamakura." Studies in Conservation 10.2: 47–52.

Toomer, G. J., ed. and trans. 1984. Ptolemy's Almagest. Duckworth Classical, Medieval, and Renaissance Editions. London: Duckworth.

Tracy, S. V. 2009. "Dating by Lettering in Greek Epigraphy." In Estudios de epigrafía griega. Edited by Á. Martínez Fernández, 105–12. La Laguna, Santa Cruz de Tenerife: Servicio de Publicaciones, Universidad de La Laguna.

Trümpy, C. 1997. Untersuchungen zu den altgriechischen Monatsnamen und Monatsfolgen. Bibliothek der Klassischen Altertumswissenschaften, n.s. 2.98. Heidelberg, Germany: Universitätsverlag C. Winter.

Tsaravopoulos, A. 2004–2009. "Η επιγραφή IG V 1, 948 και οι ενεπίγραφες μολυβδίδες του Κάστρου των Αντικυθήρων." Ηορος 17–21:327–48.

Tselekas, P. 2012. "The Coins." In The Antikythera Shipwreck: The Ship, the Treasures, the Mechanism; Exhibition Catalogue, National Archaeological Museum April 2012–April 2013. Edited by N. Kaltsas, E. Vlachogianni, and P. Bouyia, 216–26. Athens, Greece: Kapon.

Tsipopoulou, M., M. Antoniou, and S. Massouridi. 2012. "The 1900–1901 Investigations." In The Antikythera Shipwreck: The Ship, the Treasures, the Mechanism; Exhibition Catalogue, National Archaeological Museum April 2012–April 2013. Edited by N. Kaltsas, E. Vlachogianni, and P. Bouyia, 18–31. Athens, Greece: Kapon.

van Helden, A. 1985. Measuring the Universe: Cosmic Dimensions from Aristarchus to Halley. Chicago: University of Chicago Press.

Vicars, E. 1903. "A Rescued Masterpiece: The Finds at Anticythera." Pall Mall Magazine 29:551–62.

Vlachogianni, E. 2012. "Sculpture." In The Antikythera Shipwreck: The Ship, the Treasures, the Mechanism; Exhibition Catalogue, National Archaeological Museum April 2012–April 2013. Edited by N. Kaltsas, E. Vlachogianni, and P. Bouyia, 62–115. Athens, Greece: Kapon.

Vyzantinos, G. 1901a. "Εἰς τὸν βυθὸν τῶν Ἀντικυθήρων." Παναθήναια 1: 224–7.

Byzantinos [Vyzantinos], G. 1901b. "From the Bottom of the Sea." *The Independent* 53.2730: 704–6.

Weinberg, G. D., V. R. Grace, G. R. Edwards, H. S. Robinson, P. Throckmorton, and E. K. Ralph. 1965. *The Antikythera Shipwreck Reconsidered*. Transactions of the American Philosophical Society, n.s. 55.3. Philadelphia: American Philosophical Society.

Wright, M. T. 1990. "Rational and Irrational Reconstruction: The London Sundial-Calendar and the Early History of Geared Mechanisms." *History of Technology* 12:65–102.

Wright, M. T. 2002a. "A Planetarium Display for the Antikythera Mechanism." *Horological Journal* 144.5: 169–73.

Wright, M. T. 2002b. "Antikythera Error." *Horological Journal* 144.6: 193.

Wright, M. T. 2003a. "Epicyclic Gearing and the Antikythera Mechanism: Part I." *Antiquarian Horology* 27.3: 270–9.

Wright, M. T. 2003b. "In the Steps of the Master Mechanic." In *Η Αρχαία Ελλάδα και ο Σύγχρονος Κόσμος: 2ο Παγκόσμιο συνέδριο, Αρχαία Ολυμπία, 12–17 Ιουλίου 2002; Πρακτικά*. 86–97. Patras, Greece: University of Patras.

Wright, M. T. 2004. "The Scholar, the Mechanic and the Antikythera Mechanism: Complementary Approaches to the Study of an Instrument." *Bulletin of the Scientific Instrument Society* 80:4–11.

Wright, M. T. 2005a. "Counting Months and Years: The Upper Back Dial of the Antikythera Mechanism." *Bulletin of the Scientific Instrument Society* 87:8–13.

Wright, M. T. 2005b. "Epicyclic Gearing and the Antikythera Mechanism: Part II." *Antiquarian Horology* 29.1: 51–63.

Wright, M. T. 2005c. "The Antikythera Mechanism: A New Gearing Scheme." *Bulletin of the Scientific Instrument Society*. 85:2–7.

Wright, M. T. 2006. "The Antikythera Mechanism and the Early History of the Moon-Phase Display." *Antiquarian Horology* 29.3: 319–29.

Wright, M. T. 2007. "The Antikythera Mechanism Reconsidered." *Interdisciplinary Science Reviews* 32.1: 27–43.

Wright, M. T. 2011. "The Antikythera Mechanism: Reconstruction as a Medium for Research and Publication." In *Reconstructions: Recreating Science and Technology of the Past*. Edited by K. Staubermann, 1–20. Edinburgh: NMS Enterprises.

Wright, M. T. 2012. "The Front Dial of the Antikythera Mechanism." In *Explorations in the History of Machines and Mechanisms: Proceedings of HMM2012*. Edited by T. Koetsier & M. Ceccarelli, 279–92. Dordrecht, The Netherlands: Springer.

Wright, M. T. 2013a. "Archimedes, Astronomy, and the Planetarium." Paper presented at a conference titled "Archimedes in the 21st Century," held at the Courant Institute, New York University, New York, May 31–June 1, 2013. https://www.cs.drexel.edu/~crorres/Archimedes/AWC/video_wright.html

Wright, M. T. 2013b. "The Antikythera Mechanism: Compound Gear-Trains for Planetary Indications." *Almagest* 4.2: 4–31.

Wright, M. T., A. G. Bromley, and H. Magou. 1995. "Simple X-Ray Tomography and the Antikythera Mechanism." In *Archaeometry in South Eastern Europe: Second*

Conference in Delphi, 19th–21st April 1991. Edited by I. Liritzis and G. Tsokas, 531–43. PACT 45. Rixensart, Belgium: Council of Europe.

Yavetz, I. 1998. "On the Homocentric Spheres of Eudoxus." *Archive for History of Exact Sciences* 52.3: 221–78.

Yavetz, I. 2001. "A New Role for the Hippopede of Eudoxus." *Archive for History of Exact Sciences* 56.1: 69–93.

Zafeiropoulou, M. 2006. "Συλλογέ Χαλκών: Ο Μηχανισμός των Αντικυθήρων." In *2º Διεθνές Συνέδριο Αρχαίας Ελληνικής Τεχνολογίας: Πρακτικά / Proceedings of the 2nd International Conference on Ancient Greek Technology*. Edited by P. Tasios and C. Palyvou, 829–32. Athens, Greece: EMAET Technical Chamber.

Zapheiropoulou [Zafeiropoulou], M. 2012. "Old and New Fragments of the Antikythera Mechanism and Inscriptions." In *The Antikythera Shipwreck: The Ship, the Treasures, the Mechanism; Exhibition Catalogue, National Archaeological Museum April 2012–April 2013*. Edited by N. Kaltsas, E. Vlachogianni, and P. Bouyia, 241–8. Athens, Greece: Kapon.

Zahariadis, G. 2008. "Ο θείος μου 'ψάρεψε' τον αρχαίο υπολογιστή." *Τα Νέα* (October 29): 16.

Zeeman, E. C. 1986. "Gears from the Greeks." *Proceedings of the Royal Institution of Great Britain* 58:137–56.

Ziegler, K. 1969. *M. Tullius Cicero Scripta quae manserunt omnia: Fasc. 39, De re publica librorum sex quae manserunt*. 7th ed. Leipzig: Teubner.

Index